BACK ON THE STREET

ROBERT M. CARTER

and

MALCOLM W. KLEIN

University of Southern California
Los Angeles

BACK ON THE STREET
The Diversion
of Juvenile Offenders

PRENTICE-HALL, INC., Englewood Cliffs, New Jersey

75064

Library of Congress Cataloging in Publication Data

Main entry under title:

Back on the street.
   Includes bibliographical references and index.
   1. Juvenile justice, Administration of—United
States—Addresses, essays, lectures. 2. Social
work with delinquents and criminals—United States—
Addresses, essays, lectures. 3. Police services
for juveniles—United States—Addresses, essays,
lectures. I. Carter, Robert M. II. Klein,
Malcolm W.
HV9104.B33   362.7'4   75-22449
ISBN 0-13-055319-0

© 1976 by Prentice-Hall, Inc.,
Englewood Cliffs, New Jersey

10   9   8   7   6   5   4   3   2

Printed in the United States of America

Prentice-Hall International, Inc., *London*
Prentice-Hall of Australia, Pty. Ltd., *Sydney*
Prentice-Hall of Canada, Ltd., *Toronto*
Prentice-Hall of India Privated Limited, *New Delhi*
Prentice-Hall of Japan, Inc., *Tokyo*
Prentice-Hall of Southeast Asia (Pte.) Ltd., *Singapore*

For

Mike, Dayna, Steve and Dave
and
Laurie and Leigh

CONTENTS

PROLOGUE *xi*

SECTION 1
DIVERSION: ISSUES AND VIEWS *1*

1

THE JUVENILE JUSTICE SYSTEM *4*

President's Commission on Law Enforcement
and Administration of Justice

2

ALTERNATIVES TO JUDICIAL HANDLING *25*

Task Force Report: Juvenile Delinquency

3

DIVERSION FROM THE CRIMINAL JUSTICE SYSTEM *32*

National Institute of Mental Health

4

YOUTH SERVICES SYSTEMS *55*

Robert J. Gemignani

5

DIVERSION: BACKGROUND AND DEFINITION *67*

Donald R. Cressey and Robert A. McDermott

75064

6

ISSUES IN POLICE DIVERSION OF JUVENILE OFFENDERS   *73*

Malcolm W. Klein

SECTION 2
LABELING   *105*

7

THE LABELING PERSPECTIVE; THE DELINQUENT, AND THE POLICE: A REVIEW OF THE LITERATURE   *109*

John L. Hagan

8

INSTEAD OF COURT: DIVERSION IN JUVENILE JUSTICE   *123*

Edwin M. Lemert

9

THE ORGANIZATIONAL BUILDING-UP OF STIGMATIZING LABELS   *156*

Kenneth Polk and Solomon Kobrin

10

PERCEPTIONS OF STIGMA FOLLOWING PUBLIC INTERVENTION FOR DELINQUENT BEHAVIOR   *159*

Jack Donald Foster, Simon Dinitz and Walter C. Reckless

11

THE LABELING PROCESS: REINFORCEMENT AND DETERRENT?   *167*

Bernard A. Thorsell and Lloyd W. Klemke

SECTION 3
POLICE DISCRETION   *175*

12

JUVENILE DETENTION: PROTECTION, PREVENTION OR PUNISHMENT?   *179*

Elyce Zenoff Ferster, Edith Nash Snethen and Thomas F. Courtless

13

POLICE ENCOUNTERS WITH JUVENILES *197*

Irving Piliavin and Scott Briar

14

POLICE DISCRETION: THE NEED FOR GUIDELINES *207*

Richard W. Kobetz

15

GUIDES FOR LAW ENFORCEMENT AND PROBATION OFFICERS *216*

National Council on Crime and Delinquency

SECTION 4
SELECTED PROGRAMS *219*

16

LAW ENFORCEMENT SCREENING FOR DIVERSION *221*

Peter J. Pitchess

17

PLANNING FOR DIVERSION: A CASE EXAMPLE *234*

Donald Graham and Rebecca Wurzburger

18

POLICE HELP YOUTH *239*

Patricia Ann Hunsicker

19

EARLY DIVERSION FROM THE CRIMINAL JUSTICE SYSTEM: PRACTICE IN SEARCH OF A THEORY *248*

Elizabeth W. Vorenberg and James Vorenberg

20

THE CURRENT STATUS OF YOUTH SERVICE BUREAUS *263*

J. A. Seymour

21

THE CHALLENGE OF YOUTH SERVICE BUREAUS *276*

Youth Development and Delinquency Prevention Administration

SECTION 5

EVALUATION AND EMPIRICAL DATA. *299*

22

IMPLICATIONS FOR RESEARCH AND POLICY *302*

Donald R. Cressey and Robert A. McDermott

23

ON THE FRONT END OF THE JUVENILE JUSTICE SYSTEM *307*

Malcolm W. Klein

24

POLICE PROFESSIONALIZATION AND COMMUNITY ATTACHMENTS AND DIVERSION OF JUVENILES *314*

Richard A. Sundeen, Jr.

25

JUVENILE REFERRAL AND RECIDIVISM *321*

Suzanne Bugas Lincoln

· 26

PREVENTING DELINQUENCY THROUGH DIVERSION *329*

Roger Baron, Floyd Feeney, and Warren Thornton

INDEX *365*

PROLOGUE

Seldom in the history of American criminal justice has a concept erupted on the scene and generated as much interest as that of diversion. Given major impetus by the 1967 President's Commission on Law Enforcement and Administration of Justice and reinforced and emphasized by the 1973 Law Enforcement Assistance Administration-sponsored National Advisory Commission on Criminal Justice Standards and Goals, diversion has generated responses ranging from enthusiasm through anxiety and uncertainty to hostility. The diversity of responses to diversion may be, in large measure, a product of definitional understandings. Diversion generally is described in one of two ways: a process which *minimizes penetration of the offender into the criminal justice system* or as *an alternative to entry into the criminal justice system.* These two conceptualizations of diversion themselves have numerous variants and each has significant implications for the operations of criminal justice agencies.

Caught in a web of definitional variations, there is a distinct possibility that we may overlook the single and critically important fact that diversion, however it is or has been defined, has long been part of the American criminal justice process. For example, if one accepts the "alternative to entry" definition, there is a long precedent of police officer discretion as relates to decisions to arrest or not-arrest. Indeed, nationwide, approximately one half of all juveniles arrested are "counseled and released" or are "handled within the department." These juveniles are clearly diverted *from* entry into the juvenile justice system, even if a majority of them are not diverted *to* some other system as an alternative.

If, on the other hand, the "minimize penetration" perspective is utilized and we view the criminal justice system as one in which offenders are sequentially arrested, charged, prosecuted, convicted and sentenced to prison, any behavior on the part of criminal justice system personnel, be it in the law enforcement, judicial or correctional components, which terminates the sequence short of completion of the prison sentence could be classified as diversion. And, in fact, police frequently release offenders without arrest, prosecutors for a variety of reasons do not always prosecute, judges use probation far more often than imprisonment, and paroling authorities release prison inmates before completion of the sentences. Thus, even under the "minimize penetration" concept, diversion has long been part of our justice system heritage.

We do not wish to belabor the definitional problem here, but must emphasize that diversion is not a new concept; diversion in one form or another has been part of our justice system from the beginning. Given the fact that diversion in practice, if not by label, is part of our justice tradition and that there may be a variety of reasons and methods for encouraging "new" diversion which make it explicit, efficient, and effective, we may appropriately ask about the basis for the current expanded concern about a process which heretofore has been more or less commonplace. It appears that three factors have generated the current interest in diversion: (1) increasing recognition of deficiencies in the criminal justice system, (2) rediscovery of the ancient truth that the community itself significantly impacts upon behavior, and (3) growing demands of the citizenry to be active participants in the affairs of government.

Although there has been and continues to be considerable discussion and writing by academicians, administrators, practitioners and researchers about the system of criminal and/or juvenile justice, the United States does not have a single system of justice. Each level of government, indeed each jurisdiction, has its own unique system. These many "systems," all established to enforce the standards of conduct believed necessary for the protection of individuals and the preservation of the community, are a collectivity of thousands of law enforcement agencies and a multiplicity of courts, prosecution and defense agencies, probation and parole departments, correctional institutions and related community-based organizations. It is clear that our approach to criminal and juvenile justice sacrifices much in the way of efficiency and effectiveness in order to preserve local autonomy and to protect the individual.

The many systems of justice in existence in the United States in the 1970's are not the same as those which emerged following the American Revolution. Indeed, this 200 year evolution has not been uniform or consistent; some of the innovations and changes in our systems have been generated by judicial decisions and legislative decrees; others have evolved more by chance than by design. Trial by jury and the principle of bail, for example, are relatively old and date back to our European heritage in general and the English Common Law in particular. Probation and parole began in the nineteenth century and the juvenile court is a twentieth century innovation.

Coupled with the numerous criminal and juvenile justice arrangements in the United States and their uneven development is the separation of functions within the systems. There are similar components in all systems ranging from apprehension through prosecution and adjudication to correction. Although in fact interwoven and interdependent one with the other, these components typically function independently and autonomously. This separateness of functions, which on one hand prevents the possibility of a "police state," on the other leads to some extraordinary and complex problems. Not the least of these is that the systems of justice are not integrated, coordinated, and effective entities, but rather are fragmented, with agencies tied together by the processing of an increasing number of adult and juvenile offenders.

These "non-systems" are marked by an unequal quality of justice, inadequate fiscal, manpower, and training resources, shortages in equipment and facilities, lack of relevant research and evaluation to provide some measure of effectiveness and, until recently, a general indifference and apathy on the part of the public which the systems were designed to serve.

Society deals with crime in a manner which reflects its beliefs about the nature and cause of crime. Many centuries ago, for example, when crime was believed to be the product of the possession of the mind and body by an evil spirit, the primitive response was simple: drive the devil out of the body by whatever means were available for such purposes. The American tradition as relates to the etiology of crime has focused, until recently, upon the individual as a free agent—able to choose between good and evil and aware of the differences between right and wrong. Our "treatment" of crime accordingly reflected the simplistic notion that criminality was housed solely within the psyche and soma of the offender. Regardless of whether the prevalent philosophy was revenge, retaliation, retribution or rehabilitation, the individual was seen as being of primary importance.

We have long assumed that the criminal or delinquent either willfully disregards legitimate authority by his illegal acts or suffers from some personal defect or shortcoming. There is much to learn, however, about the mysteries by which a society generates abnormal responses within its own circles. But this has become increasingly apparent: society itself contributes significantly to such behavior. Indeed, it is the self-same social structure expressing its force and influence in an ambivalent manner which helps create on one hand the conforming individual—the person respectful of the social and legal codes—and on the other the deviant and lawbreaker who is disrespectful of the law. We have only recently become aware that crime and delinquency are symptoms of failures and disorganization of the community as well as of individual offenders. In particular, these failures may be seen as depriving offenders of contact with those social institutions which are basically responsible for assuring the development of law-abiding conduct.

Note, for example, that it has become increasingly common to discuss the "decline in respect for law and order." In every quarter, and with increasing intensity, we hear that the citizenry, for reasons as yet unclear, is not only failing to honor specific laws, but also displays a mounting disregard for the "rule of law" itself as an essential aspect of the democratic way of life. But even as this concern is echoed, it is not clear that we are all agreed as to what is meant by "decline in respect for law and order" or precisely to whom or to what we are referring. It may be that a large amount of what we observe and label as "disrespect for law" in a wide range and diversity of communities is in fact a normal reaction of normal persons to an abnormal condition or situation.

As knowledge expands to recognize the role of society in the creation of deviance, justice systems themselves will be modified. The implementation of knowledge, of course, always lags behind the development of knowledge.

Concurrent with the recognition that (1) the justice system is a fragmented system and (2) the community itself has an enormous impact upon the crime problem, there has been—particularly within the past decade

—the emergence of mass disaffection of a large segment of our population. This disaffection with the American system is often described in terms which suggest that citizens are not involved in decision-making and are acted upon by the government rather than impacting upon government. The disaffection has been manifested in many communities and in various ways.

We have, for example, been witness to mass civil disorder unparalleled in recent times. We have seen our young people in revolt against the war in Vietnam, the grape industry, selective service, marijuana laws, prison administration, presidential and congressional candidates, supreme court nominees, and Dow Chemical. We have observed rebellion against the establishment ranging from burning ghettos and campuses everywhere to looters in the North, freedom riders in the South, and maniacal bombers from East to West. Young and old, black and white, rich and poor have withstood tear gas and mace, billy clubs and bullets, insults and assaults, jail and prison in order to lie down in front of troop trains, sit-in at university administration buildings, love-in in public parks, wade-in at nonintegrated beaches and lie-in within legislative buildings. The establishment has been challenged on such issues as the legal-oriented entities of the draft, the rights of Blacks to use the same restrooms and drinking fountains as whites, the death penalty, and free speech. Young people have challenged socially-oriented norms with "mod" dress and hair styles, language, rock music, and psychedelic forms, colors and patterns. We have seen the emergence of the hippy and yippy, the youthful drug culture, black, yellow, red, and brown power advocates, and organizations such as the Panthers, Women's Lib, the Third World Liberation Front, and the Peace and Freedom Party.

But this disaffection or unrest is not restricted to youth alone. Increasingly, adults are rebelling against the system. One need look no further than the recent slowdowns, work stoppages and strikes of such tradition-oriented groups as police and fire officials, military personnel, social workers, school teachers, and indeed even prison inmates. Adult participation in protest has generally been more moderate than that of youth; some has been through membership in political organizations of a left wing orientation; others have joined conservative right wing organizations such as the Birch Society or Minutemen. Millions of Americans protested against the political establishment by voting for a third or fourth party or not voting at all in recent elections. The disaffection, indeed open distrust of government, reached its peak with the Watergate affair.

These three phenomena—recognition that the community impacts significantly upon behavior, the uncertainty as to the effectiveness or quality of justice in the current system of justice, and the growing desire of the citizenry for active, relevant and meaningful participation in every area of governmental affairs and community life—are moving the responses to the challenge of crime in new directions.

The diversion of offenders from the criminal justice system and a parallel development of alternatives to justice system processing of offenders is seen as prologue to "absorbtion," a more extensive process in which communities engage in a wide variety of deviant behavior, including crime and delinquency, without referral to traditional establishment agencies or with only minimum contact. Absorption is adaptive behavior within communities in which alternative strategies are developed for engaging social problems. Diversion is clearly such adaptive behavior, minimizing referral to or penetration of the established justice system and its processes and providing alternatives for addressing that deviant behavior labeled crime and delinquency.

SECTION 1

DIVERSION:
ISSUES AND VIEWS

It would be difficult to make a case for any tightly knit theoretical structure underlying the practices referred to as "diversion." We do include in Section 2 materials on labeling theory, but even that perspective is used more to rationalize or justify diversion than it is to implement or direct it. We can, however, specify some of the *assumptions* that seem most pertinent to diversion. Indeed, as the reader progresses through the papers in Section 1, he will find these assumptions not only implicit in the arguments, but often explicit as well, as if the assumptions were, indeed, facts. We can list these simply as follows:

1. *Evils of the System.* Officials, offenders, and mere visitors can all attest to sometimes occasional and sometimes common problems which suggest that the criminal justice system is in a sorry state. Time delays, personal abuses or brutalities, horrendous conditions in penal institutions, exposure of the naive offender to the teachings and predations of criminal sophisticates, miscarriages of justice, release of the guilty—these and similar items provide sufficient cause for many persons to justify early diversion from the system.

2. *Overloads.* In many jurisdictions, the number of cases processed exceeds the capacity of the system to provide just and expeditious service. Paradoxically, this can lead both to premature releases and to undue retentions of suspects and detainees. It also presumably leads to a deterioration of service—enforcement, judicial, and correctional—which, in turn, presumably results in a still greater volume of criminal behavior, requiring yet more service. Diversion, it is suggested, may at least serve to avoid, if not to correct, such overload problems.

3. *Labels and Stigmatization.* There are really three subassumptions here: that the labels applied by the system to the suspect or offender are uniformly negative; that they indeed have an effect on behavior; and that this effect is sufficiently damaging to exacerbate the original problem. Diversion, by avoiding the label, is presumed thereby to avoid a worsening of the problem behavior.

4. *System Ineffectiveness.* Depending on the component of the system involved and the type of criminal or delinquent behavior referred to, one hears that our system leads to recidivism rates as high as 80 to 90 percent; or that 50 percent recidivism is a success rate; or that the second-time offender is a goner, beyond repair. Those who find the system at least partially to blame for this find diversion to be an essential starting point for reversing the pattern.

5. *Community Responsibility.* Whatever the faults or products of the criminal

justice system, many people feel that it has become the dumping ground for problems which the community is unwilling to face or to handle within its own informal institutions—moral, religious, familial, or charitable. For these people diversion represents less a solution to a series of problems than a reassertion of the responsibility of communities to their members.

These five assumptions make up a rather formidable picture. Listing them helps us to understand the very great interest, indeed the genuine enthusiasm, which has mushroomed in the past half-decade. But as is suggested in the paper by Cressey and McDermott, this enthusiasm has mounted at such an accelerated rate that we may now be dealing with something dangerously close to a *fad*. Fads are infectious, bringing unreasoned compliance and acceptance. In the justice and social welfare areas, we can ill afford such unreasoned patterns. How do we protect ourselves from a fad?

To a considerable extent, the papers in Section 1 suggest some answers and serve to prevent us from too eagerly jumping on the diversion bandwagon. Several strategies seem in order. First, we must determine the *progenitors* of diversion, seeking out its earlier forms and the experiences with them. Second, we must analyze the current pattern of diversion statements and programs for their *uniqueness* and for the implications of these unique elements. Third, we must be wary of and develop defenses against *overenthusiasm*. Finally, we must develop criteria for judging both the good *and* the bad *consequences* of diversion; that is, we must be prepared not only to praise and proselytize but also to decry and to terminate our new programs. This goes against the natural inertia of social programming.

In the final analysis, however, our best protection against faddism lies in the same direction as the greatest opportunity for progress—coming to a mutual understanding of the conceptual and practical foundations of diversion. The papers in Section 1, presented approximately in their order of publication, aid in this process not only by virtue of their separate contents but also by illustrating a typical developmental pattern in social programming.

The first two papers, taken from the reports of the President's Commission on Law Enforcement and Administration of Justice, 1967, present the call for action and spell out recommendations for specific forms of action. The third and fourth papers, emanating from separate governmental agencies, may be seen as official and formal responses to the Commission's call for action; but note that the emphasis is still programmatic, as if to say, "We know the problem, so here's what we need to *do* about it."

The fifth and sixth papers, and to a lesser extent the fourth as well, come not from official agencies but from "the academy." They represent the initial attempts of social scientists to come to grips with the Commission's challenge and its aftermath. These latter papers represent an academic grappling for *clarification* rather than immediate guidelines for action.

Throughout this developmental pattern over a period of six years, one can easily discern a growing preoccupation with definitional (and therefore conceptual) issues rather than with action imperatives. This is a developmental trend to be sure, but it also represents alternative strategies to the construction of effective programs for delinquency control and reduction.

We would do well to keep these two strategies in focus. The first makes more assumptions about what is now known and moves ahead rapidly to implement new programs. The second is more skeptical about current knowledge and would defer immediacy of action pending more research and experimentally oriented action programs.

These strategies are in no way unique to the matter of diversion. They are visible, and the developmental pattern is repeated in every social "war" that we undertake. If the reader wishes to align himself with one strategy over the other, he can do so by recalling his reaction to the "war" on poverty of the middle 1960s, the "war" on crime of the late 1960s and early 1970s, and at present the developing "wars" on pollution and the energy crisis.

Diversion is not a unique phenomenon. Many of the general issues raised by its appearance as a popular strategy in delinquency control are similar to those raised in the past by other popular strategies. Hopefully, we are beginning to learn from these repeated patterns. And hopefully, if we can adopt a slightly skeptical stance, we can more judiciously judge the specifics of the diversion strategy as raised in succeeding sections of this book.

1

THE JUVENILE JUSTICE SYSTEM*

The President's Commission on Law Enforcement
and Administration of Justice

The President's Commission on Law Enforcement and Administration of Justice is one of the few federal commissions that has had a genuine impact on the nation. At the very least, it has led to the formation of a whole new bureaucracy with a federal center and literally hundreds of local and state branches. At its best, the commission has forced a rethinking of criminal justice philosophies and programs. The following excerpt from the Commission's report has set the stage for developments referred to as diversion, especially for the establishment of youth service bureaus throughout the nation. Three points in particular are commended to the reader: (1) the move toward diversion is based more on dissatisfactions with the present system than on clear benefits for the community at large; (2) the Commission clearly sees the police mandate as including active community involvement, not merely starting with suspect contacts and ending with case dispositions; and (3) diversion can proceed at various points in the system through such procedures as preliminary conferences, consent decrees, and so on —that is, police diversion fits into a general pattern designed for the entire system.

---

* From *The Challenge of Crime in a Free Society*, The President's Commission on Law Enforcement and Administration of Justice (Washington, D.C.: U.S. Government Printing Office, 1967), pp. 78–89.

All three parts of the criminal justice system—police, courts, and corrections—have over the years developed special ways of dealing with children and young people. Many police departments have sought to develop specialists skilled at the difficult decisions that must be made about the many young people with whom the police have contact. Officers have organized and participated in athletic and other programs to help improve police relations with youth and enrich life in the community. Corrections systems have established separate institutions for juveniles and have emphasized probation over institutionalization for juveniles more than they have for adults. The juvenile court—even where it shares its judge with other tribunals or is not physically distinct—has a philosophy and procedures of its own and markedly unlike those of the adult criminal court.

Although its shortcomings are many and its results too often disappointing, the juvenile justice system in many cities is operated by people who are better educated and more highly skilled, can call on more and better facilities and services, and has more ancillary agencies to which to refer its clientele than its adult counterpart. Yet the number of cases referred to juvenile courts continues to grow faster than the juvenile population, the recidivism rate continues to increase, and while there are no figures on how many delinquents graduate to become grownup criminals, it is clear that many do.

4

THE POLICE: INITIAL CONTACT POINT
WITH THE JUVENILE JUSTICE SYSTEM

Whether or not a juvenile becomes involved in the juvenile justice system usually depends upon the outcome of an encounter with the police. Such encounters are frequent, especially in the crowded inner city.

Some of them grow out of a criminal act of significant proportions: The juveniles have been caught in the act, or are being sought, or there is reason to believe that they answer the description given by a complainant. In such instances, the contact is very likely to lead to further processing by the juvenile justice system.

On the other hand, many encounters are based on a relatively minor violation, or not on a specific crime at all but on the policeman's sense that something is wrong. He may suspect that a crime has happened or is about to happen. Or he may believe the juvenile's conduct is offensive, insolent, or in some other way improper. On such occasions, the policeman has a relatively great range of choices. He can pass by. He can stop for a few words of general banter. He can ask the juveniles their names, where they live, where they are going. He can question them about what has been happening in the neighborhood. He can search them, order them to disperse or move on, check with the station for records and recent neighborhood offenses. He can send or take them home, where he may warn their parents to keep them off the street. Suspicion, even perhaps without very specific grounds for it, may on occasion lead him to bring them in to the station for further questioning or checking.

In any given encounter the policeman's selection among alternatives may vary considerably among departments and among individual officers. It is governed to some extent by departmental practice, either explicitly enunciated or tacitly understood. Such policies are difficult to evolve—indeed, in many instances they could not be specific enough to be helpful without being too rigid to accommodate the vast variety of street situations. Nevertheless, it is important that, wherever possible, police forces formulate guidelines for policemen in their dealings with juveniles.

Besides the nature of the situation and departmental policy, however, police-juvenile encounters are shaped by other, less tangible forces.

One such influence is the character of the police force as a whole. In a recent field study of two police forces—one putting particularly great emphasis on education and training, merit promotions, centralized control; the second relying more heavily on organization by precinct, seniority, on-the-job experience—significant differences were found between the two in handling delinquents. In the first city, the one with the more professionalized force, rates of both processing (police contact not amounting to arrest but requiring the police officer to make an official record) and arrest (formal police action against the juvenile either by ordering him to appear before a court official or by taking him into custody) were more than 50 percent higher than those in the second city. In other words, meetings between policemen and juveniles had formal, official, recorded consequences much more frequently in the first city, with its more highly trained and impersonal police force, than in the second. At the conclusion of his study on the police the researcher, noting how little is known about the actual effects on juveniles of different handling methods, speculates about the various arguments that might be made:

> *The training of a police force apparently alters the manner in which juveniles are handled. The principal effect of the inculcation of professional norms is to make the police less discriminatory but more severe. . . . Plausible arguments can be advanced . . . to the effect that certain, swift punishment (in this case, certain, swift referral to a court agency) is an excellent deterrent to juvenile crime. Youths are impressed early, so the argument might go, with the seriousness of their offense and the consequences of their actions. Equally plausible arguments can no doubt be adduced to suggest that arresting juveniles—particularly first offenders—tends to confirm them in their deviant behavior; it gives them the status, in the eyes of their gang, of "tough guys" who have "been downtown" with the police; it throws them into intimate contact with confirmed offenders, where presumably they become "con-wise" and learned in the tricks of the thievery trade; and (somewhat contradictorily) since sentencing is rarely severe, it gives them a contempt for the sanctions available to society.[1]*

The reactions and attitudes of individual officers are also influential when they are dealing with juveniles. As numerous observers and students of police work have pointed out, a policeman in attempting to solve crimes must employ, in the absence of concrete evidence, circumstantial indicators to link specific crimes with specific people. Thus policemen may stop Negro and Mexican youths in white neighborhoods, may suspect juveniles who act in what the policemen consider an impudent or overly casual manner, and may be influenced by such factors as unusual hair styles or clothes uncommon to the wearer's group or area. Naturally, the adolescents involved are aware of such police distinctions. They are at a notoriously sensitive age and are ready to see themselves as victims of police harassment. In the words of one boy: "Them cops is supposed to be out catching *criminals*. They ain't paid to be looking after my hair!" When boys are actually stopped by policemen, their own attitudes and their demeanor appear often to play a part in what happens next. Some observers have suggested that those who act frightened, penitent, and respectful are more likely to be released, while those who assert their autonomy and act indifferent or resistant run a substantially greater risk of being frisked, interrogated, or even taken into custody.

Informal street handling of juveniles creates conflicts that are extremely difficult to resolve. Juveniles commit large numbers of offenses. Some of the circumstances that lead policemen to suspect given juveniles often do stem from criminal conduct. The policeman's dependence upon the sort of information juveniles provide in informal encounters is real and unlikely to be satisfied elsewhere.

On the other hand, abuse of authority—real or imagined—may seriously

---

[1] James Q. Wilson, in *The Police: Six Sociological Essays*, ed. David J. Bordua (New York: Wiley, 1967).

impair young people's respect for constituted authority and produce deep resentment. Informal investigatory police encounters with juveniles are inevitable, but it is of the utmost importance that juveniles receive treatment that is neither unfair nor degrading.

The Commission recommends:

To the greatest feasible extent, police departments should formulate policy guidelines for dealing with juveniles.

All officers should be acquainted with the special characteristics of adolescents, particularly those of the social, racial, and other specific groups with which they are likely to come in contact.

Custody of a juvenile (both prolonged street stops and stationhouse visits) should be limited to instances where there is objective, specifiable ground for suspicion.

Every stop that includes a frisk or an interrogation of more than a few preliminary identifying questions should be recorded in a strictly confidential report.

THE JUVENILE COURT AND RELATED AGENCIES

Juvenile courts are judicial tribunals that deal in special ways with young people's cases. They exist in all jurisdictions. Their cases include delinquency (both conduct in violation of the criminal code and truancy, ungovernability, and certain conduct illegal only for children), neglect, and dependency. The juveniles with whom they deal are those below a designated age, usually between sixteen and twenty-one; court authority over the child extends until he reaches his majority. They differ from adult criminal courts in a number of basic respects, reflecting the philosophy that erring children should be protected and rehabilitated rather than subjected to the harshness of the criminal system. Thus they substitute procedural informality for the adversary system, emphasize investigation of the juvenile's background in deciding dispositions, rely heavily on the social sciences for both diagnosis and treatment, and are committed to rehabilitation of the juvenile as the predominant goal of the entire system.

Studies conducted by the Commission, legislative inquiries in various States, and reports by informed observers compel the conclusion that the great hopes originally held for the juvenile court have not been fulfilled. It has not succeeded significantly in rehabilitating delinquent youth, in reducing or even stemming the tide of delinquency, or in bringing justice and compassion to the child offender. To say that juvenile courts have failed to achieve their goals is to say no more than what is true of criminal courts in the United States. But failure is most striking when hopes are highest.

One reason for the failure of the juvenile courts has been the community's continuing unwillingness to provide the resources—the people and facilities and concern—necessary to permit them to realize their potential and prevent them from acquiring some of the undesirable features typical of lower criminal courts in this country. In some jurisdictions, for example, the juvenile court judgeship does not have high status in the eyes of the bar, and while there are many juvenile court judges of outstanding ability and devotion, many are not. One crucial presupposition of the juvenile court philosophy—a mature and sophisticated judge, wise and well versed in law and the science of human behavior—has proved in fact too often unattainable. A recent study of juvenile court judges in the United States revealed that half had no undergraduate degree; a fifth had received no college education at all; a fifth were not members of the bar. Almost three-quarters devote less than a quarter of their time to juvenile and family matters, and judicial hearings often turn out to be little more than attenuated interviews of ten to fifteen minutes' duration.

Similarly, more than four-fifths of the juvenile judges polled in a recent survey reported no psychologist or psychiatrist available to them on a regular basis—over half a century after the juvenile court movement set out to achieve the coordinated application of the behavioral and social sciences to the misbehaving child. Clinical services to diagnose and to assist in devising treatment plans are the exception, and even where they exist, the waiting lists are so long that their usefulness is more theoretical than real.

The dispositional alternatives available even to the better endowed juvenile courts fall far short of the richness and the relevance to individual needs envisioned by the court's founders. In most places, indeed, the only alternatives are release outright, probation, and institutionalization. Probation means minimal supervision at best. A large percentage of juvenile courts have no probation services at all, and in those that do, caseloads typically are so high that counseling and supervision take the form of occasional phone calls and perfunctory visits instead of the careful, individualized service that was intended. Institutionalization too often means storage—isolation from the outside world—in an overcrowded, understaffed security institution with little education, little vocational training, little counseling or job placement or other guidance upon release. Intermediate and auxiliary measures such as halfway houses, community residential treatment centers, diversified institutions and programs, and intensive community supervision have proved difficult to establish.

But it is by no means true that a simple infusion of resources into juvenile courts and attendant institutions would fulfill the expectations that accompanied the court's birth and development. There are problems that go much deeper. The failure of the juvenile court to fulfill its rehabilitative and preventive promise stems in important measure from a grossly overoptimistic view of what is known about the phenomenon of juvenile criminality and of what even a fully equipped juvenile court could do about it. Experts in the field agree that it is extremely difficult to develop successful methods for preventing serious delinquent acts through rehabilitative programs for the child. What research is making increasingly clear is that delinquency is not so much an act of individual deviancy as a pattern of behavior produced by a multitude of pervasive societal influences well beyond the reach of the actions of any judge, probation officer, correctional counselor, or psychiatrist.

The same uncritical and unrealistic estimates of what is known and can be done that make expectation so much greater than achievement also serve to justify extensive official action and to mask the fact that much of it may produce more harm than good. Official action may actually help to fix and perpetuate delinquency in the child through a process in which the individual begins to think of himself as delinquent and organizes his behavior accordingly. That process itself is further reinforced by the effect of the labeling upon the child's family, neighbors, teachers, and peers, whose reactions communicate to the child in subtle ways a kind of expectation of delinquent conduct. The undesirable consequences of official treatment are maximized in programs that rely on institutionalizing the child. The most informed and benign official treatment of the child therefore contains within it the seeds of its own frustration and itself may often feed the very disorder it is designed to cure.

The limitations, both in theory and in execution, of strictly rehabilitative treatment methods, combined with public anxiety over the seemingly irresistible rise in juvenile criminality, have produced a rupture between the theory and the practice of juvenile court dispositions. While statutes, judges, and commentators still talk the language of compassion and treatment, it has become clear that in fact the same purposes that characterize the use of the criminal law for adult offenders—retribution, condemnation, deterrence, incapacitation—are involved in the disposition of juvenile offenders too. These are society's ultimate techniques for protection against threatening conduct; it is inevitable that they should be used against threats from the young as well as the old when other resources appear unavailing. As Professor Francis Allen has acutely observed:

In a great many cases the juvenile court must perform functions essentially similar to those exercised by any court adjudicating cases of persons charged with dangerous and disturbing behavior. It must reassert the norms and standards of the community when confronted by seriously deviant conduct, and it must protect the security of the community by such measures as it has at its disposal, though the available means may be unsatisfactory when viewed either from the standpoint of the community interest or of the welfare of the child. [2]

The difficulty is not that this compromise with the rehabilitative idea has occurred, but that it has not been acknowledged. Juvenile court laws and procedures that can be rationalized solely on the basis of the original optimistic theories endure as if the vitality of those theories were undiluted. Thus, for example, juvenile courts retain expansive grounds of jurisdiction authorizing judicial intervention in relatively minor matters of morals and misbehavior, on the ground that subsequent delinquent conduct may be indicated, as if there were reliable ways of predicting delinquency in a given child and reliable ways of redirecting children's lives. Delinquency is adjudicated in informal proceedings that often lack safeguards fundamental for protecting the individual and for assuring reliable determinations, as if the court were a hospital clinic and its only objective were to discover the child's malady and to cure him.

The Commission does not conclude from its study of the juvenile court that the time has come to jettison the experiment and remand the disposition

[2] Francis A. Allen, *The Borderland of Criminal Justice* (Chicago: Univ. of Chicago Press, 1964), p. 53.

of children charged with crime to the criminal courts of the country. As trying as are the problems of the juvenile courts, the problems of the criminal courts, particularly those of the lower courts that would fall heir to much of the juvenile court jurisdiction, are even graver; and the ideal of separate treatment of children is still worth pursuing. What is required is rather a revised philosophy of the juvenile court, based on recognition that in the past our reach exceeded our grasp. The spirit that animated the juvenile court movement was fed in part by a humanitarian compassion for offenders who were children. That willingness to understand and treat people who threaten public safety and security should be nurtured, not turned aside as hopeless sentimentality, both because it is civilized and because social protection itself demands constant search for alternatives to the crude and limited expedient of condemnation and punishment. But neither should it be allowed to outrun reality. The juvenile court is a court of law, charged like other agencies of criminal justice with protecting the community against threatening conduct. Rehabilitation of offenders through individualized handling is one way of providing protection, and appropriately the primary way in dealing with children. But the guiding consideration for a court of law that deals with threatening conduct is nevertheless protection of the community. The juvenile court, like other courts, is therefore obliged to employ all the means at hand, not excluding incapacitation, for achieving that protection. What should distinguish the juvenile from the criminal courts is their greater emphasis on rehabilitation, not their exclusive preoccupation with it.

This chapter outlines a series of interlocking proposals aimed at what the Commission believes are basic deficiencies in the system of juvenile justice. Those concerning early stages in police handling of juveniles have already been set forth. The essence of those relating to the juvenile court and institutions closely connected with it is as follows:

> The formal sanctioning system and pronouncement of delinquency should be used only as a last resort. In place of the formal system, dispositional alternatives to adjudication must be developed for dealing with juveniles, including agencies to provide and coordinate services and procedures to achieve necessary control without unnecessary stigma. Alternatives already available, such as those related to court intake, should be more fully exploited.

> The range of conduct for which court intervention is authorized should be narrowed.

> The cases that fall within the narrowed jurisdiction of the court and filter through the screen of pre-judicial, informal disposition modes would largely involve offenders for whom more vigorous measures seem necessary. Court adjudication and disposition of those offenders should no longer be viewed solely as a diagnosis and prescription for cure, but should be frankly recognized as an authoritative court judgment expressing society's claim to protection. While rehabilitative efforts should be vigorously pursued in deference to the youthfulness of the offenders and in keeping with the general commitment to individualized treatment of all offenders, the incapacitative, deterrent, and condemnatory purposes of the judgment should not be disguised. Accordingly, the adjudicatory hearing should be consistent with basic principles of due process. Counsel and evidentiary

restrictions are among the essential elements of fundamental fairness in juvenile as well as adult criminal courts.

Pre-judicial disposition outside the court. It is a salient characteristic of the American criminal law system that substantial numbers of those who, on the basis of facts known to the authorities, could be dealt with by the formal machinery of justice are in fact disposed of otherwise. The pressures and policies responsible for development of pre-judicial dispositions in the juvenile system are in part the same as those that have led to the use of alternatives to the adult criminal process. The felt overseverity of the formal process in the circumstances of the particular case, the broad reach of the definition of the forbidden conduct beyond what is appropriately dealt with by the criminal or juvenile justice system, and the sheer volume of workload are among the most important considerations.

Informal and discretionary pre-judicial dispositions already are a formally recognized part of the process to a far greater extent in the juvenile than in the criminal justice system. The primacy of the rehabilitative goal in dealing with juveniles, the limited effectiveness of the formal processes of the juvenile justice system, the labeling inherent in adjudicating children delinquents, the inability of the formal system to reach the influences—family, school, labor market, recreational opportunities—that shape the life of a youngster, the limited disposition options available to the juvenile judge, the limitations of personnel and diagnostic and treatment facilities, the lack of community support—all of these factors give pre-judicial dispositions an especially important role with respect to juveniles.

Consequently, the informal and pre-judicial processes of adjustment compete in importance with the formal ones and account for a majority of juvenile dispositions. They include discretionary judgments of the police officer to ignore conduct or warn the child or refer him to other agencies; "station adjustment" by the police, in which the child's release may be made conditional on his complying with designated limitations on his conduct; the planned diversion of alleged delinquents away from the court to resources within the school, clinic, or other community facilities, by such groups as mental health, social, and school guidance agencies; pre-judicial dispositions, at the intake stage of the court process, by probation officers or sometimes judges exercising a broad screening function and selecting among alternatives that include outright dismissal, referral to another community agency for service, informal supervision by the probation staff, detention, and filing a petition for further court action. In many courts the court intake process itself disposes of the majority of cases.

There are grave disadvantages and perils, however, in that vast continent of sublegal dispositions. It exists outside of and hence beyond the guidance and control of articulated policies and legal restraints. It is largely invisible—unknown in its detailed operations—and hence beyond sustained scrutiny and criticism. Discretion too often is exercised haphazardly and episodically, without the salutary obligation to account and without a foundation in full and comprehensive information about the offender and about the availability and likelihood of alternative dispositions. Opportunities occur for illegal and even discriminatory results, for abuse of authority by the ill-intentioned, the prejudiced, the overzealous. Irrelevant, improper considerations—race, nonconformity, punitiveness, sentimentality, understaffing, overburdening loads—may govern officials in their largely personal exercise of discretion. The consequence may be not only injustice to the juvenile but diversion out of the formal channels of those whom the best interests of the community require to be dealt with through the formal adjudicatory and dispositional processes.

Yet on balance, it is clear to the Commission that informal pre-judicial handling is preferable to formal treatment in many cases and should be used more broadly. The possibilities for rehabilitation appear to be optimal where community-based resources are used on a basis as nearly consensual as possible. The challenge is to obtain the benefits of informal pre-judicial handling with a minimum of its attendant evils. The following recommendations are offered to that end.

(a) Pre-Judicial Handling by the Police. The police should promptly determine which cases are suitable for pre-judicial disposition. Where there are juvenile specialists, they should be present at the stationhouse for as many hours of the day as possible and available on call when absent, to facilitate speedy pre-judicial decisions. The police should have written standards for release, for referral to nonjudicial sources, and for referral to the juvenile court. The standards should be sent to all agencies of delinquency control and should be reviewed and appraised jointly at periodic intervals. They should be made the basis for inservice training that would consider, besides the decision-making duties of the police, materials pertinent to increasing understanding of juvenile behavior and making more effective use of nonjudicial community resources.

In cases where information on the child is needed, it should be sought through home visits as well as from official records, and the police should be aided, or replaced, by paid case aides drawn from the neighborhood within the police district and selected for their knowledge of the community and their ability to communicate easily with juveniles and their families.

In addition to outright referral to nonjudicial agencies the police should have the option to refer directly to the juvenile court specified classes of cases, including those of more serious offenders, repeated offenders for whom other and persistent redirecting efforts had failed, and certain parole and probation violators. The police should not undertake to redirect juveniles by such means as conducting quasi-judicial hearings or imposing special duties or personal obligations.

Police practices following custody thus should continue as at present but with two significant changes: Cases deemed suitable for adjustment would be referred to a youth-serving agency within a neighborhood service center (the Youth Services Bureau proposed herein and described in detail subsequently), and the categories of cases that could be referred by the police directly to juvenile court would be restricted. Exercise of discretion to release outright would be encouraged, as now, so that minor offenses not apparently symptomatic of serious behavior problems could be dismissed at the earliest stage of official handling, and even more serious offenses could be adjusted by referral to a Youth Services Bureau or other organization if, in the judgment of the police, there was no immediate threat to public safety.

The Commission recommends:

Police forces should make full use of the central diagnosing and coordinating services of the Youth Services Bureau. Station adjustment should be limited to release and referral; it should not include hearings or the imposition of sanctions by the police. Court referral by the police should be restricted to those cases involving serious criminal conduct or repeated misconduct of a more than trivial nature.

(b) Community Agencies. There should be expanded use of community agencies for dealing with delinquents nonjudicially and close to where they live. Use of community agencies has several advantages. It avoids the stigma of being processed by an official agency regarded by the public as an arm of crime control. It substitutes for official agencies organizations better suited for redirecting conduct. The use of locally sponsored or operated organizations heightens the community's awareness of the need for recreational, employment, tutoring, and other youth development services. Involvement of local residents brings greater appreciation of the complexity of delinquents' problems, thereby engendering the sense of public responsibility that financial support of programs requires.

Referrals by police, school officials, and others to such local community agencies should be on a voluntary basis. To protect against abuse, the agency's option of court referral should terminate when the juvenile or his family and the community agency agree upon an appropriate disposition. If a departure from the agreed-upon course of conduct should thereafter occur, it should be the community agency that exercises the authority to refer to court. It is also essential that the dispositions available to such local organizations be restricted. The purpose of using community institutions in this way is to help, not to coerce, and accordingly it is inappropriate to confer on them a power to order treatment or alter custody or impose sanctions for deviation from the helping program.

Those recommendations could be put into effect in the near future, with existing organizations. Long-term recommendations for enhanced use of community service agencies, however, would require the creation of new social institutions. An essential objective in a community's delinquency control and prevention plan should therefore be the establishment of a neighborhood youth-serving agency, a Youth Services Bureau, with a broad range of services and certain mandatory functions. Such an agency ideally would be located in a comprehensive community center and would serve both delinquent and nondelinquent youths. While some referrals to the Youth Services Bureau would normally originate with parents, schools, and other sources, the bulk of the referrals could be expected to come from the police and the juvenile court intake staff, and police and court referrals should have special status in that the Youth Services Bureau would be required to accept them all. If, after study, certain youths are deemed unlikely to benefit from its services, the Bureau should be obliged to transmit notice of the decision and supporting reasons to the referral source. A mandate for service seems necessary to insure energetic efforts to control and redirect acting-out youth and to minimize the substantial risk that this population, denied service by traditional agencies, will inevitably be shunted to a law enforcement agency.

A primary function of the Youth Services Bureau thus would be individually tailored work with troublemaking youths. The work might include group and individual counseling, placement in foster homes, work and recreational programs, employment counseling, and special education (remedial, vocational). It would be under the Bureau's direct control either through purchase or by voluntary agreement with other community organizations. The most significant feature of the Bureau's function would be its mandatory responsibility to develop and monitor a plan of service for a group now handled, for the most part, either inappropriately or not at all except in time of crisis.

It is essential that acceptance of the Youth Services Bureau's services be voluntary; otherwise the dangers and disadvantages of coercive power would merely be transferred from the juvenile court to it. Nonetheless, it may be necessary to vest the Youth Services Bureau with authority to refer to the court within a brief time—not more than sixty and preferably not more than thirty days—those with whom it cannot deal effectively. In accordance with its basically voluntary character, the Youth Services Bureau should be required to comply with the parent's request that a case be referred to juvenile court.

In many communities there may already exist the ingredients of a Youth Services Bureau in the form of community or neighborhood centers and programs for juveniles. All communities should explore the availability of Federal funds both for establishing the coordinating mechanisms basic to the Youth Services Bureau's operation and for instituting the programs that the community needs.

The Commission recommends:

Communities should establish neighborhood youth-serving agencies—Youth Services Bureaus—located if possible in comprehensive neighborhood community centers and receiving juveniles (delinquent and nondelinquent) referred by the police, the juvenile court, parents, schools, and other sources.

These agencies would act as central coordinators of all community services for young people and would also provide services lacking in the community or neighborhood, especially ones designed for less seriously delinquent juveniles.

The juvenile court.   (a) Intake—Pre-Judicial Disposition in Court. Prejudicial disposition is no newcomer to the juvenile court. Some courts today, as noted above, dispose of more than half the cases referred to them by means short of adjudication. It is in the court, therefore, where problems of lack of accurate, up-to-date information about needs and alternatives; lack of coordination among available services; and lack of systematic ways to bring the juvenile and the service together are particularly acute.

To meet those difficulties, the court intake function of pre-judicial disposition should be more systematically employed and more formally recognized and organized. Written guides and standards should be formulated and imparted in the course of inservice training. Staff resources should be augmented where necessary to keep abreast of service opportunities and programs in the community and to make inquiries into the backgrounds of juveniles sufficiently comprehensive to select intelligently among alternatives. Overly informal methods of control (such as informal probation with filing of a petition as the penalty for violation), subject as they are to abuse, should be abandoned in favor of institutionalized nonadjudicatory disposition.

More specifically, the Commission commends to the attention of juvenile courts the preliminary conference recently adopted by both New York and Illinois, through which voluntarily attended discussions among court personnel, juvenile, parents, complainants, and other involved parties are used to resolve grievances without adjudication. Safeguards essential to such a procedure are that it occur within a specifically limited time, to eliminate the indirect coercion of an indefinite threat that a petition will be filed at some later date, and that use of statements made at the conference be inadmissible in subsequent court proceedings.

The Commission recommends:

Juvenile courts should make fullest feasible use of preliminary conferences to dispose of cases short of adjudication.

Another method of employing the arbitrating and treating authority of the juvenile court without the disadvantages of adjudication is the consent decree. Consent decree negotiations, too, would be conducted by intake officers and would involve the juvenile and his parents and lawyer (the presence of whom, unless waived, would be required) and a probation officer assigned to the case. The consent decree would be embodied in writing and attested to by the parties and would be effective only upon approval of its terms by the juvenile court judge. It would prescribe a treatment plan but could not commit to an institution. Its duration would be limited, preferably to a year. Negotiations would be subject to the same protections as the preliminary conference procedure. If negotiations failed or the consent decree were violated, the same possibilities—dismissal, referral to a nonjudicial agency, and filing of a petition—would be available as were available prior to the decree. In case of violation of the consent decree, the charge would be the one that initially gave rise to the proceedings. Violation of the decree would be relevant only to disposition.

The Commission recommends:

Juvenile courts should employ consent decrees wherever possible to avoid adjudication while still settling juvenile cases and treating offenders.

(b) Legislative Standards for Juvenile Court Intervention. A hallmark of the juvenile court has traditionally been the inclusion in its jurisdiction of a very diverse group, sometimes characterized as children in trouble —whether the trouble consists of youthful criminality, truancy or other conduct wrong only for children, or a parent's inadequacy or abusiveness. The basic philosophy of the juvenile court was considered antithetical to narrow, restrictively specific jurisdictional requisites, and so they were discarded in favor of all-encompassing formulations intended to bring within the court's jurisdiction virtually every child in need of help, for whatever reason and however the need was manifested. To the chancery court's traditional clientele of neglected children was added the category of underage criminal lawbreakers, who were, however, not to be designated or considered as such and toward whom, despite their considerably more threatening behavior, the judicial attitude was to be equally solicitous. In accordance with the protective and rehabilitative theories of the juvenile court, the definition of conduct making one eligible for the category of delinquency was not limited by conduct criminal for adults but rather amounted virtually to a manual of undesirable youthful behavior. And in addition to enforcing the penal law, the commonly accepted standards of conduct for youth, and the basic obligations of parents to children, the juvenile court also undertook to reinforce the duties owed parents and schools by children. Thus truancy was included among the bases for juvenile court jurisdiction, as was a catch-all state variously called incorrigibility, ungovernability, uncontrollability, or simply "beyond control," which basically means defying parental authority.

The rationale for this comprehensive array of jurisdictional pegs generally emphasized the growth of social as opposed to legalistic justice and the new efforts to bring the law out of isolation and into partnership with the ascending social and behavioral sciences. The juvenile court was to arrest the development of incipient criminals by detecting them early and uncovering and ameliorating the causes of their disaffection.

Experience of over half a century with juvenile courts has taught us that these aspirations were greatly over-optimistic and chimerical. The court's wide-ranging jurisdiction thus has often become an anachronism serving to facilitate gratuitous coercive intrusions into the lives of children and families. Recent legislative revisions in several states, including California, Illinois, and New York, have significantly restricted the court's jurisdictional bases.

The Commission recommends:

The movement for narrowing the juvenile court's jurisdiction should be continued.

Specifically, the Commission recommends as follows: Any act that is considered a crime when committed by an adult should continue to be, when charged against a juvenile, the business of the juvenile court.

The conduct-illegal-only-for-children category of the court's jurisdiction should be substantially circumscribed so that it ceases to include such acts as smoking, swearing, and disobedience to parents and comprehends only acts that entail a real risk of long-range harm to the child, such as experimenting with drugs, repeatedly becoming pregnant out of wedlock, and being habitually truant from school. Serious consideration, at the least, should be given to complete elimination of the court's power over children for non-criminal conduct.

Traffic violations by juveniles should be dealt with by traffic courts, except for serious offenses such as vehicular homicide and driving while under the influence of alcohol or drugs.

The neglect jurisdiction of the juvenile court should be retained since it involves conflicts between the parents' right to custody and the child's physical and mental well-being.

Dependency jurisdiction should be abolished since such cases involve inability rather than willful failure to provide properly for children and can adequately and more appropriately be dealt with by social, nonjudicial agencies.

Careful consideration should be given proposals to create family courts that, by dealing with all intrafamily matters including those now generally handled by juvenile courts, would provide one means of achieving the consistency and continuity of treatment now too often undercut by fragmented jurisdiction.

(c) Procedural Justice for the Child. The original humanitarian philosophy of the juvenile court was believed to require a significant change in the manner in which courts determined which children to deal with and how to deal with them. The formalities of criminal procedure were rejected on the ground that they were not needed in juvenile court proceedings and that they would be destructive of the goals of those proceedings. In their place was to be substituted a wholly informal and flexible procedure under which, by gentle and friendly probing by judge, social worker, parent, and child, the roots of the child's difficulties could be exposed and informed decisions made as to how best to meet his problems. Informality in both procedure and disposition thus became a basic characteristic of juvenile courts.

In recent years, however, there has been a mounting reaction against this commitment to informality, stemming principally from profound concern about the potential arbitrariness and unfettered judicial discretion in dealing with human lives that informality establishes. This reaction is only one manifestation of much broader concern about protection of the rights of persons threatened with state intervention in their daily lives, particularly insofar as those who are involved live in poverty at the margin of American life and have not in the past had full protection. But there are special considerations applicable to the juvenile court that are of immediate importance.

First, efforts to help and heal and treat, if they are to have any chance of success, must be based upon an accurate determination of the facts—the facts of the conduct that led to the filing of the petition and also the facts of the child's past conduct and relationships. The essential attributes of a judicial trial are the best guarantee our system has been able to devise for assuring reliable determinations of fact.

Second, we are committed to the value of individual self-determination and freedom. The fact that the state's motives are beneficent and designed to provide what, at least in its view, the child and its parents need, should not be allowed to obscure the fact that in taking a child from his parents or placing him in an institution or even subjecting him to probation and supervision, the state is invoking its power to interfere with the lives of individuals as they choose to lead them.

Third, it has proved to be true for a variety of reasons that the promise of the juvenile courts to help the child, to rehabilitate him, to lead him into a healthy and constructive life has not been kept. This has been partly because of lack of community support; but as was observed above, it has in addition been because of considerations beyond society's power to alter. Therefore, the major rationale for the withdrawal of procedural safeguards ceases to exist. The point was made recently by the U.S. Supreme Court, which observed:

> *There is evidence, in fact, that there may be grounds for concern that the child receives the worst of both worlds: that he gets neither the protections accorded to adults nor the solicitous care and regenerative treatment postulated for children. Kent v. United States, 383 U.S. 541 (1966).*

Fourth, in point of fact, the welfare and the needs of the child offender are not the sole preoccupation of the juvenile court, which has the same purposes that mark the criminal law. To the extent that this is so, the justification for abandoning the protective procedural guarantees associated with due process of law disappears.

Fifth, there is increasing evidence that the informal procedures, contrary to the original expectation, may themselves constitute a further obstacle to effective treatment of the delinquent to the extent that they engender in the child a sense of injustice provoked by seemingly all-powerful and challengeless exercise of authority by judges and probation officers.

These challenges to the departure from procedural regularity in the juvenile courts make the case for bringing juvenile court procedures into closer harmony with our fundamental commitments to due process of law. What is entailed is not abandonment of the unique qualities of the juvenile court or adoption of the precise model of the criminal trial but rather accommodation of the dual goals of due process and welfare by instituting procedures permitting the court effectively to pursue humane and rehabilitative aims within the framework of a system that recognizes the indispensability of justice to any coercive governmental venture into the lives of individuals. Many of the issues here considered are raised by the case of *Gault* v. *United States,* now pending before the U.S. Supreme Court. Any procedural formulations and alterations must of course conform with its decision.

Counsel. The Commission believes that no single action holds more potential for achieving procedural justice for the child in the juvenile court than provision of counsel. The presence of an independent legal representative of the child, or of his parent, is the keystone of the whole structure of guarantees that a minimum system of procedural justice requires. The rights to confront one's accusers, to cross-examine witnesses, to present evidence and testimony of one's own, to be unaffected by prejudicial and unreliable evidence, to participate meaningfully in the dispositional decision, to take an appeal have substantial meaning for the overwhelming majority of persons brought before the juvenile court only if they are provided with competent lawyers who can invoke those rights effectively. The most informal and well-intentioned of judicial proceedings are technical; few adults without legal training can influence or even understand them; certainly children cannot. Papers are drawn and charges expressed in legal language. Events follow one another in a manner that appears arbitrary and confusing to the uninitiated. Decisions, unexplained, appear too official to challenge. But with lawyers come records of proceedings; records make possible appeals which, even if they do not occur, impart by their possibility a healthy atmosphere of accountability.

Fears have been expressed that lawyers would make juvenile court proceedings adversary. No doubt this is partly true, but it is partly desirable. Informality is often abused. The juvenile courts deal with cases in which facts are disputed and in which, therefore, rules of evidence, confrontation of witnesses, and other adversary procedures are called for. They deal with many cases involving conduct that can lead to incarceration or close supervision for long periods, and therefore juveniles often need the same safeguards that are granted to adults. And in all cases children need advocates to speak for them and guard their interests, particularly when disposition decisions are made. It is the disposition stage at which the opportunity arises to offer individualized treatment plans and in which the danger inheres that the court's coercive power will be applied without adequate knowledge of the circumstances.

Fears also have been expressed that the formality lawyers would bring into juvenile court would defeat the therapeutic aims of the court. But informality has no necessary connection with therapy; it is a device that has been used to approach therapy, and it is not the only possible device. It is quite possible that in many instances lawyers, for all their commitment to formality, could do more to further therapy for their clients than can the small, overworked social staffs of the courts. A lawyer—especially a poverty program or legal aid lawyer or other practitioner specializing in criminal matters—is often familiar with the various rehabilitative and preventive programs and organizations available in his community. He might already know the youngster's family or neighborhood. Thus he often would be, in other words, in a position to assist the court in developing a plan of disposition and treatment appropriate for the individual juvenile and, more important, in seeing that it is carried out: in making the appointments and taking the other specific steps that the press of business may force the probation officer to leave to the reluctant child or his bewildered parents. There are not nearly enough lawyers now with the skills to perform this role, but the fact that there are some argues that there could be more if there were more calls for their services. To suggest that lawyers perform these tasks is not to suggest that they become social workers. It is to suggest that in many instances lawyers can, and do, perform services for their clients that go beyond formal court representation.

The Commission believes it is essential that counsel be appointed by the juvenile court for those who are unable to provide their own. Experience under the prevailing systems in which children are free to seek counsel of their choice reveals how empty of meaning the right is for those typically the subjects of juvenile court proceedings. Moreover, providing counsel only when the child is sophisticated enough to be aware of his need and to ask for one or when he fails to waive his announced right are not enough, as experience in numerous jurisdictions reveals.

The Commission recommends:

Counsel should be appointed as a matter of course wherever coercive action is a possibility, without requiring any affirmative choice by child or parent.

Adjudication and disposition. Perhaps the height of the juvenile court's procedural informality is its failure to differentiate clearly between the adjudication hearing, whose purpose is to determine the truth of the allegations in the petition, and the disposition proceeding, at which the juvenile's background is considered in connection with deciding what to do with him. In many juvenile courts the two questions are dealt with in the same proceeding or are separated only in the minority of cases in which the petition's allegations are at issue. Even where adjudication and disposition are dealt with separately, the social reports, containing material about background and character that might make objective examination of the facts of the case difficult, are often given to the judge before adjudication. Practices vary on disclosure of social study information to the juvenile and his parents and lawyer, if he has one.

Bifurcating juvenile court hearings would go far toward eliminating the danger that information relevant only to disposition will color factual questions of involvement and jurisdictional basis for action.

The Commission recommends:

Juvenile court hearings should be divided into an adjudicatory hearing and a dispositional one, and the evidence admissible at the adjudicatory hearing should be so limited that findings are not dependent upon or unduly influenced by hearsay, gossip, rumor, and other unreliable types of information.

To minimize the danger that adjudication will be affected by inappropriate considerations, social investigation reports should not be made known to the judge in advance of adjudication. As is recommended for adult presentence reports, in the absence of compelling reason for nondisclosure of special information, those facts in the social study upon which the judge relies in making the disposition decision should be disclosed to the child, his parents, or his lawyer.

Notice. The unfairness of too much informality is also reflected in the inadequacy of notice to parents and juveniles about charges and hearings.

The Commission recommends:

Notice should be given well in advance of any scheduled court proceeding, including intake, detention, and waiver hearings, and should set forth the alleged misconduct with particularity.

Detention. Detention appears to be far too routinely and frequently used for juveniles both while they are awaiting court appearance and during the period after disposition and before institution space is available. In theory a juvenile is detained only when no suitable custodian can be found or when there appears to be a substantial risk that he will get into more trouble or hurt himself or someone else before he can be taken to court. A study for the Commission found, however, that in 1965 two-thirds of all juveniles apprehended were admitted to detention facilities and held there an average of twelve days at a total cost of more than $53 million. Furthermore, for nearly half the Nation's population there is no detention facility except the county jail, and many of the jails used for children are unsuitable even for adult offenders.

The Commission recommends:

Adequate and appropriate separate detention facilities for juveniles should be provided.

For children for whom detention is made necessary only by the unavailability of adequate parental supervision, there should be low-security community residential centers and similar shelters.

The Commission recommends:

Legislation should be enacted restricting both authority to detain and the circumstances under which detention is permitted.

Such legislation should require that only the probation officer be authorized to detain, except for those periods of time between the beginning of police custody and the arrival of a probation officer; that detention pending a detention hearing be restricted to situations in which it is clearly necessary for the child's protection or to keep him in the jurisdiction; that a detention hearing be required within no more than forty-eight hours of initial detention; and that the judge be required to release the juvenile when a detention hearing shows that the probation officer was without authority to order the initial detention.

Confidentiality of court records. Confidentiality of juvenile court records, both legal and social, is a particularly difficult issue. Privacy of proceedings and secrecy of information are basic to the court's objectives of avoiding stigma and improving rather than worsening the juvenile offender's chances to succeed in society. And the fact that damaging information is to be recorded only in the interest of assisting the juvenile is advanced to justify elimination of the check on court action that publicity would provide. In practice, however, while most juvenile courts bar or restrict attendance of uninvolved persons and limit that which may be publicly reported, the confidentiality of records is far from complete.

Employers, schools, and social agencies have an understandable interest in knowing about the record of a juvenile with whom they have contact. On the other hand, experience has shown that in too many instances such knowledge results in rejection or other damaging treatment of the juvenile, increasing the chances of future delinquent acts.

The Commission believes that legal reports should be available only to official agencies of criminal justice except when the juvenile court judge is satisfied that the information will not be used against the juvenile's interest. Social reports—which often contain the most personal of information and may incorporate the investigator's subjective interpretations—should be available only on a strictly limited basis to those agencies that need and will use the information for the same purpose for which it was originally gathered. Thus, social reports would be available only to agencies such as criminal court probation departments, mental health clinics, social agencies dealing with the delinquent.

The above recommendations on procedure must be seen as part of a whole pattern of recommendations concerning the juvenile court, particularly those with respect to pre-judicial handling and standards for legislative intervention. The major impact of these proposals would be to deemphasize adjudication as the primary method for dealing with difficult children. Most of those who did filter through to adjudication would be youths who had already proved resistant to helping services or whose conduct was so repetitive or so clearly dangerous to the community that no other alternative seemed feasible. A schematic representation of the proposed system appears on page 24.

The Commission strongly believes that all of these proposals will improve the effectiveness and the fairness of the juvenile justice system. But the fairest and most effective method for determining what treatment is needed cannot guarantee the availability of that treatment. In the last analysis, therefore, it is developing and establishing treatment methods and programs that must particularly engage the immediate and continuing efforts of communities concerned about juvenile delinquency and youth crime.

CONCLUSION

Society's efforts to control and combat delinquency may be seen as operating at three levels. The first and most basic—indeed, so basic that delinquency prevention is only one of the reasons for it—involves provision of a real opportunity for everyone to participate in the legitimate activities that in our society lead to or constitute a good life: education, recreation, employment, family life. It is to insure such opportunity that schools in the slums must be made as good as schools elsewhere; that discrimination and arbitrary or unnecessary restrictions must be eliminated from employment practices;

that job training must be made available to everyone; that physical surroundings must be reclaimed from deterioration and barrenness; that the rights of a citizen must be exercisable without regard to creed or race.

The pursuit of these goals is not inconsistent with the need to strengthen the system of juvenile justice. Some young offenders are dangerous repeaters, responsible for holdups, muggings, aggravated assaults—the crimes that frighten people off the streets. Others, while less threatening, have already shown themselves resistant to noncoercive rehabilitating efforts. Dealing with these youths so as to protect society requires—at least at this point in our understanding of human behavior—custody, adjudication of fact, and imposition of sanction. Those measures depend upon an effective, efficient system of juvenile justice. Swift apprehension, thorough investigation, prompt disposition—carried out by persons carefully selected and trained for their functions—should maximize the system's deterrent impact and the respect accorded the law it upholds. Insofar as the juvenile justice system does deal with delinquency, its dealings should be characterized by these attributes.

Further, the system should operate with all the procedural formality necessary to safeguard adequately the rights that any person has when he is subject to the application of coercive power. Juveniles should be represented by counsel; they should be able to confront those complaining of their conduct; their fate should not be determined by hearsay or gossip. They should not be unnecessarily detained.

Between these two aspects of delinquency control—the first relevant to all young people, the second reserved for those who appear to need the coercive authority of the court—there is a third: response to the special needs of youths with special problems. They may already have delinquency records. They may be delinquent but not seriously so. They may be law-abiding but alienated and uncooperative in making use of education or employment or other opportunities. They may be behavior or academic problems in school, or misfits among their peers, or disruptive in recreation groups. Whatever the nature or degree of the difficulty, today they are all too likely to be excluded by most agencies and institutions, which find these youngsters, whom ostensibly they exist to help, in fact more than their limited resources can manage. They may restrict the participation of such youths in extracurricular school activities, keep them segregated from their fellows in special classes, eliminate them from recreation groups, rate them ineligible for certain sorts of therapy.

For such youths, it is imperative to furnish help that is particularized enough to deal with their individual needs but does not separate them from their peers and label them for life. Providing sufficiently specialized services while yet avoiding destructive labeling and stigma poses one of the central dilemmas in the delinquency prevention area. The Commission has attempted herein to suggest some methods of meeting it—by minimizing the separation in special classes of children who need additional help in school and by returning them to regular routine as soon as possible; by involving whole groups of young people, rather than just the troublemakers, in community activities; by requiring that the Youth Services Bureau accept and deal with all youth and encouraging it, by means of specially earmarked funds, to develop intensive programs for delinquents. Whatever the specific methods chosen, the problem must be attacked, for it is with these young people that most youth-serving agencies today are having the least success.

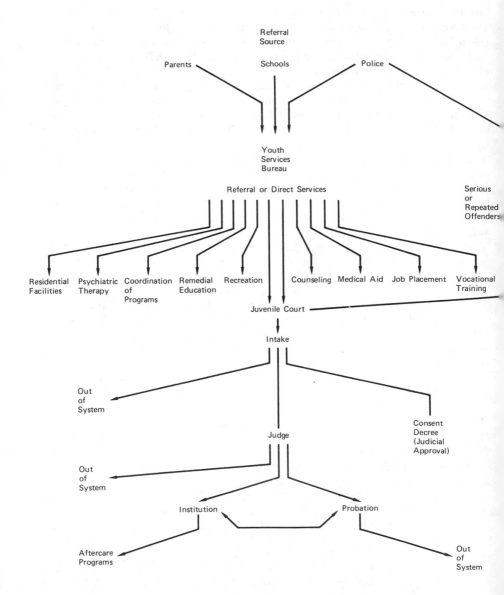

Figure 1   Proposed Juvenile Justice System

75064

2
ALTERNATIVES
TO JUDICIAL HANDLING*

The President's Commission on Law Enforcement
and Administration of Justice

Taken from the Commission's Task Force Report on Juvenile Delinquency, the following paper provides more detail on the avenues for change suggested by the President's Commission. The reader might note in particular the three categories of suggested change: (1) decriminalization as a means of ridding the criminal justice system of petty and noncriminal matters; (2) strong community involvement by means of absorption of juvenile offenders and even advocacy for them; and (3) diversion away from the juvenile justice system and the mechanics for achieving this. It is important to remember that diversion is thus recommended as part of a "package"; it is not set forth as a solution by itself.

* From *Task Force Report: Corrections*, The President's Commission on Law Enforcement and Administration of Justice (Washington, D.C.: U.S. Government Printing Office, 1967), pp. 396–399. The Commission is indebted to William Sheridan, Ass't Director, Division of Juvenile Delinquency Services, Children's Bureau; Margaret Rosenheim and Richardson White, Jr., of the President's Commission on Law Enforcement and the Administration of Justice, for many of the ideas presented here.

The line between the prevention of delinquency and its correction is not always discernible. This is as it should be, for the goal of prevention is embodied in all corrective measures pertaining to juveniles. Standing on that critical line between prevention and correction is our juvenile justice system. While this system, and alternatives to it, are discussed more completely elsewhere in the Commission report, the development of planned alternatives to judicial handling deserves to be seen as an important preventive device in its own right.

As we have mentioned, the deleterious effect of labeling youth as delinquents is the most obvious argument for limiting the number of youth thrust within the jurisdiction of our courts. Other experience at the points where police and court officials determine the disposition of young offenders supports the argument for the avoidance of stigmatization as a delinquency preventive measure.

INADEQUACY OF CURRENT NONJUDICIAL PROCEDURES

Many of the current procedures for nonjudicial handling of putative delinquents from prearrest to intake in the court system are inadequate and defective. Few formal guidelines are available to those who are responsible for exercising discretion in determining which youngsters should be sent deeper into the judicial process. Where those guidelines do exist, their relevance and justice is open to question. Frequently, those who make such decisions, by dint of inadequate experience or training, lack the capacity and the resources to make those decisions wisely. Hampered by the unavailability of resources which can serve as alternatives to court referrals, youngsters are sent to court when they need not be, or referred to resources lacking the capacity to offer the necessary help. Sometimes, extralegal sanctions are imposed which deprive due process. And without a system for the periodic review and correction of criteria and decision-making practices in this area, such practices are infrequently refined and frequently arbitrary.

THE UNFULFILLED PROMISE OF JUVENILE COURT

Added to this are the defects in the juvenile court system as a whole. Few would argue that the court has fulfilled its promise, whether they believe that the current system needs more effective implementation, or that basic changes are required.

Some suggest that the unfulfilled promise of the court is related to factors outside its control and the inadequacy of resources necessary to implement its concept effectively, such as the limited capacity of the court to effect necessary changes in conditions external to the individual, or the failure to provide the court with needed resources, e.g., trained probation officers, hearing officers and lawyers, diagnostic clinics, shelters, and treatment facilities.

Others, while admitting to the inadequate resources, suggest that the limited success has been due to problems within the system and the law which guides it. Cited here are: (1) assumptions that the problem lies within the individual, with insufficient allowance made for his social conditions, and (2) that attempts to mete out justice on an individual basis frequently lead to decisions with at least the appearance of consistency. Beyond this are discretionary matters, such as the use of records and hearsay as evidence, the lack of use of counsel, confusion of jurisdictional and dispositional issues, the overuse of detention facilities, and the continued reliance upon referral to correctional institutions with a proven inability to correct.

The generality of jurisdiction of the juvenile court—based on its desire to help children in trouble and its belief in its ability to do so, rooted in its partnership with the social and behavioral sciences, and reinforced by the increasing specialization of the helping disciplines which serve it—brings countless young people into the system who might be better served elsewhere.

To some extent, these problems have reinforced the alienation of young people and their lack of confidence in the justice of the system.

GROWING UP HELPS

One further reason for care in the use of court intervention is related to the growing doubt among experts about the connection between juvenile delinquency and adult criminality. Many individuals who engage in delinquent activities do not continue into delinquent or criminal careers. The normal and gradual process of maturation appears to be a major curative factor, even in serious cases of delinquency. Given time and some tolerance, many youngsters will simply abandon their participation in delinquent activities as they grow up, join the Army, get married, or obtain a job.

The positive effects of any intervention, especially official intervention, are usually accompanied, and to some extent vitiated, by potential negative consequences. Keeping this fact in mind, we should use every means to avoid exacerbating situations by unnecessary intervention, and allow every opportunity for normal growth processes to take the "kicks" out of antisocial behavior and reveal its uselessness.

CURRENT USE OF NONJUDICIAL PROCEDURES

A search for improved means of nonjudicial handling should not suggest that a large number of reputed delinquents are not currently handled outside the judicial process, for, in fact, they are. Such handling is based on a variety of reasons—the backlog in the juvenile courts, the desire to reduce costs, the disenchantment with the treatment and capabilities of the juvenile court system, the growth of specialized units within police departments, special efforts by the school system to cope with the behavior problems, and our general national belief in the redemptive potential of young people. As a consequence, it should be clear that only a minority of putative delinquents are processed as adjudicated delinquents. About half of all police juvenile contacts are settled without court referral. The police account for the vast majority of all juveniles appearing in court. For the other major sources of court referral—schools and parents—such referrals are usually used as a last resort. And of all cases received at court, about 50 percent are eliminated through informal probation, referral to other agencies, and dismissal at intake.[1]

The issue at hand, then, is not the establishment of a totally new practice; it is to refine and improve our practices in this area, and to expand the number of youngsters who are handled outside the court and correction systems. This requires that we redefine the delinquency jurisdiction of the court, supplementing that new definition with improved referral procedures and alternative means of dealing with juveniles. The goal of all such efforts would be to keep the juvenile functioning in the family and community without recourse to the official sanctioning system for as long as feasible, consonant with the needs of community safety and his own welfare. Given the absence of evidence of the beneficial effects of official contact, as well as the potentially harmful consequences of such contact, the burden of proof must be on the side of those who believe that official intervention is clearly necessary for the safety of the community and welfare of the juvenile.

[1] William Sheridan, "Why in Corrections?" Paper prepared for the President's Commission on Law Enforcement and the Administration of Justice.

RECOMMENDATIONS

Recommendations to improve our system of planned nonjudicial handling for reputed delinquents fall into three categories: First is the further limitation of referrals into the juvenile court system and the ability of that system to accept such referrals. Second is the creation and the strengthening of alternative agencies and organizations to deal with putative delinquents. Third is the development of an improved capacity on the part of the police and juvenile court system to make appropriate dispositions and refer putative delinquents to alternative agencies and organizations.

Limiting Referral and Jurisdiction

A major distinction should be made between those youngsters who have committed acts which would be crimes if they were committed by adults, and those youngsters whose alleged offenses would not be criminal if committed by adults. Even in the first category, every effort should be made to keep youngsters out of the judicial and correctional systems if they have committed what might be termed minor offenses which do not result in serious danger to themselves or to the community. In the latter category, legislation, preceded by such administrative action as necessary to test feasibility, should be encouraged to limit police referral and court jurisdiction.

Within the latter group are: (1) youngsters who have violated specific ordinances or regulatory laws which are applicable only to children, such as curfew violation, truancy, profanity, illegal use of alcohol or tobacco; and (2) those who have broken no law but who are designated as "beyond control," "ungovernable," "incorrigible," "runaway," or "minors in need of supervision" as in Illinois, or "persons in need of supervision" as in New York State.[2]

Generally the same dispositions are permitted for these youngsters as for those who may have indulged in criminal conduct. The number of children in these categories who appear before the courts is considerable. A conservative estimate, based upon national juvenile court statistics for 1964, indicates that these groups comprise about a quarter (approximately 185,000) of the total number of children's cases coming before the juvenile courts for conduct classified as delinquent. About one out of every five boys' delinquency cases, and over half of all girls' delinquency cases, were within these categories. A summary review of the populations of nearly twenty correctional institutions for delinquent children indicates that between 25 and 30 percent of their populations is composed of children whose offenses would not be classified as criminal if they were adults. A review of State and local detention programs showed that of 1,300 who were detained in jail pending hearing, about 40 percent fell in this group, and of 8,200 who were held in detention homes, approximately 50 percent fell within the same group.[3]

Since there is no evidence that such behavior necessarily leads to real

---

[2] Sheridan, *op. cit.*

[3] Sheridan, *op. cit.*

delinquency or criminality, or that court intervention and correctional treatment is effective in rehabilitation and prevention of further delinquency, it is recommended that the jurisdiction of the court in delinquency cases be limited to children who have broken laws which are applicable to all ages, that police be denied the authority to refer to court for detention, adjudication, and filing of a petition, any youth not suspected of criminal conduct.

We recognize that sometimes young people who have not committed delinquent acts may require the intervention of the court. In such instances as when a child may be neglected or in need of supervision, court action should be clearly differentiated from its action in delinquency cases. Although the fact that a youth needs supervision may eventually take on its own invidious characteristics, the record should make clear that the youngster has not broken the law. Since it also seems desirable that police activities in such instances be restricted and that youngsters have access to appropriate community services, it is recommended that police make referrals to a nonjudicial resource in the first instance, and that the authority to file petitions alleging nondelinquent behavior be limited to school officials, or representatives of public or private agencies providing services for children and families.

Further, the youth brought before the court on allegations other than delinquency should not be detained pending court proceedings, and the range of dispositions open to the court should be limited. The present Standard Family Court Act and the Standard Juvenile Court Act delimit the placement of neglected children and children who are incorrigible or beyond control.[4] It is recommended that this limitation be extended so that no youth whose acts would not be considered criminal if committed by an adult may be placed in an institution designed for delinquents. It is further recommended that when legal custody is vested in any agency or institution, such an agency should be prohibited from placing or transferring such youths to facilities designed for the care and treatment of delinquents.

Consideration also should be given to limiting delinquency proceedings in the juvenile court to children above the age of ten or possibly twelve. Children of younger age would, in no instance, be adjudicated as delinquent, nor placed in an institution designed to house delinquents.

In order to assure the limitation on referrals and court action, increased legal protection and other methods should be provided, such as the provision of counsel at all stages, the review of petitions to test their legal sufficiency, the requirement that juvenile hearing officers be members of the bar, and the tightening of procedural regularity, such as separate hearings on the issue of jurisdiction and disposition.

Alternatives to Judicial Handling

Obviously, the limitation on police action and the jurisdiction of the court is dependent upon a concomitant increase in the capacity of community in-

---

[4] U.S. Department of Health, Education, and Welfare, Welfare Administration, Children's Bureau, 1965.

stitutions to deal effectively with young people in trouble. Many of our recommendations point in that direction, as well as toward broader delinquency prevention goals:

In the increased effort to include young people in the decision-making processes and service operations of their community, a new set of standards is required. Such opportunities, for which achieving youngsters primarily have had priority in the past, should be increasingly available to "predelinquent" and delinquent youth as a way of tying them into the community system rather than locking them out.

In addition to the general upgrading of educational efforts on the part of schools in areas of high delinquency, specific attention should be paid to developing the schools' capacity to deal more effectively with youngsters presenting academic failure and behavior problems. Particularly, the schools will need to become less dependent upon the courts for their handling of truancy cases and should develop new mechanisms for dealing with cases of truancy and other serious behavior (see school section).

The mobilization of citizen groups should be encouraged so that (1) they may be more effective in their direct dealings with young people in their community and increase their capacity to provide incentives and sanctions, and (2) they may more competently deal with community agencies and institutions in order to make their services more appropriate.

Existing youth-serving agencies should be encouraged to make their programs more relevant to the lives of young people by integrating them with educational, social service, and social action efforts, and they should be urged to include in these programs more youngsters whose behavior problems and predelinquent patterns are now frequent cause for exclusion.

Funding policies should be established which offer incentives to educational and youth-serving agencies on the basis of their increased capacity to provide opportunities for young people who now tend to be excluded.

The neighborhood service centers should provide special services for potential delinquents or those who have had early contact with the law. Services should include not only diagnosis and clinical treatment, but legal assistance and educational and vocational help.

The new youth services agencies mentioned earlier should be established, wherever possible, in conjunction with other community service centers. Easily accessible, they should have local governing boards with heavy youth representation on them.

These agencies should be required to accept all referrals from police and courts, but care should be taken to avoid the possibilities of stigmatization by making sure that these centers are not for delinquent or "predelinquent" youth alone. They should be centers available for all community youth with the provision that problem youth and youth referred by official agencies are not excluded. Young people in the youth service agencies should not be treated on the basis of their alleged offense; they should be treated as full-fledged members of the community who have a right to and a need for certain kinds of service. Youth service agencies should be empowered to refer cases to court within sixty days of initial contact when necessary.

Advocacy should be increasingly recognized as a legitimate community function on behalf of youth. Each of the service agencies mentioned above should perceive its role, in part, as falling within this area. Opportunities exist within the multipurpose centers, the youth service agencies, and the schools for increased advocacy on behalf of youth whose behavior or social situation makes them suspect and denies them full access to community services and opportunities. Experimentation with the Ombudsman concept should be encouraged in the community centers and in the schools. Greater use of attorneys and legal service aides is warranted as advocates of improved community service for youth from social agencies and schools.

While new funds will be required to assure the availability of many of the alternative resources suggested above, much can be accomplished with a modification of attitudes and existing programs currently operative in the community.

The Police and the Court

Formal guidelines need to be drawn for use by police in the exercise of their discretion, in accordance with the newly established rules suggested above. These guidelines would encourage police to make greater use of nonjudicial means of handling and, where appropriate, to avoid the call for any intervention at all.

The extralegal hearing practices of youth aid officers should be evaluated to determine their effect and effectiveness.

On an experimental basis, police should be provided with simple predictive criteria (similar to those utilized in establishing bail upon recognizance and summons in lieu of arrest) as supplements to their other standards for referral to courts.

Training should be instituted for patrolmen and youth aid officers to acquaint them with youth services available in the community as well as provide them an insight into the problems and needs of young people. Such training would enable the police not only to refer youth to these agencies, but also to alert the agencies to individuals and groups who could use their help. Training would also acquaint police officers with the new referral rules.

Informal adjustment practices should be reviewed periodically; such reviews should involve private agencies, adult and youthful citizens, and schools, as well as police and courts.

Alternatives to detention, such as supervision in the community by youth service agencies and shelter facilities, should be explored.

Juvenile court intake staff should be authorized to dismiss or adjust, without referral, cases which are directly referred to them.

Court intake officers should be familiarized with community alternatives to the court system and encouraged to rationalize their screening of cases for petitioning.

The option of a new mechanism—the consent decree—should be provided in accordance with other papers prepared for the Crime Commission.

This section has tried to stress the importance, for preventive purposes, of a planned approach for the nonjudicial handling of young people who are now sent to court. It seems simplistic to state that if we adjudicate fewer youngsters as delinquents, we would reduce the delinquency rate. But evidence about the effects of adjudication suggests that this is more than a statistical gimmick. It is a way of reducing the official escalation of noncriminal offenses into real delinquency.

3

DIVERSION FROM
THE CRIMINAL JUSTICE SYSTEM*

National Institute of Mental Health

This paper, issued by the National Institute of Mental Health, deals with the entire criminal justice system, adult as well as juvenile. It provides a broader context within which to understand juvenile diversion, its similarities to and differences from adult diversion practices. After all, we have already logged a considerable amount of relevant experience in the diversion of drunks, drug addicts, and the emotionally or mentally disturbed. It helps to consider delinquency within this broader context of deviant behavior. Doing so, and looking at diversion programs designed for these other deviant "types," allows us to bridge the gap to issues of social control and to avoid placing all our emphasis on the actor or delinquent.

* From *Diversion from the Criminal Justice System,* National Institute of Mental Health (Washington, D.C.: U.S. Government Printing Office, 1971), 1–26.

The *diversion* of persons from the criminal justice system has long been practiced in the United States, largely because the system allows—in fact, requires—considerable discretion on the part of the police, with regard to decisions to arrest or dismiss and court referral or informal disposition, and on the part of the prosecutor or intake worker, with regard to official or unofficial processing. Diversion from the justice system may occur, of course, at any stage of judicial processing; but concern over the tremendous burden placed on courts and the injustices associated with the inability of the courts to handle the volume of cases, compounded by evidence that criminal processing often does more harm than good, has resulted in a focus on diversion of certain groups of offenders before court processing.

Informal preadjudication disposition occurs in both the juvenile and the adult justice systems, for many of the same reasons. First, even with the best legislative formulation, definitions of criminal conduct are not likely to be completely unambiguous.[1] The decision to divert an individual from judicial proceedings is affected by many factors, including the nature of the offense, the circumstances of its commission, the attitude of the victim, and the character of the accused.[2] The use of discretion is affected also by the consideration that the stigma of official processing might seriously limit the accused's social and economic opportunities or impose on him a deviant role, leading to further antisocial acts. Further, the huge volume of cases would seem to require some screening of those less serious, to allow concentration of law enforcement resources on what are considered to be major crimes.

The issue of screening out less serious cases is germane to the two areas in

[1] President's Commission on Law Enforcement and Administration of Justice, *Task Force Report: Juvenile Delinquency and Youth Crime,* Washington, D.C., the Commission, 1967, p. 10.
[2] *Ibid.*

which diversion as a conscious policy currently is given most attention: minor noncriminal "delinquent" behavior, and adult conduct which is socially disapproved but which might be more appropriately handled by social agencies or public health authorities. While it is clear that considerable numbers of persons are diverted from the criminal justice system as a result of official discretion, the assumption that less serious offenders are screened out is questionable. Arrest data and court statistics indicate that "most of the cases in the criminal courts consist of what are essentially violations of moral norms or instances of annoying behavior, rather than of dangerous crime,"[3] and that many juveniles contacted by police for truancy, waywardness, or "incorrigibility" end up in juvenile court with an adjudication of delinquency. It is difficult to see how these might be viewed as "major crimes." Diversion does occur; but its use is so informal, unstructured, and lacking in principle that it tends to depend on the personal inclination of the individual official.

Arguments against informal pre-judicial processing are: (1) that broad powers of discretion may be abused; (2) that enlarged discretionary power results in inconsistent law enforcement and disrespect for law; (3) that discretionary power may be used to further staff convenience at the expense of other goals of crime prevention and control. These are valid criticisms of "diversion" as it might operate if informal discretionary powers were merely extended. The proponents of diversion, however, are advocating that pre-judicial disposition be made a conscious and clearly defined policy, that the processes of diversion be given some procedural regularity, and that decisions be made on the basis of explicit and predetermined criteria. Assuming that alternate resources are made available and that nonjudicial procedures are defined, the extended use of unofficial or informal disposition need not necessarily result in an increase in "invisible" decision-making by individuals with great discretionary authority.

Diversion from the criminal justice system, whether in accordance with an explicit policy or in the form of case-by-case exceptions to the rule, occurs primarily because of official concern that application of the full criminal process is not always possible or appropriate. In the past, consideration of the need for diversion and special handling of some classes of deviants led to the establishment of the juvenile court and a noncriminal procedure to be used "in the interest of the child" as well as to the sanctioning of civil commitment "for treatment" of mentally ill offenders either adjudged incompetent to stand trial or after dismissal of criminal charges because of insanity. Experience with these measures has demonstrated that humanitarian intentions do not guarantee either more humane treatment of the individual or more successful rehabilitation. Juvenile court procedures have been found to infringe on the rights of the child and adjudication of a person as mentally ill proved to involve problems of stigma as harmful —some say even more—as a criminal record. Civil commitment procedures have been attacked for their failure to protect individual rights as well as on the grounds that adequate treatment is often not provided and the custody

[3] President's Commission on Law Enforcement and Administration of Justice, *The Challenge of Crime in a Free Society,* Washington, D.C., the Commission, 1967, p. 14.

involved generally becomes the equivalent of penal incarceration. Despite the criticisms of such noncriminal court measures, there has been considerable interest in broadening the use of civil commitment as an "enlightened" alternative for narcotic addicts and alcoholics, and since the early days of the juvenile court there has also been an increased use of the delinquency adjudication for relatively minor misbehavior or for such vaguely defined statutes as "incorrigibility."

In more recent years, there has been a noticeable shift in emphasis from lightening the impact of either civil or criminal court processing on certain groups of social deviants[4] to removing such persons entirely from the judicial process. The American system has a general tendency to rely too heavily on the law and legal process for the solution of pressing social problems. In particular, the arbitrary assignment to the criminal law and its processes of a variety of human conduct and conditions has come to be regarded as a problem of "overcriminalization." The problems associated with "overcriminalization" and the growing concern for the consequences associated with the expansion of the "sick" role have resulted in a body of literature and some experimentation with direct referral to community agencies, transfer of responsibility for certain groups to public health authorities, and legal reform to *remove* some kinds of minor misconduct of victimless "crimes" from the criminal statutes. Recent attempts to find alternatives outside of the legal process have been most evident in the cases of juveniles brought to court for noncriminal misconduct—drug users and drunkenness offenders; "status" offenders such as addicts, alcoholics, and vagrants; and mentally ill offenders.

These two opposing trends—the expanded use of civil and criminal procedures for an increasing variety of behavior and the countering attempt to eliminate the option of reliance on official coercion and thus transfer responsibility for some less socially injurious conduct to other authorities —currently are both evident and the issues are still being debated. Three types of social response to deviant, but not clearly criminal, behavior can be distinguished according to degree of involvement of law enforcement, courts, and correction: (1) penal sanction and criminal processing; (2) legal reform and transfer to public health authorities or social welfare agencies (the "sick" role); and (3) the compromise solution—civil processing and compulsory commitment.

From the very extensive literature on both present practices and proposed changes in these areas, several issues emerge as predominant: civil commitment or compulsory court-ordered treatment; the use of health resources and other nonpenal measures for purposes of social control and individual treatment (referral to clinics or Youth Service Bureaus and provision of outpatient or other voluntary treatment for addicts and alcoholics); and constitutional and statutory reform (to "legalize" abortion, homosexuality, vagrancy, or drunkenness not accompanied by other illegal activity).

---

[4] Throughout this monograph, the term "deviant" is used to suggest nonconforming or socially disapproved behavior, whether illegal or not. No implication of mental or emotional disorder is intended.

Civil commitment generally is described as a noncriminal process by which a sick or otherwise dependent person is involuntarily committed to a nonpenal institution for care, custody, or treatment.[5] As such, it is often represented as a useful and human means of diverting selected types of deviants from the criminal justice system. However, closer inspection reveals that the affirmative aspects of diversion exist only in theory.

The rationale for civil commitment, as it is generally phrased, is at first difficult to resist. The putative offender (juvenile, mentally ill, sexual psychopath, or addict) is "diverted" to a noncriminal proceeding and subsequently hospitalized for treatment rather than sentenced to prison or otherwise punished. At the same time, society is protected against whatever dangers such persons might present if left at liberty and, through rehabilitation, against the possibility of repetition of disapproved behavior upon release. Everyone seems to benefit and, since few people these days support the punishment of ill persons or children, such a plan of "treatment" appeals to contemporary notions of justice.

Why, then, is civil commitment the subject of such controversy? Much of the criticism—of the civil processing of offenders designated as ill and the so-called processing of juveniles—has been focused on the lack of adequate procedural safeguards, the absence of the treatment which is supposed to justify commitment, or the injustice of the longer confinement often imposed under civil as compared with criminal law. For example, one writer argues that most involuntary civil commitment laws do not adequately safeguard the rights of the individual because of almost insurmountable problems of definition[6]; another stresses the fact that the New York compulsory commitment statute fails to supply the alleged addict with the basic protections to which one in danger of losing his liberty is entitled and recommends that a task force be established to survey known treatment methods and design a program to be used throughout New York institutions[7]; a third implies that the major issue in question is whether the method of treatment is capable of producing a lasting cure.[8] The President's Crime Commission accepted involuntary civil commitment as offering "sufficient promise to warrant a fair test" but restricted itself simply to warning that such programs "must not become the civil equivalent of imprisonment," that the best possible treatment should be provided, and that length of confinement should not exceed that which is "reasonably necessary."[9] In the field of juvenile justice, similar arguments are found: the principle of civil intervention leading to involuntary treatment for alleged conditions and behavior that are noncriminal generally is accepted, while criticism is focused

---

[5] In practice, however, some commitments are to penal institutions and the proceedings often follow suspension of criminal proceedings.

[6] Kaplan, Leonard V., Civil commitment "As you like it," *Boston University Law Review*, 49(1):14–45, 1969.

[7] Due process for the narcotic addict? The New York compulsory commitment procedures, *New York University Law Review*, 43(6):1172–1193, 1968.

[8] Steinan, Leslie, Commitment of the narcotic addict convicted of crime, *Albany Law Review*, 32(2):360–387, 1968.

[9] *Op. cit., supra* note 3, p. 229.

on the need for the safeguards of procedural due process, the imprecision of definitions, inadequate theory, inadequate resources, lack of data, etc. Although these may all be important areas of concern, the emphasis is unfortunate in that attention to specific problems of procedure and adequacy of treatment tends to mask or at least divert attention from the more basic issue of the validity of civil commitment itself.

Sol Rubin has pointed out that the concept of civil commitment in "quasi-criminal" cases (defendants acquitted of crime for insanity, sex offenders, addict violators of drug laws, or juvenile and youthful offenders) raises more than one question of legal and social soundness.[10] He distinguishes these civil commitments from others (quarantine of persons with contagious disease, commitment of mentally incompetent persons) which are well established and well based in law, explaining that "it is the concepts of these better-established civil commitments that serve as the rationale for the more recent forms."[11] The power of the state in both of these older forms of commitment is derived from two legal doctrines: the sovereign's power of guardianship over persons under disability (*parens patriae*), and the police power to take steps necessary for the protection of the populace. These powers are not absolute. The statutes merely define the class of persons who are committable; the determination of whether a particular case meets the criteria must be made by means of a judicial or administrative proceeding. Rubin explains that, since the protective functions must be related to the real needs of the individual or the community, the element of dangerousness or helplessness must be found. In those civil commitments which Rubin calls quasi-criminal (and which are commonly considered a *diversion* from the criminal justice system by reason of the "civil" label), the criterion for commitment usually is not the test of dangerousness or helplessness, but the criminal act.[12] While these commitments are sustained, usually by reference to *parens patriae* or the police power, they are not civil commitments in the sense of quarantine[13] or the commitment of mental incompetents. It becomes obvious that, as Rubin so clearly demonstrates, "the 'civil' character of the quasi-criminal commitments is, in brief, a legal fiction."[14]

The essential problem with this fiction is not that it allows the incarceration of ill persons and children in what is essentially penal custody, or that it permits circumvention of due process requirements of the criminal law, or even that it disguises the fact that civil "treatment" is often more punitive than criminal "punishment." Although all of these charges are serious enough, to stress these points implies that were these defects removed (through provision of better treatment, less prison-like facilities, greater

---

[10] Rubin, Sol, *Psychiatry and Criminal Law: Illusions, Fictions, and Myths*, Dobbs Ferry, N.Y.: Oceana, 1965. See especially pp. 139–170.

[11] *Id.*, p. 141.

[12] *Id.*, p. 142.

[13] The rationale for civil commitment of addicts, however, frequently draws on this analogy, maintaining that drug addiction is "contagious" and spreads from social contact with the addicts. For example, see Kuh, Richard H., Civil commitment for narcotic addicts, *Federal Probation*, 27(2):21–23, 1963.

[14] *Op. cit., supra* note 10, p. 142.

attention to procedural regularity and individual rights), then civil commitment of, say, the addict offender would be the admirable innovation it was intended to be. The essential point is rather that existing commitment statutes, in permitting the "civil" incarceration of classes of persons for treatment of illness without a finding that the individual is *also* clearly dangerous or helpless, are unjustifiable. In fact, such statutes are penal in nature. A statute which prescribes the consequences (whether these are called treatment or punishment) that will attend certain behaviors or conditions has been described as a *penal* statute even if it is specifically classified as nonpenal.[15] Where a proceeding is truly nonpenal, then the question of whether a defendant is subject to control should depend on whether his condition is serious enough (dangerous, helpless) to require intervention by the State.

The courts usually have been willing to support the legislatively determined distinction between civil and criminal commitment—and to do so without careful scrutiny. The Supreme Court of the United States, in *Robinson* v. *California* (1962), decided that drug addiction is a disease and that an addict cannot constitutionally be dealt with as a criminal on the basis of his addiction. While it found penal imprisonment for addiction to be cruel and unusual punishment, the decision did not rule on the civil commitment (imprisonment?) of these same individuals. Rubin stresses that the decision only implies that civil commitment of a sick person would be proper, but that its language on this point is dicta and no precedents are cited.[16] While this dictum states that "a State might establish a program of compulsory treatment for those addicted to narcotics . . . [which] might require periods of involuntary confinement . . . [and] penal sanctions might be imposed for failure to comply with established compulsory procedures," the Supreme Court still has not handed down a decision on the civil commitment of ill offenders, and the substance of civil commitment statutes has not been examined to establish its "civil" nature. Meanwhile, the persistence of the label "civil" attached to procedures to commit ill persons for compulsory treatment, even though they have not been proven to be dangerous or incompetent, allows us to believe that these persons are being properly diverted from the criminal justice system.

The case for civil commitment of ill persons in lieu of criminal processing is seriously challenged by the Supreme Court decision in *Powell* v. *Texas* (1968). The Court upheld the criminal conviction of Powell, an alcoholic, on the grounds that he had committed an illegal act—being drunk in public —whereas in *Robinson* the issue had been that of a condition—being an addict—which could not in itself be viewed as criminal. Most interesting was the cautionary attitude of the Court toward civil commitment as opposed to penal incarceration.[17] The Court in *Powell* claims that "one virtue of the criminal process is, at least, that the duration of penal incarceration typically

---

[15] *Id.,* p. 149.

[16] Rubin, Sol, Civil commitment of addicts and alcoholics, Paper presented to the Governors' Conference on Drug and Alcohol Abuse, January 12–13, 1970, Miami Beach, Florida: New York, NCCD, 1970.

[17] *Ibid.*

has some outside limit. . . . 'Therapeutic civil commitment' lacks this feature; one is typically committed until one is 'cured.' " It is also objected that there is as yet no known generally effective method of treating alcoholics and that facilities for their treatment are "woefully lacking." Thus, in the space of a few years the Court has moved from a position of invitation to one of deep suspicion.

As Rubin points out, each of the Court's objections to civil commitment of alcoholics holds true for the drug addict.[18] The case for civil commitment, both in terms of legality and of social value, obviously is still unsettled.

COMPULSORY TREATMENT AS A "NONPENAL" ALTERNATIVE

Civil commitment is not the only sticky problem in the diversion of individuals from the criminal justice system. Several contemporary beliefs have converged around compulsory treatment: (1) that offenders should be treated instead of punished; (2) that some conditions—alcoholism, addiction—are not criminal but manifestations of illness; (3) that some persons, because of their condition—youth, mental illness—should be given special consideration or dealt with less severely; and (4) the belief that the State has a right and obligation to intervene where the individual or society is endangered. The quasi-criminal "civil" measures (civil commitment, juvenile court procedure, or compulsory treatment of the noncrime enforced by the prospect of penal processing for a crime) come into operation to satisfy the requirements of these beliefs. The supposed diversion of persons to civil processing whose condition or behavior is held noncriminal appears to be an attempt to have it both ways: the individual, not being criminal, is not subject to penal sanction *but,* for the protection of all concerned, he may be subjected to similar measures classified as nonpenal.

The point on which this whole structure should rest is the power of the State to intervene in cases where no penal sanction exists, a power which is, or should be limited by the requirements that there be sufficient danger either to other individuals or to the populace and sufficient helplessness[19] of the individual. To achieve analytical clarity, then, it is necessary that dangerousness and helplessness be clearly distinguished from the existence of a condition such as addiction or mental illness.[20] Lady Wooten notes, "The concept of illness expands continually at the expense of the concept of moral failure."[21] That the State's power to intervene in civil cases is clearly limited

---

[18] *Ibid.*

[19] As Rubin has suggested, "helplessness" rather than mere disability should be the criterion. *Op. cit., supra* note 10. It might even be argued that a completely disabled person is not helpless as long as he has someone to take care of him. Thus, the question may become: Under what circumstances should the State be permitted to deprive a person of the power to make decisions about himself?

[20] This point has been argued by a number of authors with reference to mental illness, addiction, and other conditions. A finding of addiction, for example, would be considered a necessary but not sufficient condition for commitment. See: Civil commitment of narcotic addicts, *Yale Law Journal*, 76(6):1160–1189, 1967.

[21] Wooten, Barbara, Sickness or sin, *Twentieth Century*, 159:433–434, 1957.

must be recognized, not merely because ignoring this fact leads to abuse, but because without constant attention to the weaknesses in such thinking, any behavior might be convincingly described as "harmful to self or others," given a particular value system. An extreme example, but one which differs only in degree from official disapproval of the "incorrigible" child who persists in disobeying parents, teachers, and police, is that of the adult individual whose "wrong thinking" is considered a danger to himself and others and whose incarceration for "reeducation" is thus justified.

Society cannot have it both ways. If a deviant behavior or condition is to be defined as not criminal, then it would seem that an individual should not be compelled to accept treatment for that condition or behavior unless the condition is ruled inherently dangerous, and he should not be committed for other reasons except on a determination that he himself is dangerous or helpless.

If society decides that certain nondangerous offenders should be diverted from the criminal justice system, then it should not be satisfied with the substitution of measures which differ only in their description as "nonpenal" or "treatment."

There are other alternatives for handling the noncriminal juvenile, the narcotic addict, the alcoholic, and other nondangerous deviants. These might be discussed together because the principle is essentially the same: in the case of a noncriminal deviance, where the individual is not otherwise committable under State power (i.e., neither dangerous nor helpless), he may be released to the community; where a crime has been committed and the defendant is also a noncriminal deviant, he may be dealt with by the penal process for his offense. In either case, society may be more adequately protected by laws relating specifically to dangerous offenders.[22] Despite the similarities, the different offender groups will be discussed separately here because they usually are dealt with as such in the literature.

NARCOTICS ADDICTS

There has been relatively little experimentation in the United States with the diversion of addicts from the criminal justice system. While the ruling that an addict cannot constitutionally be labeled a criminal for his addiction would suggest a step in this direction, in practice this has not been a large concession. Civil commitment statutes have functioned to retain the State's ability to incarcerate or otherwise intervene in the lives of both the addict offender and the addict nonoffender. Rather than reducing the number of persons subject to State intervention, civil commitment ironically has greatly increased this number by bringing into the system that population of otherwise noncriminal persons whose only "offense" is their illness.

Both California and New York, the states with the largest addict popula-

---

[22] The Model Sentencing Act, adopted by NCCD's Advisory Council of Judges, establishes criteria for identifying dangerous offenders and provides for the sentencing of an offender upon a finding of dangerousness, where such an offender has been convicted of a felony. Advisory Council of Judges, *Model Sentencing Act,* New York: National Council on Crime and Delinquency, 1963, p. 16.

tions, have enacted civil commitment statutes and both have developed extensive rehabilitative programs based on civil incarceration.[23] While both the California Rehabilitation Center Program and the program of New York State's Narcotic Addiction Control Commission (NACC) are described in terms of rehabilitation, treatment, and hospitalization of "patients," neither is based on the medical model. Both programs depend for their identification as "nonpenal" and "medical" on the distinction between treatment and punishment, with no apparent recognition of the fact that treatment can be provided as well in a penal institution. There is nothing inherently nonpenal about a treatment facility.

AN ALTERNATIVE: THE MEDICAL MODEL

What has come to be called "the British system"[24] of narcotics control and treatment of addiction—in which the addict is viewed as an ill person to be treated, if he feels the need, by the medical profession—is statutorily, though not in practice, the American system as well. The legislative enactments of both countries appear the same: narcotic drugs may be prescribed by physicians, in the course of professional practice only, for the treatment of addiction. The essential difference is that in Britain the determination of proper treatment of addiction rests with the medical profession, while in the United States the definition of professional practice has been rigidly established by nonmedical authorities.

An account of the intimidation of the medical profession by the Narcotics Division of the Treasury Department following its merger with the Prohibition Unit in 1920 may be found in several sources.[25] Narcotics Bureau regulations still provide for the penal sanction of physicians who administer drugs to addicts,[26] although this regulation is in clear violation of both the Harrison Act[27] and the Supreme Court ruling in *Linder* v. *United States* (1925).[28] The *Linder* decision set forth what is still the Supreme Court's interpretation of the Harrison Act, ruling that physicians may, in the course of proper professional practice, prescribe drugs to addicts for the treatment of their addiction. The Court states that the Harrison Act "says nothing of 'addicts' and does not undertake to prescribe methods for their medical

---

[23] For a brief description of the establishment of the New York program, see: Kuh, *op. cit., supra* note 13. On the California program, see: Wood, Roland W., New program offers hope for addicts, *Federal Probation*, 28(4):41–45, 1964.

[24] E.g., Lindesmith, Alfred R., The British system of narcotics control, *Law and Contemporary Problems*, 22(1):138–154, 1957.

[25] For example, see: Rubin, *op. cit., supra* note 10: Advisory Council of Judges, *Narcotics Law Violations*, New York: National Council on Crime and Delinquency, the Council, 1964; U.S. Department of Health, Education, and Welfare, Juvenile Delinquency and Youth Development Office, *A Community Mental Health Approach to Drug Addiction*, by Richard Brotman and Alfred Freedman, Washington, D.C.: U.S. Government Printing Office, 1968.

[26] *Code of Federal Regulations*, Title 26, Sec. 151; 392, 1961 Supp. 1963.

[27] Act of December 17, 1914, ch. 1, 38 Stat. 785, as amended, 26 U.S.C. Sec. 4701-36 (Int. Rev. Code).

[28] *Linder* v. *United States*, 268 U.S. 5 (1925), at 22.

treatment." It also states that "if the Act had such scope [to prohibit administration of drugs by physicians to treat addiction] it would certainly encounter grave constitutional difficulties."

The medical model, in which the medical profession has the authority to determine and to administer proper treatment to ill persons, is clearly prescribed, in regard to narcotics addiction, by the present law. It is only the nature of administrative enforcement by the Narcotics Bureau and the collaboration of the A.M.A. which deters physicians from administering drugs to treat (not necessarily maintain) addiction. The Supreme Court in *Robinson* stated that "the narcotic drug addict is a sick person, physically and psychologically, and as such is entitled to qualified medical attention just as are other sick people."[29] This decision has been viewed as a significant advancement in its prohibition of penal imprisonment for addiction, yet it has done nothing to enhance the treatment of addicts as "sick people." Addicts will not receive the treatment to which they are "entitled" until the Bureau of Narcotics and Dangerous Drugs, U.S. Department of Justice regulations are amended to conform with the law, and physicians feel free to provide qualified medical attention to addicts just as they do to other sick people.

The Advisory Council of Judges of the National Council on Crime and Delinquency has issued a policy statement on narcotics law violations in which this recommendation is made.[30] The Council advises that the necessary action be taken, either by statute or by the appropriate bureaus and departments to have the interpretation of the Harrison Act as set forth in *Linder* carried out administratively and the Bureau of Narcotics regulations amended. The ACJ also states that sick persons do not need criminal or civil process for medical care to be available to them (although some are subject to civil commitment) and that a drug addict "should have access to medical care, in or out of a hospital, without so-called civil commitment, unless he is, in fact, unable to take care of himself despite medication."[31] While recognizing that narcotics traffic is properly controlled by legislation and penal sanction, the Council states that the addict should be directed to medical help and should not be criminally prosecuted.[32] The fact that many addicts currently are subject to criminal prosecution for illegal possession arises from the unavailability of "legal" drugs by prescription from physicians. The tragedy of the enforcement policy of the U.S. Department of Justice is that it creates criminals out of sick persons by denying them legal access to treatment.

If the medical model in its voluntary aspect is put into effect in this country, most communities would not be prepared to deal with addiction as a social problem. Private physicians obviously would be unable to handle the large numbers of addicts needing legal access to drugs, yet hospital and clinic

---

[29] *Robinson v. California*, 370 U.S. 660 (1962).
[30] Advisory Council of Judges, *op. cit., supra* note 25, p. 14.
[31] *Id.*, p. 13.
[32] *Id.*, p. 14.

facilities for the treatment of addiction are at present generally lacking. The New York State Planning Committee on Mental Disorders, in their report of the Task Force on Addictions (alcohol and drugs), observes that in New York State, at least, little progress had been made in the treatment of addicts within the structure of the general hospital, even as emergencies in the dangerous state of acute intoxication; that within the community mental health board structure the problem has remained as the lowest priority; and that the police, the courts, and correction have continued to handle the problem by default.[33] The Committee suggests that the new approach of the community mental health center will have little impact on the problems of drug dependence unless the medical share of the responsibility is accepted and programs commensurate with the magnitude of the problem are instituted.

There have been a number of other references to the community mental health center as an appropriate structure for the treatment of the addictions. The Office of Juvenile Delinquency and Youth Development has issued a publication entitled *A Community Mental Health Approach to Drug Addiction,* authored by two professionals in the fields of psychiatry and community health.[34] The community mental health approach is described in detail and its application to the field of addiction, including treatment, research, and training, is outlined. The goals of treatment are expressed in terms of the individual's diagnosed level of dysfunction in different areas. Improved adaptation or functioning becomes the central goal, with particular phased subgoals assigned on the basis of individual characteristics. Addiction is viewed as a chronic condition and "success" in treatment is defined individually, as is the case with other chronic conditions. This approach is in stark contrast to the present requirements of compulsory treatment programs in which one relapse is taken to denote failure.

Other types of treatment facilities, with which there has been some experimentation, are residence facilities (Daytop Lodge, Synanon); hospital programs; and outpatient treatment in clinics. Daytop and Synanon are similar in that both are administered by ex-addicts and both utilize reality therapy and the communal unit in rehabilitation. Synanon appears to have been successful with many addicts. However, one writer argues that Synanon's success is only partial since it functions to support a dependent individual indefinitely in a protective community; it does not rehabilitate in the sense of improved ability to function in the outside community.[35]

An increasing number of State and municipal hospitals are adding local hospitalization facilities specifically for addicted persons admitted voluntarily. In the community program of New York City's Metropolitan Hospital, addicts are detoxified by the methadone-substitution method and placed in a rehabilitation ward for a period of four weeks, although they may sign

[33] New York (State) Planning Committee on Mental Disorders, Report of the Task Force on Addictions, Albany, 1965, 36 pp.

[34] Department of Health, Education, and Welfare, *op. cit., supra* note 25.

[35] Sternberg, David, Synanon House: a consideration of its implications for American correction, *Journal of Criminal Law, Criminology and Police Science,* 54(4):447–455, 1963.

themselves out at any time.[36] Major emphasis is placed on aftercare, including financial, family, and housing services, legal advice, recreation, and vocational counseling. The hospital program is associated with two local neighborhood agencies which work with addicts and ex-addicts.

Experience with outpatient care of addicts is more recent but the results obtained so far with the methadone-maintenance method appear encouraging. At New York's Bernstein Institute of Beth Israel Medical Center, addicts are given daily dosages of liquid methadone which eliminate the craving for drugs while blocking the effects of any opiates if they are taken. It is reported that individuals in the program have been able to adjust satisfactorily in terms of work, school, and normal community life and that the need for criminal activity to obtain drugs has been eliminated.[37] A new methadone program was recently established in Brooklyn, scheduled to treat 5,000 hard-core addicts over a five-year period. The clinic is operated by a private organization, the Addiction Research and Treatment Corporation, with grants from Federal and city governments. Many patients are referred from courts and prisons, but adult addicts may come in off the street. To obtain the methadone, an addict must cooperate with staff, come to the center daily, and refrain from any criminal activity. The research program will test whether methadone is more effective alone, or in combination with counseling, job assistance, vocational training, and group therapy.[38]

The Community Service Society of New York recently has issued a publication describing four voluntary agency programs for addicts in New York, including three clinics and a therapeutic community residence which offers an outpatient program as well.[39] All focus their efforts on the individual addict with emphasis on improved health and decreased antisocial behavior. The treatment goal of the programs examined is abstinence, as opposed to the maintenance approach of other clinic programs. The relative value of maintenance vs. abstinence as a means or a goal of successful rehabilitation is a fundamental issue which will be settled only by further research and experimentation.

There has been a growing tendency to classify drugs and alcohol together, both for purposes of analysis and in the design of programs of public health treatment of dependency and addiction. The New York State Planning Committee on Mental Disorders included alcohol and drug dependence under a single heading for consideration in planning in mental health. A Special Commission to study the use of harmful and illegal drugs in Massachusetts described alcoholism as a "type of drug abuse the social consequ-

[36] Freedman, Alfred H.; Sager, Clifford J.; and Rabiner, Edwin L., A voluntary program for the treatment of narcotic addicts in a general hospital, New York, Metropolitan Hospital Center, 1962, 14 pp.

[37] Dole, Vincent P., and Nyswander, Marie, A medical treatment for diacerylmorphine (heroin) addiction, *Journal of American Medical Association*, 193(8):646–650, 1965.

[38] *New York Times*, Sunday, October 12, 1969.

[39] Community Service Society of New York, A study of four voluntary treatment and rehabilitation programs for New York City's narcotic addicts, by Judith Calof, New York, 1967, 52 pp.

ences of which are virtually incalculable" and advised that both be handled within a total program of mental health for both individuals and society on a community basis.[40] A World Health Organization report on services for the prevention and treatment of dependence on "alcohol and other drugs" acknowledged the important differences between types of drug dependence but recommended that the two be considered together because of similarities of causation, interchangeability of agent, and thus similarity in measures required for treatment and prevention.[41] Combined services for persons dependent on alcohol and other drugs are provided in Toronto, Canada, by the Alcoholism and Drug Addiction Research Foundation. The comprehensive program developed for alcoholic dependence, including research, public education, training, and rehabilitation services, was extended to other drugs in 1963.[42]

The above are only some of the ways in which addiction might be handled as a public health problem by medical authorities without the use of civil commitment or other compulsory or penal measures. It is important to stress that drugs need not be "legalized" for the treatment of addiction to be carried out in the community. The legal basis for the administration of narcotics to addicts under a physician's care already exists; it is necessary only to make enforcement conform to law.

CHRONIC DRUNKENNESS OFFENDERS

While alcoholism and drug addiction may be considered together for the purposes of designing a public health approach to prevention and treatment, alcoholism presents a slightly different problem for the diversion of offenders from the criminal justice system. This difference was demonstrated in the Supreme Court ruling in *Powell* v. *Texas*. Alcoholism itself is not an offense, and rarely is possession of alcohol by an adult, but being drunk in public almost always is, and it is the public drunkenness charge which provides the basis for intervention to control alcohol. While removal of drug addicts from the justice system requires primarily a change in enforcement practices and the development of community facilities for treatment, in the case of the chronic drunkenness offender—the "visible" alcoholic —diversion requires a change in law. Civil commitment is not as popular a solution for the public drunk. The drunkenness offender usually is put in jail—as was deemed the lesser of two evils, by the Court in *Powell*.

Legal reform to make public drunkenness no longer an offense is now a respectable and widely voiced recommendation. The President's Crime Commission recommended that public drunkenness, unaccompanied by

[40] Massachusetts, Special Commission to Make a Study Relative to the Extent of the Use of Harmful, Injurious, and Illegal Drugs Within the Commonwealth, *Report*, Boston, the Commission, 1968, 127 pp.
[41] World Health Organization, Expert Committee on Mental Health, Services for the prevention and treatment of dependence on alcohol and other drugs (Technical Report Series No. 363), Geneva, 1967, 45 pp.
[42] *Id.*, p. 28.

other illegal behavior, not be considered a crime.[43] The Pennsylvania Crime Commission's Task Force on alcohol and the criminal justice system reports that handling public drunkenness through criminal processes amounts to the "misguided criminalizing of a social problem."[44] It is fairly commonly agreed that while commission of a criminal act by an intoxicated person requires criminal handling, the problem of drunkenness requires effective treatment rather than an adjudication of guilt.

It is at this point that the problems of addiction and alcoholism become similar, at least with respect to the goal of diversion of persons for whom State intervention for control is unnecessary or undesirable. If it is stated that these persons *require treatment* rather than punishment, the tendency is to suggest that they must be treated, even if it is necessary to incarcerate or otherwise compel acceptance of these services. The labeling of such a disposition as "treatment" only hinders recognition of the similarity between treatment and punishment under conditions of compulsion.

Also, some few voices now are being heard to argue that it may be more sensible to take a protective shelter-maintenance approach to the problem. That is, it is suggested that the costs involved and minimal success possible in attempting to cure the alcoholic require a different approach. It may be that neither the "sick" role nor the "bad" role is appropriate and the State should rethink its function along the lines of providing temporary shelter for those who are rendered temporarily helpless and—the more controversial aspect—actually supply alcoholic beverages of good quality to the skid row alcoholic. Obviously, this approach is novel and controversial and needs a great deal of additional thought and research.

The arguments against compulsory civil measures for narcotics addicts also apply to the alcoholic. However, until civil commitment of the drunk becomes acceptable practice, the major problem is not civil incarceration but compulsory treatment for an illness condition manifested by the existence of a closely related behavior—public appearance and/or disorderly conduct—which are considered to be crimes. Compulsory treatment involves placement on probation under conditions of abstention and requires attendance for treatment or suspension of criminal charges in exchange for participation in treatment and its successful completion.[45] There is here, as with compulsory treatment for drug addiction, a hint of double-think. *Addiction (drugs or alcohol) is considered a "noncrime," albeit associated with offense behaviors under present law—yet intervention concerns itself less with the offense than with the illness held to be not punishable.*

Not only is involuntary treatment for alcoholism a questionable practice, [as alluded to earlier] there are indications that it also is ineffective. The San

[43] President's Commission on Law Enforcement and Administration of Justice, *Task Force Report: Drunkenness* (Annotations, consultants' papers and related materials), Washington, D.C., 1967, 131 pp.

[44] Pennsylvania, Crime Commission, Task Force report: alcohol and the criminal justice system, Harrisburg, Pennsylvania, 1969, 48 pp.

[45] Even here there are sophisticated legal problems to be dealt with. In *Sweeney v. United States,* F.2d 10, 11 (7th Cir. 1095) the Court decided that it was unreasonable and therefore unenforceable to impose the typical "no drinking" condition on a chronic alcoholic placed on probation.

Diego Municipal Court has been studying the relative effectiveness of treatment and punishment of chronic drunkenness offenders for several years.[46] During this time there have been various reports of municipal court programs in the United States which utilize such approaches as probation with referral to clinic treatment, Alcoholics Anonymous, court-sponsored honor classes, halfway houses, and camps in lieu of jail sentences. However, the San Diego Court felt that generalizations could not be made from the results of these programs because of the absence of adequate control studies. Previous research by court staff had suggested that probation with suspended sentence would be effective in getting the chronic drunkenness offender into treatment and reducing the likelihood of rearrest. To test this proposition, a controlled study was undertaken to compare the effectiveness of three different treatments following suspended sentence: (1) referral to an alcoholic clinic; (2) required participation in Alcoholics Anonymous; and (3) no treatment. The results of this carefully controlled study revealed no statistically significant differences among the three in terms of recidivism rate, number of rearrests, or time elapsed before rearrest. In fact, no treatment obtained slightly, though not significantly, better results. It was concluded that enforced referral to treatment was no more effective than no treatment at all. One explanation offered for this result is that the conditions of court-imposed referral confronted the offender with an anxiety-producing situation which may have increased the likelihood that he would resume his previous drinking pattern. Whatever the explanation, the concluding advice of this study must be considered: "The present data offer no support for a general policy of forced referrals to brief treatment."[47]

What are the alternatives? The President's Commission Task Force on Drunkenness recommended that communities establish detoxification units, as part of comprehensive treatment programs, to which inebriates might be brought by police for short-term detention under the authority of civil legislation[48]; yet the Commission also recommended that drunkenness not be treated as a criminal offense, thus bringing up the problem of compulsory civil detention for a noncrime.

The Vera Institute of Justice in New York City proposed and instituted a voluntary alternative—the Manhattan Bowery Project.[49] Following staff research into existing alcoholism programs in various parts of the country and the needs of homeless alcoholics in New York City, the Vera Institute concluded that there was an urgent need for emergency street rescue and sobering-up services for homeless alcoholics, effectively related to existing long-term rehabilitative programs. It was also concluded that all efforts and services on behalf of these men should operate on a voluntary basis without the use of either arrest or involuntary commitment. In its first year of

[46] Ditman, Keith S., et al., A controlled experiment on the use of court probation for drunk arrests, *American Journal of Psychiatry*, 124(2):64–67, 1967.

[47] *Id.*, p. 67.

[48] *Op. cit., supra* note 43, p. 4.

[49] The proposal for the Project is included in Appendix D of the President's Commission Task Force report on drunkenness, *op. cit., supra* note 43, pp. 58–64.

operation, the Project's primary goals were to test whether Bowery alcoholics would accept a voluntary program of alcohol detoxification; whether such a program would be workable in a nonhospital setting; and whether on completion of detoxification, these men would accept referral to other types of programs for ongoing care. The results so far indicate that the majority of debilitated alcoholic Bowery men approached by a medically oriented street patrol voluntarily agree to detoxification.[50] The Project also has found that Bowery men undergoing detoxification are manageable, both medically and behaviorally, in a well-staffed nonhospital facility, and that at completion of detoxification the majority of the patients are willing to seek further treatment. It is stressed that a voluntary program is preferable to a compulsory program because patients are more cooperative and managerial problems created by a compulsory program are avoided.

Another program providing an alternative to the police-correctional handling of the homeless alcoholic is the Boston South End Center for Unattached Persons. Assistance is offered to skid row inebriates approached on the streets. An official of the program has estimated that 80 percent of the men approached in this manner respond willingly.[51] The Center acts as a referral unit for existing community agencies providing medical, job placement, housing, and welfare services.

These programs suggest that the belief that most chronic inebriates require compulsion to "motivate" them to accept treatment is not well founded; they also refute the argument that police arrest is necessary as a case-finding tool. Through the concerted efforts of public and private social agencies, a large number of alcoholics may be provided voluntary treatment and welfare services before an offense has been identified by police. If an essentially unavoidable situation (such as public drunkenness is for many homeless and destitute alcoholics) is no longer treated as an offense, an even greater number of these persons might be "diverted" from the criminal justice system.

In areas where help has been extended to the skid row alcoholic by such organizations as the Salvation Army, the need for arrest and detention in order to provide social services and "control" of the situation has been considerably reduced.[52] Were such services and facilities supplemented by other public and private agency efforts, including "aggressive casework" types of casefinding, and treatment offered on a voluntary basis to this group, "prearrest" diversion might be successfully implemented on a large scale.

Postarrest diversion presents other problems, similar in principle to those involving the commitment for treatment of the addicted offender. The literature on the alcoholic offender reflects a growing support for the

[50] Manhattan Bowery Project, *First Annual Report,* New York, the Project, 1969. 68 pp.

[51] *Op. cit., supra* note 43, pp. 4–5.

[52] A survey of Wayne County (Michigan) detention needs and jail practices reported that "much of the credit for the absence of alcoholics in Wayne County Jail must go the Salvation Army, which makes shelter available for more than 600 persons daily, the majority of whom are indigent alcoholics." National Council on Crime and Delinquency, Adult detention needs in Wayne County, Michigan: a survey of the Wayne County Jail, New York, 1968.

postarrest "diversion" of offenders, for purposes of treatment, to institutional or other compulsory treatment. Most widely recommended are brief, involuntary detention in civil detoxification centers following arrest,[53] involuntary commitment to an inpatient facility for treatment,[54] and enforced treatment of offenders on probation.[55] These measures may be found effective in getting the alcoholic offender to accept treatment—or even to cure him; and they may be an improvement over the usual jailing and punitive detention; but they cannot really be considered a diversion except in name, and their compulsory nature may well be unjustified if a right to refuse treatment is established. Closer examination reveals that these measures involve the use of community resources in penal treatment, the adoption of a treatment orientation in correction, or the substitution of nonpenal hospital/patient terminology, rather than an actual removal of the offender from the justice system. The goal of providing more humane treatment should not be confused with diversion.

That the intent to retain control remains the same is revealed by the wording of a recommendation found in the report of the Michigan Crime, Delinquency, and Criminal Administration Commission. The Commission supports the provision of a "statutory alternative" (to replace criminal arrest when this authority no longer exists) which would authorize forty-eight-hour protective civil custody in a medical facility for those drunks who endanger only themselves.[56] Those who endanger others, of course, could be arrested and held under criminal sanction. In other words, when a nondangerous inebriate can no longer be arrested for public drunkenness, he might be "diverted" to a facility classed as nonpenal, under identical conditions of intervention for control, except that this time such a disposition is for his own good. While on the surface such handling might be significantly more humane, it is easy to see that no substantive difference exists.

Examination of current practices and proposals concerning alternatives to penal sanction of the alcoholic offender supports the conclusions suggested by the literature on the narcotic addict: civil incarceration is not a diversion or "alternative" and thus it is difficult to justify; commitment or other compulsion for purposes of treatment, rather than because of dangerousness, is questionable; and there are voluntary alternatives involving a considerable saving in police, court, and correctional resources which are more consistent with a policy of diversion.

Prerequisite to the removal of the drunk or alcoholic offender from the justice system will be the development and expansion of community resources, including medical, welfare, and other assistance. The nonoffender drunk (where public drunkenness is not an offense in itself) then may be referred directly to social agencies for voluntary treatment or other services.

[53] Op. cit., supra note 43, p. 5.

[54] Tao, L. S., Legal problems of alcoholism, Fordham Law Review, 37(3):405–428, 1969.

[55] Mills, Robert B., and Hetrick, Emery S., Treating the unmotivated alcoholic, Crime and Delinquency, 9 (1):46–59, 1963.

[56] Michigan; Crime, Delinquency, and Criminal Administration Commission, Report and Recommendations of the Commission, N.P., 1967.

An alcoholic who has committed an offense may be handled by the penal system, in which treatment for his condition might be offered. If his offense is not considered serious (disorderly conduct, disturbance of the peace), he might be routinely handled in a special program for misdemeanants, involving police warning, rather than arrest, and referral to community agencies for voluntary treatment or other assistance. The difference is an invitation to virtue rather than coercion to virtue.[57]

PETTY MISDEMEANANT OFFENDERS

Evidence that the overload on the courts is caused largely by the huge volume of minor offenses, plus the fact that penal sanctions do not seem to deter such offenses, makes the petty misdemeanant offender the most obvious case for removal from the criminal system. Here we do not deal as directly with the conceptual problems inherent in the "sick" role—"bad" role dichotomy—but other problems abound. The President's Crime Commission states that such behavior (the almost half of all arrests which are "essentially violations of moral norms or instances of annoying behavior") generally is considered too serious to be ignored, but its inclusion in the criminal justice system raises questions deserving examination.[58]

It is widely accepted that new procedures for handling these offenders—procedures which would avoid prosecution, would not result in a more serious "civil" disposition, and would not contribute to a criminal record—could and should be devised. One such procedure, proposed by Hugh Price, is especially relevant to the misdemeanor problem because of its recognition of the social class bias of many arrests for petty offenses. Price proposes the establishment of neighborhood police offices in ghetto areas, staffed by community affairs officers (not necessarily career policemen, but trained in police-community relations) and several neighborhood aides.[59] All persons arrested for petty offenses such as family disputes, nonserious disturbances of the peace, loitering or trespass, or public drunkenness, would be brought initially to a neighborhood office where the officer would check the police "blacklist" of multiple offenders who are not to be handled by the informal procedure. A person would be blacklisted if he has been detained and released by the police or prosecutor three or more times in the past year or if he has failed to appear for a prosecutor's or family relations hearing during the past year. A blacklisted offender would be formally booked and presented in court for prosecution. An offender who is not found to be blacklisted would be recorded in a police log book but not formally "booked," so no arrest would be entered on a criminal record card. The community affairs officer then would meet with the offender and attempt to determine the problems which led to the violation. Any statement

---

[57] See J. S. Kolnick, Coercion to virtue: the enforcement of morals, *Southern California Law Review*, 41, 588 (1968).

[58] *Op. cit., supra* note 3.

[59] Price, Hugh B., A proposal for handling of petty misdemeanor offenses, *Connecticut Bar Journal*, 42(3):55–74, 1968.

on the part of the subject could not be used by the State in any proceeding, and the police could not use these interviews for interrogation about other crimes. Once the community affairs officer has assessed the severity of the offense and the nature of its origin, he may recommend that the parties contact a mental health, employment, or legal aid agency, but such referrals would not be binding on the parties. The officer may choose among several dispositions: outright release; release with warning; or referral to the prosecutor or family relations officer for conference. The last disposition would be used in cases where the facts of the violation are more serious, where the causative factors appear deep-seated, or where the offender has committed the limit of violations prior to blacklisting. At these hearings, further possibilities for referral to social, legal, or other agencies would be explored and again the dispositions of release, release with warning, and referral (not binding) to other agencies are available. At this second stage, the hearings officers also would be authorized to issue an order for arrest. Up to this point, however, no arrest has been recorded.

The proposed misdemeanor procedure is offered as a means of minimizing the impact of petty crimes on the courts and on the offender without impairing the ability of the police and courts to maintain law and order. It is also proposed as a means of reforming the unequal and discriminatory manner in which petty offenses now are processed at the police station. The new system would "interject guidelines and predictability into the existing practices and apply them to a broader range of offenses."[60] The necessary statutory revisions are described and solutions to possible procedural and administrative problems are discussed.

This proposed model is a true example of diversion of offenders from the criminal justice system. Every attempt is made to handle the minor offender in alternate ways before an arrest is made. Where offenses such as public drunkenness or vagrancy are not removed from the criminal statutes, and to the extent that casefinding and provision of services are not offered before police contact, such a procedure exists as a possible alternative. One runs the risk, however, that by implementing this sort of a program one also reduces the possibility of removing some of these questionable laws from the books.

NONCRIMINAL JUVENILES

Although the juvenile court was established, ostensibly, as a means of removing the juvenile offender from the criminal justice system, this "nonpenal" alternative has functioned (as has the civil commitment procedure) in such a way as to draw even more persons into the system of control by State intervention. That the juvenile justice system has not fulfilled the need for an alternative to the penal system is demonstrated by the current demand for new ways of handling the problem juvenile through diversion from juvenile court processing.

The concern of the juvenile court with disposition in the interest of the

[60] *Ibid.*

child, rather than with direct reference to the alleged offense, as well as the vagueness of statutory descriptions of behaviors requiring intervention, has necessitated the use of broad discretion by police and court officials and has resulted in the present informal system of preadjudication diversion of many potential subjects of formal court action. Police "station adjustment," referral to community resources, or other intradepartmental handling by police has been reported to occur nationally in 45 to 50 percent of all juvenile contacts.[61] However, the criteria for selection of disposition generally are not explicitly defined, ordered in priority, or systematically reviewed for administrative purposes.[62] A study of differential handling by police and selection of juvenile offenders for court appearance in four different Pennsylvania communities revealed wide variations in rates of arrest and court referral.[63] Disposition, including whether a juvenile was diverted from formal processing, was related not only to offense, but to age, race, sex, and residence. Differential handling was found to be related to attitudes of the policeman toward the juvenile, his family, the juvenile court, and his own role as a policeman, and his perception of community attitudes toward delinquency.

Some critics of the existing system of informal disposition have argued that the observed arbitrary and discriminatory factors in the selection process be eliminated through professionalization of the police, the setting of explicit standards by police departments, training of officers in juvenile behavior, police-community relations programs or police-juvenile liaison schemes, or other means of improving police discretionary judgments. Certainly such efforts are important, especially since the police are often the first to come in contact with juvenile misconduct.

However, the screening of serious offenses from simple misconduct or other nonserious behavior should not be primarily a police responsibility. The police, for the most part, attempt to do what they believe the community—or important segments of it—expect them to do.[64] If the public relegates to law enforcement and the courts responsibility for what are essentially child-rearing functions (discipline, guidance, moral instruction, protection), it is not the task of the police to decide that arrest and court processing are not meeting these needs.

Much of the literature on the removal of juveniles from the jurisdiction of police and the courts recognizes the extent of community responsibility in the area of social control. Many writers have urged that the definition of

[61] *Op. cit., supra* note 1, p. 12. However, one writer argues that national data on police disposition of juveniles suggest that the size of the police dismissal category is not half as large as has been alleged. Monahan, Thomas P., National data on police dispositions of juvenile offenders, *Police*, 14 (1):36–45, 1969.

[62] *Op. cit., supra* note 1, p. 14.

[63] Goldman, Nathan, *The Differential Selection of Juvenile Offenders for Court Appearance*, New York, National Council on Crime and Delinquency, 1963, 133 pp.

[64] *Ibid.* Goldman states that an important determinant of police discretion is perception of community attitudes toward delinquency. Also, Wilson describes police as acting according to perceived public expectations. Wilson, James Q., *Varieties of Police Behavior*, Cambridge, Massachusetts: Harvard University, 1968.

delinquency be narrowed to exclude a variety of behaviors which if committed by an adult would not constitute a violation of law (truancy, disobedience, school behavior problem, bad companions, etc.), implying not only
that court processing for such conduct is unjust but that handling of noncriminal deviance by community agencies and individuals is more appropriate. It has been argued that juvenile court statutes which use terms such
as "incorrigible" or "disobedient" might be nullified on the grounds of
vagueness or "status" criminality.[65] It also has been suggested that judges
simply stop accepting the dependent, neglected, or nondangerous child for
detention, probation, or commitment, thus diverting such children to family
and child-welfare agencies or social and mental health services[66] and forcing
the public to accept responsibility for their problems. It is commonly acknowledged that many children in the United States who have not committed
crimes and whose conduct does not present a threat to the community are
being drawn into the correctional system, to the serious detriment of both
the child and the system itself. If it is public apathy or tacit acceptance of this
situation which allows it to continue, then a broad effort should be made to
make it understood that existing practices are neither effective nor necessary.

The Youth Services Bureau has been offered as a major alternative to
social control by the criminal justice system. The concept of Youth Services
Bureau was given official recognition by the President's Crime Commission,
which recommended that such bureaus be established in the community to
provide and coordinate programs and services for delinquents and
nondelinquents.[67] The stated purpose of these bureaus is to facilitate the
diversion of children and youth from judicial processing to social services. It
is suggested that the nature of services provided and the specific operation
of the bureaus will vary with the community because of local differences in
the incidence and characteristics of delinquency and the resources
available.[68] Presumably, local definitions of delinquency and interpretations
of situations requiring intervention also will affect the nature and extent of
service.

Although the concept of the Youth Services Bureau has only recently
become popularized, the idea of employing the local community agency to
develop and coordinate youth services is not entirely new. For example, ten
years ago a local community action program was initiated in Oakland
County, Michigan, to coordinate the efforts of individuals and social agencies in the development and delivery of services to youth.[69] From this
developed the Oakland County Protective Services Program, involving the

---

[65] McKay, Malcom V., Juvenile court jurisdiction over noncriminal children, unpublished
paper, Cambridge, Massachusetts: Harvard Law School, 1969.
[66] Rector, Milton G., Statement before the U.S. Senate Subcommittee to Investigate Juvenile
Delinquency, *Crime and Delinquency*, 16(1):93–99, 1970.
[67] *Op. cit., supra* note 3, p. 83.
[68] California, Delinquency Prevention Commission, Youth Service Bureaus: standards and
guidelines, Sacramento: Youth Authority Department, 1968, 30 pp.
[69] Moore, Eugene Arthur, Youth services bureaus: local community action program prevents
delinquency, *Judicature*, 52(3):117–119, 1968.

court, municipal government and school board, local agencies, and volunteer citizens in delinquency prevention activities, both for youth in general and on an individual basis. In Philadelphia, essentially the same function is fulfilled by the Youth Referral Program, in operation since 1944.[70] In this program, youths between the ages of seven and seventeen who have had minor contacts with police are identified and adult neighborhood volunteers work to achieve parental acceptance of responsibility for supervision of their children, cooperation among parents, educators and community leaders in child guidance, and sponsorship of programs based on studies of environmental conditions affecting child behavior. While there are differences between these programs and the Youth Services Bureau, as it is currently described, the basic ideas are there: community responsibility for handling minor misconduct and development of alternatives to court processing as a means of providing services to youth.

The experiences of the more recently established Youth Services Bureaus, such as those now in operation or underway in nine California communities,[71] have not yet been assessed by research. Reports of their establishment and operation are enthusiastic and expectations are high. It appears likely that whatever problems do arise, many juveniles nonetheless will be removed from the juvenile justice system and a variety of alternative dispositions will be demonstrated as feasible.

Two possible sources of problems in this type of organization and delivery of rehabilitative services are apparent: (1) that pressures to accept "treatment," even where it is unwanted, might develop; and (2) that the effort to provide services to those who are presumed to need them may prevent recognition of the fact that for much of what now is labeled as deviance, the problem is *not* how to treat it but how to absorb or tolerate it—or even encourage it. Not all deviant behavior requires treatment, whether in or out of the criminal justice system, yet the mere presence of a functioning mechanism of community services, with none of the more obvious drawbacks of the penal system, is likely to result in the "treatment" of many more individuals by official agencies. A rational policy of diversion, especially if the goal involves more than individual "cures," would seem to require that society broaden its definition of acceptable behavior rather than merely extend its control efforts to include treatment and provision of services. Some diversion should result in simple release from any system of intervention or control.

CONCLUSION

From a study of factors related to differential rates of delinquency, Victor Eisner has concluded that our present delinquency problem stems from our

[70] Philadelphia, Division of Youth Conservation Services, A review of the Youth Referral Program, 1944–1969, Philadelphia, 1969, 13 pp.

[71] California, Youth Authority Department, Community Services Division, California's youths services bureaus: a study in community action and cooperation, by William A. Underwood, Sacramento, the Department, 1969, 9 pp.

cultural intolerance of diversity and variability and our overly restrictive boundaries on acceptable behavior.[72] His observations with regard to the repression and resultant alienation of adolescents in American society could be more generally applied, not only to youth and lower-class black communities, but to many groups on the fringe of and outside the mainstream of society.

> Our laws are made by only one segment of this culture, for whom many of the laws are unnecessarily restrictive. As a result we have alienated large groups of people, and we have applied a delinquency label to many of them. . . . Our high delinquency rates are evidence that our boundary-maintaining mechanism has excluded too many. . . .[73]

An understanding of this basic intolerance of diversity, increasingly apparent in the United States today, is prerequisite to the recognition of a major weakness in our efforts to prevent and control crime, and especially in the current emphasis on diverting offenders from the criminal justice system to agencies of civil and social control. Criminal statutes may be revised (to "legalize" public drunkenness, vagrancy, victimless sex offenses); control and surveillance of minor violations may be achieved without arrest (in special misdemeanant programs or youth guidance services); and health and welfare services may be made accessible to those who need them (clinics for treatment of addiction; employment services for youth and the poor; housing and other assistance for the skid row alcoholic). All such measures are likely to result in fewer persons entering the criminal justice system. But as long as mainstream America continues to view all deviations from a narowly defined acceptable norm as evidence of pathology requiring some kind of control response (whether punitive or rehabilitative), diversion is likely to remain largely a technique of enforcing conformity by alternate means. The "crisis of overcriminalization" might be more accurately understood as a crisis of *overcontrol,* because to construe it as merely a problem of the criminal law is to conceal the injustices inherent in a more general policy of social exclusion.

---

[72] Eisner, Victor, *The Delinquency Label: The Epidemiology of Juvenile Delinquency,* New York: Random House, 1969, 177 pp.

[73] *Id.,* pp. 132–133.

4

YOUTH SERVICES SYSTEMS*

Robert J. Gemignani

In some ways, this next paper is the most interesting of all in this section. It reports a *governmental* strategy that emerged from *academic* consultations, a relatively uncommon occurrence. This particular strategy has a heavily sociological flavor and emphasizes an organized approach to prevention. In some ways, it has less to do with diversion than with community *absorption*, that is, preventing youngsters from entering the juvenile justice system, from even a first contact with the police. Specifics aside, however, the critical aspect of this paper is its exposition of a governmental, structural (bureaucratic) translation of abstract principles. Thinking before acting is often urged but less often observed. The reader must judge for himself whether this instance constitutes a good advertisement for such a strategy.

* From "Youth Services Systems," *Delinquency Prevention Reporter*, Youth Development and Delinquency Prevention Administration, U.S. Department of Health, Education, and Welfare (Washington, D.C.: U.S. Government Printing Office, July–August 1972), pp. 1–7.

This paper discusses a *national strategy* for the prevention of juvenile delinquency which has evolved over the past two years.

The broad outlines of the strategy were developed at a meeting called by the Youth Development Delinquency Prevention Administration early in 1970. Those who attended were representative of the professions most concerned about youth problems and included law enforcement officials, educators, sociologists, and practitioners and researchers in the fields of juvenile delinquency and youth development.

Their recommendations reflected analyses of past failures and successes in juvenile programs and appraisals of the roles of youth in our society today.

Subsequently, the strategy has been refined, and actions designed to implement it have been taken by the legislative and executive branches of Federal and State governments. Pilot programs have been launched in twenty-three communities throughout the Nation. Additional programs are being initiated this fiscal year (1972).

The strategy calls for the establishment, Nationwide, of youth services systems which will divert youth, insofar as possible, from the juvenile justice system by providing comprehensive, integrated, community-based programs designed to meet the needs of all youth, regardless of who they are or what their individual problems may be.

Although the need for direct work with individuals and families is not overlooked, the national strategy focuses primarily upon creating changes in our social institutions so that they become more effective in providing legitimate roles for all youth.

Included in the paper are current and projected statistics which highlight the need for the strategy, as well as details of the strategy itself and the administrative, fiscal, legislative, and other factors involved in carrying it out.

THE PROBLEM

Scope. In 1970, the number of juvenile delinquency cases handled by juvenile courts reached an all-time high of 1,052,000. The figure, however, represents only a part of the total number of youth involved in the juvenile justice system. It is estimated, conservatively, that almost 4,000,000 youth had a police contact in 1970 and that 2,000,000 of those contacts resulted in arrests, half of which were referred to juvenile courts. Of the million referred to juvenile courts, about half were counseled and released with no further action; the other half were handled officially through some form of court hearing.

Until 1970, the number of youth processed through juvenile courts was increasing by a higher and higher rate each year. In 1970, however, the *rate of increase* declined—from 10 percent in 1969 to 6 percent in 1970. Although this drop is encouraging, it does not yet indicate a trend and therefore any projection of the extent of the problem that can be prepared at this time must assume a rate of increase of at least two-tenths of a percent each year.

Using this conservative estimate of rate of increase on actual figures from 1965 through 1970, it can be expected that, unless more effective strategies are adopted, *there will be nearly 1,500,000 juvenile delinquency cases handled by juvenile courts in 1977.* The following table is a projection of the scope of the problem for the years 1971–1977.

I. Rate of Referrals to Juvenile Court 1971–1977—A Projection

Year	Child Population 10–17	Rate (%)	Court Delinquency Cases
1971	32,614,000	3.1	1,011,000
1972	32,788,000	3.3	1,082,000
1973	32,962,000	3.5	1,154,000
1974	33,136,000	3.7	1,226,000
1975	33,311,000	3.9	1,299,000
1976	33,049,000	4.1	1,355,000
1977	32,787,000	4.3	1,410,000

Cost. No precise data on the cost of handling delinquency problems through the juvenile justice system are currently available, although an accurate analysis of such costs is now being undertaken by the Youth Development and Delinquency Prevention Administration (YDDPA).

The best figures available at present are based on reports made by States to the YDDPA. Although these are believed to be low, they are the figures used in the following projections of the cost of continuing present methods

and the savings that could be expected from a concerted effort to divert young people from the juvenile justice system.
These projections indicated that, by 1977, almost *$1.5 billion could be saved* in official court costs by the adoption of a strategy for diversion. This is not a net savings, of course, because it does not take account of the cost of diversion programs. Tables II, III, and IV show the basis for this estimate of savings.

The total costs shown in Table IV under "Actual Costs in Juvenile Justice System" include intake costs for 100 percent of the cases, the cost of probation service for 25 percent, training schools for 10 percent, and community services for 10 percent.

II. Annual Cost per Youth Processed Through the Juvenile Justice System

Referral and intake	$ 100.00
Probation service	500.00
Training schools	5,700.00
Other residential commitments	1,500.00
(foster care, group homes, halfway houses)	

III. Estimated Diversion of Youth—Years 1972–1977
(suggested % decrease in rate)

	Rate	Decrease in Rate (from 1972)	Youth in Court Delinquency Cases	Youth Diverted from Court (Projection)
1972 base yr.	3.30	—	1,082,000	
1973 1st yr.	3.23	−2	1,065,000	89,000
1974 2nd yr.	3.10	−6	1,027,000	199,000
1975 3rd yr.	2.90	−12	966,000	333,000
1976 4th yr.	2.70	−18	892,000	463,000
1977 5th yr.	2.50	−25	820,000	590,000

IV. Cost Savings of a Suggested Plan of Diversion

Year	Actual Costs in Juvenile Justice System	Diversion Rate (%)	Revised Costs in Juvenile Justice System	Savings
1973	$ 981,000,000	2	$905,000,000	$ 76,000,000
1974	1,042,000,000	6	873,000,000	169,000,000
1975	1,104,000,000	12	821,000,000	283,000,000
1976	1,152,000,000	18	758,000,000	394,000,000
1977	1,199,000,000	25	694,000,000	505,000,000
			Cumulative savings	$1,427,000,000

THE STRATEGY

Options. Basically, there are four program approaches which can be chosen for emphasis in planning a strategy for preventing juvenile delinquency.

1. Programs based on behavior modification.
2. Programs based on improving institutional services to delinquents.
3. Programs based on developing new services and delivery systems to predelinquents and delinquents.
4. Programs that address themselves to the processes in communities that propel children into the juvenile justice system.

The first, which deals with modification of behavior, is extremely limited. It presupposes early identification and is a highly individualized and expensive process. The state of the art is developing rapidly, however, and the approach might be used to work with youth already identified as being alienated from the social system.

The second and third are approaches that have been and are currently being utilized. They both deal with previous efforts at reform and frequently address themselves to narrow issues like training of institutional staff, reducing caseloads, and innovative treatment programs. Efforts in these areas would have a minimal impact because they tend to oversimplify the problem and do not deal with those community processes that are responsible for most delinquency.

The fourth is the strategy discussed in this paper. It is advocated for Nationwide adoption because it offers two avenues for diverting young people from the juvenile justice system: first, by providing prevention programs; and second, by offering community-based rehabilitation programs as alternatives to placement of delinquent youths in traditional correctional facilities.

Strategy development. The adoption of this strategy was first recommended by a group of national experts who were invited to YDDPA to meet in Scituate, Massachusetts, in June 1970, to consider how the Nation might cope with its juvenile delinquency problem more effectively. A short document produced at that meeting stated:

> We believe that our social institutions are programmed in such a way as to deny large numbers of young people socially acceptable, responsible, and personally gratifying roles. These institutions should seek ways of becoming more responsive to youths' needs.

Any strategy for youth development and delinquency prevention, the statement urged, should give priority to:

> . . . programs which assist institutions to change in ways that provide young people with socially acceptable, responsible, personally gratifying roles and assist young people to assume such roles.

The group's conclusion that the important element in any strategy is *institutional* rather than individual was based upon the premise that effective youth development programs must *start* with a consideration of the institutional forces which impinge on youth and shape their behavior. This was made more explicit in a document, the "National Strategy for Delinquency Prevention," which evolved after the meeting at Scituate:

> These propositions furnish a basic perspective on the problem of delinquency by linking it firmly to specific types of failure on the part of specific social institutions as they seek to relate to young people, and, in turn, to the negative reactions of young people to such institutions when they find them wanting. It follows from this that the development of a viable national strategy for the prevention and reduction of delinquency rests on the identification, assessment, and alteration of those features of institutional functioning that impede and obstruct a favorable course of youth development for all youths, particularly those whose social situation makes them most prone to the development of delinquent careers and to participation in collective forms of withdrawal and deviancy.

YDDPA role. The need for centralizing national leadership in advancing the new strategy was early recognized by both the executive and legislative branches of the Federal government as indicated by the following actions.

In 1971, YDDPA analyzed its program and recommended a sharper delineation of the responsibilities assumed by the Law Enforcement Assistance Administration (LEAA) of the U.S. Department of Justice and those assumed by YDDPA. As a result, papers were exchanged between the Attorney General and the Secretary of Health, Education, and Welfare. Both agreed that YDDPA should be the Federal focal point for prevention and rehabilitation activities *outside* the juvenile justice system, and that LEAA should perform a similar function in relation to activities *within* the juvenile justice system.

The House Committee on Education and Labor picked up this new delineation of responsibilities in its report on the *Juvenile Delinquency Prevention and Control Act Amendments of 1971*, outlining the YDDPA role as follows:

> The committee suggests that this role be that of funding preventive programs which are administered outside the traditional juvenile justice system, that is, the police, the courts, the correctional institutions, detention homes, and probation and parole authorities. These programs might include community-based halfway houses, after-school and summer recreation programs, foster home or group home care, youth service bureaus, volunteer programs within schools, or other community services. Such programs would be provided principally for those youths who have not become enmeshed in the traditional juvenile justice system, but they could also be provided for delinquent youth under the control of this system if the service or care itself were not under the direct administrative control of the traditional agencies and institutions. The committee hopes that the Department will concentrate its efforts during fiscal 1972 on funding such programs and that this experience will serve as the basis for recommendations for a complete revision of the present Act.

The House report quoted the House Select Committee on Crime, which concluded that the programs under the Juvenile Delinquency Prevention and Control Act should *not* be merged with those funded under the Omnibus Crime Control and Safe Streets Act:

We feel that basic law enforcement techniques are not the correct procedure for dealing with the juvenile delinquency problems confronting us. There must be more understanding, research, conceptualization, and experimentation. Arrest and incarceration are not the answer to juvenile delinquency problems. They have their place, but it is not with young people.

The House report stated the Committee agreed with this view and extended the Juvenile Delinquency Prevention and Control Act for one year ". . . with the hope that the Department of Health, Education, and Welfare will concentrate on refocusing it to fulfill the great need for preventive programs. The committee notes the Department's recent efforts at redirecting the program and would hope for a continued interest by the Department in the program."

Subsequently, the Senate report on the 1971 amendments pointed to the report on the original Act which states that the legislation should not be just another categorical program that is administered in relative isolation from much larger efforts such as the community action program, model cities, and the Manpower Development and Training Act. Moreover, the committee called for effective coordination with the Justice Department, and asked that programs administered under the Act be used to further coordination of all Government efforts in the area of juvenile delinquency and to provide "national leadership" in developing new approaches to the problems of juvenile crime.

Prior to the Senate's report, the Department of Health, Education, and Welfare had begun coordination efforts with the Department of Justice.

With its responsibilities more clearly defined by both the Department of Health, Education, and Welfare and the Congress, YDDPA adopted the mission of: (1) functioning as the Federal focal point for delinquency prevention, helping to achieve coordination, improving existing programs and developing new programs: (2) acting as a youth advocate and providing technical assistance; and (3) developing youth services systems.

Action plan.   The key factor in implementing a nationwide strategy of institutional change is the establishment of youth services systems. These systems offer comprehensive services to the population at risk and are jointly planned and funded by local, State, and Federal agencies, utilizing YDDPA expertise, its relative neutrality among functional service providers, and some of its leverage money to identify gaps and provide bridges between those service providers. This arrangement makes optimal use of public and private resources. It minimizes the risk of further stigma to the target population by integrating programs that meet their specific needs into services offered to the total youth population.

Federal coordination. Over the past few years, organizational arrangements have been made within the executive branch of the Federal
government which help YDDPA to assure that, while the activities that
comprise a youth services system will continue to be supported by various
Federal agencies, it will be possible for States and communities to pool funds
from these Federal sources in developing their youth services systems. Many
of the necessary services—such as welfare, vocational rehabilitation, medical
assistance—are administered at the Federal level by the Social and Rehabilitation Service (SRS) of the Department of Health, Education, and Welfare.
YDDPA, as a part of SRS, works closely with the other Administrations in
that unit. Coordination with other parts of HEW and with other Federal
departments and agencies that administer programs affecting youth is assured by an Interdepartmental Council to Coordinate Juvenile Delinquency
Activities in the Federal Government. This Council was formed in 1971 and
the YDDPA Commissioner serves on it.

THE YOUTH SERVICES SYSTEM

All communities have some form of available youth services. Serious deficiencies exist, however, in a community's efforts to meet the needs of its
young people. The following are *eight major problem areas and a remedial
response* to each of them. These responses comprise the basic characteristics
of a *Youth Services System.*

1. In most communities, services for youth are very much fragmented. For
example, a family with multiple problems is often seen by several different
agencies at the same time. Rarely does one agency know what the other is doing. It
is not uncommon for one agency to be working at cross-purposes with another.
    RESPONSE: INTEGRATED SERVICES. Agencies funded under a youth services
system work together to achieve common objectives. Contractual and other formal agreements are utilized to insure a coordinated and integrated approach.
2. As they are currently operated, many agencies find it difficult to adapt their
services to the constantly changing social scene. For example, a project concerned
with school truancy and failure may be unable to refocus its services to include the
sudden intrusion of a drug abuse problem.
    RESPONSE: ADAPTABILITY. Through the interaction of the agencies that
comprise the youth services system, a viable program evolves which can meet the
needs of youth, regardless of the precipitating problem. Agencies are asked to
assure a flexible and adaptive posture rather than maintaining a traditionally
more comfortable and static position.
3. A major failure of youth services programs is that they are geared to helping
only a portion of youth with problems, instead of potentially helping all youth. In
some instances, many youngsters are not eligible for services or, when eligible,
must become part of a long waiting list.
    RESPONSE: SCOPE. A youth services system must have scope, must be able to
provide services to *all* youth within the project area, regardless of who they are
and regardless of the type of problem. In such a system, the youth who just "walks
in" is as important as the youth referred by a traditional agency.

4. Past efforts at coordination of services have failed. Involving interested agencies in an effort to work together to meet common objectives has not always met with lasting success.

RESPONSE: JOINT FUNDING. It is necessary to get a commitment of resources and/or implement a purchase of services plan. The youth services system must be jointly funded to assure that agencies will indeed work together.

5. The development of jointly funded programs at the local level can be a difficult process, since most funds flow through a variety of State agencies. Comprehensive plans (developed by such agencies as the Welfare Department, Department of Vocational Rehabilitation, the Office of Education, the Criminal Justice Planning Agency, and the Department of Mental Health) reflect the local community's basic needs in each respective area.

RESPONSE: MULTIGOVERNMENTAL PARTICIPATION. It is important that a youth services system be multigovernmental. It is essential that appropriate State agencies, and their Federal counterparts at the Regional level, be *convened formally*, to aid in developing coordinated youth services, and to assure adequate joint funding.

6. An additional problem with past youth services has been an *inadequate* capacity for extracting knowledge. And what knowledge was learned was usually inadequately transmitted to others. Thus duplication of effort is often the rule, and one program's errors are repeated by other programs throughout the country.

RESPONSE: EVALUATION AND TRANSFER OF KNOWLEDGE. A critical characteristic for a youth services system is its capacity for *evaluation* and its ability to *transfer* knowledge. Much of this evaluation and transfer is being accomplished, but it needs to be greatly augmented Nationwide through a strong program of technical assistance at the State and Federal levels.

7. Technology and new knowledge often fail to be translated rapidly into effective action programs because agencies do not receive the information and technical assistance that will enable them to use the new approaches.

RESPONSE: USE OF ADVANCED TECHNOLOGY. One of the great advantages of a Nationwide network of youth services systems is that positive results from a program in one area can more easily be adopted by other States and communities.

8. There is a great amount of justified criticism that youth *themselves* are rarely consulted and utilized in planning and carrying out programs and services that directly affect them.

RESPONSE: YOUTH INVOLVEMENT. Youth, as the consumer, must be heavily *involved* in all phases of programs that affect them. We must provide them with leadership training and help them to assume decision-making roles at all levels of government.

Chart A is a flowchart demonstrating how integrated youth services work to achieve maximum results. *(Note: This is only for purposes of example. Differing configurations of services and structure are possible in meeting individual community needs).*

In this case the Mayor's office is the grantee agency. The boy is a school dropout, with no job skills, and he is estranged from his family, and experiencing the effects of an overdose of LSD. He refuses traditional professional help. However, he comes in contact with the project when he calls its youth-manned HOTLINE, reporting that he is on LSD and wants to talk to someone about his problem. A sympathetic youth talks him into visiting the

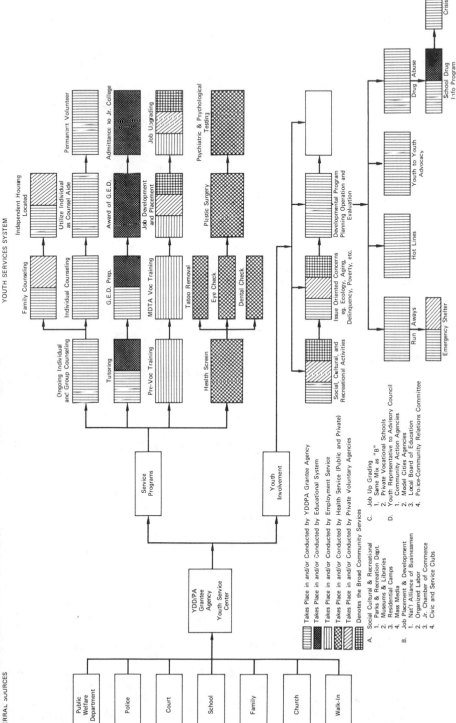

YOUTH SERVICES SYSTEM

REFERRAL SOURCES

| Public Welfare Department |
| Police |
| Court |
| School |
| Family |
| Church |
| Walk-In |

YDD/PA Grantee Agency Youth Service Center

Service Programs

Youth Involvement

Independent Housing Located

Permanent Volunteer

Family Counseling

Utilize Individual as Counsel Aide

Individual Counseling

Admittance to Jr. College

Ongoing Individual and Group Counseling

Award of G.E.D.

Job Upgrading

Tutoring

G.E.D. Prep.

Job Development and Placement

Pre-Voc Training

MDTA Voc Training

Psychiatric & Psychological Testing

Health Screen

Tatoo Removal

Plastic Surgery

Eye Check

Dental Check

Social, Cultural, and Recreational Activities

Issue Oriented Concerns eg. Ecology, Aging, Delinquency, Poverty, etc.

Developmental Program Planning Operation and Evaluation

Run Aways

Hot Lines

Youth to Youth Advocacy

Drug Abuse

Emergency Shelter

School Drug Info Program

Crisis Center

Takes Place in and/or Conducted by YDDPA Grantee Agency
Takes Place in and/or Conducted by Educational System
Takes Place in and/or Conducted by Employment Service
Takes Place in and/or Conducted by Health Service (Public and Private)
Takes Place in and/or Conducted by Private Voluntary Agencies
Denotes the Broad Community Services

A. Social Cultural & Recreational
   1. Parks & Recreation Dept.
   2. Museums & Libraries
   3. Residential Camps
   4. Mass Media

B. Job Placement & Development
   1. Nat'l Alliance of Businessmen
   2. Organized Labor
   3. Jr. Chamber of Commerce
   4. Civic and Service Clubs

C. Job Up Grading
   1. Same Mix as "B"
   2. Private Vocational Schools

D. Youth Representative to Advisory Council
   1. Community Action Agencies
   2. Model Cities Agencies
   3. Local Board of Education
   4. Police-Community Relations Committee

63

HOTLINE's adjunct drug crisis center. The center finds the youth to be under heavy influence of LSD. An ex-addict counselor is brought in to help the youth accept hospitalization. Within a few days of intensive contact with the ex-addict, the young man decides to accept some professional help.

A plan is developed with him by the social worker at the center. It includes counseling for both him and his family; tutoring to prepare him for a GED; prevocational training; and the removal of unwanted tattoos from his hands. The counseling is rendered by the social worker at the center. The system's central information retrieval bank shows that the parents are already being seen by a local private agency, and a communication on the case is established with that agency. Tutorial services for the GED are supplied by a teacher from the local school assigned to work at the center. The prevocational training is rendered in the facilities of the local Department of Employment. The tattoo removal takes place in the plastic surgery clinic of a local private hospital, improving the youth's appearance and self-confidence.

As a result of the counseling program, the young man is able to understand his problems and begin to do something about them. Although a reconciliation with his family is unsuccessful, a suitable independent living arrangement is made in a local boarding house. He is eventually awarded a GED. He gains some vocational skills and through the cooperation of the local chapter of the Junior Chamber of Commerce he is placed on a job. In this case, the young man continues his relationship with the program following his rehabilitation. He donates two nights a week to answering the HOTLINE telephone—a service to others that returns great satisfaction to him.

YDDPA helped the local community in planning, developing, and financing the youth services system and in making a broad range of community services an integral part of that system.

The State Vocational Rehabilitation Agency sought out and selected this particular community and brought it to YDDPA's attention as a locality where youth and adults had worked together (in establishing a HOTLINE). YDDPA's technical and financial assistance helped support the administration of the program and the development of the evaluation component. In addition, YDDPA funds supported the program in the drug crisis center, as well as the salary for the ex-addict counselor. YDDPA also assisted in developing the system of joint funding. The components of the program were worked out as follows:

1.   For the youth hospital service, special educational tutoring, and prevocational training, YDDPA had worked out prior agreements with other units of the U.S. Department of Health, Education, and Welfare (the Health Services and Mental Health Administration and the Office of Education) and with the U.S. Department of Labor, which facilitated local arrangements.

2.   Programs providing plastic surgery, family casework, and employment placement had been developed with YDDPA providing technical assistance to the local United Way, family service agency, and private hospital.

YDDPA, through its grantee agency, helped to make a big difference in the way this community responds to problems, and in the life of the seventeen-year-old youth. Prior to the establishment of the youth services system, the available services for youth in the community were fragmented and lacking in necessary components. There was a HOTLINE program, operated by a local church group. If the seventeen-year-old boy with the drug problem had called for help, there was no youth-operated drug crisis center to which he could be referred. Even if one had existed, it is doubtful that a working arrangement between such a drug center and the local hospital would have been made. Further, the ability to coordinate a remedial service program for a multi-problem family would have been extremely difficult. Such is the reality in the majority of our American communities today.

YDDPA's legacy to the community. Many demonstration projects have resulted in a short-term integration of services. However, when Federal funds were no longer available, integration was not maintained. YDDPA wants to institutionalize mechanisms which do *not* require the presence of Federal funds for their continuation.

YDDPA's action steps for such insurance are as follows:

1. All programs that provide services under a youth services system will ultimately be accountable to YDDPA's prime grantee. The grantee organization will be responsible for seeing that services are coordinated and that they are comprehensive.

2. YDDPA's prime grantee will also be responsible for seeing that the system performs advocacy functions, seeing that youth's interests and needs are considered in all community planning activities.

3. YDDPA's role in youth services systems is a developmental one. Its financial resources are used as leverage to attract from $3 to $4 for every $1 it invests. YDDPA's dollar essentially buys administration, technical assistance, and program components necessary for inclusion of those youths who are otherwise ineligible for participation in the range of services planned. These costs are to be assumed by the community and State agencies once the system and the cost effectiveness of integrated youth services have been demonstrated.

4. To insure continuity and full integration of youth services, the development process involves not only a joint planning effort among participating service providers, but agreements or contracts for providing services in which specific numbers and types of services are identified and dollars are committed. These agreements may require changes in the respective State plans (e.g., State Welfare Plan, State Criminal Justice Plan). Once in place, however, the service pattern becomes part of approved and continuing state plans under various formula grants. The integrated services plan then becomes institutionalized to the point where it becomes a natural mechanism for accepting general revenue sharing support. YDDPA's prime grantee is responsible for planning and monitoring the effort to assure that the agreements for services and dollars are honored.

MEASURABLE OBJECTIVES

The decision to adopt a Nationwide strategy focused upon institutional change, and to use youth services systems as the instrument for carrying out this strategy, was based upon thoughtful analyses of the deficiencies of present efforts to curb delinquency and careful appraisals of the potentialities of the new approach.

However, the actual value of this approach can only be determined by setting forth clear and specific objectives that the system must achieve if it is to be counted a success and by devising ways of measuring the extent to which those objectives are being reached.

The objectives decided upon and the methods to be used to measure their achievement are as follows:

1. Provide more socially acceptable and meaningful roles for youth. One of the reasons why most youth don't get into trouble is that they have access to a variety of positive, socially acceptable roles, such as student, family member, peer group member, club group member, employee. The community process opens up progressively wider roles for youth as they successfully perform their present role functions. It is at the point where the denial of access to increasingly responsible roles occurs that delinquency is more apt to become an option. The denial of completing the student role (i.e., suspension from high school or dropping out) makes it extremely difficult for the ex-student to fulfill the employee role since a high school diploma is a minimal requirement for most jobs. In addition, the loss of the student role creates a strain on the existing family roles, peer group roles, and club group roles which often results in the process of alienation from those social institutions which have in effect "closed their doors."

A program-by-program analysis will be completed whith will indicate whether the youth services system succeeds in providing the socially acceptable roles that are necessary to "make it" in our society. Criteria are: the reduction of dropout rates, the opening of job opportunities, the process of youth involvement, and participation in community life.

2. Divert youth away from the juvenile justice system into alternate programs. The measure for this objective will be a statistical procedure reflecting a reduction in the annual rate of referrals to juvenile courts.

3. Reduce negative labeling. A great deal of interest has legitimately been generated over the process of labeling, particularly the labeling that attaches a stigma. The process of searching for an approach to eliminate the negative labeling of youth leads directly to those agencies and institutions which apply the labels, most notably the schools, welfare departments, juvenile courts, employment services, and some private agencies that stress eligibility determinations. An evaluative paradox occurs, for instance, in the schools; special dropout prevention programs have been instituted which in themselves denote a very positive effort. Nevertheless, the programs rely on certain predictors which identify potential dropouts for special services. In effect, the children and youth selected for special services to keep them in school are labeled as potential dropouts and very shortly their peers are aware of the distinction despite official silence.

Labeling that occurs at the juvenile court is being addressed by YDDPA's efforts to divert youth away from the court and the subsequent "delinquent" label. The problem to be addressed yet is how to provide alternative youth services that do not label by their presence in the community. YDDPA's comprehensive youth services systems, with a wide range of participants, not just delinquent or predelinquent youth, offer a viable alternative. The measurement problem in this area is a field of conceptual exploration at present, to be followed by formal research in the future.

4. Reduce youth-adult alienation. Criterion measurements for this objective are in the process of assembly and development. The measures of a reduction in alienation will necessarily be a part of each program's internal monitoring system and will apply to observed behavioral patterns of the youth being served in that system. The assumption is that a reduction in youth-adult alienation will bring about an increased participation by youth in the total community's activities and will be reflected in lower rates of official delinquency.

5
DIVERSION:
BACKGROUND AND DEFINITION*
Donald R. Cressey and Robert A. McDermott

The following paper, excerpted from a larger monograph concerned with juvenile corrections, is aimed more at diversion at the court intake locus than with police diversion. Nonetheless, the principles are similar. For us, it emphasizes two major points. First, through analogy and simplification (or perhaps oversimplification) it emphasizes the main features of the diversion trend and labels it as such—a trend or fad. Second, it focuses once again on the definitional problems in diversion. It is difficult to come away from papers like this as confirmed diversion addicts; this in itself seems a worthwhile outcome.

---

* From *Diversion from the Juvenile Justice System,* National Assessment of Juvenile Corrections (Ann Arbor: University of Michigan, June 1973), pp. 1–8. Reprinted by permission of the authors and publisher.

Only a few years ago, most American chief probation officers and other juvenile justice administrators used the words "research" and "breakthrough" constantly if they wanted good marks from their superiors and their colleagues. In large cities, especially, ratings of "excellent" went to the men who frequently used this rhetoric and who developed the corresponding research programs. Now the word is "diversion," and it is diversion programs that win the accolades.

In 1967 the President's Commission on Law Enforcement and Administration of Justice recommended establishment of alternatives to the system of juvenile justice. Service agencies capable of dealing with certain categories of juveniles who routinely come into contact with agents of the juvenile justice system should have juveniles diverted to them:

> The formal sanctioning system and pronouncement of delinquency should be used only as a last resort.
>
> In place of the formal system, dispositional alternatives to adjudication must be developed for dealing with juveniles, including agencies to provide and coordinate services and procedures to achieve necessary control without unnecessary stigma. Alternatives already available, such as those related to court intake, should be more fully exploited.
>
> The range of conduct for which court intervention is authorized should be narrowed, with greater emphasis upon consensual and informal means of meeting the problems of difficult children.[1]

By implication, these recommendations are highly critical. They say that contact with the juvenile justice system is bad, or not as good as it should be, so alternative programs should be utilized or invented.

The Commission and its staff probably synthesized several delinquency causation theories in order to establish a foundation for its recommendations. Or perhaps some of the parties to the recommendations simply were sick of seeing juvenile delinquents mucked about, and demanded change on that ground rather than on the ground of sociological or social psychological theory. In any case two basic theories of delinquency might have provided the gunpowder for the explosive recommendation.

The first is labeling theory, as developed by George Herbert Mead, Frank Tannenbaum, Herbert Blumer, Edwin McC. Lemert, Howard S. Becker, and others.[2] The basic contention of labeling theory is that individuals stigmatized as delinquent become what they are said to be. Initial deviation (primary deviance) occurs rather haphazardly, as does apprehension, arrest, and labeling as delinquent. Once caught and labeled, however, the child is stigmatized, forced out of interaction with the value system of nondelinquents and shunted into association with juveniles similarly labeled. Delinquency after labeling (secondary deviance) is a direct result of the labeling process.

Clearly, in this theoretical perspective, the agencies established to deal with delinquency contribute to its incidence even as they try to cope with it. Policemen, juvenile court judges, probation officers, institution workers, and other juvenile justice administrators create or "cause" delinquency. It should be noted, however, that police departments have long been "divert-

---

[1] President's Commission on Law Enforcement and Administration of Justice, *Task Force Report: Juvenile Delinquency and Youth Crime* (Washington, D.C.: U.S. Government Printing Office, 1967), p. 2.

[2] For summary statements of labeling theory, see John I. Kitsuse, "Societal Reactions to Deviant Behavior: Problems of Theory and Method," *Social Problems* 9 (1963), pp. 247–256; and Jack P. Gibbs, "Conceptions of Deviant Behavior: The Old And the New," *Pacific Sociological Review* 9 (1966), pp. 9–14.

ing" the vast majority of the delinquents they encounter. Perhaps eight out of ten youths encountering the police are released without any formal processing or recording. They are lectured, ignored, threatened, or even punished administratively, but they are not arrested or booked. Most diversion thus takes place at the police level.

The second theoretical justification stems from differential association theory, as developed by George Herbert Mead, W. I. Thomas, Herbert Blumer, Edwin H. Sutherland, Lloyd E. Ohlin, Daniel Glaser, James Short, Albert Cohen, David Matza, and others.[3] Stated simply, this theory holds that individuals engage in delinquent behavior because they experience an overabundance of interactions, associations, and reinforcements with behavior patterns favorable to delinquency. Many nondelinquents, including parents, carry such infectious values. The principal Typhoid Marys, however, are other delinquents: a foundation stone underlying diversion practices is the notion that "naive" or "potential" delinquents should not be cast into interaction with more experienced ones.

Now, if a policy maker looks at the juvenile justice system through the lens of these two theories, he is bound to see that it contains everything necessary to make an individual into a "hard-core" delinquent, and even into a career criminal. There, within the system's processing and record-keeping procedures, is the labeling and stigmatizing machine; its offices, programs, and institutions are the die-makers of hard-core young crooks, naive delinquents, and children exhibiting "delinquent tendencies."

We are not sure the criminal justice system stigmatizes, labels, or infects with criminality many of the children it processes. Surely it "corrects" a lot of them, meaning that they go away and don't come back. Now, if a humanitarian with political power sees juvenile delinquents floating down a river of juvenile justice programs toward a Niagara of criminal careers, he is likely to try his hand at diverting them toward some tributary leading to noncriminality. If he doesn't have the money, time, or energy to divert everyone, he will probably concentrate on the children far upstream—those "predelinquents" displaying only "delinquent tendencies."

Such reasoning is in fact taking hold in many states, resulting in the creation of a variety of types of diversion programs designed to sidetrack youths judged to be other than "hard core" delinquents. Official attention is being given to alternative procedures for juveniles considered "beyond the control" of their parents or guardians, or who are in danger of leading what one state law refers to as "an idle, dissolute, lewd, or immoral life." In many states, diversion efforts are also carried out farther downstream in order to sidetrack some of the children who break the law in ways that, if the child were an adult, would be called criminal. Such sidetracking supposedly

[3] For summary statements of differential association theory, see Donald R. Cressey, "Epidemiology and Individual Conduct: A Case from Criminology," *Pacific Sociological Review* 3 (1960), pp. 47–58; Robert L. Burges and Ronald L. Akers, "A Differential Association-Reinforcement Theory of Criminal Behavior," *Social Problems* 14 (1966), pp. 128–147; and Melvin DeFleur and Richard Quinney, "A Reformulation of Sutherland's Differential Association Theory and a Strategy for Empirical Verification," *Journal of Research in Crime and Delinquency* 3 (1966), pp. 1–22.

avoids labeling or stigma in the form of an "official" record and minimizes association between "predelinquents" and "lawbreakers."

In line with the national trend, the state we studied (hereafter referred to as the Mountain State) has developed an impressive array of diversion programs for juveniles *at the law enforcement level*. Some of these successfully avoid the undesirable labeling and associational processes they were set up to avoid, but we are not sure how many manage this because we did not look at them. Our focus is on diversion occurring *after* initial court contact and *prior* to adjudication. Most diversion at this level takes place immediately after the "initial court contact," with an officer employed by a probation department—but who functions as an intake officer for the juvenile court.

Such initial contact, and the dispositional decisions made immediately following it, occur in a bewildering variety of ways, reflecting the organizational structure and correctional philosophy of the probation department involved, as well as of the ideology, training, and personality of the person making the decision. The disposition of juvenile cases is left almost entirely to the discretion of the individual probation officer serving as intake officer. Probation officers at this level probably account for better than 90 percent of all probation department diversion, regardless of one's definition of diversion.

The problem juvenile may encounter a diversion program at his school, in the local police department, in the probation department unit doing intake work, and in the probation department unit investigating his eligibility for probation. But the further he proceeds into the juvenile justice system, the less the chances that he will be diverted. Thus, a juvenile who "fails to take advantage" of a police diversion program is likely to find himself before a probation intake officer with a narrower range of diversion options. If at this level the juvenile "fails" or in some other way foregoes his chance at avoiding the juvenile justice system, his case will most likely become truly "official." Probably an official petition or request for a court appearance will be filed. However, the petition papers go to a probation investigating officer (not to a juvenile court judge or referee) and this officer has a degree of dispositional discretion. Once a juvenile's case is officially "petitioned," his chances of being diverted are greatly reduced. When, after completion of the investigation, the juvenile appears in court, there is only a very slight chance that he will be "diverted" by the referee or judge. By then he will have had so many contacts with the juvenile justice system that it is doubtful whether the "diversion" action can be called diversion without putting the word in quotation marks.

DEFINITIONAL PROBLEMS

The most perplexing problem we encountered in our explorations was to decide what should or should not be called diversion. The term is bandied about by social scientists, law enforcement officers, judges, correctional personnel, community service workers, and others. One would think that a concept that has become so in vogue had been readily and precisely defined. It has not.

Consider the following definition presented in a California report on diversion programs:

The process whereby problems otherwise dealt with in a context of delinquency and official action will be defined and handled by other means.[4]

Such an apparently clear-cut definition is fraught with difficulties, chiefly because the definition is not clear at all to individuals charged with administering diversion programs. How and when does one decide whether his handling of a problem is outside the realm of "delinquency and official action"? Even if he does decide that his action has this characteristic, how does he know his decision is correct? It seems reasonable to believe that a public official assigned the task of diverting delinquents will find it quite impossible to do so without first identifying the delinquent as delinquent. Further, it seems reasonable to believe that any action he undertakes or performs as a required or "normal" part of his responsibility is going to be official, no matter what he calls it.

Further problems arise when one considers the implications of "other means." Must they always be unofficial, or may they include official acts somehow interpreted as less official than other acts?

A simplistic interpretation of the definition would insist that in order for diversion to occur, individuals known as public officials concerned with delinquency—police, probation officers—must refrain from all direct action except that of referring the juvenile to individuals or agencies capable of handling the problem by "other means." They would have to do this, somehow, unofficially. Such diversion may be identified as "true" diversion, even if the official unofficially calls the juvenile's problem one of delinquency rather than one of, say, "acting out," "resenting authority," or "interfering with the property rights of another."

If "true" diversion occurs, the juvenile is safely out of the official realm of the juvenile justice system and he is immune from incurring the delinquent label or any of its variations—predelinquent, delinquent tendencies, bad guy, hard core, unreachable. Further, when he walks out the door from the person diverting him, he is technically free to tell the diverter to go to hell. We found very little "true" diversion in the communities studied.

To take this further: The juvenile justice system offers the juvenile certain official helping services, including warnings and lectures, informal probation, court adjudication and dispositional services, formal probation, and rehabilitation in a correctional facility. It makes sense to say that diversion programs try to avoid enmeshing the juvenile in such official acts by employing alternatives or "other means." The child is diverted away from the juvenile justice system and to "other means." Ideally, he doesn't get into the system. If he does, he gets sent somewhere else, unofficially. Simply ignoring him or dismissing his case isn't handling him by other means. Doing nothing is not customarily considered a positive act of diversion.

If one is willing to delimit the notion of "official," as we are, he can get on

---

[4] Elaine Duxbury, *Youth Service Bureaus in California* (Sacramento, Calif.: Youth Authority Progress Report No. 3, 1972), p. 5.

with the job of exploring diversion programs. Now the villains are merely courtroom ceremonies, their offspring, and their aftermath, not the whole juvenile justice system. "We" are all right, and "we" must divert from "them." Now "diversion" begins to make sense since any positive action, official or unofficial, that keeps the juvenile from going through that courtroom door may properly be viewed as diversion. Now the child need not be sent to the waiting arms of nonofficial users of "other means." The official diverter can send him to any of the programs maintained by the system at any sequential level short of official court action. The juvenile may consequently find himself diverted from the courtroom and to informal probation, a Diversion Unit for Predelinquents, a Drug Abuse Program, etc.

Most of the juvenile justice system representatives we interviewed were quick to identify various action programs as "diversion" if they kept juveniles out of courtrooms. This consensus is reflected in official language used to describe government programs receiving children whose "delinquent tendencies" are evident in such behavior as playing truant, running away from home, hitchhiking, or raising hell in school. These programs are called "diversion units," and they generally are intended to short-circuit the need for court appearance.

That the "diverted" juvenile remains within the juvenile justice system was normally regarded as irrelevant, if unfortunate, by the persons interviewed. When we pushed the question, however, most individuals acknowledged that assignment or even referral to a program that is part of the juvenile justice system is not "true" diversion but rather an attempt to reduce incursion of stigma, or to keep the juvenile out of the bureaucracy. "Minimization of penetration" has become a popular phrase used for identifying diversion occurring *within* the juvenile justice system *from* court *to* another official or semiofficial program. We think it means that the juvenile doesn't get mucked about as much, or as well, as he would if he penetrated to the maximum.

What all this says to a researcher is that the simple term "diversion" means many different things to many different people. We looked at anything anyone said was a diversion program; but before any full-scale national study is begun—particularly one employing quantitative methodology—the boundaries of the definition must be decided upon.

We would favor the choice of a working definition along the lines of what has been called "true" diversion; we know, however, that if a study is limited to events occurring after initial court contact, little such diversion is likely to be found, at least in Mountain State. The reasons for the paucity of "true" diversion programs will be explored later. Here, we merely note that once "initial court contact" is made, the juvenile and one or more court officials get attached—like flies to flypaper. There is not much "true" diversion to study.

However, if the definition of diversion is expanded to include "minimization of penetration," any researcher will find himself the guest of many justifiably proud administrators anxious to show him their "diversion" programs. We recommend that, in research studies to come, this expanded conception of diversion be adopted.

We make this recommendation knowing full well that the organizational variety of such programs is apt to wreak havoc upon any sophisticated quantitative research model. We also know that adopting the expanded definition as the basis of a large-scale national study will wreak havoc with attempts to test the theories that spawned "diversion" practices in the first place. "Diversion" programs have, among other things, diverted away from the juvenile justice system the damning accusations that the system has inadvertently been harming young children and teen-agers as well as help-ing them.

Study of the effects of "true" diversion would enable policy makers to decide on the basis of fact whether using "other means" to define and process young people's problems is better, or less harmful, than using the official actions of the juvenile justice system.

Study of "minimization of penetration" could conceivably determine whether use of a new piece of official juvenile justice machinery is better, or less harmful, than using the older equipment. In this case, however, policy makers utilizing the research results would find it necessary to use their best judgment as to whether the new machinery is in fact just a piece of the old juvenile justice apparatus with a few nuts and screws removed.

6
ISSUES IN POLICE DIVERSION
OF JUVENILE OFFENDERS*

Malcolm W. Klein

This final paper in Section 1 provides a rather extensive coverage of many of the major issues in diversion. It was written originally for police juvenile bureau commanders. As such, it was specifically designed to be argumentative in part and to stress the limits of our knowledge about diversion issues. The reader might note, in addition, the attempt to deal with definitional issues once again, including the distinctions among diversion, referral, absorption, and normalization.

---

* Manuscript prepared for the Center for the Administration of Justice, University of Southern California, Los Angeles, 1973.

Since the establishment of her State Almshouses and Reformatories, Mas-sachusetts has assumed the guardianship of many thousands of indigent and unfortunate children, large numbers of whom have disappeared in the ever-varying currents of human destiny, no accurate record of their locality, condition or life, having been preserved. Of their hopes and their struggles, their successes and their fate, no history exists. How many of them went forth to honor or to dishonor, to virtue or to vice, cannot now be known. (416)[1]

[1] All quotations at section headings are taken from Wiley B. Sanders (ed.), *Juvenile Offenders for a Thousand Years*, Chapel Hill, N.C., University of North Carolina Press, 1970.

This paper is designed more as a catalogue than as a manual. I am concerned not so much with techniques of diversion as with making explicit some of the problems raised by the philosophies and practices of diversion. My hope is that the paper can serve to spark and drive discussion so that those in a position to affect diversion procedures will do so on rational, well-considered grounds. My experience over the past few years suggests that there is great need in this area for more considered and less doctrinaire approaches.

Before proceeding further, five critical terms require definition so that writer and reader can be in at least temporary accord on meanings. For the purpose of this paper:

1. We shall mean by *diversion* any process employed by components of the criminal justice system (police, prosecution, courts, corrections) to turn suspects and/or offenders away from the formal system or to a "lower" level in the system. This avoidance of greater involvement of the offender in the sequential components of the system can be and is practiced by each of the components, but this paper is concerned only with the diversion of juveniles by police agencies.[2]

2. We shall mean by *insertion* any process employed by components of the criminal justice system or by nonmembers of the system to introduce suspects and/or offenders into the system or into "higher" components of the system. Complaints, arrests, bookings, petition filings, correctional placements, and many other acts exemplify this simplistic notion of insertion. Since at every decision point in the criminal justice process there is a diminishing of the suspect/offender pool, it is obvious that the insertion rates at sequential decision points almost always decline; i.e., diversion constantly reduces the size and changes the quality of the offender population.[3]

3. We shall mean by *referral* any process by which a diverting agent initiates the connection of the diverted suspect or offender to another agent or agency, usually within the offender's community. Thus referral goes beyond the most common police diversion practice of "station adjustment," "warning," or "counsel and release," in which the youngster is released without further significant action. A police officer who *refers* a youngster takes active steps to attach that youngster to someone else for preventive, rehabilitative, or reintegrative purposes.[4]

[2] Useful discussions and reviews of related issues in the areas of court diversion and juvenile detention can be found in two recent publications: Elyce Zenoff Ferster, Thomas F. Courtless, and Edith Nash Snethen, "Separating Official and Unofficial Delinquents: Juvenile Court Intake," and Ferster, Snethen, and Courtless, "Juvenile Detention: Protection, Prevention, or Punishment." Both papers are reprinted in *Diverting Youth from the Correctional System*, Youth Development and Delinquency Prevention Administration, Department of Health, Education and Welfare, Washington, D.C., 1971.

[3] A dramatic illustration of this sequential process has been provided by Philip H. Ennis, "Crime, Victims, and the Police," *Trans-action, 4*, No. 7 (June 1967), pp. 36–44. Using a survey of potential crime victims, Ennis and his colleagues identified 2,077 victimizations. Of these, 1,024 were reported to the police, 787 received a police visit in response, 593 were called a crime by the police, 120 led to arrest, 50 proceeded to court trials, and 26 resulted in convictions. Note the critical role here of the several police diversion procedures (the decisions not to respond or not to define the incidents as a crime).

[4] A very useful distinction is made by Empey between reformation (rehabilitation) and reintegration, the latter term placing greater emphasis on the role of the community and the offender/community relationship in fomenting and preventing further criminal involvement. See LaMar T. Empey, *Alternatives to Incarceration*, Office of Juvenile Delinquency and Youth Development, Department of Health, Education and Welfare, Washington, D.C., 1967.

4. We shall mean by *absorption* the processes by which institutions in the community (family, educational, religious) or agencies (scouts, clinics, Big Brothers, etc.) take on offenders or suspects rather than reporting them or their acts to the police. To the best of my knowledge, the concept of *community absorption* was first explicated by Carter, who defined it as ". . . the attempt of parents, schools, neighborhoods, indeed, the communities, to address the problem of delinquent and deviant youth by minimizing referral to one of the official state or county agencies designated to handle such youth; or, if there has been a referral to one of these agencies, the attempt to remove the offender from the official process by offering a solution, a technique, or a method of dealing with the offender outside the usual agency channels."[5]

5. Finally, we shall mean by *normalization* the treatment of behavioral acts often thought of as deviant or criminal as though they were not deviant or criminal and therefore not calling for sanctions or criminal processing. The reduction of criminal sanctions for marijuana possession is a move toward normalization, as is the treatment of alcoholism as a disease. The move to expunge consenting homosexuality, prostitution, and juvenile status offenses (acts which are not crimes if committed by adults) from the books represent pressures toward normalization. Fist fights among boys, petting among minors, and tearing down goalposts after a football victory are actionable behaviors ordinarily normalized by officials who recognize such behavior as "par for the course" in adolescence. The general spirit of normalization is captured in this statement: "Given the relatively minor, episodic, and perhaps situationally induced character of much delinquency, many who have engaged in minor forms of delinquency once or twice may grow out of this pattern of behavior as they move toward adulthood. For these . . . *a concerned policy of doing nothing* may be more helpful than active intervention, if the long-range goal is to reduce the probability of repetition of the acts."[6]

Obviously, the distinctions among these terms must remain a bit blurred. There is a certain arbitrariness in any set of nominal definitions. Sufficient clarity can be maintained if we remember that insertion is an act calling for further *formal* action; that the progression from diversion to referral to community absorption represents increasing levels of *nonformal* action; and that normalization represents a decision to deny the necessity for *any* action.

Given this foundation, there are two additional caveats to be mentioned before proceeding to the cataloging of issues in diversion. The first is that the current national intellectual trend toward diversion practices and policies is taking place in the absence of definitive proof that insertion is an *unsuccessful* policy. In almost every treatise on the criminal justice procedure, we read about the ineffectiveness of the deterrence and correctional apparatus of enforcement agencies, the judiciary, and especially correctional institutions and practices. Recidivism figures are cited to indicate a discouraging, even frightening, failure of the system to deal with delinquent

---

[5] This definition, evolving from work in two highly absorbing communities in California, is found on page 22 of Robert M. Carter, *Middle Class Delinquency: An Experiment in Community Control,* School of Criminology, University of California at Berkeley, April 1968.

[6] This approach, as a technique, is attributed by the authors to "labeling theorists" such as Lemert, to whom we shall refer often in this paper. The quote is taken from a very useful little paper by Stanton Wheeler, Leonard Cottrell, Jr., and Anne Romasco, "The Labelling Process," in Donald R. Cressey and David A. Ward (eds.), *Delinquency, Crime, and Social Process,* New York, Harper & Row, 1969, pp. 608–613.

and criminal populations. Indeed, the failure may be as advertised, but in all honesty we must admit that we cannot *know* this because we haven't tried genuine experiments *without* invoking punitive and restraining sanctions. To say that some percentage—50, 60, 80—of prison parolees eventually recidivate tells us little about what that percentage would be without imprisonment.

We live in a society—similar to most—in which genuine experimentation with immediate or early release of offenders is deemed unacceptable. Thus we turn to diversion practices for two reasons. First, we can compare their outcomes to those associated with normal insertion rates to determine comparative effectiveness among less serious offenders.[7]

Second, controlled field experiments are more feasible at those stages of the criminal justice process where diversion is currently legitimated. But let us remember as we proceed that the pressure toward diversion is more a function of our frustration with insertion than of any proof of its failure. We must turn to diversion in the spirit of testing its potential, not of accepting its preferability—not yet, at least.

The second caveat to keep in mind is that even as this is written and certainly as it is read, constant change is occurring in the legal foundations of the criminal justice system. Some of these changes can have momentous effects upon police diversion practices. Two examples will suffice.

From Florida comes a report of a new state law that accords to judges the discretion to release offenders convicted of felonies in their county. This is as close as we have ever come in modern times to being in a position to test the use of such discretion and its results on both the felon and the community.[8]

From the California Supreme Court comes a ruling (*T.N.G.* v. *Superior Court*, S.F. No. 22777) that prohibits criminal justice agencies, without express approval of the Juvenile Court, from releasing information to *any* other agencies about juveniles who have never been the subject of wardship proceedings. Thus, presumably, for the roughly 50 percent of juveniles arrested by police but released without the filing of a petition, no referral to other police or community agencies can be made which would identify the youngster as a police contact. The more aggressive diversion practices now employed by some police departments are seemingly endangered by this ruling.[9]

The reader may easily think of other changes, recent or impending, that

[7] For the reader seriously interested in working toward a comprehensive evaluation of the effectiveness of the criminal justice system, see Malcolm W. Klein, Solomon Kobrin, A. W. McEachern, and Herbert Sigurdson, "Systems Rates: An Approach to Comprehensive Criminal Justice Planning," *Crime and Delinquency* (October 1971), in press; and also see Alfred Blumstein and Richard Larson, "Models of a Total Criminal Justice System," *Operations Research, 17*, No. 2 (March–April 1969), pp. 199–232.

[8] Preliminary analysis of this situation involves a description of the characteristics of cases to which this discretionary action has been applied; see Theodore G. Chricos, Phillip D. Jackson, and Gordon P. Waldo, "Inequality in the Imposition of a Criminal Label," Department of Criminology, Florida State University, 1971 (mimeo).

[9] In Los Angeles County as this report is being written, a cross-agency effort is being undertaken to obtain blanket approval from the juvenile court to release information for referral purposes to an extended list of approved absorption agencies.

would affect the subject of this paper. The important point does not lie within any specific change—somehow we always manage to adjust—but rather in maintaining the flexibility of mind, of policy, and of practice that takes maximum advantage of such changes instead of being inhibited by their inevitability.

I. THE APPROPRIATENESS OF DIVERSION AS POLICE WORK

It will not do to let them go unpunished; but it seems useless and endless, to inflict punishments which produce no reformation. . . .

Mayor C. D. Colden of New York City,
December 29, 1819 (330)

On the walls of a sheriff's station in a western U.S. county hang signs saying "Think Referrals." When told of this, reactions of police officials range from good-humored disbelief to enthusiastic approval. Whether diversion of juveniles is proper police work, to say nothing of how much and of what kind, is anything but a closed issue. If we can take departmental figures as an indication of policy and practice, then the lack of agreement on diversion becomes apparent in diversion rates. In 1969, a study of forty-eight police agencies in Los Angeles County revealed diversion rates ranging from a high of 82 percent to a low of 2 percent.[10] In this latter case, it was the policy of the department to insert *all* arrested juveniles into the system. Asked about the 2 percent who seemed to escape insertion, the chief suggested that this might have been a clerical error.

That such variation in practice (and therefore presumably in philosophy) is widespread is shown in studies by Goldman (with insertion rates ranging from 8.6 to 71.2 percent),[11] Bordua (nationwide data showing a range from less than 5 to more than 95 percent diversion),[12] and McEachern and Bauzer (revealing not only departmental but officer-to-officer variation as well).[13] In view of such data, it would be foolhardy to maintain dogmatically, as I have heard many police officials do, that either diversion *or* insertion is "obviously" the appropriate police tactic. There is nothing obviously correct about either position, nor, for that matter, about the more popular in-between position often stated as "well, it depends on the circumstances of each individual case."

This much *is* clear, however; a perusal of the available professional

---

[10] Malcolm W. Klein, "Police Processing of Juvenile Offenders: Toward the Development of Juvenile System Rates," 1970 report prepared for and available from the Los Angeles County Criminal Justice Planning Board.

[11] Nathan Goldman, "The Differential Selection of Juvenile Offenders for Court Appearance," in William J. Chambliss (ed.), *Crime and the Legal Process*, New York, McGraw-Hill Book Company, 1969, pp. 264–290.

[12] David J. Bordua, "Recent Trends: Deviant Behavior and Social Control," *Annals of the American Academy of Political and Social Science, 359* (January 1967), pp. 149–163.

[13] A. W. McEachern and Riva Bauzer, "Factors Related to Disposition in Juvenile Police Contacts," in Malcolm W. Klein (ed.), *Juvenile Gangs in Context: Theory Research and Action*, Englewood Cliffs, N.J., Prentice-Hall, 1967, pp. 148–160.

literature shows a preponderant preference for diverting youngsters at the point of police intake. Eldefonso cites a survey undertaken by the International Association of Chiefs of Police documenting the low level of active diversion practices. The kind of action diversion recommended by Eldefonso is illustrated in this excerpt:

> In preparing a child and his family for referral, the officer should do a constructive job of explaining the functions of the agency. He should describe the special skills of the workers employed in the agency and explain how they are able to help children and parents with specific problems. The officer should make it clear that problems can be solved only through the joint efforts of the agency and the child or his parents, and that the agency cannot undertake to help them without their active interest and participation.
>
> The officer should also provide specific information as to the name and address of the agency, the telephone number, and the person to contact. This information should be written on a card for the child and his parents. Once they have expressed their desire for help, the officer may telephone the agency to explain the case and, in certain instances, to make an appointment for them. A brief written summary of the case, as seen by the officer, may also be of value to the agency.[14]

In much the same vein, Kenney and Pursuit in their perennially popular text on juvenile procedures outline ten steps to be taken in the referral of diverted youngsters.[15] Like Eldefonso and many others, Kenney and Pursuit raise no question about the appropriateness of the diversion process. In his work *Alternatives to Incarceration*,[16] Empey cites the position of the Second United Nations Congress on the Prevention of Crime and Treatment of Offenders (1960), urging both the normalization of juvenile status offenses and the diversion of all such problems as truancy, neglect, and incorrigibility with referrals to schools and other noncriminal justice system agencies. The International Association of Chiefs of Police has also endorsed diversion practices in its Policy Guide No. 30.[17]

Interestingly, it is the juvenile justice system itself, and especially the police, that in some sense may gain the most from successful diversion practices. This point is made nicely in a report prepared for the California Council on Criminal Justice:

> Concerning the responsibility of juvenile justice agencies, there is a growing conviction that any youngster who interacts with the juvenile justice apparatus is thereby stigmatized and, hence, any prevention program that is launched from a juvenile justice base may be self-defeating. Still, it is that same juvenile justice

[14] Edward Eldefonso, *Law Enforcement and the Youthful Offender: Juvenile Procedures*, New York John Wiley & Sons, 1967, p. 102.

[15] John P. Kenney and Dan G. Pursuit, *Police Work with Juveniles and the Administration of Juvenile Justice*, 4th ed., Springfield, Ill., Charles C Thomas, 1970, pp. 223–225.

[16] Empey, *op. cit.*, p. 24.

[17] See Richard W. Kobetz, *The Police Role and Juvenile Delinquency*, Gaithersburg, Md., International Association of Chiefs of Police, 1971.

system that has, perhaps, the greatest motivation to launch preventive efforts, for it stands to reap the ugly product of society's failure to prevent.[18]

Finally, there is an important point—almost a twist of the policeman's logic—made by Carter. Many police officers decry diversion practices—especially diversion without referral—as being antithetical to police goals and of no rehabilitative value. In fact, it is often suggested that to release youngsters without further action is tantamount to *rewarding* them or showing them that they *can* get away with their legal transgressions. Carter, viewing the situation in part from the offender's perspective, suggests a different outcome, one which puts the officers "one up" over the offender.

It appears that the police have a "probation system" which is a specific expression of the policeman's discretionary power by which certain youth who come into contact with law enforcement agencies and are not formally proceeded against are placed "on probation" to the police (to individual officers and the total agency). Violations of police "probation" by arrest for a new offense may result in entry of the offender into the official system for processing juveniles. While "police probation" is generally informal, records of contacts with youth who were handled informally and returned home may be recorded in "unofficial" pocket-size notebooks for further reference. The police "probation system" is quite simple, and the dialogue from officer to youthful offender runs along the lines of "I'm going to let you go this time, but if you get into more trouble, you will be processed as a delinquent." The violation of "police probation," flagrant cases excluded, is seemingly one of the key factors in deciding which youth are returned home without formal action and those which are moved forward into the juvenile justice system.[19]

Lerman, in a variation on this theme, sees the police as often taking the role of "Dutch uncles." He says "as a matter of historical fact, the hallmark of the American system is the intriguing combination of limitless scope of our delinquency statutes and enormous discretion granted in their enforcement and administration. Our statutes appear to reflect the image of the stern Puritan father, but our officials are permitted to behave like Dutch uncles—they are so inclined."[20]

The question remaining, of course, is *how* to play this discretionary role. We can use the past as one guideline, useful at least in that it demonstrates directions which diversion might take. Lerman cites data from the U.S. Children's Bureau that at least a quarter of the cases reaching juvenile courts involve juvenile status offenses—offenses which are not criminal, not punishable if committed by adults. Further, these data reveal that from 40 to 50 percent of the detentions awaiting dispositional hearings do not involve criminal acts and that 25 to 30 percent of the commitments to juvenile correctional institutions do not involve criminal acts.[21] The implications for increasing diversion levels are obvious.

[18] *Juvenile Delinquency: The Core Problem,* Sacramento, California Council on Criminal Justice (Task Force on Juvenile Delinquency), July 1970, draft prepared by Howard Ohmart and staff.
[19] Carter, *op. cit.,* p. 61.
[20] Paul Lerman, "Child Convicts," *Trans-action, 8,* No. 9–10 (July–August 1971), p. 37.
[1] *Ibid.*

Other guidelines come from reviewing the factors which seem to account for diversion rates. As one example, one can cite Goldman's analysis. Describing diversion/insertion decisions as depending upon ". . . the attitudes of the policeman toward the offender, his family, the offense, the juvenile court, his own role as a policeman, and the community attitudes toward delinquency," Goldman specifies thirteen sets of influencing factors which certainly are not part of any legislative intents.

1. *The policeman's attitudes toward the juvenile court.* This may be based on actual experience with the court or on ignorance of court policies. The policeman who feels the court unfair to the police or too lenient with offenders may fail to report cases to the court since, in his opinion, nothing will be gained by such official referral.

2. *The impact of special individual experiences in the court, or with different racial groups, or with parents of offenders, or with specific offenses, on an individual policeman.* This may condition his future reporting of certain· types of offenses or classes of offenders.

3. *Apprehension about criticism by the court.* Cases which the policeman might prefer, for various reasons, not to report for official action may be reported because of fear that the offense might subsequently come to the attention of the court and result in embarrassment to the police officer.

4. *Publicity given to certain offenses either in the neighborhood or elsewhere may cause the police to feel that these are too "hot" to handle unofficially and must be referred to the court.* In the discussion of police interviews it was indicated how this factor might operate to bring into court an offense of even a very insignificant nature.

5. *The necessity for maintaining respect for police authority in the community.* A juvenile who publicly causes damage to the dignity of the police, or who is defiant, refusing the "help" offered by the police, will be considered as needing court supervision, no matter how trivial the offense.

6. *Various practical problems of policing.* The fact that no witness fees are paid policemen in juvenile court was mentioned by a small number as affecting the policy of some police officers with respect to court referral of juveniles. The distance to the court and the detention home and the availability of police personnel for the trip were likewise indicated as occasionally affecting the decision of the policeman.

7. *Pressure by political groups or other special interest groups.* Such pressure may determine the line of action a policeman will follow in a given case. He considers it necessary to accede to such pressures in order to retain his job.

8. *The policeman's attitude toward specific offenses.* The reporting or nonreporting of a juvenile offender may depend on the policeman's own childhood experiences or on attitudes toward specific offenses developed during his police career.

9. *The police officer's impression of the family situation, the degree of family interest in and control of the offender, and the reaction of the parents to the problem of the child's offense.* A child coming from a home where supervision is judged to be lacking, or where the parents—especially the mother—are alcoholic, or one whose parents assume an aggressive or "uncooperative" attitude toward the police officer, is considered in need of supervision by the juvenile court.

10. *The attitude and personality of the boy.* An offender who is well mannered, neat in appearance, and "listens" to the policeman will be considered a good risk for

unofficial adjustment in the community. Defiance of the police will usually result in immediate court referral. Athletes and altar boys will rarely be referred to court for their offenses. The minor offenses of feebleminded or atypical children will usually be overlooked by the police. Maliciousness in a child is considered by the police to indicate need for official court supervision.

11.   *The Negro child offender is considered less tractable and needing more authoritarian supervision than a white child.* He is generally considered inherently more criminal than a white offender. Exceptions to this general attitude were found in the upper-class residential area and also among white policemen in the crowded Negro slum area of Pittsburgh. The statistical data, except for the small mill town, do not corroborate these discriminatory attitudes expressed by the police.

12.   *The degree of criminal sophistication shown in the offense.* The use of burglar tools, criminal jargon, a gun, or strong-arm methods, or signs of planning or premeditation, are generally taken by the police to indicate a need for immediate court referral.

13.   *Juvenile offenders apprehended in a group will generally be treated on an all-or-none basis.* The group must be released or reported as a whole. Some police may attempt to single out individuals in the gang for court referral. Such action, however, exposes the policeman to the censure of the court for failing to report the others involved in the offense.[22]

Goldman's list might be looked upon as a cafeteria of topics from which one could choose implications for changing diversion rates. Such a cafeteria makes it abundantly clear that one cannot retain any mythology about police response to juvenile offenses being a function only of the nature of those offenses.

If it is true that there has been much written on the advisability of diversion, and as we have seen there is much leeway for changing current diversion rates, we might next look at some of the specific pros and cons so that they may be weighed against each other. The task force on delinquency under the President's Crime Commission notes the following as the primary issues:

With respect to the pre-judicial function of the police, it can be argued that discretionary power increases their influence over the behavior of juveniles. Deployed about the city and county, the police have frequent contacts with juveniles and stand a better chance to identify the serious crime risks than do officials more removed; it follows that they may judge more wisely which juveniles to leave alone and which to divert to nonjudicial tracks. This line of reasoning suggests that police discretion should be enlarged in cities where existing policy requires automatic court referral for many crimes and other types of misbehavior.

Opponents of substantial discretionary police powers argue that informal dispositional duties divert police from primary law enforcement tasks. The authoritative mantle of the police, moreover, is said to make them appear to the public as figures of control, hence unlikely agents of help. Internal bureaucratic pressures may produce a predominantly punitive ethic. The subtle character of screening

[22] Goldman's work probably merits reading in full, since it seems to have been one of the most influential studies in this area. See Nathan Goldman, "The Differential Selection of Juvenile Offenders for Court Appearance," reprinted in Chambliss (ed.), *op. cit.,* pp. 264–290.

judgments calls for different personalities and preparation and for administrative checks of a sort than can be monitored more efficiently within the juvenile court.[23]

Other arguments in *favor* of police diversion include the clear fact that lack of diversion would quickly overload the courts, the belief among police generally that one offense still leaves room for reformation, and the opinion of many that insertion into the courts is insertion into an ineffective deterrence and rehabilitation system.[24] The possibility of stigmatizing youngsters through insertion is an additional major argument which will be treated throughout this paper.

Additional arguments *against* diversion include the observation that police departments are not well organized for the referral aspect of the diversion process, the view that diversion does not fit with the "normal" role assigned to enforcement personnel, and the growing absolutist or universalistic principle that all offenders should be treated alike, without attention to individual case differences.

A few additional points need to be considered. For instance, my own experience indicates that police chiefs are not, as a rule, very concerned with nor interested in juvenile matters. More often than not, they delegate most of the responsibility for juvenile matters to others, so that rewards for increasing diversion or community referrals are seldom forthcoming.

Another consideration is that diversion with referral should also involve follow-up procedures and activity to increase referral resources, i.e., aggressive rather than passive diversion. But such activity requires time and effort that presumably could otherwise go into more direct detection, apprehension, and enforcement activities.[25]

Finally, this point: discussions that this writer has had with juvenile officers and commanders have revealed a common tendency to equate diversion with treatment, or at least to confuse the two. Diversion does *not* mean treatment; those police officials who shy away from diversion practices because they object to the treatment role for police make an understandable error of logic. Diversion can be seen as a legitimate exercise in police discretion. Whether or not it results in treatment is a function of the absorption end of the spectrum, to be discussed later.

II. SEPARATISM VERSUS A PLACE IN THE SYSTEM

There has been a marked tendency among the various components of the criminal justice system to draw clear boundaries between the mandates and

[23] *Task Force Report: Juvenile Delinquency and Youth Crime,* Washington, D.C., The President's Commission on Law Enforcement and Administration of Justice, 1967, p. 18.

[24] This latter point, along with the frequent paucity of community resources, were presumably instrumental in developing such police *treatment and prevention* activities as police athletic leagues and the juvenile aid bureaus in cities like New York and Philadelphia. These developments are discussed on pp. 54–70 of Edwin M. Lemert, *Instead of Court: Diversion in Juvenile Justice,* Washington, D.C., National Institute of Mental Health, 1971 (available as PHS Publication No. 2127).

[25] The surprisingly low level of follow-up in one study can be found in Malcolm W. Klein, "Police Processing of Juvenile Offenders," *supra.*

practices of each. More recently, the emphasis has been upon breaking through these boundaries to facilitate a full *system* of criminal justice administration. Among the police, the separatist approach has been strengthened by an increasing interest in police professionalization. The professionalized department has been described by James Q. Wilson: "A 'professional' police department is one governed by values derived from general, impersonal rules which bind all members of the organization and whose relevance is independent of circumstances of time, place or personality."[26]

In comparing data from two cities, Wilson illustrates that the more professional department of the two ended up processing and arresting a far greater proportion of juveniles, although the crime rates were almost identical. Careful scrutiny of Wilson's data[27] suggests that the more professional department normalizes and diverts less, inserting more juveniles into the court system. I would suggest that this results in part from a narrow reading of appropriate police work in the more professional department. A broader perspective, stressing the police as a part of a larger processing mechanism which starts in the community, would lead to greater diversion rates. In particular, it is police/community connections which require strengthening. Many components of the community—the potential absorption agencies and institutions—should be viewed as part and parcel of the juvenile justice system.[28] As an example of separatism, we can report that in thirty-one interviews with juvenile officers in the two largest police agencies in Southern California, fully one-fourth of the officers could name *no* community resources and only two of the thirty-one used direct referral practices. Forty-five percent said they made *no* referrals, direct or indirect.

We can contrast these figures with postadjudication referrals reported by community agencies. In a survey of these agencies in Los Angeles County, 119 returns yielded an annual figure of five referrals from these two police agencies but 6,142 from probation, court, and correctional components of the system.

That the diversion rate can be increased substantially has been demonstrated recently by a special project in Los Angeles. The Sheriff's Department and the County Department of Community Services have launched a pilot project at a Sheriff's station in East Los Angeles. In 1969, this station had a below-average diversion rate of 38.6 percent, and made only an occasional juvenile referral to a church or to the Salvation Army.

During the pilot project, a Sheriff's Lieutenant was placed in the station with the explicit mandate to see what might be done to increase the diversion rate. He investigated potential resources in the community and worked closely with the juvenile officers. Within the first forty days of the project, thirty-five youths were diverted to ten agencies, a remarkable change in

---

[26] James Q. Wilson, "The Police and the Delinquent in Two Cities," in Stanton Wheeler (ed.), *Controlling Delinquents*, New York, John Wiley & Sons, 1968, p. 11. The entire selection by Wilson should be read and pondered; if somewhat overstated, it nevertheless provides a highly valuable perspective on the consequences of increased police professionalization.

[27] *Ibid.*, pp. 15–17.

[28] This viewpoint is expanded in Klein et al., *op. cit.* (footnote 6).

organizational behavior. Only three of these failed to make the agency connection.[29]

We cannot afford to discount the importance of this project by the Sheriff's Department. A report of the State of California reveals that almost two-thirds of all prevention agencies in the state are private.[30] Thus successful diversion with referral *requires* making viable connections between the private and public components of the justice system, specifically between absorption agencies and police agencies.

Of the public agencies, the schools represent the greatest potential as absorbers of diverted youngsters and therefore a prime target for working to break down separatist attitudes. MacIver reports results of a police-school liaison project in Flint, Michigan. After introduction of the liaison, the area encompassed by the project reportedly yielded one-eighth as many offenses among school students as was the case in outside areas.[31]

This is not to say, of course, that increasing the connections between police and community raises no problems. Cicourel, for example, has illustrated very clearly that departmental procedures with juveniles can be and often are affected by local politics and by internal administrative wrangles occasioned by reaction to those politics.[32] The President's Crime Commission adds to this the point that: "From an administrative perspective the enlargement of discretionary power entails dangers of .' . . inconsistent law enforcement and the resultant evils of disrespect for and distrust of legal institutions."[33] But negative experiences and *possible* dangers seem insufficient justification for withdrawal from the community. Such withdrawal usually leads to an increase in numbers of insertions into the system, as has recently happened in California,[34] and the effect of this system overload is desired by none. Here, the Crime Commission makes our point quite convincingly:

> Discretionary judgment also provides a necessary steam valve in the juvenile justice system. Just as the administration of criminal justice is strained by growing criminal populations, so too the increasing volume of juvenile offenders builds up pressure within police departments, juvenile courts, and all of the other institutions with responsibility to control delinquency. Neither police ranks nor the number of judges and auxiliary staff of juvenile courts has expanded at a rate commensurate with the increase in recorded delinquency. Informal determinations as to which cases demand official action are inevitable, and in the process many juveniles are diverted to nonjudicial sources of control and service.[35]

---

[29] These data and their implications are summarized in Malcolm W. Klein, "On the Front End of the Juvenile Justice System," paper delivered at the meetings of the Pacific Sociological Association, 1971, available upon request.

[30] *Juvenile Delinquency: The Core Problem, op. cit.*, p. 44.

[31] Robert M. MacIver, *The Prevention and Control of Delinquency*, New York, Atherton Press, 1966, p. 143.

[32] Aaron V. Cicourel, *The Social Organization of Juvenile Justice*, New York, John Wiley & Sons, 1968.

[33] Task Force Report, *op. cit.*, p. 10.

[34] *Juvenile Delinquency: The Core Problem, supra*, p. 8.

[35] Task Force Report, *op. cit.*, p. 11.

The Commission's report also points out (p. 16) that greater diversion can lead to distinct advantages for the police, the prosecution, and the courts because of the additional time and energy freed up for ". . . greater emphasis on official handling of the more serious and intractable offenders. Improvements in the several stages of the predispositional process would result in more selective and discriminating judgments as to those who should be subjected to formal and authoritative surveillance in the interest of community protection."

All of this points to some restructuring, modifying, or change in emphasis in the police role with juveniles in a number of departments. In particular, it calls for the police to conceive of community components as a part of "their" juvenile justice system, to conceive of the police not as the first or entry component of the system but as the second component, following the absorption components. Lohman's statement suggests much of the same emphasis:

> The juvenile police officer's role as a professional is to be reconstructed so that he functions as a catalytic agent, through whom the resources, services, and institutions of the community can be activated in behalf of the needs of problem children. Hence, the target is no longer the act, nor its perpetrator, but "the condition of the child." The answer is no longer a single type of agency solution but those aspects of the community's total resources which relate to a particular child's needs.
>
> In short, we should increase the capacity of the community to serve the needs of its problem children by increasing the capacity of the police to draw upon the totality of the community's resources.[36]

What we have suggested, then, is this: Greater emphasis on police professionalism has led to more restricted conceptions of the policeman's role. In the case of juvenile work, these restricted conceptions have seen the police separating themselves from those community components feeding youngsters into the police and capable of absorbing them in the diversion process. The result is an increase in the insertion of youngsters further into the juvenile justice system. This progression is particularly interesting because ordinarily the term "professionalism" is associated with a *maximum* amount of individual discretion. Professionals are credited with the knowledge and skills to make discretionary decisions where nonprofessionals are not. In the case of police, the notion of professionalism seems to have been misconstrued, leading to less use of discretion and more ritualistic, legalistic behavior. Wilson draws the conclusion very succinctly:

> If this analysis is substantially correct, it will suggest several things to the policy maker. First, decisions with respect to "professionalizing" big city police forces should not be taken without consideration of their effect on the justice meted out in discretionary cases. It is not possible—as we should have known all along

---

[36] Joseph D. Lohman, statement before the Subcommittee to Investigate Juvenile Delinquency, of the Committee on the Judiciary, U.S. Senate, 86th Cong., 1st Sess., S. res., pt. 2, "Juvenile Delinquency," pp. 116–117, quoted in Irving A. Spergel, *Community Problem Solving: The Delinquency Example*, Chicago, University of Chicago Press, 1969, p. 208.

—simply to make a police force "better"; these questions must first be answered: "better for what?" and "better for whom?" Students of public administration have argued long and correctly that "efficiency" or "management" can rarely be "improved" without some effect on the substantive goals of the organization. It should not be surprising that, in police departments, as elsewhere, means are almost never purely instrumental but have their consequences upon ends.

The second implication directly concerns the problem of juvenile delinquency. The training of a police force apparently alters the manner in which juveniles are handled. A principal effect on the inculcation of professional norms is to make the police less discriminatory but more severe. As a political scientist, I cannot pretend to know whether, from the standpoint of "solving" or "treating" the "delinquency problem," this is good or bad. I find it difficult, however, to believe that the issue is settled.[37]

III. DIVERSION AND COURT DECISIONS

One point omitted in the previous section is the effect of recent court decisions on police diversion. These decisions, particularly in the cases of *Gault* and *Miranda*, have been taken as supporting insertion as opposed to diversion practices. They have also been interpreted as forcing diversion-oriented police to abandon their approach in favor of insertion as a means of getting youngsters into treatment facilities. A similar trend among judges has been noted by Wheeler et al.: the more liberal juvenile court judges more often sent convicted youngsters to institutional facilities, presumably because of the greater treatment potentials in those settings.[38]

Gault, Miranda, and similar appellate decisions have, in effect, brought juvenile handling more in line with that of adults. The stress has been at the same time to reinforce concern with the civil rights of juvenile suspects and to deny the past efficacy of the treatment-oriented procedures of juvenile courts. Discussions with scores of police juvenile officers and commanders have suggested that some essentially ignore any import of these decisions. A larger number have been influenced by them to use their field and dispositional discretion with greater care concerning civil rights issues.

However, the most striking (although I do not claim the most common) reaction has been to "use" the court decisions as a *post hoc* justification for preferred actions—insertion actions. The logic goes something like this: "The courts have told us kids should be treated like adults, so if that's what they want, that's what we'll do; no more treatment or getting off easy. They can go to court with their lawyers like anyone else. Our job is to make a good case for the prosecution."

This logic is *not* inherent in the court decisions; these decisions do not

---

[37] Wilson, *op. cit.*, p. 28.

[38] Stanton Wheeler, Edna Bonacich, M. Richard Cramer, and Irving K. Zola, "Agents of Delinquency Control: A Comparative Analysis" in Wheeler, *op. cit.*, pp. 31–60. Some readers may be surprised by the suggestion of a substantial police interest in treatment for juvenile offenders. However, our Los Angeles interviews revealed that, of those officers desiring more resources than were available in their community, the overwhelming majority sought individual or family counseling services, emphasizing the psychogenic bias of proper treatment for the divertable young and minor offender.

pertain to police dispositions, but to adjudication procedures. But they have been used by police separatists to help rid themselves of difficult and sometimes displeasing diversion practices. Accepting the logic has been a very human reaction, but not a particularly professional one in the usual sense of the term. Among other things, it has overlooked the fact that a large proportion of juvenile arrests are for *juvenile status* offenses, those which have no adult counterparts.[39] Finally, it does suggest a danger inherent in the continued professionalization of the police (as described above) and the continuing tendency of the courts to provide for juveniles more and more of the trappings of adult criminal justice procedures: namely, that we may be turning away from some of the most potent preventive resources in our repertoire—those of the community itself. The detached policeman responding to the legalistic dicta of the court will be hard-pressed to serve as liaison between the juvenile offender and his community. Failure in this direction may well increase our recidivism rates to the point where "diversion" will remain only a footnote in the history of juvenile justice.

IV. NORMALIZATION

In this connection it may be noted that the proportion of children's cases compared with those of adults in the Old Bailey sessions is extremely small. In many sessions of the court no children appeared. In one collection of proceedings covering seventeen Old Bailey court sessions during the period February 1683/4–January 1702, only four boys, and no girls, were reported among the six hundred and fifty-four criminals on whom sentences were passed.

From accounts available in the British Museum (21)

Normalization, the attitude of responding to possible deviance as nondeviant, seems to raise at least three types of questions. First, is it appropriate for police to adopt a normalization attitude? Second, how do we determine a "proper" amount of normalization; i.e., what is normal and who decides this? Third, what are the major arguments for and against having the police increase their current normalization stance?

For purposes of our discussion, these three questions all pertain to what Lemert most recently has referred to as the "Overreach of Law."[40] Available data[41] make it obvious that the police *are* normalizers. They know that the law "overreaches" and dismisses from serious action the vast majority of juvenile behavior which *could* fall within the bounds of actionable behavior as defined by current statutes. The fact that there is great variation between officers and between departments in the amount of normalizing undertaken is witness to the conception that delinquency is a function not only of the

---

[39] For one prominent judge's recommendations in this area, see Ted Rubin, *Law as an Agent of Delinquency Prevention*, Washington, D.C., Youth Development and Delinquency Prevention Administration, Department of Health, Education and Welfare, 1971.

[40] Lemert, *op. cit.*: note that in this context Lemert cites the words of Roscoe Pound written in 1916!

[41] In addition to studies cited earlier, see those (e.g., Terry, Bodine) cited in Don C. Gibbons, *Delinquent Behavior*, Englewood Cliffs, N.J., Prentice-Hall, 1970, especially pp. 36–39.

actor but of the reactor. "Normal" is a definition, not an act. Lerman puts this into its proper context:

> While many judgments about the seriousness of these offenses may appear to be based on the merits of the individual case, delinquency definitions, in practice, employ shifting cultural standards to distinguish between childhood troubles, play fads and neighborhood differences. Today, officials in many communities appear more tolerant of profanity and smoking than those of the 1920s, but there is continuing concern regarding female sexuality, male braggadocio and disrespect of adult authority. In brief, whether or not a youth is defined as delinquent may depend on the era, community and ethnic status of the official as well as the moral guidelines of individual law enforcers.[42]

Different communities and different subcultures define as "normal" a surprisingly wide range of behaviors, with the definitions often in conflict. Each group, of course, considers its definitions to be most proper, whether the group be ghetto residents, suburban housewives, police officers, or used car salesmen. In his novel *The New Centurions*, Los Angeles Police Sergeant Joseph Wambaugh illustrates the changes in the definition of "normal" that can take place from year to year in a policeman's career.[43] Police must be very careful, therefore, to avoid assuming that *their* sense of normal and acceptable behavior is the only sense upon which to act or not act. They must be alert to other definitions, including even those of their suspects. This means, once again, *greater* use of discretionary powers.

The dangers of failing to normalize many minor infractions have been discussed earlier, and revolve principally around the issues of stigmatizing youngsters and overcrowding the juvenile justice system. Here, we might look more directly at the dangers of too *much* normalizing. For example, noting the large number of youngsters on whom no significant action is taken, Terry suggests that normalization may have the effect of denying access to treatment for many youngsters until it is too late for treatment to curb delinquent careers.[44] David Matza adds an interesting variation with the suggestion that going from the ignoring (normalization) of a first offense to an increasingly more serious response to succeeding offenses may, as a pattern, habituate the offender to minor increments of "pain" that lose their deterrent value.[45] This escalation of sanctions may be analogous to the slow increasing of heat under water holding small animals. The frog, if subjected to slow increases in the heat of a pot of water, never reacts or hops out but dies as the boiling point is reached. Unlike the case of the frogs, the juvenile offender lives in a peer culture in which his experience is viewed by his comrades. If the slow escalation of sanctions serves as a poor deterrent for him, his comrades will learn the same lesson without the need themselves of jumping in the same pot.

[42] Lerman, *op. cit.*, p. 37.

[43] Joseph Wambaugh, *The New Centurions*, Boston, Little, Brown, 1970.

[44] Robert M. Terry, "The Screening of Juvenile Offenders," *The Journal of Criminal Law, Criminology, and Police Science, 58* (1967), pp. 173–181.

[45] David Matza, *Delinquency and Drift*, New York, John Wiley & Sons, 1964, pp. 186–188.

Other arguments include those suggested by Wheeler et al.[46] concerning breaking the cycle of antisocial behavior which tends to develop if its rewards go unchallenged; setting limits for behavior by reacting to that which goes too far; seeking early identification of delinquency-prone youngsters in order to provide early treatment; and the ever-present belief in sanctions and deterrents. None of these arguments is new, but they do make it clear that the issues around normalization are clearly two-sided and not to be discounted easily.[47]

V. DIVERSION CRITERIA[48]

Generally the Chamberlain sought to smooth out difficulties rather than pronounce judgements. He preferred to arbitrate or admonish and only when these measures proved unavailing did he commit to prison, and even then was ever ready to release the penitent. In the middle of last century the Clerk of the Chamber stated that he, personally, was able to "arrange" five cases out of six without troubling the Chamberlain. (6)

Enough solid empirical work has now been carried out that hunches or prejudices about the use of police discretion can be replaced by factual descriptions. While there is obviously much research yet to be done, it seems fair to dispute the earlier statement from the Crime Commission report: "At this point we know little more than that a multitude of factors governs discretionary judgment. One source of the difficulty in evaluating pre-judicial disposition is the vast range of pertinent considerations."[49] The discretionary pattern emerges from a listing of major findings reported over the past decade.

1.   Goldman[50] cites the primary factors determining diversion/insertion as the subject's age, sex, race, and the seriousness of the alleged offense. Offense seriousness emerged as the single most important factor.

2.   McEachern and Bauzer[51] found significant factors to be age, sex, family status, number of prior offenses, probation status, and offense seriousness, but not race. Additionally, they found significant differences from year to year, department to department, and officer to officer. Again, the primary factor was offense seriousness, with departmental and interofficer differences having secondary importance. Other differences were minor.

3.   Sellin and Wolfgang cited a whole series of factors, summarized by Gibbons[52]

---

[46] Wheeler, Cottrell, and Romasco, op. cit.

[47] Lemert's general handling of the issue, while comprehensive and logically sound, seems to suffer from a somewhat one-sided presentation of the merits of normalization; Lemert, op. cit.

[48] A brief but concise review of processes relevant to this issue can be found in Frank W. Miller, Robert O. Dawson, George E. Dix, and Raymond L. Parnas, The Juvenile Justice Process, Mineola, N.Y., The Foundation Press, Inc., 1971.

[49] Task Force Report, op. cit., p. 17.

[50] Goldman, op. cit.

[51] McEachern and Bauzer, op. cit.

[52] Gibbons, op. cit., p. 40.

into eight categories: (a) prior record, (b) type of offense and subject's role in the offense, (c) attitude of victim or complainant, (d) family status, (e) community resources, (f) demeanor and attitude of the subject, (g) availability of detention facilities, and (h) estimates of likely court action.

4. Piliavin and Briar[53] reported initial differences in diversion according to the subject's race but indicated that this could be accounted for by differences in demeanor. Minority youths exhibited more antagonistic attitudes toward the police officers and those with such attitudes—whites or blacks—were more likely to be processed officially.

5. Black and Reiss[54] found particular significance in dispositions of juveniles in the factors of offense seriousness, levels of situational evidence, attitudes (and presence or absence) of a complainant, and attitudes of the subject. This latter finding, in contrast to that of Piliavin and Briar, indicated that an antagonistic attitude *or* an obsequious or overcompliant attitude would tend to bring about an arrest.

6. Speaking specifically to the question of attitudes, Adams[55] lists these as critical questions: "What does he (the subject) say about his involvement? What are his standards of value? Is he remorseful and do his actions indicate that he is not likely to repeat the offense? Is he defiant and likely to form a delinquent behavior pattern? What is his attitude toward authority—the police and the court? Are there any feelings of resentment, animosity, or remorse with regards to his victim?" As a police lieutenant and an instructor in police science courses, Adams' questions exhibit the same fine discrimination in his subject as in the skier's discrimination between a half-dozen types of snow or the gourmet's discrimination among wine bouquets. In the absence of hard data, it increases our confidence that such differences make a difference.

7. Lemert,[56] in noting the great differences in diversion rates among departments, suggests (but fails to document) that "such differences are largely a function of differences in police organization and in the degree to which they are integrated in a cultural sense with the community areas whose populations they police. They are also associated with cultural differentiation of the police themselves and with variable policies of departments as to what kinds of deviance will or will not be adjusted internally."

Similarly, Wilson[57] has attempted to illustrate diversion differences as a function of departmental policies and styles of operation. Unfortunately, my own research[58] and that of Sundeen[59] largely fail to substantiate these claims despite a determined effort in the attempt. There does seem to be

[53] Irving Piliavin and Scott Briar, "Police Encounters with Juveniles," *American Journal of Sociology, 70,* No. 2 (September 1964), pp. 206–214.

[54] Donald J. Black and Albert J. Reiss, Jr., "Police Control of Juveniles," *American Sociological Review, 35,* No. 1 (February 1970), pp. 63–77.

[55] Thomas F. Adams, *Law Enforcement: An Introduction to the Police Role in the Community,* Englewood Cliffs, N.J., Prentice-Hall, 1968, p. 180.

[56] Lemert, *op. cit.,* p. 62.

[57] Wilson, *op. cit.*

[58] Klein, *op. cit.*

[59] Richard A. Sundeen, Jr., *A Study of Factors Related to Police Diversion of Juveniles: Departmental Policies and Structures, Community Attachment and Professionalization of Police,* unpublished Ph.D. dissertation, University of Southern California, 1971.

some cause-and-effect residue in the arena of departmental policy, but it is diffuse and weak, suggesting a multitude of causative agents rather than a few. This leaves room for concerted policy efforts to have substantial impact. Summarizing the data from studies similar to the above, Gibbons draws the conclusion quite properly:

> These four studies add up to a picture of the police operating in a "legalistic" fashion, rather than in terms of prejudices and biases of one kind or another. Apparently the police are more impressed by the nature and seriousness of offenses than by any other factors. The major route to the juvenile court appears to be heavily traveled by those juveniles who are most persistently involved in lawbreaking. The four investigations certainly do not provide much factual underpinning for claims than the principal determinants of police action center about such things as economic status or racial characteristics.[60]

It also seems clear that social-psychological factors constitute a second major but secondary category of determinants of police dispositions. Here one could include the attitudes of the victim, offender, complainant and officer, the demeanor of the offender, and the behavioral interactions among the participants in any incident.

The third, but perhaps least clear, category would relate to the police departments themselves—their policies, their styles, their relations to the community, their knowledge and use of resources, etc. In England, Walker[61] suggests that next to age, "The extent to which cautioning is used as a method of dealing with young offenders depends on the policy and instructions of each Chief Constable, and varies remarkably from one police area to another."

Of course, to suggest that dispositional factors can be reduced to these gross categories (the behavioral-legalistic, the social-psychological, and the departmental-community) does not tell us which *ought* to be given priority. Nor does past practice answer the question of what *ought* to be given priority. This is where *professionalism* should come into play, exercising the available discretion among the available alternative actions by consideration of the appropriateness of the three categories of determining factors. Only further research which relates these to recidivism can adequately deal with the "ought" in this issue. Meanwhile, the role of the *trained* juvenile officer must clearly include the exercise of his discretion in such a way as to counterbalance the inexperienced or untrained exercise of discretion employed by field officers in the initial contacts with juveniles.

One cautionary note will conclude this section. Interviews and observations undertaken by my colleagues and me have revealed a rather consistent tendency among police officers to adopt a narrow perspective on suitable diversion and referral cases. The preferred case is a girl, a younger subject, a first offender, a transgressor of a nonserious statute, or some combination of these. The preference should, of course, be in these directions for both empirical and value reasons. But the perspective is too often *too* narrow. If

[60] Gibbons, *op. cit.*, p. 39.
[61] Nigel Walker, *Crime and Punishment in Britain*, Edinburgh, Edinburgh University Press, 1968 (rev.), p. 179.

forced, I would conjecture that a broader definition of divertable youngsters could double the numbers released without undue damage to youth or society. At least, the case for or against a broader perspective could be tested.

VI. COMMUNITY TOLERANCE

The methods now employed to dispose of delinquent children failing either to reform them or relieve society from their presence, it is certainly expedient a new experiment should be tried.

London, 1829 (137)

Diverting youngsters back to the community is obviously highly dependent upon the community's willingness to report them to the police in the first place and to absorb them following diversion. The greater the community's tolerance, the less diversion needs to take place. In the city of Flint, Michigan, Gold reports that parental knowledge of offenses admitted to researchers was about eight times the knowledge of the police; parents were aware of about one-fourth of their children's offenses, while the police were aware of only 3 percent.[62] This is a measure of one form of tolerance.

Other forms have been described in Carter's report on the communities of Lafayette and Pleasant Hill.[63] Even though absorption levels were already high in those two communities, the project reported by Carter seemed to demonstrate the feasibility of increasing tolerance levels as an approach to delinquency control.

One of the most significant issues in diversion is the question of how actively the police themselves should seek to increase community tolerance. Most would agree that the police (although not necessarily juvenile officers) should attempt to increase the community's receptiveness to referrals. Fewer would agree to more direct intervention. For example, during the Ladino Hills project[64] in Los Angeles, a sixteen-year-old gang member who had for several years involved himself in minor transgressions was picked up once again for trespassing on school grounds. The investigating juvenile officer learned that the boy had recently been fired (not for the first time) by the manager of a car wash. The officer called the manager, convinced him to rehire the youngster, and then released the boy with the expected admonishments. A similar instance is recorded by Spergel:

Officer J. recalled one case in which a youngster had two charges of robbery against him. The employer refused to hire the youngster. The officer checked the record and found that the youngster had been booked twice in a southern town on suspicion of robbery. But on neither occasion had anything been proved against

---

[62] Martin Gold, *Delinquent Behavior in an American City*, Belmont, Calif., Brooks/Cole Publishing Co., 1970.

[63] Carter, *op. cit.*

[64] Malcolm W. Klein, *Street Gangs and Street Workers*, Englewood Cliffs, N.J., Prentice-Hall, 1971. This work includes very extensive discussions and examples of attempts at referrals and absorption.

him. The police officer was able to get the employer to change his mind and hire the youngster.[65]

When I have described such instances to juvenile officers, the reactions have been quite mixed. The reaction most pertinent to the issue discussed here is that such interventions by the police seem in danger of *forcing* community tolerance. Whether such forcing is actually possible is problematic, but at least the illustrations highlight the issue of just how aggressive the police ought to be in getting the community to adopt a more tolerant stance toward juvenile misconduct.

Additional tests of the police role are emerging in the wake of newer efforts at coordinating community absorption potentials. Youth Service Bureaus, as centralized referral junctions in the juvenile justice network, can only succeed with the active participation of the police. Their very formation forces the issue of the police role in community and agency tolerance.

A similar forcing of the issue would result from Judge Rubin's suggestion[66] of establishing Neighborhood Juvenile Conference Committees to deal with juvenile status ("predelinquent") offenses. These Committees would tie juvenile dispositions directly to local cultures and situations. This approach, along with Rubin's plea for minority-based absorption agencies, would truly test the universalistic, separatist trend adopted by so many police agencies.

VII. ABSORPTION MECHANISMS

The Marine Society apprentices vagrant and delinquent boys to sea service on warships.

1759 (52)

Edwin Lemert has provided a rather thorough review of the absorption potentials represented by the schools, the welfare system, and community organization programs. In each case, he concludes that much is lacking both in operation and in potential.[67] We will be concerned here with four subproblems, each of which seems to call for discussion of how police activity might yield some improvement. We can label these problems (1) acceptability, (2) suitability, (3) availability, and (4) accountability of absorption agencies.

Acceptability. If a police officer is to divert youngsters, he can best do so on the assumption that there is someone or something "out there" that will help prevent that youngster's reappearance. If he is to go beyond this and make an agency referral, he must know of agencies which *he*, the officer, finds acceptable. Ohmart's analysis of California State survey data[68] reveals

[65] Irving A. Spergel, *Community Problem Solving: The Delinquency Example*, Chicago, University of Chicago Press, 1969, p. 210.

[66] Rubin, *op. cit.*, pp. 9–12.

[67] Lemert, *op. cit.*

[68] *Juvenile Delinquency: The Core Problem, supra*, pp. 44, 45.

the content of reported community programs to be, in order: drug treatment and prevention, service center or teen center, and "hotline." Significantly, many police are highly skeptical of just these types of operations. Thus there is a gap between what is available and what is acceptable to the referring officers.

Our interviews with Los Angeles officers[69] revealed a very consistent negative view of free clinics and similar informal drug facilities. Similarly, these officers shied away from involvement (other than intelligence!) with self-help agencies, ghetto agencies run by residents, agencies with a taste of militancy or radicalism, and so on. Agencies emphasizing lay or volunteer rather than professional staffs were viewed with considerable skepticism. Finally, whether by design or by inadvertent omission, these officers, representing seventy-seven police jurisdictions, failed to mention employment resources even once.

In other words, just as the juvenile police have a constricted view of the types of youngsters who might be diverted and referred, so they have a very constricted view of the kinds of absorption agencies that could be acceptable as resources for them. Add to this that the sorts of agencies officers prefer, such as family service agencies and counseling clinics, are few and far between. Then finally add the strong suspicion that the usual "character-building" program—YMCA, Girl and Boy Scouts, Boys' Club, church groups, recreation clubs—have consistently failed to manifest any significant impact on delinquents. The conclusion which emerges is inescapable; the police must broaden their view of acceptable referral resources.

Suitability.   About this problem there is little dispute; a large number of potential community resources have limited suitability because of their policies and practices. Many will not accept certain kinds of cases. Others have hours, such as 9:00 A.M. to 6:00 P.M., which are unrelated to patterns of juvenile misconduct or police referral needs. Still others have restrictive fee schedules, long waiting lists, insufficient personnel and budgets, and so on. The only issue here is whether the police should tolerate and gripe about this situation, or take on a more aggressive role to facilitate the necessary changes.

Availability.   The Crime Commission has noted the problem of resource availability. Among recommendations to deal with the problem, the Commission included the development of auxiliary staff for the police to increase both available resources and knowledge of them, better training for juvenile officers, and the development of Youth Service Bureaus.[70] These recommendations do indeed seem responsive to juvenile officers' needs. Officers to whom community resources seem unavailable often report that they will insert youngsters into the system—send them on to court —specifically to ensure that some form of treatment will be available to them.[71]

[69] Klein, 1971, *op. cit.*

[70] *Task Force Report*, p. 19.

[71] In a search of the relevant literature, I find very few writers who acknowledge this rationale from juvenile officers, although it is one I hear quite often. An exception is Wayne R. LaFave in "Noninvocation of the Criminal Law by Police," in Cressey and Ward, *op. cit.*, pp. 185–208.

But there are two additional problems here. The first is that the availability of a resource is no guarantee of the amount or quality of help a youngster will receive. For many referred youngsters, this "help" turns out to be superficial and unresponsive to *delinquency* prevention. A study by Teele and Levine in Boston[72] illustrates an unfortunately common situation in which referrals (in this case, from the court) simply do not lead often enough to useful consistent intervention. Teele and Levine conclude sadly that delinquency referrals ". . . do not seem to be a central concern of child-guidance clinics" (p. 125).

The second problem is that of the low level of police knowledge of available resources. Our Los Angeles interviews revealed a surprising lack of information concerning local resources (despite the presence of up-to-date catalogues of such resources often to be found on the shelves in the Juvenile Bureau). Many of our interviewers were taken from a county coordinating agency, and their knowledge of resources for juvenile police work vastly exceeded that of the juvenile officers. Juvenile officers do not seek out, nor are they urged to seek out, suitable referral agencies. By the same token, few private agencies offer themselves as willing absorbers of delinquency. Thus the modal number of private agencies known to our smaller-city juvenile officer respondents in 1970 and 1971 was two! In six cities, the officers in 1970 could not name a single private agency to which youngsters might be referred.

Nor is this "accidental" or temporary ignorance of resources. Exactly half of the 1971 respondents reported *belonging to no* community organizations in the communities they served. Half did not live in the community served. Yet the median number of police associations for the same officers was two and one-half.

Accountability. The final problem in this section is so obvious that it can be stated by noting the contrast between two statements. The first, by MacIver, states the need, while the second, from the Crime Commission, states the reality. In referrals, accountability gets translated as follow-through. Without it, when no one is accountable for the process and outcome of the referral, one can legitimately question the value of any referral.

The selection of an agency should be discriminating and the communication with it fully informative, and there should always be a follow-up to find out what, if anything, has been done. The trained juvenile unit officer is best qualified to undertake this task.[73]

The absence of follow-through also has ramifications with respect to juveniles referred for nonjudicial handling. Typically the official agency gets in touch with a clinic, social agency, youth board, or other similar organization. But the time to explain a referral to the juvenile or a member of his family is short, and in the impersonal, populous districts of an urban area the referral case is often lost. The juvenile may not arrive at the selected place of service, or he may be refused service without the referring official's finding out in time to take other steps. Even

---

[72] James E. Teele and Sol Levine, "The Acceptance of Emotionally Disturbed Children by Psychiatric Agencies," in Wheeler, *Controlling Delinquents, supra,* pp. 103–126.

[73] MacIver, *op. cit.,* p. 145.

where there is a well-articulated referral system with smoothly operating procedures, sheer number of cases may substantially lessen its effectiveness. If the time
lapse between apprehension and referral is a matter of days, the subsequent
follow-up by a selected community resource may occur at a point when the
juvenile and his family have surmounted their initial fear, anger, or regret and
concern, and the contact is regarded as an unwelcome reminder of past unpleas-
antness instead of an avenue of help in time of crisis.[74]

VIII. OLD STIGMATA FOR NEW

The next issue is quickly stated and easily illustrated, but not currently
resolvable because the requisite data have not been collected. It is the
question of whether diversion away from the justice system and referral into
another system—welfare, mental hygiene, scholastic—may not simply avoid
one stigmatizing context by adopting another. In terms of the youngster's
perspective of himself and others' views of him, do such labels as "delinquent," "in trouble," or "bad" do more harm or good than labels like "sick,"
"unstable," "weak," or "stupid"?

Because of this problem, Wheeler et al.[75] suggest that ". . . it is not clear
that doing something is better than doing nothing, or that doing one thing is
better than doing another." Lemert[76] has summarized the case of the "special schools" which have been developed by school systems in major cities
such as New York, Chicago, and Los Angeles, schools designed to deal
specifically with recalcitrant and delinquent youths. He concludes very
tentatively that they may indeed decrease antisocial behavior related specifically to schools (truancy, vandalism, resistance to teachers), but that the
physical, financial, and social costs involved may not be justified by the
approach or the results. Even more to the point, Lemert points to the
problem in these and in regular schools of the labeling process of selecting
out youngsters as (negatively) "special":

> If the teacher feels strongly enough she refers the child to the vice principal,
> sometimes with the objective of ridding herself and the class of the child's pres-
> ence. This, of course, is an old practice. What is comparatively new is the bureau-
> cratization of these procedures, with the possibility of additional referrals to
> school counselors, psychologists, social workers, and sometimes psychiatrists.
> Cicourel and Kitsuse have concluded from research on this question that the
> addition of such professionalized service workers to the schools enhances the
> probability that problems will be perceived in students and that the farther they go
> along the referral chain, the more serious the problem is likely to be seen. This
> accrues from the specialized perspectives held by professional clinical people and
> their reliance on accumulated records about the child from within and outside of
> the school. Professionals, like teachers, are less likely than lay persons to normalize
> unusual behavior or deviance, but for different reasons and with differing con-
> ceptions of the kinds of problems they "find" in the students.[77]

---

[74] *Task Force Report,* p. 18.
[75] Wheeler, Cottrell, and Romasco, *op. cit.,* p. 611.
[76] Lemert, *op. cit.,* pp. 27–30.
[77] *Ibid.,* p. 24.

Thus, to divert an offender from the juvenile court and its institutions may lead to his insertion into another equally enveloping system of labels and stigmata. If there is any validity to the notion of the self-fulfilling prophesy in delinquency labeling—that being handled as a delinquent will increase one's penchant for delinquent behaviors—why should not the same be true in the case of labeling as in need of guidance, therapy, or other intervention forms? This is an issue which cries out for critical research studies, but pending these there is certainly great room for careful consideration of the various alternatives within the police officer's discretionary repertoire.

IX. STIGMATIZATION: THE BURDEN OF PROOF

At this moment, if a child is brought before myself, for example, as a magistrate, I have no power not to award punishment; I am bound to do it; I should be glad to have the power of sending the child to school, instead of sending it to prison. The sending a child to prison is a very serious matter. When you come to reflect upon it; you destroy his or her character probably for life; if you once give them the taint of a prison mark, it is very difficult for them to shake it off; and it is a very great hardship upon a poor infant that he should have this stigma upon him.

1853 (236)

We have referred throughout this work to the concept of stigmatization or labeling. Lemert[78] defines it as ". . . a process which assigns marks or moral inferiority to deviants; more simply it is a form of degradation which transforms identities and status for the worse." Labeling Theory, as it has come to be known recently, may rank as the most widely accepted unsupported proposition in the criminology of the 1960s and 1970s. The problem lies not in the fact of labeling but in its consequences. It is widely accepted that these consequences are largely negative, that in the delinquency field in particular they comprise a further commitment to delinquency and a step down the path to an adult criminal career.

The data available to support or refute these consequences are largely nonexistent, although speculation abounds. Labeling theory seems to constitute one of those instances in criminology—much like Lombroso's work in an earlier era—in which the proposition fits the needs and biases of the field so well that careful empirical investigation has been largely bypassed. The following constitute the bulk of the directly pertinent research.

1. Schwartz and Skolnick[79] have reported on two studies. In the first, job applicants were falsely identified as having court records in a demonstration that such labeling does evoke negative reactions from potential employers. In the second, physicians sued for malpractice were not particularly harmed by the experience. In some instances, in fact, their fellow physicians directed more patients to them as a means of counteracting the effects of the suit. These studies, although often cited and reprinted in the literature, throw little if any light on our problem.

[78] *Ibid.,* p. 11.

[79] Richard D. Schwartz and Jerome H. Skolnick, "Two Studies of Legal Stigma," *Social Problems, 10,* No. 2 (Fall 1962), pp. 133–140.

2.   Gold, in his Flint, Michigan, study, matched twenty youngsters who had been apprehended with twenty who had not but who were equated on their prior offenses (self-reported), age, and sex. Those who had been apprehended were found to commit further offenses in a ratio of eleven to four for their nonapprehended peers. On the basis of these data and others, Gold suggests four processes which might be involved in moving the original apprehension/stigmatization to further apprehensions:

> I suggest that a youngster in this situation is exposed to at least four kinds of pressures to commit more delinquent acts. First, to stop engaging in delinquent behavior constitutes his agreement that he has indeed behaved badly and, by implication, that he is bad; he withholds his agreement and rejects this judgment by offending again. Second, if he stops in the face of threat, he's "chicken": and if he dares again, he's a cool player of the odds (which usually pays off—rarely are youngsters caught twice). Third, his motives for committing the delinquent act in the first place, whatever they may have been, are seldom changed by the processes invoked by his apprehension; they remain to provoke him. Finally, his apprehension may have just made him mad; so he strikes out.[80]

3.   Contrary data are reported by McEachern and his associates.[81] They reported on offenders inserted upward by the police who were or were not made court wards and, in each case, were or were not given probation treatment. They found that labeling (i.e., being made a court ward) was associated with *lower* subsequent recidivism while receiving treatment (i.e., being seen by a probation officer) was associated with higher subsequent recidivism. The condition most directly related to lower recidivism was wardship without treatment, suggesting that labeling may in fact deter further delinquency if it is not reinforced by further actions.

The same study deals with the possible effects of juvenile detentions. The authors conclude: ". . . while these figures cannot be read to suggest that detention is a cause of improvement (on probation), they can be read as evidence that detention, in these counties, does not constitute a serious obstacle to improvement." Further on, the authors suggest that ". . . those who contend that detention is an effective deterrent for delinquents have no support from our findings. Nor can we conclude that detention itself is harmful . . . the effects of detention, so far as simple recidivism is concerned, are still obscure" (p. 27).

4.   Finally, the issue of detention in a juvenile hall has been investigated by O'Connor.[82] He found that alienation among boys with higher delinquency orientations was increased by detention, but otherwise the findings were quite mixed. O'Connor's conclusions emphasize *differential* responses to detention, suggesting a complex interaction between institutional factors and personality variables of the detainees.

Since these studies constitute the bulk of our specific empirical knowledge of the effects on offenders of stigmatization, and since these studies yield

---

[80] Gold, *op. cit.*, especially p. 108.

[81] A. W. McEachern, Edward M. Taylor, J. Robert Newman, and Ann E. Ashford, "The Juvenile Probation System: Simulation for Research and Decision-Making," *American Behavioral Scientist, 11,* No. 3 (January–February 1968), pp. 1–45. See pp. 17–18 and in particular Tables 24, 25, and 26 and the associated text.

[82] Gerald G. O'Connor, "The Impact of Initial Detention upon Male Delinquents," *Social Problems, 18,* No. 2 (Fall 1970), pp. 194–199.

such equivocal conclusions, our own conclusion is obvious. We don't know about the good or the harm of stigmatization, even though we use our *suppositions* about such good or harm to justify policies and practices in the disposition of juvenile cases. Surely it is time to admit our collective ignorance, to hold in abeyance the lessons we *believe* we have learned from personal experience, and to support or undertake some definitive research.

X. DIVERSION: THE BURDEN OF PROOF

By an arrangement which has been in operation at the Birmingham sessions from the beginning of the year 1841, young convicts who are not hardened in crime are, after trial, delivered to the care of their employers or parents, as the case may be.

These persons enter into an engagement to superintend the conduct of their young wards, and to furnish them with the opportunity of earning or assisting to earn their livelihood.

Both guardians and wards are visited from time to time by one of the superior officers of police, for the purpose of ascertaining the conduct of the parties.

The results of this treatment up to October last were as follows: 113 convicts had been so delivered up. Of these, 44 were reformed, 40 relapsed, and of 29 the conduct was doubtful.

The majority of these 29 there was reason to fear had relapsed. But all having left their masters, and many having left the town, nothing certain was known of them.

This experiment, which at all events is inexpensive, may be called satisfactory, when it is considered that from the moment the young offender leaves the bar, the Court has no legal control either over him or his guardian, who of course acts gratuitously.

London, 1847 (179–180)

When I first started my studies of juvenile gangs, the door through which I entered the study of the criminal justice system, I made a point of visiting the juvenile court to learn how it functioned. I was immediately struck by the sermons, admonishments, lectures, and advisements given youths in court by their judges and referees. But when I asked these gentlemen what they hoped to accomplish with their statements, each *without exception* said that they probably accomplished nothing, yet it seemed like the appropriate thing to do. Here, then, we have a case of acting according to the expectations for a role with full knowledge that it is a matter of form, not of substance. Is it only judges who find themselves in this position? Consider the following statement:

Compared with the possible need of a youth for psychotherapy, how effective can be the solemn little sermon with which a judge or referee in court embellishes his announcement of the disposition of a case? As contrasted with the need to reverse subcultural attitudes fostering delinquency, of what value can be the two or three hours of interviewing and possible advice-giving by a police officer?

Despite the apparent superficiality of such devices, court workers and police officers will continue to do what they see as within their power. Even if found to be ineffectual, they still would be strongly inclined to continue to do these things.

Yet, in the overall design of delinquency prevention programs by communities it may be significant to know what real contribution to delinquency reduction can be achieved by the relatively "superficial" means. If it is a major contribution then these should be viewed more seriously as components in a community's efforts. If they are useless, there is no point in encouraging well-meaning individuals to fritter away badly needed time and energy going through meaningless motions.[83]

The authors of this quote undertook a study of "effective" and "ineffective" juvenile officers. They found that, contrary to the question they themselves raised, officer behavior does indeed make a difference. Some officers consistently act as deterrents more than others. Additionally, evidence suggested that both uniformly high diverters and uniformly low diverters failed to deter recidivism as effectively as officers who, through careful use of their discretion, ended up with medium diversion rates.

Strangely, however, a search of the literature turns up no further empirical rather than speculative work on the effectiveness of diversion procedures. My own research group is now in the middle of such research even as this is written, but even this may be more suggestive than definitive. Still, we have hopes; our research involves the active collaboration of almost fifty different police departments, many of whom, historically, have been wary of social research. We can at last agree with Wheeler et al. that the opportunity for turning issue into policy is upon us:

There was a time when many police organizations were assumed to be distrustful of social scientists and others concerned with delinquency, and they, in turn, assumed that police attitudes toward juveniles were harsh and punitive. The climate of relations is apparently changing in at least some communities. Knowledgeable authorities report that many police organizations are eager to cooperate in efforts to solve the complicated problems of delinquency control. The time seems ripe, therefore, for a renewed examination of the relation between the delinquent, police, and community agencies.[84]

XI. YOUTH SERVICE(S) BUREAUS

Of all the proposals to implement police diversion policies, the Crime Commission's suggestion for Youth Services Bureaus has captured the greatest attention (and funding). The spirit of the Commission's recommendation has been captured by Seymour: ". . . the proclamation of a policy to deal with as many juveniles as possible informally obviously requires the development of a flexible, pre-judicial system able to cope with a wide range of problem children. Hence the importance of youth services bureaus in the re-shaping of juvenile justice."[85]

---

[83] William W. Wattenberg and Noel Bufe, "The Effectiveness of Police Youth Bureau Officers," *Journal of Criminal Law, Criminology, and Police Science, 54,* No. 4 (December 1963), pp. 470–475.

[84] Stanton Wheeler, Leonard S. Cottrell, Jr., and Anne Romasco, "Juvenile Delinquency: Its Prevention and Control," Appendix T of the *Task Force Report, op. cit.,* see p. 420.

[85] John A. Seymour, *Youth Services Bureau,* prepared for a seminar sponsored by the Center for the Study of Welfare Policy and the Center for Studies in Criminal Justice, University of Chicago, January 24 and 25, 1971 (mimeo), p. 4. Seymour's background paper is a marvelously comprehensive review of the issues in the development of the Bureau concept. For those wishing a full and excellently reasoned review, the Seymour paper is by far the best available.

The general nature of the Commission's recommendation can be gleaned from Lemert's brief summary and from the Commission's chart placing the Youth Services Bureau in the organizational structure of the juvenile justice system (Figure 1).[86]

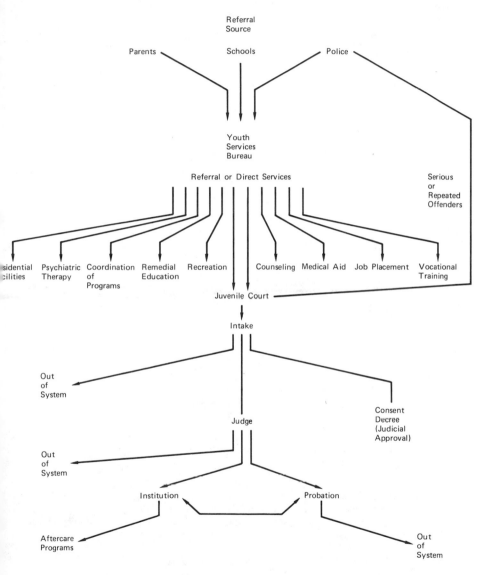

Figure 1   Proposed Juvenile Justice System

[86] Figure 1 is taken from page 89 of *The Challenge of Crime in a Free Society*, the summary report of the President's Commission on Law Enforcement and Administration of Justice, Washington, D.C., 1967. Relevant descriptions can be found in the *Task Force Report, op. cit.*, pp. 20–21.

Describing the bureaus, Lemert noted:

These were proposed to be local agencies, or part of neighborhood centers, supplying a broad range of services for "trouble-making" youth, referred to them by police, probation departments, schools, and community agencies, or brought in by parents. Suggested services were to be obtained gratis from community agencies, or by contract if necessary. The recommendations for the Bureaus stressed the need to "work out plans" for the rehabilitation of troubled minors through their voluntary participation and that of parents. No detailed means were given for solving the problems of agency coordination but the Bureau staff would be required to observe the principle of accountability in its interagency contacts.[87]

A recent paper by Polk[88] cites a report by the National Council on Crime and Delinquency authored by Sherwood Norman[89] which listed three major functions which Youth Services Bureaus might serve: linking youths to services available to them, developing new resources in the community, and modifying current aspects of the juvenile justice, welfare, educational, and other pertinent systems. The NCCD study also identified five rather distinct models which YSBs had adopted, identified as (1) a cooperating agencies model, (2) a community organization model, (3) a citizen action model, (4) a street outreach model, and (5) a systems modification model.[90] The fact that Polk was then able to suggest five somewhat different functions for the bureaus[91] is clear evidence of the ambiguity attendant upon the whole concept.

Even in the few years of active consideration of these bureaus, a number of dangers and failures have been noted by various observers. Among these are the following:

1. A report from the National Institute of Mental Health notes: ". . . the major problem seems to be that coordination of resources—where there are no resources—does not help things very much."[92]

2. Another NIMH report notes two dangers which could apply to any formal referral mechanism. The first is that there might evolve some undue pressure on

[87] Lemert, *op. cit.*, p. 93. Useful statements on purposes and organizations of YSBs can also be found in John M. Martin, *Toward a Political Definition of Juvenile Delinquency*, Washington, D.C., Youth Development and Delinquency Prevention Administration, Department of Health, Education, and Welfare, 1970, pp. 11–15, and G. David Schiering, "A Proposal for the More Effective Treatment of the 'Unruly' Child in Ohio: The Youth Services Bureau" in *Diverting Youth from the Correctional System*, Youth Development and Delinquency Prevention Administration, Department of Health, Education and Welfare, 1971.

[88] Kenneth Polk, "Delinquency Prevention and the Youth Service Bureau," paper delivered at the University of Massachusetts, Juvenile Delinquency Prevention Seminar, October 1970 (mimeo).

[89] Sherwood Norman, *The Youth Service Bureau*, New York, National Council on Crime and Delinquency, 1971.

[90] Polk, *op. cit.*, pp. 18–21.

[91] *Ibid.*, pp. 23–33.

[92] *The Juvenile Court: A Status Report*, Washington, D.C., National Institute of Mental Health (Public Health Service Publication No. 2132), 1971.

the diverted youth and family to accept unwanted treatment. The second is the inadvertent reduction of normalization through what we might here refer to as the "overreach of treatment." As noted in the NIMH report, ". . . for much of what is now labeled as deviance, the problem is *not* how to treat it but how to absorb or tolerate it. . . ."[93]

3. Rubin[94] has described the development of one type of Youth Services Bureau in Denver, but indicates that police referrals to the Bureau had not as yet been built into its program or structure. Obviously, such a situation defeats the very design of a diversion program.

4. Lemert has suggested several problems, best stated in his own terms:

  a. "The ubiquitous risk is that such Bureaus will become just one more community agency following popular or fashionable trends in youth work, muddying the waters a little more and falling into obscurity."

  b. "California's labors so far suggest that something less than stark innovation characterizes planning for its Bureaus."

  c. "It is hard to escape the impression of old ideas being recycled when looking at the organizational pattern of some of the Bureaus."[95]

5. Polk[96] cites the NCCD study of five bureaus and adds his own review of an additional four to point out the diversity of approaches which makes reasonable evaluations problematic at best. A brief résumé of the NCCD findings is not encouraging:

  Public and private agencies generally resist working with acting-out children and youth. Existing Youth Service Bureaus tended to limit functions to short-term counseling and referral without follow-up, or failed to develop missing community resources. Only one bureau focused on modifying systems that contributed to delinquent behavior.[97]

6. A two-year progress report on the California Bureaus[98] makes no mention of impact, only of information gathering and things the evaluator "will do." Seymour's paper, however, specifically mentions low police referrals as a major problem in the first year of the California Bureaus.[99]

7. Finally, a report by Seymour of a national conference of scholars and practitioners makes it painfully clear that the development of Youth Services Bureaus

---

[93] *Diversion from the Criminal Justice System*, Washington, D.C., National Institute of Mental Health (Public Health Service Publication No. 2129), 1971.

[94] Rubin, *op. cit.*, pp. 14–15.

[95] Lemert, *op. cit.*, p. 93.

[96] Polk, *op. cit.*

[97] *Research Relating to Children*, Bulletin 27, ERIC Clearinghouse on Early Childhood Education, item 27-KK-1, Washington, D.C., June 1970–February 1971.

[98] *The Status of Current Research in the California Youth Authority: Annual Report, 1971*, Sacramento, Department of the Youth Authority, 1971, pp. 24–26. An earlier report goes into far greater detail on implementation of the California Bureaus. Unfortunately, no impact data were yet available and the data on diversion varied so widely and were of such unequal value that no clear conclusions could fairly be said to have emerged. See Elaine B. Duxbury, *Youth Service Bureaus in California: A Progress Report*, Sacramento, Department of the Youth Authority, January 1971.

[99] Seymour, *op. cit.*

has been haphazard, inadequately coordinated, unresponsive to critical issues, and so on.[100]

Given all of the above, it is no wonder that solid data on the process and outcome of Bureau operations are not as yet available. While this final section of the report might hopefully have reported the results of a major diversion mechanism, we find instead that it can only caution against high expectations. If the value of these bureaus is to be fairly assessed, it may be that the police themselves must see to it that their programs are adequately implemented *with* ample police referrals. Failing this, we have made no gains in the face of increasing pressures to provide some kind of answer to the increasing tide of delinquency.

---

[100] John A. Seymour, "Report on Youth Services Bureau Seminar," Chicago, Center for the Study of Welfare Policy and Center for Studies in Criminal Justice, University of Chicago, 1971 (mimeo).

SECTION 2

LABELING

Marshmallow Not "Deadly Weapon"

The felony arrest records of two youths arrested on Halloween for assault with a deadly weapon—miniature marshmallows—was ordered expunged Wednesday by Superior Judge Campbell M. Lucas.

R._____ C._____, a student at College of the Canyons, and R._____ K._____, a hospital employee, claimed in their civil suit that the criminal record had damaged their reputation and careers.

They were arrested by Los Angeles Police Officer _____, Van Nuys Division, and released the next day without being charged. Any records, they said, should state "detention only, not an arrest."

The young men said in the suit that the marshmallows, fired from slingshots, weighed less than half a gram each and were not dangerous.

"None of the victims of the assault were hit with anything harder than a soft marshmallow, shot at a distance with slow speed over the heads of the victims, which popped down and hit the victims on the head," the suit stated. "That would be misdemeanor battery at most."

Assault with a deadly weapon is a felony offense.

—article appearing in the Los Angeles *Times*, January 3, 1974

The case of the "deadly marshmallows" is one of those few instances of labeling and stigmatization that provides us with some comic relief. For the most part, however, the process and outcome of being labeled and stigmatized are taken as a serious matter. Much of the stimulus for diversion programs comes from the desire to avoid an unhealthy stigmatization of young offenders, and the question of stigmatization is directly tied to the social psychological approach known as "labeling theory." The papers in this section have been carefully chosen to describe labeling theory, to illustrate its importance to diversion, and to call attention to certain dangers inherent in labeling as a theory and in diversion as a practice.

In order to highlight some of the issues raised in these papers, we can draw particular attention here to several critical points. For example, it is very important to distinguish between the terms "label" and "stigma." A label applied to an individual may have a positive, negative, or neutral value to that person, and the same or different value to those who learn of this label. For example, the word "cop" may be evaluated quite positively or negatively, depending upon who applies it and to whom.

For the most part, labeling theory is concerned with negatively valued labels, and thus we often substitute the word "stigma" to indicate this negative connotation. Lemert, in a recent article,[1] reviews the terminology of the labeling theorists and reports such phrases as modern organization of taboo, dramatization of evil, scapegoating, ceremonial degradation, stigmatization, victimization, exclusion, and conferral of an invidious property.

Such phrases make our point rather dramatically. Offenders are not diverted from the justice system in order to avoid labels generally—some labels can be positive, or at least they can be neutral.[2] Rather, offenders are diverted in order to avoid *stigmatizing* labels. To make the point clear, let's take the example of many youngsters arrested for possession or use of marijuana. Such arrests may indeed provide labels, but given the widespread skepticism over the moral legitimacy of current marijuana laws, the arrested juveniles and others around them often fail to accept any stigmatization as a result of such an arrest. Thus arrests on such charges cannot be expected to produce deterrence, nor perhaps should they lead to diversion practices justified by reference to avoidance of stigmatization. The shoe simply doesn't fit.

Now let's move one step further. While some juvenile offenders become adept at shrugging off the stigma attached to the processes of arrest and police labeling, we can fairly assume that many—probably most—do not. Diversion programs are based on this assumption, that it is indeed stigmatizing to be labeled as car thief, pot head, truant, incorrigible, delinquent, or "heading for serious trouble." Thus the most common form of diversion is to turn away from insertion into the juvenile justice system (with a court petition) via a referral of the offender to a counselor or counseling agency. This avoids stigmatization and provides help for the youngster. Or does it?

Several papers in this volume will look at this question from different vantage points, but to set the stage, let's raise the issue here. What is the reaction of a youngster (and his family, his friends, his teachers) when he finds himself enrolled as a "client" in something called the Community Mental Health Center, or Psychological Services, Inc., or The Youth Counseling Service, or The Drug Abuse Clinic, or The Family Therapy Group? May he not feel that he has left the frying pan for the fire, given up being "bad" for being "maladjusted"?

If he has avoided the *system* of juvenile justice, with all that this implies, there is a danger that the offender may merely enter an "alternative encapsulation," becoming enmeshed in a mental health or social services *system*. One can quite easily be surrounded by helpers, so surrounded in fact, that he cannot escape the implication—the stigma—that he is in need of help, is "sick," or is trapped in an unhealthy family environment. What we do not

---

[1] Edwin M. Lemert, "Beyond Mead: The Societal Reaction to Deviance," *Social Problems, 21*, No. 4 (April 1974), p. 459.

[2] In fact, the process of "neutralizing" potentially negative labels may be a major cause for the failure of a presumed stigmatizing label to produce deterrence of future deviance.

know, but may legitimately fear, is the degree to which this alternative encapsulation will itself lead to more deviance in a fashion quite similar to that being "avoided" by the diversion program.

There is a corollary issue involving labeling and stigmatization, namely the assumption that these are "bad." However, we can mention two very major uses of labels that suggest quite a different interpretation. First and most obvious is the use of the label as a deterrent. We use labels on many occasions specifically because the implied stigma can deter; we say: "You don't want people to think you're a thief, do you?" or "Do you want people to call you fatty (or lazy, or stupid, or mean)?" Anyone who has participated in or observed juvenile arrests and station counseling knows how often the label-as-deterrent device is used. Its use assumes its effectiveness.

A second positive use of negative labels takes place in certain rehabilitative programs which insist that the client must first acknowledge his deviance before he can be helped. Examples include Alcoholics Anonymous, Synanon and many other drug projects, and Weight Watchers. In each case, the client's acceptance of a deviant identity—the admission of the applicability of the stigma—is seen as the first step in the adjustment process. Although it may seem a weak analogy, we suggest that this process is not much different from a common police belief and practice in work with juveniles. The admission of guilt is often taken as a sign that an offender may be deterred from further delinquent involvement. Denial of the offense, by the same token, suggests the likelihood of a commitment to delinquency. Thus in many police diversion programs, the denier is not eligible for referral to a counseling resource while the youngster who admits his guilt is eligible. In other words, a program designed to avoid labeling insists as a first step that the label be accepted.

Another related point seems too obvious to require discussion, yet we often lose sight of it. It is the fact that the labeling process is far from automatic. Specifically, the fact that a police officer arrests a juvenile and that a proper disposition is arrived at is merely the starting point. For these acts by potential labelers to eventuate in further delinquency—especially in the development of a delinquent career—certain intervening processes must presumably take place.

First, there are processes which reinforce the application of the label; for example, its application by other justice officials, school or agency personnel, parents, and peers. Further, one should look for consistency among the label applications; inconsistencies will be more likely to weaken the process.

Second, there are levels of the label's acceptance or rejection by the juvenile. Minimally, one would include here the content of the label, its "favorableness" or degree of stigma, and the juvenile's self-expectations for his behavior (an accepted label for which the expected behaviors are unknown or unclear will be less likely to lead to recidivism).

Finally, even if label application is high and label acceptance is high, impact of these processes on subsequent behavior (new offenses, new arrests) may depend on the process being repeated several times. That is, the entire process may be cumulative over several arrest episodes but unlikely to be very evident after only one.

This caution, that the impact of labeling may not be evident until after several arrest episodes, leads to the last point to be raised here. This has to do with the severity of cases to which a diversion program is applied. This volume deals primarily with police diversion, and within that arena there is still some confusion as to when a "release" is a "diversion."

It is generally conceded that police release rates of arrested juveniles are around 50 percent nationally; i.e., police departments typically decide against taking further action in about half of their cases. There is wide variation around this figure, however, so that it cannot be said to be a fixed standard. If diversion means merely the turning away or releasing of arrested youngsters prior to a possible insertion further into the justice system, then we have a national diversion rate of about 50 percent. If we include those "informally" diverted—especially by patrol officers—prior to arrest, then the rate is much higher. Here we combine street diversion with normal station diversion.

However, many writers currently take diversion to refer only to *increased* releases above and beyond the normal rates. If a department with an annual release rate of 50 percent wishes to launch a diversion program to increase its rate, then it can only do so by releasing some of the offenders on whom it has been the practice to file a petition request, i.e., refer on to *court*. Referring normally released youngsters to community treatment agencies is *not*, from this point of view, the same as diverting them. Referral does not equal diversion, but is a step which can take place independently of it. Again, from this point of view, diversion *as an increase in release rates* is what is called for by labeling theory, and this can only happen by sending fewer offenders on for court processing.

Police departments with new involvements in the referral of released youngsters to community agencies tend to see themselves as participating in the new diversion emphasis of the 1970s. They are not, because they are not diverting at a higher rate than before. They are referring more of their minor offenders for treatment. This may or may not be good, but it clearly is not based on labeling theory; it is not designed to decrease stigmatization; it is, as a number of cynics have pointed out, a good way to get one's hands on federal or state funds.

7

THE LABELING PERSPECTIVE, THE DELINQUENT, AND THE POLICE: A REVIEW OF THE LITERATURE*

John L. Hagan

Although this first paper in Section 2 has a strong Canadian flavor, it applies equally well to the United States. It presents a rapid yet competent review of specifically relevant research. Among others, the reader might note three points. (1) Most juvenile contacts are initiated not by the police, but by citizens in the community. Thus police response is often not to an offense, but to a complaint about an offense. (2) Given this fact, one could maintain that the labeling of a community's juveniles as delinquent is brought about by the community itself, not by the police, who may often serve merely as the instrument of the community's labeling process. (3) The reader's reaction to this paper may be colored by the type of police force with which he is familiar. Hagan's depiction of the police in this paper reminds one of an older style of police, less professional than many current departments, featured by greater reliance on the use of force and a heightened sense of alienation from the community.

* From "The Labeling Perspective, the Delinquent, and the Police: A Review of the Literature," *The Canadian Journal of Criminology and Corrections*, 14, 2 (1972): pp. 150–165. Reprinted by permission of the author and the publisher. Special thanks from the author are due to Professor James Hackler for many useful suggestions which are incorporated in this article.

A currently popular approach to the problem of juvenile delinquency is expressed in a trend of thought variously designated as the "societal reactions school," the "underdog philosophy," and, most commonly, as the "labeling perspective." Basic to this thoughtway is the assumption that it is not the actor alone, but also the "reactors," or the agents of social control, who are partially responsible for the problems of delinquency. The application of this perspective to the study of police response to juvenile behavior is reviewed, with special attention given to empirical studies of police-juvenile encounters, juvenile demeanor and police response, police bias and minority group relations, and the organization of police work. It is concluded that the labeling perspective may have the potential of directing us into the type of research that will inform us as to what the police "really do" and what the consequences of these actions "really are."

THE SOCIAL TRANSFORMATION OF JUVENILE BEHAVIOR

If "beauty lies in the eyes of the beholder," then it may also be that "delinquency exists in the reactions of social control agencies." If all this is true, then perhaps it is agencies of social control, instead of delinquents, that sociologists should be studying.

The thought pattern expressed in the above paragraph represents in synoptic form a unique and currently popular approach to the study of delinquent behavior. This approach is variously known as the "societal reactions school," the "underdog philosophy," or, most commonly, the "labeling perspective." The premise most basic to the labeling approach is the assumption that it is *the process of getting caught and labeled* which separates official delinquents from their nondelinquent contemporaries.[1] Thus it is thought to be a process of "social transformation," instigated by agencies of social control, that molds juvenile delinquency from more ordinary juvenile behavior.[2] Bending our thoughts to this frame of reference, we stop asking of the delinquent, "Why did *you* do it?" and begin asking of ourselves, "Why do *we* react so strongly to what he has done?"

Various authors have, in different ways, called our attention to the labeling viewpoint.[3] Although there are both advantages and disadvantages in using the labeling perspective to study delinquent behavior,[4] this essay will focus on the potential benefits of such an approach. Hackler has argued that there are at least three useful consequences of the labeling approach:

1. It leads us to focus our attention on the process by which society defines and reacts to deviance.

2. It allows us to correct a false impression that deviance is a characteristic of the individual alone.

3. It forces us to recognize and critically observe the agents involved in the process of defining deviance.[5]

The goal of this essay will be to incorporate these insights of the labeling perspective into an attempt to determine just *how much* and in *what directions* the police, as an agency of social control, influence the character of delinquency.

ENCOUNTERS: POLICEMAN VS. DELINQUENT

The link that ties the labeling perspective into an analysis of social control agencies is the decision-making process utilized in the handling of juveniles.

[1] Gwynn Nettler, "An Outline of Contemporary Theories of Criminogenesis," mimeographed (Edmonton, Alberta: University of Alberta, Department of Sociology, 1969).

[2] Cf. H. Taylor Buckner, "Transformations of Reality in the Legal Process," *Social Research* 37 (Spring 1970): 88–101.

[3] See, for example, Howard Becker, *Outsiders* (New York: Free Press, 1963); *idem, The Other Side* (New York: Free Press, 1964); Emile Durkheim, *The Rules of the Sociological Method* (New York: Free Press, 1938); Edwin Lemert, *Social Pathology* (New York: McGraw-Hill, 1951); *idem, Human Deviance, Social Problems and Social Control* (Englewood Cliffs, N.J.: Prentice-Hall, 1967); George Herbert Mead, "The Psychology of Punitive Justice," *American Journal of Sociology* 23, no. 5 (1918): 577–602; Frank Tannenbaum, *Crime and Community* (New York: Columbia University Press, 1938).

[4] See, for example, David J. Bordua, "Recent Trends: Deviant Behavior and Social Control," *The Annals of the American Academy* 369 (January 1969): 149–163; Jack P. Gibbs, "Conceptions of Deviant Behavior: The Old and the New," *Pacific Sociological Review* 9 (Spring 1966): 9–14; John L. Hagan, "Psychologies Exposed: The Unexamined Premises of a Popular Explanatory Model in Deviance" (Master's thesis, University of Alberta, 1970); Edwin M. Schur, "Reactions to Deviance," *American Journal of Sociology* 75 (November 1969): 309–322.

[5] James C. Hackler, "An 'Underdog' Approach to Correctional Research," *Canadian Journal of Corrections* 9, no. 1 (1967): 5–6.

As the delinquent encounters each of the various social control agencies, decisions are made that influence the direction that his "career" will take. Representatives of three agencies attain particular significance in the delinquent career: the police, court officials, and probation officers. The remainder of this essay will provide an in-depth look at perhaps the most important of these agencies—the police. Our focus will be on the role played by police encounters with juveniles in the social transformation of juvenile behavior.

FIELD OBSERVATIONS OF POLICE-JUVENILE ENCOUNTERS

The most impressive research carried out in the area of police-community relations to date has been organized by Donald Black and Albert Reiss, Jr.[6] Perhaps the most useful aspect of this research effort is the fact that it has concentrated on actual field observations of police-delinquent encounters. Black and Reiss utilized in this field study thirty-six trained observers (persons with law, law enforcement, and social science backgrounds) to record observations of police work in three of North America's largest cities. The observers rode in patrol cars and walked with policemen on their beats on all shifts each day of the week, for seven consecutive weeks, in each of the three cities. Precincts were selectively chosen so as to maximize observation of lower socioeconomic, high crime rate, racially homogeneous, residential neighborhoods. In the end, 5,713 incidents were observed and recorded in "incident booklets" filled out by the observers. The results of this research effort provide information on a number of important problems.

A basic point made by the Black–Reiss study comes in the form of empirical support for an insight provided earlier by Reiss and Bordua.[7] This insight consists of the simple observation that the police operate in a "reactive" rather than a "proactive" manner. In other words, the police do not aggressively *seek out* delinquent behavior, but rather they more often *respond* to complaints *about* juvenile behavior. Black and Reiss introduce this point by referring to two basic types of mobilization of the police: *"citizen-initiated"* or *"reactive mobilization,"* and *"police-initiated"* or *"proactive mobilization,"* depending upon who makes the original decision that police action is appropriate.[8] The folk image of police work is that of constant and penetrating efforts at surveillance that continuously result in the discovery of deviance—even when it doesn't exist. The common feeling is that where there is no deviance to be found in a particular jurisdiction, the police will simply go out and cultivate their own "new business"—persecuting and prosecuting as they go. There may be a serious error in this pattern of thought, however, for there never seems to be an end to the citizenry's capacity to find new supplies of deviance to complain about. In this context, there is little opportunity for proactive police work.

[6] Donald J. Black and Albert J. Reiss, Jr., "Police Control of Juveniles," *American Sociological Review* 35 (February 1970): 63–77.

[7] Albert J. Reiss, Jr. and David J. Bordua, "Organization and Environment: A Perspective on the Municipal Police," in *The Police: Six Sociological Essays*, ed. David J. Bordua (New York: Wiley, 1967).

[8] Black and Reiss, *loc. cit.*

The mobilization of police control of juveniles is then overwhelmingly a reactive rather than a proactive process. Hence it would seem that the moral standards of the citizenry have more to do with the definition of the juvenile deviance than do the standards of policemen on patrol.[9]

The implication of this finding is that the "people" are the source of police intervention in the lives of others.

Thus it is the people of the community, and not the policeman, who initiate the social transformation of juvenile behavior. However, once past this stage of initiation, the policeman rapidly becomes the central figure in an unfolding social drama. It is his role to introduce order into a degenerating and/or socially disorganized situation. The policeman must do this with the aid of specialized techniques he has developed for restructuring potentially chaotic situations. The basic tactic for accomplishing this goal is to "take charge." If successfully carried out, this tactic "freezes" the situation and avoids escalation of the offense involved. The basic instrument utilized in the "take charge" strategy is the verbal and body behavioral expression of authority. The importance of the successful implementation of the "take charge" strategy is revealed in the fact that when it fails, force is imposed to compensate for the unsuccessful expression of authority.[10] So it is in the process of attempting to gain control of a disorganized social situation that brutality and arrest are likely to take place.

To summarize, the policeman reacts to *citizen* complaints about juvenile behaviors. Once on the scene, however, it is the policeman who dominates a developing social drama. His role is to reintroduce structure into the situation by means of a display of authority. It is within this context that police encounters with juveniles must be understood.

JUVENILE DEMEANOR AND POLICE RESPONSE

We have noted that authority is an extremely important quality in police control of disorganized situations. It is not surprising, then, that police are tremendously sensitive to the "respect" they receive in their encounters with juveniles. Any slippage in the amount of respect an officer is receiving may be perceived as a warning signal that he is losing his authoritative edge. As our previous discussion has indicated, the likely outcome of such a situation is that the officer will turn to the use of force.

William Westley,[11] currently at McGill University, was alarmed at the apparent willingness of the police to resort to the use of violence, and designed a study to discover just how great the tendency to rationalize the use of brutality is. In pursuing his study, Westley found that the police regard the public as their enemy, feeling that their occupation puts them in conflict with the community. The policeman apparently sees himself as a social pariah who is assigned an essential, yet intensely disliked, role in our

---

[9] *Ibid.*, pp. 66–67.
[10] Cf. Reiss and Bordua, *op. cit.*, pp. 47–48.
[11] William A. Westley, "Violence and the Police," *American Journal of Sociology* 59 (1955): 34–47.

society. This is not the full extent of the patrolman's problems; there are additional pressures with which to contend. Among these are the competition between patrolmen and detectives for important arrests, the publicity value associated with *solved* cases, and public pressures for the strict control of certain offenses (e.g., sexual assaults and drug abuse). All of these factors combine in pressuring officers to enlarge upon the area where violence is legally prescribed. The results, Westley contends, are police secrecy, an attempt to coerce respect from the public, and a belief that almost any means arc legitimate in completing an important arrest.

Evidence for Westley's conclusions come in the form of questionnaire responses secured from members of a large urban police force in the United States. After analyzing his data, Westley reports that "37% of the men believed that it was legitimate to use violence to coerce respect."[12] The implication is, of course, that violence may all too readily be utilized in an effort to coerce an attitude of respect from the public.

A hypothesis that easily suggests itself from the Westley study is that it would be juveniles who do *not* show respect for the police who are most likely to be caught and labeled as delinquents. Just this sort of hypothesis formed the basis for a study by Piliavin and Briar.[13] Observations reported in this study appear to have been gathered both on the street and the precinct level of police operations. Stressed throughout the study is the belief that it is the "demeanor" of juveniles that forms the basic set of cues used by the police to make their decisions as to final disposition of juvenile cases. Thus the authors report that both the decision on the street (i.e., whether to take the juvenile in) and the decision made in the station (i.e., whether to release or detain) are contingent upon the more salient personality and background characteristics of the juvenile in question. Among the influential factors involved here are: group affiliation, age, race, grooming, and dress. Further, it is found that other than previous prison record, it is the juvenile's general "demeanor" that is the most crucial determinant of his fate. In other words, Piliavin and Briar indicate that it is specifically the degree of "contriteness" projected by the juvenile that determines whether he is to be labeled a delinquent or nondelinquent. Piliavin and Briar conclude that the ". . . official delinquent is the product of a social judgment made by the police."

The provocative implication of the Piliavin and Briar study is an implicit explanation for higher arrest rates among juveniles from minority groups. In short, Piliavin and Briar suggest that racial imbalance in the severity of police decisions is attributable to the fact that Negroes in large American cities demonstrate a demeanor that provokes punitiveness on the part of the police. Ferdinand and Luchterhand[14] provide some inferential support for this hypothesis in a study of 324 teenagers from six inner-city neighborhoods of an eastern American city. In particular, Ferdinand and Luch-

---

[12] *Ibid.,* p. 39.

[13] Irving Piliavin and Scott Briar, "Police Encounters with Juveniles," *American Journal of Sociology* 70 (September 1964): 206–214.

[14] Theodore N. Ferdinand and Elmer G. Luchterhand, "Inner-City Youth, the Police, the Juvenile Court, and Justice," *Social Problems* 17 (Spring 1970): 510–527.

terhand find that offenders against property who express verbal rejection of authority in questionnaire responses receive more severe dispositions in their encounters with police. The inference is that a failure to demonstrate "contriteness" in interactions with police officers may result in Negro property offenders receiving harsher treatment.

In other words, both the Piliavin–Briar study and the Ferdinand–Luchterhand research effort seem to suggest that the severity of punishments distributed to Negro juveniles may be a function of little more than their behavior in the company of police during their detention or interrogation. If this were true of American Negroes, then it might also be true of Canadian Indians.

An indication that this may be the case is provided in a survey prepared by the Canadian Corrections Association:

> It is . . . obvious that the Indian people, particularly in cities, tend to draw police attention to themselves, since their dress, personal hygiene, physical characteristics, and location in run-down areas make them conspicuous. This undoubtedly results in more frequent arrests.
>
> The feeling is widespread among the Indian and Metis people that the police push them around and arrest them on the slightest provocation.[15]

Quite clearly, the question that emerges is whether cultural or class factors are an explanation for the differential handling of juvenile offenders. Unfortunately, this question remains unanswered with specific reference to the Canadian scene; however, implications can be drawn from a review of American research on this question.

POLICE BIAS AND MINORITY GROUP RELATIONS

The question that is posed by the Piliavin and Briar study is similar to a theme that runs throughout theoretical discussions of "labeling." In fact, advocates of the labeling perspective have commonly assumed the factuality of a social class bias in police work without the benefit of an adequate empirical test.[16] Fortunately, there are by now a number of studies that test this assumption. The results are in some respects surprising.

In evaluating the findings of the various studies of class bias in police work, it will be useful to call on two sources. First, we can utilize Bordua's able summarization of several studies pertaining to this question. Second, we will report the most recent findings in this area as described in a study, referred to earlier, by Black and Reiss.

Bordua[17] has included four studies in his summarization. Each of these research efforts involved an attempt to determine the factors most often

---

[15] Canadian Corrections Association, *Indians and the Law* (Ottawa, 1967), p. 37.

[16] Cf. Aaron V. Cicourel, *The Social Organization of Juvenile Justice* (New York: Wiley, 1968), p. 67.

[17] Bordua, *loc. cit.*

associated with police disposition in juvenile cases. In other words, the researchers sought an answer to the question, "What determinants operate in police decisions regarding the handling of juveniles taken into custody?"

The studies cited by Bordua are those conducted by Goldman,[18] McEachern and Bauzer,[19] Bodine,[20] and Terry.[21] Bordua reaches the following conclusion regarding those factors that *did* influence disposition of juvenile cases in three of the four studies:

> If we put together the findings of McEachern and Bauzer and of Bodine we find that offense type, arrest record, probation status, age, department and officer all seem to affect disposition of the factors common to these studies, and also in Goldman's, offense and previous record seem the most securely established.[22]

The fact that stands out in Bordua's summary is that social class factors achieve *no consensual recognition* as influences in the final police disposition of juvenile cases.

The final study included in Bordua's summarization is a recent analysis by Ralph Terry of police work in Racine, Wisconsin. The results of this research project are perhaps the most convincing yet considered.

> . . . Terry found that offense, previous record, and age held up as correlates of disposition decision out of twelve factors studied. Terry points out that his results imply a rather "legalistic" handling of juveniles and also that the much claimed socio-economic bias of the police simply does not appear.[23]

By way of conclusion, Bordua offers some compelling comments as explanation for the failure of class bias to show up in police statistics. The police are severely constrained in the number of juveniles that they can refer to court and, beyond the court appearance, there is very little in the way of institutional space for juveniles. Thus the police know that they are going to have to return the great majority of juveniles to the community. As an example, in Terry's study nearly 90 percent of the juveniles were returned to the community without a court appearance. It appears that the police must reserve the use of court referrals for only the most severe cases. Thus Bordua concludes that we should not be surprised at the failure of class bias to show up in police figures:

[18] Nathan Goldman, *The Differential Selection of Offenders for Court Appearance* (New York: National Council on Crime and Delinquency, 1963).

[19] A. W. McEachern and Riva Bauzer, "Factors Related to Disposition in Juvenile Police Contacts," in *Juvenile Gangs in Context: Theory, Research, and Action*, ed. Malcolm W. Klein (Englewood Cliffs, N.J.: Prentice-Hall, 1967).

[20] George E. Bodine, "Factors Related to Police Dispositions of Juvenile Offenders" (Syracuse University Youth Development Center, 1964).

[21] Ralph M. Terry, "The Screening of Juvenile Offenders: A Study in the Societal Reaction to Deviant Behavior" (Ph.D. diss., University of Wisconsin, 1965).

[22] Bordua, *op. cit.*, p. 158.

[23] *Ibid.*

. . . in order for socio-economic bias to appear, it would have to be monumental since after all the police must pay *some* attention to the law.[24]

The findings reported by Black and Reiss[25] in their most recent study allow us to look beyond the more general problem of class bias to the possible details of racial discrimination. Again, the findings contain some surprises. Black and Reiss begin their discussion of the racial question in police work by noting that police encounters with Negro juveniles involve legally more serious incidents than police encounters with whites. In particular, Negro juveniles are more often involved in felonies. Since in this study only 15 percent of the police-juvenile encounters result in arrest, the more serious nature of the offenses committed by Negroes will influence the dispositional pattern of police decisions. However, the results of this study reveal that the difference in arrest rates of Negro and white juveniles taken into custody (21 percent for Negroes, 8 percent for whites) is not alone a consequence of the larger number of legally serious incidents that occasion police-Negro contacts.

Another major factor that influences higher arrest rates for Negro juveniles is whether or not a *citizen complainant* participates in the encounter. As Black and Reiss point out, "A complainant in search of justice can make direct demands on a policeman with which he must comply."

Of particular interest, in the case of complaints about Negro juveniles, is the fact that the complainants seeking severe dispositions are themselves Negro. The white officer acting without a Negro complainant is considerably more lenient. Further, when no complainant is involved in the police-juvenile encounter, the racial difference in arrest rates nearly disappears (14 percent for Negroes, 10 percent for whites).

An extended quote from the Black and Reiss study may help place the whole question of police discrimination against Negroes into its proper context.

. . . it is evident that the higher arrest rate for Negro juveniles in encounters with complainants and suspects is largely a consequence of the tendency of the police to comply with the preferences of complainants. This tendency is costly for Negro juveniles, since Negro complainants are relatively severe when they are compared to white complaints vis-à-vis white juveniles. . . . Given the prominent role of the Negro complainant in the race differential then, it may be inappropriate to consider this pattern an instance of discrimination on the part of policemen. While police behavior follows the same *patterns* for Negro and white juveniles, differential *outcomes* arise from differences in *citizen* behavior.[26]

The results of this study bring us back once again to what would appear to be a rather unfashionable conclusion: police powers seem to reside, for better or worse, in the hands of the "people."

[24] *Ibid.*
[25] Black and Reiss, *loc. cit.*
[26] *Ibid.*, pp. 71–72.

A paradox of the finding that the police themselves seem to instigate little, if any, class or racial discrimination in their work is the fact that police do *verbalize* racial prejudice in their attitudinal expressions. Thus in an earlier report, Black and Reiss[27] indicate that during the observation period included in the study, a large majority of the policemen expressed anti-Negro attitudes in the presence of observers.

One attempt to account for this paradox suggests that police bias may be acted out at some stage in the police-citizen encounter *before* the arrest takes place. The feeling here is that the police may stop a disproportionate number of Negroes, heap verbal or physical abuse on them, and then release them because they have no evidence for arrest. Research findings available at the present time do not support this contention. For example, Black and Reiss[28] suggest that if the police tended to stop a disproportionate number of Negroes on the street in minor incident situations, then we might infer the presence of discrimination. However, their findings provide no evidence in support of such a proposition. Similarly, Black and Reiss also suggest that if a higher proportion of the total Negro encounters were police-initiated than that of the total white encounters, we again might conclude in favor of police discrimination. However, evidence is also lacking here in that rates are identical for both racial groups.[29] It would appear that there may be a quite large slippage between police expression of verbal attitudes and their actual overt behavior.

The most convincing evidence for the preceding conclusion is to be found in another portion of the above study.[30] Using data gathered in the previously described research, Reiss has tabulated the infliction of brutality by both white and black policemen. The finding that emerges is that only 33 percent of the citizens victimized by white policemen were Negro, while fully 71 percent of the citizens victimized by Negro policemen were Negro. In other words, Negro policemen inflict more than twice as much brutality on Negroes as do white policemen.

> Though no precise estimates are possible, the facts just given suggest that white policemen, even though they are prejudiced toward Negroes, do not discriminate against Negroes in the excessive use of force.[31]

There seems to be no escape from the persistent paradox of a sharp disparity between police beliefs and police behaviors. Perhaps we should not be surprised. If one takes the time to think about the irony of the situation, it will probably be acknowledged that the disparity between thought and

[27] Donald J. Black and Albert J. Reiss, Jr., "Patterns of Behavior in Police and Citizen Transactions," in President's Commission on Law Enforcement and Administration of Justice, Studies in Crime and Law Enforcement in Major Metropolitan Areas, Field Surveys III, Volume 2 (Washington, D.C.: U.S. Government Printing Office, 1967), pp. 1–139.

[28] Black and Reiss, "Police Control," *loc. cit.*

[29] *Ibid.*, p. 68.

[30] Albert J. Reiss, Jr., "How Common Is Police Brutality?" *Transaction* (July–August 1968).

[31] *Ibid.*, p. 17.

action is a recurring theme in the human experience.[32] And at least in this case we seem to be the better for it.

The findings reported above, and the conclusions reached, seem to counsel against any easy solution to the problems of police work among the native peoples of Canada. For example, a recent suggestion[33] that an increase in the number of band constables used to patrol Indian communities would produce improved police/Indian relations has yet to be supproted by empirical research. As we have seen, the inferences to be drawn from American research in this area are not nearly so sanguine.

THE ORGANIZATION OF POLICE WORK

Concern for the quality of police work has, in many communities, stimulated recent attempts to "professionalize" or "modernize" police departments. These efforts have been the result of seemingly humanitarian concerns, they have utilized what would appear to be reasonable assumptions, and they have involved expenditures of large sums of money. The hope has been that the "new policeman," a well-educated and extensively trained public servant operating in a highly organized department, would be less prone to brutality and other forms of punitiveness. James Wilson has attempted to evaluate this "new look" in the organization of police work.[34]

Wilson begins his study by observing that juvenile codes allow considerable discretion on the part of authorities in their handling of delinquency. The result is that the organization of a department can make a large difference in the disposition of juvenile cases. Wilson's study characterizes two departments, one in a Western city and another in an Eastern city, and compares their respective styles in the handling of juvenile cases. Western City operates a "professional" police department. This department is described as highly organized with emphasis placed on centralization. Officers are recruited on the basis of their achieved characteristics, with particular importance attached to the level of education attained by applicants. Members of the department are often nonresidents and their training is formalized. Rules in this department are impersonal and applied across time and place; corruption is minimized.

Eastern City, on the other hand, operates a "fraternal" department. Decentralization is the organizational priority with this police force. Officers are chosen primarily for their ascribed characteristics, particularly according to their residence and recognition in the community. Training in this department is informal and characteristically of the "how to get along" variety. Rules are bent to the location, time, situation, and personality of

---

[32] Cf. Richard T. Lapiere, "Attitudes vs. Actions," *Social Forces* 13 (December 1934): 230–237; Irwin Deutscher, "Words and Deeds: Social Science and Social Policy," *Social Problems* 13 (Winter 1966): 235–254; and Allan W. Wicker, "Attitudes vs. Actions: The Relationship of Verbal and Overt Behavioral Responses to Attitude Objects," *Journal of Social Issues* 25 (Autumn 1969): 41–78.

[33] Canadian Corrections Association, *op. cit.,* pp. 37–39.

[34] James Wilson, "The Police and the Delinquent in Two Cities," in *Controlling Delinquents,* ed. Stanton Wheeler (New York: Wiley, 1968), ch. 4.

those who are involved. Corruption is rationalized as a necessary lubricant in the political machine. In short, one might summarize the situation in Eastern City and juxtapose it to the setup in Western City with the following bit of folk wisdom: "It's not what you know, but who you know."

A comparison of official statistics for the handling of juveniles in Western and Eastern cities presents some surprises. It seems that "professional" officers in Western City, invoking their impersonal standards, arrest a relatively large share of the juveniles encountered; the result being a release rate of only 53 percent. The fraternal officers in Eastern City, on the other hand, arrest far fewer of the juveniles they encounter, and in the end release 70 percent of the cases they handle. The conclusion that one must reach on comparing these figures is that Western City, and its professional department, generates a higher juvenile arrest rate.

TABLE 1

Rates of Juveniles "Processed" and Arrested in Western and Eastern City*

	Western City	Eastern City
Arrested or cited (per 100,000)	6,365 (47%)	1,910 (30%)
Processed and released (per 100,000)	7,235 (53%)	4,870 (70%)

* Table adapted from Wilson (38).

There is an exception to the above conclusions, however, and it comes in Negro neighborhoods. The professional department shows no bias in terms of class or racial factors, but the fraternal department shows a large bias in its referral rate for Negroes (i.e., Negroes, apparently, are referred to court in Eastern City at a much higher rate than are whites). It would seem, then, that professionalization of police work has accomplished the goal of reducing discrimination in racial ghettoes, while at the same time evoking the unintended consequence of increasing punitiveness in majority group neighborhoods.

Wilson has something of an explanation for the generally higher arrest rate found in the professional department. While professional departments employ officers who usually have no contact with the community they work in, other than their patrol assignment, fraternal departments more often utilize officers who have an in-depth and personalized knowledge of the community they patrol. Often the officers in Eastern City have grown up in the community to which they are assigned. The implication is that officers in Eastern City are aware of means other than arrest for solving problems in encounters with juveniles. Knowing the details of a family's situation, or having lived through similar situations himself, the officer from a fraternal department may often be able to find personalized solutions that avoid arrest. This explanation of the paradox of professionalization suggests insights worthy of investigation by advocates of efforts at modernization in police work.

Another investigation of the organization of police work is provided by John Gandy, of the University of Toronto School of Social Work, in his study of the Metropolitan Toronto Police Department.[35] Gandy begins, like Wilson, by noting the wide latitude of discretion available to authorities in the handling of juveniles. Again, the organization of a particular department is seen as exercising a dramatic influence on an individual officer's response to juvenile behavior. The basic premise of this study is, then, that the organizational structure forming the environment of police work, and the officer's "common sense" interpretation of this organizational structure, provide an explanation for the use of discretion in the handling of juveniles.

Gandy notes that in an organization as large as the Metropolitan Toronto Police Department bureaucratic subdivision is inevitable. Thus it was anticipated that in a department this large there would be several rather than only one pattern of disposition in the handling of juveniles. These patterns of disposition were, however, expected to reflect consistency within the organizational *subdivisions* of the department.

To investigate these propositions, Gandy selected three administrative subunits within the larger department, all dealing with the disposition of juveniles taken into custody by the Metropolitan Police. After analyzing responses to open-ended interviews conducted with officers in each of the organization branches investigated, Gandy found the following:

> Differences in content and outcome of police discretion regarding the disposition of juveniles were associated with the administrative sub-unit of the department to which the officer was assigned. There were significant differences between the administrative sub-units (a) in the emphasis and weight given to the same criteria in making choices among possible dispositions; (b) in their perception of the relative seriousness of certain types of behavior; and (c) in the frequency with which certain courses of action were selected.[36]

An awareness of the usefulness of these findings requires an examination of their implications for the guidance of social policy.

Gandy suggests that greater consistency would be desirable between the administrative subdivisions of the Metropolitan Toronto Police Department. Yet, one of the reasons for establishing a Youth Bureau within a large police department is to develop a different pattern for handling juveniles. Gandy also concludes:

> The lack of clearly stated departmental policies in the handling of juveniles resulted in the development of informal procedures related to the needs of the particular administrative unit.[37]

[35] John M. Gandy, *The Exercise of Discretion by the Police in the Handling of Juveniles* (1967).
[36] John M. Gandy, "The Exercise of Discretion by the Police as a Decision Making Process in the Disposition of Juvenile Offenders," *Osgoode Hall Law Journal* 8 (November 1970): 342.
[37] *Ibid.*, p. 343.

Again, one could interpret this conclusion as characteristic of a complex organization, a fact to be understood rather than something that must be changed. Clearly stated policies that do not reflect reality are frequently disregarded. Similarly, the development of informal procedures that are compatible with the needs of the particular administrative unit are inevitable. The question to be asked, of course, is whether or not these informal procedures achieve desired goals. Perhaps it would be well to examine the day-to-day working of such police units before formalizing policy. The social scientist might make his greatest contribution in this type of research if he can help those in positions of authority assess the consequences of different patterns within a social agency such as a police department. Assuming that there will always be inconsistencies within administrative subunits (as well as from individual to individual), it may be easier to funnel cases into appropriate subunits than to expect the units themselves to change.

A further conclusion reached by Gandy is that police officers make only limited use of social agencies in dealing with juvenile problems. The assumption, of course, is that social work agencies would be in a better position to help many of these juveniles—a reasonable position to be taken in a study emerging from a school of social work. Is the assumption a valid one? In their article entitled "Policeman as Philosopher, Guide, and Friend," Cumming, Cumming, and Edell[38] point out that the police provide effective social work services to lower-class clientele. Their 24-hour-a-day availability and familiarity with touchy problems where physical violence is a possibility could make the police the logical agency to deal with many problems that we traditionally think of as "social work."

The purpose of this discussion is not to argue in favor of a particular policy but to emphasize the point that studies of agencies dealing with juveniles do not automatically lead to clear policy decisions. Furthermore, we must resist the temptation to see studies of police forces in Canada as either devices for embarrassing the police or for whitewashing their activities.

The important insight emerging from the type of studies carried out by Wilson and Gandy is an awareness that it can make a great deal of difference where and by whom a juvenile is caught. One may conclude that identical youths engaging in the same activities in Vancouver and Toronto will likely encounter characteristically different responses from the local authorities; similarly, but on a lower level of analysis, juveniles behaving in like ways in Yorkville and Crestwood Heights will probably also meet alternative fates. Thus the social transformation from ordinary juvenile to stigmatized delinquent status seems at least partially contingent upon the particular organization orientation that the officer of first encounter is following. Certainly this should alert us to the naïveté of the universalistic and democratic values underlying our system of juvenile justice.

[38] Elaine Cumming, Ian Cumming, and Laura Edell, "Policeman and Philosopher, Guide and Friend," *Social Problems* 12 (Winter 1965): 276–286.

CONCLUSIONS

On a broader level of analysis, several types of researchable questions emerge from the various studies of police work considered in the previous phases of our discussion. For example: Would native Canadian policemen be more punitive in the patrol of indigenous communities than nonnative policemen? Do police use marijuana legislation to harass that manner of youth referred to as "freaks" or "hippies"? Do negative attitudes that many police have toward long-haired youth mean that they will automatically treat them unfairly? While many of us assume that we know the answers to such questions, the present state of our knowledge indicates that such an assumption is unjustified. Unfortunately, there are only slight stirrings in Canada indicating interest in the type of research we have suggested. Reasons for the dearth of such activity can be noted. First, granting agencies may be hesitant to face the potential pressures that might arise if they encouraged scholars to study agencies of criminal control. Second, the agencies themselves have not welcomed inquiries to study their operations, perhaps fearing the exposure of vulnerable regions of activity. Third, most researchers, with the exception of a small group of legally trained scholars in Eastern Canada, have displayed a distinct preference for the more traditional study of juveniles and their behavior rather than tread on more sensitive turf.

These observations are offered in the hope of signaling the need for an alternative mode of analysis. It is argued that, as we determine more accurately what social control agencies "really do," we will be better qualified to constructively criticize the social reality of a system called "juvenile justice." The labeling perspective may, if properly channeled, have the potential of directing us into the type of research that will investigate just this type of problem. In short, it may lead us at last to finding out what social control agencies like the police "really do" and what the consequences of these actions "really are."

8
INSTEAD OF COURT:
DIVERSION IN JUVENILE JUSTICE*
Edwin M. Lemert

The next paper includes two sections from Lemert's very comprehensive monograph. Not reproduced here, but well worth the reader's additional attention, are chapters on school, welfare, and community organization models of diversion as they pertain to labeling theory. The first section reprinted here is noteworthy for its juxtaposition of two major issues. The first of these is the bureaucratized, multipurposed "overreach" of the juvenile court system. The second is the concept of secondary deviance and its avoidance, which highlights the *definitions* of delinquency, normalization, and referrals. Both force us to consider the extent to which delinquency is *not* dependent upon the delinquents.

In the second section, the reader may feel that Lemert does not give sufficient credit for both the amount and the variety of police diversion now in existence. This is true, but not because of his error—it is a function of the enormous diversion explosion that has taken place during the four- or five-year interval between his publication and this.

* From *Instead of Court*, National Institute of Mental Health (Washington, D.C.: U.S. Government Printing Office, 1971), Chapter I (pp. 1–18), Chapter IV (pp. 54–70), and Chapter VI (pp. 94–95). Reprinted by permission of the author.

THE PROGRAM

This monograph is an effort to develop a series of models for diverting children and youth away from juvenile courts, so that their problems which otherwise would be dealt with in a context of delinquency and official action will be defined and handled by other means. It is premised on the idea that an excessive number of children are being processed by juvenile courts, that children are unnecessarily referred to juvenile courts, and that in many cases the harm done to children and youth by contacts with these courts outweighs any benefits thereby gained. Moreover, the interaction between child and court and unanticipated consequences of the processing of a child in many instances contributes to or exacerbates the problem of delinquency.

The reasons for this undertaking grow out of major shifts which have taken place in thinking and public policy in regard to the preeminent position of the juvenile court as an agency for dealing with the problems of children and youth. Vast changes have taken place in American society since the birth of the juvenile court at the beginning of the present century— changes which make reexamination of the court long overdue, both as an institution and as a working organization in a community context. One of the most striking developments in the picture of child and youth problems has been the great increase in contacts between youth, law enforcement bodies, and the juvenile court. For example, in 1966 between a million and a million and a half arrests were made of persons under 18 years of age, and it was estimated that 27 percent of all male youths can expect to have been arrested before they have reached age 18.[1] The proportion of those who actually become known to police by this age will be much greater because large numbers of youthful "offenders" are disposed of by police without record or formal action.

Approximately one-half of police arrests of juveniles result in their referrals to juvenile courts. According to several community studies, about one-fifth of the male population will have been referred to juvenile court by age 18.[2]

If these are valid measures of serious youth problems, then American society is in a critical if not moribund state. A preferred explanation is that the difficulties in reality lie elsewhere, that there is something badly wrong with the agencies which apprehend, receive, define, and process problems of children and youth. And indeed, this largely has been the tenor of the social criticism which has been directed toward police activities and juvenile procedures in recent decades. Mounting dissatisfaction and concern have been captioned by the far-reaching decision in the Gault case, in which the United States Supreme Court felt it necessary for the first time to review the work of juvenile courts. In paraphrase, the decision held that the wide powers of the juvenile court have not appreciably diminished youthful crime, that inconsistencies in its philosophy can have adverse effects upon youth under its control, and that gross injustices may result from its procedures in which youth are punished more severely than adults for comparable offenses.[3]

CRITICISM OF THE JUVENILE COURT AS AN INSTITUTION

It is unfortunate that the Supreme Court's opinion in the Gault case was reached in an atmosphere more political than scholarly, leaving a suspicion that its purpose was to invite elimination of the juvenile court. At best, the decision was a synthetic justification for extending a number of rights of criminally accused persons to juveniles. Justice Harlan, whose opinion both concurred and dissented, decried the absence of a rationale for the decision, at the same time emphasizing the need to determine the requirements of due process of law, not by criminal or civil criteria, but rather by criteria "consistent with the traditions and conscience of our people":

> The central issue here . . . is the method by which procedural requirements of due process should be measured. . . . the protections necessary cannot be determined by . . . classification of juvenile proceedings either as criminal or as civil. Both formulas are too imprecise. . . . The court should instead measure the requirements of due process by reference both to the problems which confront

[1] Alfred Blumstein, Systems analysis and the criminal justice system, *American Academy of Political and Social Science*, 1967, 374, 92–100.

[2] *Op. cit.*, p. 99.

[3] *In re Gault*, 387 U.S. I (1967), pp. 1–81.

the state and to the actual character of the procedural system which the state has created.[4]

Justice Harlan missed the fact that the juvenile court is more of a local than a State agency, but his insistence on the need to examine it as an institutional system responding to variable problems in a geographical setting reflects a sociological view: in essence that decision making and judicial outcomes in juvenile courts are phenomena of social organization rather than law per se.[5] The variation in such organization is considerable; indeed, this is one of the core difficulties in trying to understand the juvenile court. How to comprehend the protean local adaptations of the many juvenile courts and yet capture those features which make it distinctive as an institution is no mean task. Perhaps this can best be done by combining several loosely linked perspectives on the court—its institutional differentiation, its efficacy as a working organization, also as a treatment agency, its bureaucratization, the overreach of law by the court, and its consequences as a deviance-designating agency.

INSTITUTIONAL DIFFERENTIATION

A perennial problem of juvenile courts, particularly as they are seen by national, standard-conscious agencies, has been their failure to differentiate according to the early model. Much of this has been blamed on the character of juvenile court judges, many of whom took conservative views of the court or else lacked the background and special education to appreciate and fulfill its ideal goals. Many courts had no probation officers, while others had to do with untrained and poorly educated personnel; social investigation and written reports were conspicuously absent, and access to specialized services was limited or nonexistent. Years ago, Carr called attention to these facts as evidence that "most courts have to be substandard."[6] The persistent failure of courts to differentiate is born out by a 1963 study which revealed that only 71 percent of juvenile court judges had law degrees; and of "full-time" juvenile court judges, 72 percent spent a quarter or less of their time on juvenile matters. One-third of the judges had no probation officers to carry out work of the court, and but a small portion could call on psychological or psychiatric consultation services.[7]

Undifferentiated juvenile courts are much more numerous than others, but over all they serve a smaller proportion of the population. Their substandard quality appears to be directly related to the low population density of the areas they serve, where sheer economics or high per capita costs of servicing cases makes specialization difficult or impossible.

[4] Op. cit.

[5] Aaron Cicourel, The Social Organization of Juvenile Justice, New York: John Wiley & Sons, 1968, Chapters I, II.

[6] Lowell Carr, Most courts have to be substandard, Federal Probation, XIII, 1949, 22–23.

[7] Shirley McCune and Daniel S. Skoler, Juvenile court judges in the United States, Part I, Crime and Delinquency, 1965, 11, 121–131.

THE COURT AS A WORKING ORGANIZATION

In looking at juvenile courts serving large population areas which have reasonably adequate resources to differentiate along specialized, professionalized lines, different kinds of problems come to light, the most important of which is an overburden. As a juvenile court differentiates, it develops a number of interdependent relations with local and State agencies—police, sheriffs' departments, boards of supervisors, welfare departments, schools, hospitals, clinics, correctional institutions, and professional associations. While such agencies serve the court, they also make claims on it, one of the main consequences being that it receives far more referrals than it has resources to handle. Attempts are made to meet this problem by concentrating on screening cases at intake, but nevertheless their volume means that much if not most of the manpower of the court has to go into investigations and court hearings.

It has been argued that the court's case-processing methods are ill adapted to its tasks. For one thing a great deal of information often is collected which either is not used or cannot be related in any specifiable way to the kinds of decisions the courts make in particular cases. Storage and retrieval of information by hand-filing methods frequently is inadequate to the magnitude of its work. There is an absence of methods for monitoring and assessing the work of the court, nor can it forecast the direction of its movement with any accuracy. One result is that cases are not disposed in line with a continuous or clear policy: policy of the juvenile court often is a reflection of inconsistent demands being made upon it at a particular time by particular agencies. Salient among these is the effort of police to coopt the court in their jobs of maintaining public order. A comparison of the working of the juvenile court with that of the modern business corporation makes it appear poorly managed, inconsistent, duplicative, and costly in effort.[8]

THE COURT AS BUREAUCRACY

The necessity of processing large numbers of cases with diversified problems transforms juvenile courts into hierarchical organizations with divisions, departments, specialists, and routinized procedures. As such, they take on the qualities and problems of bureaucracy. Cases are passed from functionary to functionary and from one department to another; hence, decisions often are reached in piecemeal fashion or in consultations between various levels of authority. While there is a strain toward rationalized procedures, nevertheless responsibility tends to be diffused, and conflicts between individual workers or between divisions are endemic. Group interaction within the court, routines, contingencies, and organizational requirements profoundly affect the fate of cases.

[8] Robert Vinter, The juvenile court as an institution, *Task Force Report: Juvenile Delinquency and Youth Crime*, President's Commission on Law Enforcement and the Administration of Justice, 1967, Washington, D.C., pp. 84–90.

What in the early days of the juvenile court was envisioned as a quasi-personal relationship between a child and a judge or between a youth and a probation officer turns into a relationship between a child or youth and a large, complex organization. Given the overburden of cases born of external demands on the court, the exigencies of its internal operations make it extremely difficult or impossible to predict that the interests of the child will be those of any particular member of the organization or of the court as a whole. Until recently, juvenile courts failed to make any adaptations to this crucial problem, in part because ideal aspects of the original model of the court as a protectorate of children obscured its significance and in part because recognition of this kind of problem would compel fundamental changes in the design of the court itself. The problem has further ramifications, best seen in questions about the inherent limits of law as a means of social control.

THE COURT AS THE OVERREACH OF LAW

Many of the difficulties of the juvenile court revolve around its character as an enterprise originally designed to use the power and authority of law to achieve ends not amenable to legal means. These strictures were anticipated years ago by Roscoe Pound in his classic paper on the limits of effective legal action. In it he noted that this kind of question comes to the fore in epochs when efforts are made to cause law to coincide with morals. When this happens the individual becomes the unit of law and wide discretion is given to magistrates (judges). The limits of legal sanctions inhere in the intangibleness of moral duties, which although of great public concern, defy public enforcement. As cases in point, Pound observed how obligations for the care of health, morals, and education of children—even truancy and incorrigibility—were coming under the jurisdiction of juvenile courts. When these matters are committed to courts they necessarily delegate the work of enforcement to administrative agents, such as probation officers, whose capacity to achieve these ends is questionable.[9]

Although Pound remained favorable to the juvenile court idea throughout his career, he was aware of its inherent shortcomings. In his estimation there were two main threats to the juvenile court, both inherently forms of the overreach of law:

It remains to speak of two movements in current thinking which may threaten the continued development of the juvenile court. One is the movement to reach the causes of all delinquency and so particularly of juvenile delinquency through programs of official national agencies and local welfare agencies subordinate to or allied with them. . . .

Another aspect of current thinking is the move towards absolutism the world over. The subject . . . affects every agency of government which involves the exercise of discretion with reference to the interests of individuals. Especially the move-

---

[9] Roscoe Pound, The limits of effective legal action, *Twenty-Second Annual Report of the Pennsylvania Bar Association*, XXII, 1916, 221–239; ——, The juvenile court and the law, preprinted in *Crime and Delinquency*, 10, 1964, 490–504.

ment for a wide administrative criminal jurisdiction may easily be carried so far
with mistaken zeal that administrative criminal tribunals and the juvenile courts
may be pushed back or fall back into ordinary criminal courts of the old
type. . . .[10]

A critical retrospective on the establishment of the first juvenile courts
reveals them to have been less a carefully planned innovation than the
climax of a nineteenth-century reform movement to rescue children from
"depravity and immorality" of lower-class urban environments. Another
part of its impetus came from reformers who turned to the juvenile court
idea as an oblique way of attacking the evil of child labor through using the
court to enforce compulsory education laws. In its early history it was not
unusual for the court to be pressured to take custody of children as a device
to coerce parental conformity in matters of divorce, adultery, and insobriety.
Some of the early controversies between judges and welfare workers re-
volved around these issues, with conservative judges in some instances using
their considerable discretionary power to resist the zeal of reformers.[11]

The juvenile court's emergence in Illinois solved a major problem for
private charity organizations there, which had seen statutes giving them
control over delinquent children declared unconstitutional, while those
allowing control over dependent and neglected children were sustained on
appeal.[12] Combining jurisdiction over all three classes of children in a
"socialized court" theoretically civil in nature provided the much sought
legitimation of the values of the moral reformers. Unfortunately, the envisioned ideal that delinquent children would thereafter be defined and
treated as "neglected" proved false; in practice the reverse often was true,
i.e., dependent and neglected children fell under the pall of delinquency
and in many cases were subjected to the same kinds of sanctions.

THE OMNIBUS NATURE OF DELINQUENCY

Designations of delinquency in the first juvenile court laws were radical
departures from traditional principles of Anglo-Saxon criminal law, which
parsimoniously applies sanctions to conduct manifestly violating narrowly
defined laws and leaves but small scope for preventive law. Early statutes
describing juvenile delinquency were omnibus in nature, drawn with the
intent of bringing the widest possible gamut of child and youth problems
under the bind of law. They embraced juvenile law violators, but "predelinquents" as well; later statutes added those with "delinquent tendencies."
While the statutory phrasing under which juvenile courts assumed their
almost unlimited jurisdiction has varied widely, delinquency is generally
described as: (1) actions which if committed by adults would be punishable as
crimes; (2) actions or states of being applicable only to minors—special

[10] Roscoe Pound, The juvenile court and the law, p. 503.

[11] Edwin M. Lemert, *Social Action and Legal Change*, Chicago: Aldine Publishing Co., 1970,
Chapters I, II.

[12] Anthony Platt, *The Child Savers*, Chicago: Aldine Publishing Co., 1969, Chapter 5.

children's offenses such as idleness, begging, junking, smoking, using alcohol, loitering or sleeping in alleys, curfew violations, presence in a gambling place or house of prostitution, playing ball in the street, engaging in street trades, and associating with adult criminals; (3) very generalized unspecified acts or states such as truancy, incorrigibility, immorality, and being in danger of leading a lewd and lascivious life.

The passage of time has seen the elimination of long lists of outmoded acts and morally hazardous conditions from juvenile court laws in some States, but reliance on nonspecific jurisdictional categories has continued, including "runaways," "beyond control" of parents and school authorities, and actions "endangering morals and welfare." In eight States delinquency is not defined, but is left to the discretion of the juvenile courts themselves.[13]

SUBSTANCE AND SHADOW OF DELINQUENCY

Nationwide the substantive meaning of delinquency has to be restricted to the body of similar findings between jurisdictions as to what constitutes law violations by minors. Otherwise, definitions are artificial, arbitrary, and conventional.[14] The meaning of delinquency is relative, and peculiar to time and place. It must be discerned in the routine perceptions and practices within the court as effected by external claims of agencies and individuals making up. its overburden.

In courts where social work philosophy and psychiatric ideologies prevail, the shadowy nature of delinquency determinations is furthered, or perhaps validated, by the idea that wrongdoing is a symptom of underlying pathology of the person or of his family situation. This "pathology" is inferred not so much from conduct as from "patterns" or "tendencies," judged to exist or intuited by probation officers, social workers, or clinical consultants. From their view, it may be more urgent to take or retain official control over a youth who has committed a benign offense than one guilty of a law violation.

THE COURT AS A TREATMENT AGENCY

In actuality juvenile courts as a whole have not been receptive to psychiatric ideology and social work methods. Pressures on the courts to mete out punishment to delinquents and the inclination of probation officers to see themselves as surrogates of law and community interests have determined otherwise. Conceptions of treatment held by probation officers are much more likely to be correctional in nature and communicated from within their own field. The desire to do "treatment" and enthusiasm for novel ideas of therapy are often met with among probations officers, but then countered in the same breath by the occupational complaint that caseloads are too overwhelmingly large to allow time for treatment. When pushed for justification of what they do, judges and probation officers are likely to describe the

---

[13] *Comparative Survey of Juvenile Delinquency, Part I, North America,* UNESCO, No. 58, IV, 2–4.
[14] Manuel Lopez-Rey, Juvenile delinquency, maladjustment and maturity; *Journal of Criminal Law and Criminology,* 1960, 51, 31.

working dispositions of their cases as treatment or in more candid moments recognize them as expedients for disciplining unruly youth.

About one-half of all cases received by juvenile courts are dismissed or continued without a formal disposition—in other words, little more occurs than processing itself. One long-accepted justification for what otherwise might seem a meaningless spinning of its wheels by the court is that errant youth are thereby given an experience with supervening authority hitherto missing from their lives. Commonly this means a confrontation with a probation officer in the presence of parents or a stern lecture from a judge in a courtroom, and warnings of dire consequences of further misconduct.

A more painful accompaniment of these proceedings in a certain number of cases is a stay of detention. This often is a pragmatic move so that youth can "cool off" or "think things over": not infrequently it is a type of punishment decreed in lieu of other forms of incarceration. At still other times detention is a direct accommodation to needs of police who are trying to solve a crime series or recover property; no pretense of treatment is made.

Next to continuances the most frequent disposition in juvenile court cases is placement on probation. But probation often is a nominal type of control which adds up to relatively few contacts between probation officers and their wards, their average number being about one or less per month.[15] In defense of this procedure it has been argued that merely placing a youth on probation, regardless of what else happens, is in itself a form of treatment. Seen more realistically it is a form of attenuated surveillance.

Leaving aside the question of commitments to schools and institutions, what the juvenile court does by way of treatment is so intertwined with its other purposes as to defy specification and evaluation. Undoubtedly there are cases in which encounters with juvenile court personnel, stays in detention, and probationary status suffice to make youth more law abiding or at least more cautious and careful about actions likely to result in arrest or referral to the court. Those so responding are probably fortunately situated or culturally and psychologically endowed to profit from their experiences. In contrast, there are those for whom juvenile court appearances and their consequences simply add new problems to old, redefine old problems in more ominous and fateful terms, or become episodes in delinquent careers.

THE COURT AS AN AGENCY FOR DEFINING DEVIANCE

A final way of perceiving the juvenile court illuminates the way in which it designates deviance, shapes its expression, and helps to perpetuate it in secondary form.[16] It does so by redefining normal problems of children and youth as special problems requiring legal action and restraining controls. In a real sense it "causes" delinquency by processing cases of children and youth whose problems might be ignored, normalized in their original settings, or dealt with as family, educational, or welfare problems. Prima facie support-

---

[15] Lewis Dana, What is probation? *Journal of Criminal Law and Criminology*, 1960, 51, 189–204.

[16] Edwin M. Lemert, *Human Deviance, Social Problems and Social Control*, Englewood Cliffs, N.J.: Prentice-Hall, Inc., 1967, Chapter 3.

ing evidence for this conclusion comes from studies of so-called "hidden" or "unofficial" delinquency, which show that a high percentage of college students and high school students have committed acts similar to those of boys who were wards of juvenile courts or inmates of correctional schools.[17]

One difference between college students and juvenile court boys, also between high school boys and those in correctional schools, was that the officially processed boys had committed *more* actions definable as delinquent than their counterparts. This fact might allow the conclusion that the processed youths represented cases in which normalization of their actions had been tried and failed. However, close examination of these studies indicates that when both frequency and seriousness of infractions are considered, there is a good deal of overlap in the distributions of cases of official and "unofficial" delinquency. This is most readily seen in the Cambridge–Somerville study, in which a comparison is possible between youth who became juvenile court cases and those who did not. The former, the "official" cases, disclosed a-frequency range of from five cases per youth to over 323, with a median of 79 for a five-year period. During this same time the range for the frequencies of unofficial cases was from zero to 266, with a median of 30. Twelve and a half percent of the official cases fell below the median of the unofficial cases, while 21.3 percent of the unofficial cases were above the median of the officially processed offenders.[18]

The areas of overlap between official and unofficial delinquency can be assumed to embrace primarily the special children's offenses and those in nonspecific categories of "delinquent tendencies." It is in these areas that the process of redefining normal child and youth problems into those requiring court intervention meets with the least resistance. However, as will be shown, criminal statutes also may be stretched or so interpreted to accomplish the same end. The difference between official and normal delinquencies lies in their context, primarily in the values, motivations, and policy decisions of complainants seeking to define the problems whose solution lies in juvenile court intervention. The more immediate meanings behind such allegations as incorrigibility, truancy, curfew violations, and moral danger are distributive aspects of the extraneous group and individual demands which make up the overburden of the court.

For example, incorrigibility when put into its social context is a term which many times connotes little more than conflict between a teen-age youth and parents, in which unreasonable demands are made by the latter and in which a probation officer becomes a partisan. Sometimes the application of this term is merely a convenient vehicle for abdicating parental responsibility for a child. Outside the family it may mean that a teacher or vice principal has concluded that a child is a trouble-maker whom he will not tolerate further in the school. Truancy, which usually is arbitrarily defined by school policies, reflects a wide variety of situations other than willful absence by the child. A

[17] Austin Porterfield, *Youth in Trouble*, Fort Worth, Tex.: Leo Potishman Foundation, 1946, Chapter 2; Mary Shirley and Helen Witmer, The incidence of hidden delinquency, *American Journal of Orthopsychiatry*, 1946, 16, 686–696; James F. Short and F. Ivan Nye, Extent of unrecorded delinquency, *Journal of Criminal Law and Criminology*, 1958, 49, 296–302.

[18] Edwin Powers and Helen Witmer, *An Experiment in the Prevention of Delinquency—the Cambridge–Somerville Youth Study*, New York: Columbia University Press, 1951, Chapter XVIII.

study conducted in 1960 found that among other things the label of truancy was sometimes simply applied as a result of failure of parents to sent written excuses to school.[19] Curfew violations may mean many things, but typically they flow from crude police action seeking to maintain order in public places. The allegation of moral danger tends to arise out of behavior or situations, real or fancied, which arouse sufficient sexual anxieties in others to demand court action. Normal sex play of children witnessed by neighbors may suffice.

The overreach of law in converting normal problems into delinquency is even more striking when allegations of law violations are made. These range from adventitious overblown charges arising from domestic quarrels to routine use of maximum charges in ways comparable to practices in regular criminal courts. Usually these stem from strong personal involvements or from the vested interests of organizations. Consider the following, witnessed in a Northern California county juvenile court:

> Naomi, age 13, was charged with assault on her grandmother, the case against her aggressively presented by the probation officer. Under his questioning, the grandmother angrily stated that the girl had pushed her and struck her without provocation in the early morning hours in her own house. This had badly upset the grandfather, who came downstairs on the scene shortly thereafter. He verified his wife's version of the events.

> But slowly under cross examination by the defense attorney it became clear that the girl had done no more than push her grandmother down into a chair to compel her to listen to her. This was a reaction to events of the previous evening when the grandmother in the girl's presence had called her mother a whore, mainly because she was associating with an Indian, the two having gone to San Francisco the night in question. The girl was badly disturbed, brooded about the remark, finally phoned her grandmother to demand a face-to-face explanation in her house, where the alleged "assault" occurred. Further questioning made it fairly clear that the court action was one of a long series of harassments to remove the mother and girl from a small house owned by her grandmother.

The importance of vested interests in routine exaggeration of crime charges involving youths is best seen in auto thefts, which in many cities make up the lion's share of court cases involving boys. Most of these are "joy riding" offenses rather than taking with the intent of converting the property of others to personal use. The vehicles usually are abandoned after a short period, and recovery rates are quite high. Yet because of the crucial importance of automobiles and because of the special interests of insurance companies in these matters, probation officers in many jurisdictions charge the maximum statutory offense.[20] Here law typically goes beyond its province to make maximum findings because juvenile courts are not constrained by strict rules or criminal evidence.

[19] See Sophia Robison, *Juvenile Delinquency*, New York: Holt, Rinehart and Winston, 1960, pp. 148–155.

[20] Jerome Hall, *Theft, Law and Society* (2nd ed.), Indianapolis: Bobbs-Merrill Co., Inc., 1952, Chapter Six.

STIGMATIZATION

Juvenile court proceedings originally were held to be civil in nature, confidential, and to be concluded without creation of a record. Events proved them to be punitive, correctional, and stigmatizing in effect if not in intent. This came about from persistent opinion and pressures from groups that saw the court as a means of repressing crime. The location of juvenile courts within the regular system of courts, their close relations with police departments, use of jails for detention, and dispositions depriving children of their freedom all sustained the punitive and stigmatizing features of these courts.

Stigmatization is a process which assigns marks of moral inferiority to deviants; more simply it is a form of degradation which transforms identities and status for the worse. It is both implicit and explicit in formal procedures in the court. Intake interviews, and those in subsequent investigations, often are inquisitions seeking admissions of guilt or of complicity in offenses necessary to meet legal requirements of petitions, or to obtain evidence in other cases. Detention means loss of freedom, removal of personal possessions, subjugation to arbitrary security rules, and surveillance—in some juvenile halls by microphones and closed-circuit television. Girls, on admission to detention, may have to submit to routine pelvic examinations, with the implications of possible pregnancy or venereal disease.

Court hearings on many occasions are equivalents of degradation rituals in which probation officers recite in detail the moral failings or "unfitness" of children, youth, and parents. Hostile witnesses add to the condemnations, and judges often deliver sermon-like lectures, larded with threats, which confront children and parents with choices of reform or dire consequences. For emphasis, judges have been known to read incriminating facts or opinions from the probation record.

While such dramatized insults to identity and integrity cut deep for some, their impact varies and is absorbed or discounted by others. Less easy to cope with are the objective consequences of stigmatization resulting from the creation of a court and police record. While not open public records, nevertheless their contents get known. This can and does act as a handicap in seeking certain types of employment, professional schooling, and acceptance in the armed forces. A paradoxical handicap, one of special importance in the larger discussion of this report, is that once a child becomes a ward of a juvenile court, many welfare agencies will not accept him as their client.[21] Henceforth, he loses his chances of having his problems treated as welfare matters.

THE ESCALATION OF STIGMA

Probation officers, welfare workers, and others are familiar with cases of children who have come into juvenile court as dependent wards, later were

[21] Alfred J. Kahn, *A Court For Children,* New York: Columbia University Press, 1953, pp. 59–60.

classed as incorrigible, and at last typed as law violator delinquents. Court workers are very apt to look on this sequence as a kind of unfolding process in which the potential for delinquency becomes overt. Omitted from their thinking, and that which impresses many sociologists, is the influence of court experiences themselves in the generation of such sequences or careers.

A certain portion of the escalation of delinquent careers is almost purely arbitrary or results from bureaucratic responses to court overload. For example, in 1966 juvenile courts in California sent 80 minors to the Youth Authority, by reclassifying them from code section 600 (dependency, unfit homes) to 602 (law violations) without bringing them back to court for rehearings.[22] A common problem cloaked by such actions is the inability to find foster home placements or lack of other resources. This leads to the administrative expedient of legally redefining the child's problems so that he or she may be turned over to the State agency. There is no way of knowing how widespread this kind of circumvention is, but results of a 1966 survey of 15 to 20 correctional institutions showed that about 30 percent of their inmates were children committed for conduct that would not have been judged criminal for adults. Similar studies brought out the fact that 48 percent of 9,500 children in State and local detention programs had no record of criminal acts.[23]

SECONDARY DEVIANCE

One of the great paradoxes of organized society is that agencies of social control may exacerbate or perpetuate the very problems they seek to ameliorate. In so doing they foster conditions of secondary deviance. Such deviance evolves out of adaptations and attempted adaptations to the problems created by official reactions to original deviance.[24] From this point of view the sanctions, dispositions, or "treatment" imposed by the juvenile court personnel too often simply add another series of problems to original problems of parents and children, then further stigmatize the failures to cope with the new problems. The specifics of this process lie in the reactions made to special status which sets wards apart and special conduct standards which hold them accountable in ways not expected of other children. Probation exemplifies this process, wherein a youth is forbidden to associate with persons he regards as his friends, a girl is barred from seeing her boyfriend, or a child is ordered not to see an "unfit" parent.

A teenager placed in a foster home is expected to obey orders of people who are strangers; the boy placed in a ranch school must tread a narrow path hedged with rules, many of which are drawn up with his potential deviance in mind. A youth may violate rules with perfectly good motives—to show loyalty to friends, to visit with a parent, or to look for employment. In other

[22] *Proceedings of the 1966 Institute for Juvenile Court Judges and Referees,* 1966, Long Beach California Judicial Council of California, p. 22.

[23] William H. Sheridan, Juveniles who commit non-criminal acts: Why treat in a correctional system? *Federal Probation,* 1967, XXXI, 26–30.

[24] Edwin M. Lemert, *op. cit.*

cases a boy may take leave from a ranch school because of problems beyond his power to solve. Yet the court typically defines such actions as "failures" or disobedience of its orders, which become legal justification for more severe measures whose effect is to move a minor farther along the road to correctional school. Probation officers or judges sometimes are aware at the time of a disposition that it is destined to "fail," yet they will say that they have no choice when it comes to the more fateful dispositions which follow such failures.

DELINQUENCY AS A PROCESS

Becoming delinquent is not a simple aggregation of the effects of juvenile court experiences, but rather a process in which parents, neighbors, teachers, school officials, and police as well play significant roles. No less important is the subjective response of "self-reaction" which children and youths make to these significant others. While becoming delinquent is by no means a unilinear process, frequently it discloses a cumulative reinforcement of problems confronting a child in different social contexts. Parents may be loveless, punitive, or rejecting toward a child, or they may place him prematurely on his own resources. The child may be labeled as the "bad one" or black sheep of the family; neighbors may focus hostility on such a child and make him a scapegoat. Teachers may add another facet to the child's disrepute with the designation of troublemaker, or a vice principal may insist that the child be removed from his school. Finally, the police, who are the main source of juvenile court referrals, form stereotyped judgments of the child based upon fragmentary information of his family or his school record.

While there is no agreement on the precise way a child becomes delinquent, much indicates that the process consists of predominant interactions in which the child's sense of integrity and moral worth are placed in question. This is most likely to happen when relationships of trust vital to personal growth are attenuated or changed to those of distrust. When this occurs, wariness, cognizance, and surveillance replace the easy mutual acceptance of trust. There is little effort to normalize deviance or to see it as a problem amenable to ordinary solutions.

Deviance which subsequently gets defined as delinquency represents efforts by children and youth to defend their autonomy and somehow preserve character in the face of degrading interaction. For children this includes a lot of testing and retaliative behavior, often idiosyncratic in nature, which invites problematic definitions. For the adolescent, deviance is more apt to be shaped in peer group audiences which serve to validate character claims or "rep." It is not unusual for this to turn into character contests involving both police and juvenile court officials. The subjective aspects of this process have been analyzed well by Werthman elsewhere.[25] Here the main concern is with the special attributes of the institutional context which pose character problems for the child.

[25] Carl Werthman, The function of social definitions in the development of delinquent careers, Task Force Report: Juvenile Delinquency and Youth Crime, op. cit., Appendix J, 155–170.

The place of the juvenile court and that of the police differ in several fundamental ways from the family, neighborhood, school, and welfare agencies. Whereas the latter are organized primarily around presumptions of trust, the reverse is true of the police; they institutionalize distrust, suspicion, and inquisitorial methods. Distrust is problematical for primary groups, but, conversely, trust is problematical in police and court organizations. When police and probation officers cultivate trust, it is likely to be for instrumental reasons, and it easily deteriorates into exploitation. This is in contrast with the family, where parent-child relations fluctuate, get repaired, and leave room for forgiveness and mutual sharing of blame. In the school the nonconforming child may still find a basis for accommodation and trust with teachers. To a very limited degree this is even possible between police and street youth. Not so, however, for the juvenile court, whose formal decisions and actions are clothed with finality, and whose errors must be laboriously proved by appeal. There are no procedures by which a juvenile court can admit openly that it has been wrong, nor does its charter allow it to make reparations.

Awareness of the fateful nature of juvenile court processing on the part of judges and probation officers helps explain the large proportion of cases that are dismissed, continued, or assigned to informal supervision. From what has been said it seems plain that the bulk of such cases should have been previously normalized or defined as problems other than delinquency. However, their presence and processing through to disposition reflect efforts of court personnel to solve their own dilemmas. They provide means to satisfy the extraneous claims making up the overburden of the court, to validate its presumptions of treatment, and to quiet public demands for repressing delinquency. At the same time some protection and individualized consideration are given children and parents.

IMPLICATIONS FOR PUBLIC POLICY

Examination of the juvenile court from several perspectives leaves it painfully clear that too often it seeks to do things best not done; it undertakes ambitious tasks without available means and it fails to apply means at hand to clearly defined ends. Moreover, the juvenile court aggravates many problems it tries to ameliorate, and, in an undetermined number of cases, it furthers delinquent careers.

Questions of public policy raised by these criticisms are twofold: (1) whether some of the actions of children and parents now subject to definition as delinquency or unfitness should not be conceived as nonproblematical and either ignored or written off simply as part of the inevitable, everyday problems of living and growing up; (2) whether many of the problems now considered as delinquency or preludes to delinquency should not be defined as family, educational, or welfare problems, and diverted away from the juvenile court into other community agencies.

The first question resolves itself into other questions, mainly relating to what kinds of youthful actions and family situations should be used to make such determinations. The diversity of American culture and shifting public opinion makes substantive answers to these questions difficult. In general terms, however, it appears that the emphasis should be on *conduct* and its *manifest consequences*. Other criteria obviously applicable are those of *recurrency* and *injury to self and others*. The stance of the juvenile court should be nonintervention; the standards of proof should be high; the burden of proof should rest on those seeking intervention.

The second question comes with cases in which a serious problem is demonstrably present, but there is good reason to believe that it can be worked out in other than the authoritative setting of the court. Here the special laws applicable only to children should be closely reexamined, with a view primarily to their abolition or substantial revision in that direction. Leaving aside the emotionally charged topic of drug use by minors, the time is past due for overhauling laws governing the use of alcohol by minors. The same is true for laws dealing with the curfew, the possession of knives, and some forms of theft. Truancy, runaways, incorrigibility, beyond control, and lewd or immoral conduct all refer to problems which according to our line of thinking are least amenable to control by law and the most likely candidates for other kinds of social control.[26] For these problems are almost always matters of arbitrary definition; in a wide range of instances they reflect normal reactions of maturing youth to arbitrary authority or other intolerable conditions. Finally, in an equally impressive number of cases they are simply a guise for transferring or "dumping" problems from one institutional setting to another, concealing reasons which are unclear, indefensible, or both.

Changes in public policy aimed at narrowing the jurisdiction of the juvenile court and limiting the range of problems definable as delinquency can be formed by appellate rulings, legislation, and finding new ways of administering the law. In the past, appeals from juvenile court decisions have not been influential in constraining unwise action by juvenile courts, and it remains to be seen what the full effects of the U.S. Supreme Court ruling in the Gault case will be. It is more likely that relevant changes will have to come from State legislation and local administration. Yet there is risk that passage of statutes to restrict the volume of cases reaching juvenile courts may miss their targets if they do no more than describe new substantive bases for jurisdiction, for the reason that complainants as well as juvenile court personnel are likely to rationalize or define their problems in whatever terms the new statutes state. More effective constraints lie in new procedural or adjective law.

Such procedural requirements include intake screening, detention hearings, bifurcated hearings, sharp separation of findings of fact and information related to dispositions, official records, advice as to right to counsel, provision of counsel, and limitations on dispositions according to the type of jurisdiction assumed by the court. Many changes along this line have already been made in various States.

Probably the most revolutionary change under way in the present-day

---

[26] See Sol Rubin, Legal definitions of offenses by children and youths, *Illinois Law Forum*, 1960, Vinter, 512–523; Alfred Kahn, Sociology and social work—challenge and invitation, *Social Problems*, 1957, 4, 220–228.

juvenile courts is the entree and presence of counsel in a growing number of cases. Increasingly aggressive advocacy has had direct effects on procedures, among them delays, complications, and increased costs. In areas where this has been occurring—California juvenile courts, for example—a general result is to move the courts closer to a kind of negotiated, plea-bargaining justice similar to that which has evolved in adult criminal courts.[27]

Two important changes in our larger society are encouraging the exercise by juveniles and parents of their rights to counsel and vigorous defense in juvenile court, changes which combine to push the courts toward a more narrowly conceived agency, dealing primarily with serious law violations. One of these is the heightened sensitivity of minority populations to real or fancied abuses of police power and to civil rights issues. The other is the swelling numbers of youth apprehended for violating narcotics laws, many of whom have middle-class status. Among the consequences of the first change is a greater likelihood—particularly of Negroes in ghetto areas—of resistance to arrest, or even attacks on police. This means that arrests for minor offenses lead to secondary charges of interfering with police or assault. Protracted hearings follow, necessitating evaluation of conflicting testimony and extensive arguments over the law of arrest.

The situation regarding the enforcement of narcotics laws is one of imbalance, in which the stringency of penalties has outstripped the social harm of the offenses. The threat of prison makes engaging or assignment of counsel commonplace. Defense, at times helped by a sympathetic judge or prosecutor, tends to exploit technicalities of the law as a means of rebalancing the scales of justice. Hence, the excesses of legislators seeking to stamp out the "drug evil" may well have the unanticipated effects of making the juvenile court more legalistic, more like a criminal court.

However, this seems unlikely to happen solely through changes in law and increased use of counsel. Such a view overplays the influence of law in producing changes, particularly more positive and constructive changes needed to lessen the overburden of the juvenile court. It is doubtful that problems of overload and the overreach of law can be solved unilaterally so long as juvenile courts are part of a reciprocating system of community and State agencies and so long as parents and individuals can freely initiate court action. It is also questionable whether public opinion will be favorable to withdrawal of juvenile courts from many problem areas without some new forms of control coming into being.

In sociological terms it can be said that if something is removed from a reciprocating system of groups, something must be put back. Hence if the problem domain of the juvenile court is to be made smaller and more specialized, other definitions of youth problems need to be developed and new means invented to deal with them. This can be accomplished by reorganizing existing agency resources or by inventing new types of organization, or both. In both instances the organizational principle or objective will be that of bypassing the juvenile court process.

[27] See Edwin M. Lemert, *op. cit.*

THE LAW ENFORCEMENT MODEL

A community service worker, discussing with the author ways of diverting youth from juvenile courts, commented that "The police are the best delinquency prevention agency we have." This he meant in a very direct and literal sense, to wit, that since police make decisions about arrests and also make the great majority of referrals to juvenile courts, theirs is the strategic power to determine what proportions and what kinds of youth problems become official and which ones are absorbed back into the community. This becomes a very persuasive reason for constructing diversion models around police organization and operations; a further pragmatic argument in their favor is that any plan which does not allow substantial recognition and satisfaction of law enforcement values risks being ignored, indirectly undermined, or openly resisted. Police understandably are unlikely to remain quiescent if they believe that a diversion system is being used to protect serious law violators or to act as a shield behind which delinquent gangs or "subcultures" are perpetuated. Nor will police rest easy with methods of handling delinquencies which hamper their appointed tasks of clearing offenses and recovering property.

THE NATURE OF THE LAW ENFORCEMENT MODEL

In its essentials the law enforcement model consists of specialized organization and practices integral to a police department, sheriff's department, or probation department. It also includes special techniques used to adjust problems of juveniles without court action. Generally these are outgrowths of discretion police have to arrest or not arrest offenders. The most common differentiation of police organization for this purpose is in the form of juvenile bureaus or fixed assignments of juvenile officers. Characteristic methods of the exercising of police discretion in handling juveniles are screening, counseling, surveillance, and referrals.

Screening is the process whereby minors suspected of law violations or delinquent tendencies are interviewed, a search made for the existence of prior police or court contacts, records evaluated, and decisions reached about what to do with the case in hand. A rough kind of screening takes place in any or most police-juvenile contacts, but ordinarily it presupposes some kind of juvenile bureau and access to a record system. Here and there in less populated areas screening is done by consultation with a probation department. Cruiser patrolmen in large cities where electronic equipment is available can get needed information by car radio and make necessary decisions to release or take a youth to police headquarters.

Screening is a practical necessity in large urban jurisdictions because far more complaints against minors are made than action can be taken on or can be processed. However, screening is also motivated by beliefs of police that youthful offenders have a great potential for reformation or that they deserve a "second chance." Added to this is a conviction that rehabilitation is possible at the police level. Screening results in about one-half of all minors who come to the attention of police nationwide being "handled within the department," i.e., released or otherwise dealt with short of referral to juvenile court.

Ideally, screening out cases of juveniles whose infractions are not serious enough to refer them to juvenile court but not so innocuous as to dismiss should result in some kind of assistance or treatment. The choice then becomes one of the police doing the job or referring such cases to other agencies. While there are some jurisdictions, such as Los Angeles and Chicago, in which police have worked out elaborate referral systems, evidence for the Nation as a whole reveals that police referrals elsewhere than to juvenile courts are infrequent. One survey showed that 253 out of 498 police departments referred children to other agencies: to schools in 211, to religious workers in 195, and to welfare agencies in 210 jurisdictions.[28] However, such figures are misleading, because the overall national percentage of cases referred to nonlegal agencies is nominal, 1.6 percent according to an FBI estimate in 1964.[29] Police seem to be neither organized nor inclined to make referrals to outside agencies, which speaks of a possible dilemma or defect in reliance upon police diversion models.

DO-IT-YOURSELF SOCIAL WORK—SPURIOUS MODELS

Beginning sometime in the 1930s, police departments of many larger population centers began to enter the field of prevention and social treatment of delinquency. This trend probably came from a recognition of growing erosion of informal family and community self-help procedures for dealing with juvenile problems and a shortage or inappropriateness of welfare facilities for the purpose. Also, New Deal philosophy and legislation during this era undermined political patronage arrangements which had mitigated the formal procedures of dealing with juvenile crime.

Some of the direct services police undertook for minors and their families were in the form of social investigations and casework-type treatment in which women police workers played an important role. Big Brother programs were organized by police on the assumption that avuncular-type relationships between a juvenile and a policeman or other adult would keep the youth from delinquency. Capitalizing on the prevalent though questionable idea that participation in recreational activities would have a preventive effect on those inclined toward delinquency, police also sponsored athletic leagues for youth in city areas where risk of delinquency was statistically high. Finally, systematic surveillance was undertaken of special community institutions typically associated with delinquency and child neglect— junkyards, pawnshops, poolrooms, and liquor outlets.

The Juvenile Aid Bureau set up in New York City in 1930 may be

[28] *Police Services for Juveniles*, U.S. Department of Health, Education, and Welfare, 195 Washington, D.C., p. 86.

[29] *Uniform Crime Reports*, Federal Bureau of Investigation, Washington, D.C., 1964, p. 102.

regarded as a prototype of police social work. The Bureau was directed by a Deputy Police Inspector and was divided into nine geographic areas of the city. The staff included policewomen and policemen, who were given social work training. Responsibility was taken for all minors under 21 years who were brought to the attention of the police but who were not arrested. Forms were completed for each such case which was then directed to the appropriate area office. Records were consulted and if the case was active with some agency, that agency was notified and no further action followed. Otherwise, parents of the minor were contacted and admonished, or a complete social investigation was made and some kind of treatment initiated. The Bureau also sponsored a police athletic league and directed surveillance in the community.

In 1943 a program of Precinct Coordinating Councils was launched. In 1954 these became known as Precinct Youth Councils, in charge of commanding officers in precincts, who recruit Council members and direct Council activities under departmental policy of the Juvenile Aid Bureau. Programs include environmental study, community relations, education, social service, and recreation.[30]

POLICE PROBATION

Another development, less oriented to social work and more toward correctional rehabilitation, is that of police probation, also called "voluntary supervision," or "on report." This system works under informal agreements between police, juvenile law violators, and parents, whereby the minor reports periodically at police headquarters for interviews. These may be combined with arrangements for restitution and the laying down of conditions restricting the movements of the minor, such as "grounding" practiced in one city. This system requires that a youth attend school unless excused by a physician, leave his house only in the company of his parents, dress conventionally, keep his hair cut to a reasonable length, and study at home for prescribed periods daily.[31]

THE LIVERPOOL POLICE JUVENILE LIAISON SCHEME

Yet another type of police diversionary plan, midway between social work counseling and informal probation, got its start in Liverpool, England, in 1949. Its fundamentals are outlined in general directives laid down by the Chief Constable to officers singled out to give special attention to divisions of the city known to have high crime rates. They were to:

> . . . concern themselves with the prevention of juvenile crime by establishing liaison with school teachers, ministers of religion, social workers and similar people concerned with the welfare of children, seeking the cooperation of the

[30] Kenneth Beam, Organization of the community for delinquency prevention, *The Juvenile Aid Bureau of the New York City Police Department,* 1943.

[31] Juvenile delinquents: The police, state courts and individualized justice, *Harvard Law Review,* 79, 1966, 784.

Probation Service, keeping in regular contact with children who have been cautioned and where possible, introducing them into the membership of clubs or similar youth organizations. Stress also was laid on home visiting, contact and discussion with parents and regular pooling of experiences at monthly conferences presided over by the Chief or Deputy Chief Constable.[32]

Staff for the English scheme gradually expanded from an original two officers until by 1965 it had two sergeants and seventeen constables (four of them policewomen) under the direction of a Chief Inspector. Among the first effective liaisons was that set up with the managers of department stores and shops in the center of the city. This brought to attention a number of instances of shoplifting and pilfering by children, who were not being brought to juvenile court because the merchants could not afford to take the time or release staff to appear as witnesses. Recovery of stolen property at the time had sufficed.

With passing time, the juvenile liaison officers more and more focused on "near" and "potential" offenders, specifically meaning boys and girls who had truanted from school, who were "unruly," "out of control," or "frequenting undesirable places." The working patterns of the officers took shape in regular home visits to interview parents and child, school visits to check on attendance, and "keeping a watchful eye" on the local areas in order to get to know personally as many youngsters as possible, along with key people in the localities. The content of home interviews generally was a mixture of cautioning, admonition, and fatherly advice.[33]

CRITICISMS FROM WITHIN AND FROM WITHOUT

The popularity of police-style social work and police probation in the United States waxed, then waned, to the extent that many leaders in the police field reject the conceptions completely.[34] This clearly was the position of former Chief Parker of the Los Angeles Police Department, who stated that he did not believe that prevention of crime was a proper police function.[35]

Some of the criticisms which have been levied against direct treatment of delinquents by police are as follows:

1. Police officers are neither selected nor trained for preventive work.

2. Adequate treatment requires training skills and education that the average policeman cannot be expected to have.

3. A police department is best suited to apprehension and screening, making the best referral possible to existing agencies or to juvenile court.

4. If a community lacks treatment facilities, the role of the police department is to cooperate with others in an effort to gain such facilities, but not to develop them.

[32] J. B. Mays, The Liverpool Police juvenile liaison officer scheme, *The Sociological Review*, 1965, 186.

[33] *Op. cit.*, p. 188.

[34] George W. O'Connor and Nelson A. Watson, *Juvenile Delinquency and Youth Crime: the Police Role*, International Association of Chiefs of Police, 1964, p. 42.

[35] O. W. Wilson, ed., *Parker on Police*, Springfield, Ill.: Charles C Thomas, 1957, p. 12.

5. A voluntary police supervision program duplicates other services and wastes taxpayers' money.
6. Police departments are not appropriate settings for treating children.
7. Voluntary police supervision has no legal basis.
8. Voluntary police supervision complicates the work of probation departments because referrals from such probation may have to be handled as first offenders.[36]

Similar criticisms have been directed at the Liverpool liaison scheme, in addition to which some English critics point out that the scheme may be so operated to keep youth from obtaining services that they need. But despite its controversial status in England and its limited adoption there and in Scotland, the scheme continues to have its partisans. Teachers are strongly in favor of the liaison work and some in the Probation Service also have voiced their approval. Perhaps the strongest favorable argument is that timely intervention of the police at critical points into the careers of marginal or near-delinquents may lend the extra measure of help or authority needed to forestall further deviance. This argument rests upon two assumptions: (1) that the police discriminate accurately between serious deviance and trivial deviance that can be ignored, and (2) that deviance defined as marginal police problems is not transitional, will not disappear by itself, and will not be solved by other means if left alone. Yet the evolving emphasis put on "marginal" problems makes it difficult to believe that the liaison scheme does not make problems of actions which would go unheeded by the community if police held to strict legal standards of delinquency. Indeed, this seems to be avowed rather candidly:

> Thus from a very early date the J. L. O.s were concerned with a number of young delinquents who had hitherto been escaping the official net. Their work helped to draw the mesh tighter to bring to light a number of hitherto unknown and marginal-offenders.[37]

Whether police social work normalizes youthful deviance or whether it successfully treats problems which are defined as marginal or unofficial are questions yet to be researched in the United States. Some data have been published to show that trends in rates of juvenile court cases rose more slowly in Liverpool than for England and Wales as a whole following installation of the liaison scheme. Unfortunately, these figures concealed the fact that large numbers of slum-dwelling families were moved from the central city to new housing areas outside its boundaries during the years covered by the study. Crime rates in these sections soared forthwith.[38]

An important consideration in assessing the effects of police screening and various kinds of police treatment is the use to which information gathered in the process is put in subsequent police contacts and juvenile court referrals. An efficient recording system and conscientious patrolmen may mean that a police record is built up whose existence influences the way

---

[36] *Police Services for Juveniles, op. cit.*, pp. 24–27.
[37] J. B. Mays, *op. cit.*, p. 187.
[38] *Ibid.*, pp. 197–198.

in which later actions of the minor are perceived. This takes on real signifi-cance when it is recognized that decisions of officers to write up a field report for some youths and not for others may be either fortuitous or negatively biased by the nature of the area and by status factors. In a similar way, the records made of dispositions of police hearings may affect later contacts which juveniles so involved have with police or probation officers.

POLICE INTERACTION WITH JUVENILES

Research on police contacts with juveniles has shown a number of factors that affect reactions of police to juvenile suspects and their choice of disposi-tions, including the instant offense, age, sex, prior record, appearance and demeanor, and family status. A serious offense is apt to cause an officer to take a youth into custody without weighing other factors, but lacking such a charge, discretion occurs, with on-the-spot screening. In the field, informa-tion on prior record may not be available, in which case the minor's appear-ance and demeanor become decisive. Older youth, those with leather jackets, long hair, and shabby clothes, and Negroes are said to be at a disadvantage before a suspicious officer. Truculence, sullenness, posture, and gestures may mark the youth as uncooperative and cause him to be taken into custody.[39] This, of course, can be interpreted as prejudice on the part of the officer, but also as evidence of his need to act decisively once his authority is put in issue.

More precisely formulated research on police-juvenile interaction has shown that decisions to arrest juveniles are greatly affected by the presence and preferences of a complainant. Arrests are more frequent when the complainant is present and when he urges strong action. Arrests of Negro juveniles are of a much higher percentage (21 percent) in such contacts than they are of whites (8 percent) when complainants are present during the encounters. White complainants differ markedly in their preference for informal dispositions (leniency) in contrast to Negro complainants. A major-ity (69 percent) of the latter prefer to have the youth arrested or else leave their preference unclear, in contrast to whites, a majority of whom (58 percent) are amenable to informal disposition of the cases.[40]

The research referred to here does not raise the question as to why attitudes of Negro complainants are less lenient than whites. It may be speculated, however, that Negro victims of juvenile offenders are less able to absorb property losses due to delinquency, or that they have fewer resources to protect themselves from juvenile depradations, and hence are inclined to rely more on police. Again, it may be that in more Negro than white cases there is no responsible family unit to accept informal responsibility for restitution or future control.

---

[39] Irvin Piliavin and Scott Briar, Police encounters with juveniles, *American Journal of Sociology* 70, 1964, 206–214.
[40] Donald Black and Albert Reiss, Police control of juveniles, 1969, Yale Law School, Program in Law and Social Science, mimeographed.

POLICE HEARINGS

A police model for diversion probably must be constructed around whatever potential effects brief, intense, authoritative contacts with juveniles have for the deterrence and control of deviance. Police are salient agents of legal authority and are so conceived by complainants and misdoers alike. At one extreme involving adult suspects and older, serious delinquents, this authority is routinely exercised by arrest. At the other extreme, with very young children and those engaging in trivial misdeeds, there is routine normalization either by dismissal or brief custodial attention pending return of a child to parents. In between these extremes, police "treat" law violators by special definitions of their behavior and the show of authority. Definitions are characterological, that is, of the youth rather than of his behavior. This is clearly demonstrated when the same offense produces variable definitions of the individual offenders who are involved.[41] The common thrust of the attendant interaction is to secure admissions of guilt or complicity. Such admissions are believed by the police to be an indispensable first step to reformation, but their more important symbolic effect is to define the youth as a repentant deviant, and thus to validate the moral authority of the police.[42] Once this happens, police are free to exercise discretion and try to dramatize the meaning of the deviance as a two-valued antecedent to subsequent behavior: criminal versus law-abiding.

Dramatization of authority may be done in the field by patrolmen or squad car officers, who engage in a range of behavior, from clever through heated acting to acute personal involvement. In many American police jurisdictions dramatization of authority takes place through well-structured hearing procedures, which in many respects are the analogues of probation intake or juvenile court hearings. There are formal notices to parents and minors setting the time and place for the meeting with a "hearing officer" who is seated impressively behind a desk. Such officers are chosen for their special ability to charm (con) adolescents; sometimes there are two, one who plays the "bad guy," the other the "good guy."

Dispositions hinge on officers' judgments as to whether more offenses are likely to occur, or whether parents can take necessary steps to contain the problem. The hearing procedure will not work without a confession, although this does not in itself guarantee that the case will be diverted from court. Leverage both to insure attendance at hearings and for confessions derives from actual or implied threats to create a permanent police record or to refer the case to juvenile court. If a youth refuses to confess, referral to the court usually follows unless the case is so factually poor that it will be embarrassing to the police. This is done to sustain the effectiveness of the

---

[41] For a study of the processes of typification, see Aaron Cicourel, *The Social Organization of Juvenile Justice,* New York: John Wiley & Sons, 1968.
[42] See Joseph Gusfield, Moral passage: The symbolic process in public designations of deviance, *Social Problems,* 1967, 15, 175–188.

referral threat. Another reason is the possibility of judicial repercussions if the police were to insist on treatment in the face of denial of the offense.[43]

Despite good intentions of those who administer it, such a system can work to the disadvantage of lower-class youths and Negroes. For one thing, lower-class parents more than others are prone to seek police assistance in the disciplining of their children; also, misconduct of youths in slum or ghetto areas has a higher visibility than elsewhere because these areas are more heavily policed. Too, shabbily dressed youths or Negroes moving outside their own areas may be suspect because of their appearance. Outcomes of police hearings are more unfavorable to lower-class youths because they are less apt to have intact families or families which can mobilize resources to solve the problems of their deviance. Negro youth not only more than share the handicaps of low social status, they more frequently make the system work against them by their hostile and enigmatic manner in the presence of police.

POLICE AND THE COMMUNITY

Generalizations of the sort made above are subject to the serious reservation that proportions of police contacts which get normalized or handled unofficially vary greatly from one jurisdiction to another—sometimes as much as 100 percent. Such differences are largely a function of differences in police organization and in the degree to which they are integrated in a cultural sense with the community areas whose populations they police. They are also associated with cultural differentiation of the police themselves and with variable policies of departments as to what kinds of deviance will or will not be adjusted internally.[44]

Data shedding a good deal of light on how differing patterns of organization and police styles affect the processing of juvenile deviants are provided by Wilson's study of these matters in "Eastern" and "Western" cities. The key difference between police in these two cities lay in the degree of their professionalization, highly developed in Western city, weak or absent in Eastern city. This is taken to account for the high arrest rate of juveniles in the West and the low rate in the East.

Juvenile officers in Western city were recruited on a nonlocal basis, and a high percentage had out-of-State origins. They were reasonably well educated, having completed at least high school; a good portion had gone to college several years or had graduated. Western city officers were well dressed, well officed, well equipped, and in general, efficient and businesslike in their manner. All of this was in contrast to Eastern city juvenile officers. Western officers had technical training in dealing with juveniles, and generally applied universalistic, impersonal criteria to decision making

[43] The police, the State courts and individualized justice, *op. cit.*

[44] Bordua cites evidence questioning the existence of socioeconomic bias in police discretion in dealing with juveniles, which evidence points to great variation in police discretion from place to place and time to time. His impression that variation is more significant than bias seems plausible enough. David Bordua, Recent trends: Deviant behavior and social control, *Annals of American Academy of Political and Social Science*, 1967, 57, 149–163.

and action. Eastern city police received their training informally from other officers, primarily in "how to get along on the force." Their decisions tended to be particularistic, personalized, and were made by considering each case in its local context.

Organization of juvenile officers in Western city was centralized in a bureau, where investigating or arresting officers turned over cases to be processed and disposed of by other juvenile officers. Supervision and accountability were insured by a captain, lieutenant, and sergeant. Standards also were informally reinforced by continuous association with other juvenile officers; private lives of the officers were pretty much dissociated from their work.

In Eastern city individual juvenile officers were assigned to precinct stations and no centralized supervision over juvenile matters existed. Juvenile officers kept their own records as they saw fit, made decisions about their cases, and presented them in court. This lack of procedure is burdensome and tends to cut down on the number of court cases. Informal association with regular patrolmen in the precinct station deters rather than encourages taking youth into custody, because such patrolmen look down on the arrests of juveniles; they are not "good pinches," and bringing a child to the station provokes derogatory remarks or offers to help hold a "desperate criminal."

It is highly significant that many Eastern city police were "locals"; they had been recruited from the same or similar lower- and lower-middle class neighborhoods which they policed. Local lore is that "half those in such neighborhoods go to reform school and the other half join the police or fire department." Parenthetically it can be said that the ideal of "new careers" in retrospect has long been a reality among the ethnic-dominated police forces of Eastern cities.

The origins of Western city juvenile officers together with their commitment to education gave force to values placed by middle-class whites on police efficiency, honesty, freedom from political corruption, and "good government." Such values were reflected in the stress placed on procedures which were assumed could be applied by any properly trained juvenile officer. Impersonal methods were substituted for intimate knowledge of neighborhoods and of particular individuals. It thus is possible to speak of routinized alienation of Western city juvenile officers, attested to by their high arrest and detention rates for juveniles and their preferences for a hard police style, such as using official marked cars for transporting juveniles. Their techniques lead Wilson to liken them to an "army of occupation organized along paramilitary lines."[45]

While heeding the danger of romanticizing the old-style "beat cop" who played the role of the wise neighborhood mediator, it is clear that a strong tendency to normalize juvenile misconduct is closely associated with Eastern city "fraternal"-type police organization. Built into this pattern is a special

[45] James Q. Wilson, The police and the delinquent in two cities, in *Controlling Delinquents*, Stanton Wheeler, ed., New York: John Wiley & Sons, 1968, Chapter 2; George O'Connor and Nelson Watson, *Juvenile Delinquency and Youth Crime: The Police Role*, Washington, D.C.: International Association of Chiefs of Police, 1964, Chapter 6.

regard for ethnic family solidarity, missing among Western professionals. This Eastern pattern favors a greater release rate of offenders back to families, but it also militates against normalization of offenses by Negroes. Negroes fall outside of the pattern; as recent arrivals they were looked upon by Eastern juvenile officers as alien, secretive, vicious, criminally inclined, and lacking in home life. Hence their greater chance of going to juvenile court.

If this line of analysis is correct, it concludes that professionalization of police in current form is antithetical to the objective of diverting youths away from the official court system. In Western city, as in an undetermined number of other areas, it is probable that greater percentages of lower-class youth are referred to juvenile court than in Eastern city. While the percentages of arrested Negro juveniles who are referred to court does not appear to differ from corresponding percentages of white juveniles, nevertheless the rate of Negro juveniles referred to court based on population is much greater. Hence, even allowing for a possibly higher deviance rate, Negro youths are at a disadvantage under both police systems.

White lower-class youths benefit from more lenient dispositions in Eastern city in comparison to the Western city situation, but middle-class white youths seem to occupy a "good" position under both systems. From the standpoint of model building, the problem is to pull out factors or processes which operate to normalize middle-class white delinquency and see if their functional equivalents can be devised to increase chances of normalizing the behavior of Negro and lower-class white youths at odds with the law.

COMMUNITY ABSORPTION, MIDDLE-CLASS STYLE

Community absorption is the constructive aspect of police discretion. It stands for active steps taken to restore or remedy problem situations involving juveniles, parents, neighbors, victims, and complainants which have come to police attention. Absorption may be initiated by police or it may come from parental action or through the offices of mediators in the community. The following case may be taken as illustrative:

> Several teenage males changed the license plates on a small European sports car which was parked outside a garage awaiting repairs. They drove the car late at night through the suburbs of the medium-sized city where they lived and finally were stopped by the police, who cited them to the probation department on several charges, and then released them to their parents. The car was taken to the police storage. The father of the leader of the boys phoned the proprietor of the garage, who immediately travelled downtown and retrieved the car. When the car's owner showed up next day, the proprietor, who was repairing a cabin cruiser he had sold to the father, told him what had happened and added that the repairs on his car, undamaged by the boys, would cost him nothing. Mollified but curious, the car owner inquired at police headquarters about the car theft, where he was told that because no stolen car report had been filed, no charge of theft had been made. Later the boy's case was dismissed by the probation officer when it was determined that no restitution was necessary.

While the case does not exemplify diversion in a complete sense, nevertheless it shows something of how the absorption of juvenile problems is managed: quick action to take advantage of a bureaucratic police procedure, connivance between a father and self-interested proprietor, and bribing or "cooling out" the victim and potential complainant. The result was to scale down the charge for a moderately serious offense to a trivial one and forestall official action by the juvenile court.

EXPERIMENT IN COMMUNITY ABSORPTION

Possibilities of action to sustain and extend normalization by community action were brought to light in a study of two middle-class predominantly white suburbs in Contra Costa County, California—in the east San Francisco Bay Area. One community, Lafayette, is incorporated and policed by sheriff's deputies; the other, Pleasant Hill, is unincorporated, but policed by the sheriff's department under a contractual agreement. High rates of delinquency absorption in the two communities are made evident by comparison with proportions of police-adjusted juvenile cases for the Nation and State, which in 1966 ran slightly below 50 percent. In contrast, nearly 80 percent of youth cases in Lafayette and Pleasant Hill were dealt with in the sheriff's department, and then released.[46] According to the investigators, these figures indicate a pattern of reaction not confined to police, but one which permeates the whole way of life of the communities, "in their mores" as it were.

Vandalism and malicious mischief such as breaking windows, stealing bicycles, knocking over mailboxes, and discoloring swimming pools are seldom reported to the police, but instead are matters for restitution and settlement between parents, or they are written off against homeowners insurance policies. Youngsters having school difficulties customarily are transferred to military academies, parochial schools, or continuation schools. Cases of teenage pregnancy and venereal infections rarely end up in agencies for unwed mothers or official health agencies. Rather, girls are taken to foreign countries for abortions and their disease is treated by private physicians. Recidivism in these communities holds at a low rate.[47]

The experiment in question was designed to augment the deviance absorption processes in these communities, and was organized to counteract a perceptible increase in delinquency. The experiment ran more in the direction of community organization via creation of youth councils than it did toward furthering the police adjustment practices, but several of its features are worth noting as examples of deliberate efforts to redefine youthful deviance. The most impressive was the establishment of motorcycle clubs with two objectives in mind: to reshape the behavior of youthful bike riders, but also to change the ominous stereotype (Hell's Angels) of such groups held by adults. A related effort was the "legitimation" of a secret teenage

[46] Robert. Carter, *Middle Class Delinquency—An Experiment in Delinquency Control,* Berkeley: School of Criminology, 1968, p. 20.
[47] *Ibid.,* pp. 23–24.

boys club which had acquired a reputation for heavy drinking and assaultive behavior, reinforced by the death of a 19-year-old youth at a swim club dance, allegedly caused by a secret club member. Legitimation consisted of giving the club official sponsorship.[48]

The idea of community cooptation of delinquent groups and gangs is not new. What is new is the idea of bringing adult groups and deviant groups together with the idea of *mutual change* in conceptions of deviance held by adults and in the expression of deviance by the youths. Apart from a police-youth discussion group, police were not directly involved in the cooptative ventures, although their acquiescence obviously was needed. Community absorption becomes integral to the police model when it affects practices and policies in making arrests and referrals, police procedures in street contacts with juveniles, or their intervention in neighborhood and family conflicts. On these points, unfortunately, the study in question gives no details.

The increasing rationalization of police organization and the reliance of juvenile officers on a kind of one-shot interview or hearing strategy necessarily leaves a vacuum between police and the community. This is keenly felt in lower-class areas and Negro ghettoes. The problem in such places can be put as one of balancing opportunities for community absorption through the simulation and implementation of a special culture or organization that does the job for middle-class suburban areas.

THE POLICE-COMMUNITY RELATIONS AIDE MODEL

The police-community relations aide model seeks to fill in the lacunae between police and the community, linking police with the community by employing persons of lower-class and minority ethnic origins in a kind of detached police unit. These aides take up cases after the police, either finding needed services for problem youths or providing the services themselves.

Development of a unit along these lines was begun in the Oakland Police Department in 1965, largely from outside pressures; it was facilitated by funds from the Office of Economic Opportunity and a program of "new careers" for the unemployed. Police interviewed recruits while social workers supplied paraprofessional training for them: there was joint supervision by police and the project staff. At first, difficulties arose because of conflicting conceptions of the purposes of the project and a lack of real interest on the part of the police. Later the project was placed under a Human Relations Officer in the police department, which gave it consistent direction and also enlisted police motivation to support its work.

Among activities of the police aides were:

1. Mediation in neighborhood quarrels. Done by display of personal interest, marshaling local opinion, involving many people, and day-by-day overseeing of the situation.

2. Enrolling youths in clubs.

[48] *Ibid.*, p. 55.

3. Obtaining parttime work for their cases, especially for thieves.
4. Obtaining medical care or increased welfare benefits for youths and families.
5. "Cooling out" irate parents.
6. Getting a youth transferred to another school or placed in a continuation school.
7. Obtaining an early release from probation for clients.

Police-community relations aides also were used in at least one instance as observers and agents to try to eliminate open gambling in a public park, an issue which had stirred a number of complaints. As a result of their work, one boy was dispatched via juvenile court to a probation camp. However, this kind of employment of the aides brought disapproval from social workers connected with the project.

The project, like that in Lafayette and Pleasant Hill, set up police-youth discussions, with somewhat similar results. At first the police attending saw the sessions as occasions to impose rules in a didactic manner. This did not work well, but in time the police came around to letting the youths use meetings for expressive purposes. What further effects this may have had are not known.

THE LAW ENFORCEMENT BASE

Whether police departments are the best base on which to build or attach an absorption program may be questioned. In some areas where they are still viable it may be preferable to devise a model based on sheriff's departments, which historically have been more inclined to dispense a sort of informal justice in which restitution and handing back discipline to families of offenders has prevailed. Yet in some counties, sheriffs' departments have sought to pass juvenile problems on to probation departments. In the early history of the Oakland aide project, police felt that it properly belonged in the probation department. Here and there Chief Probation Officers have talked of schemes for placing a deputy or deputies at police stations so that more time could be had to investigate cases of runaways, for example, without the necessity of filing juvenile court petitions.

An inventive plan having diversionary features, which is located in a branch probation department but relies on cooperation from sheriffs' deputies, is the Watoto (Swahili for "children") project in East Palo Alto and Menlo Park, California. It came into being as a semiautonomous division of probation under direction of a Negro deputy, ostensibly to counteract the "bad image" the Department had in the black communities. Behind this was a broader purpose of enlisting community members to help in various ways to keep youths from becoming court cases or to assist those on probation. Needless to say, a strong theme of ethnicizing probation work was advanced by the black partisans of the project.

The staff of the project includes regular probation deputies, salaried new careerists, and volunteers. A sheriff's deputy is stationed at the Center, to which other deputies cite youths or bring them instead of delivering them to the county juvenile hall. At the Center youths may be counseled, in some cases by "community mothers." A variety of direct service methods not unlike those practiced by the Oakland police aides are used. Youngsters also are organized into groups and taken on recreational outings. A distinctive feature of all of this is encouragement for Negro youths to use the Center as a gathering place.[49]

In summary, this project is an elaborated informal probation system with a definite locale, serving an unincorporated area which is treated as a separate sheriff's precinct. One of the main problems in getting the project into operation was to persuade sheriff's deputies to cite youths to the Center in lieu of detention. This was accomplished by several city councilmen of East Palo Alto and the probation officer in charge, who persuaded the sheriff to give the system a trial. Police in Menlo Park did not respond with an equal degree of cooperation as did the sheriff's people.[50]

CONCLUSIONS

Indications for organizing diversion systems along the lines of a police model are strong. Police encounter youth problems more frequently than other community agencies; they meet the problems at the time of their occurrence, and they wield a great deal of coercive and symbolic authority to make deviance costly to juveniles and parents, as well as to define it on their own terms. Police methods, such as cautioning, counseling, supervision, threats, dramatized hearings, and suspended action, usually proceed from relatively uncomplicated moral conceptions of right conduct and respect for law (authority), without much specialized knowledge of human behavior and its treatment. Insofar as the net result of these is unofficial action, normalization takes place. Their effectiveness in preventing subsequent deviance probably is greatest among middle-class youths or those whose family situation and resources support remedial action. Police predictions that this will occur, in turn, affect discretion and the likelihood that adjustment rather than referral to court will be their choice.

Patterns of police organization, cultural backgrounds of juvenile officers, and the degree of their affinity and appreciation of the problems of classes of population they police all significantly affect the processes of discretion and normalization. The bias runs against lower-class youth in many areas but not in others; it seems to work most uniformly against Negroes in urban areas, but this probably is less a function of racial bias than of a number of

[49] Charles E. Range, *Watoto Project*, 1970, San Mateo Probation Department Juvenile Division, San Mateo, California, mimeographed.

[50] There are some other diversion schemes which more or less spin off from probation departments. In Los Angeles there has been discussion of using citizen professional committees to review Probation Department recommendations to see if nonofficial dispositions can be made of cases. Also, in 1945 the Monmouth County Plan was devised by probation officers in Asbury Park, New Jersey. This plan established committees appointed by the Juvenile Court judge to investigate, hear, and dispose of cases of truancy beyond control, malicious mischief, and other minor offenses. The court, police, and private parties may bring complaints. See *Manual for Guidance of Juvenile Conference Committees Appointed by the Juvenile and Domestic Relations Court*, Trenton, N.J., Administrative Office of the Courts, 1958.

other factors which interact in the discretionary process, the foremost being the presence and attitudes of complainants.

A police model of choice would reproduce conditions of normalization which work in middle-class white suburban communities. However, these conditions appear to be an inherent part of that life, albeit weakening with passing time. In slums and ethnic ghettos their equivalents must be contrived through novel means peculiar to localities. Some sort of irregular, detached unit, subordinate and responsible to law enforcement, staffed with paraprofessional workers, has a good deal to recommend it. Whether in the long run new careerists drawn from lower classes will prove adapted to the needs of such work is an open question. Their kind of work is very demanding and calls for a high level of dedication, which is difficult to sustain. Some of the things done for clients by new careerists, such as taking over welfare checks and personally making purchases, paying rent and other bills, are much like nineteenth-century social work, in which the worker "played God" to clients, and at the same time ensured continuance of their dependency.

Another more general, unsettled query confronts the militant ethnic motivations for projects like Watoto. The sectarian political emphasis raises doubts about freedom of the organization to evolve along rational lines, and it may be wondered whether individual needs are not likely to be sacrificed to political contingencies. There is a further risk that such organizations will turn into vehicles to expand opportunities for the black middle class. This contradiction is noted in the Watoto project, where new careerists turned out to be black college students. Once such projects get organized and legitimized they may follow the same dismal path as many other bureaucracies, as management finds it must compete for budget, personnel, and space; devise routines for handling large numbers of cases; and settle conflicts within the organization.

One conclusion standing out among others is that sheriffs' departments and probation departments are better foci for organizing diversion units than police, especially in less urbanized areas. This may be because they are less narrowly responsible for law enforcement and preservation of public order than are police. They are less bound by fixed policy, such as, for example, police rules that they "never adjust a felony."

The existence of gang delinquency and disturbances of public order by mass aggregations of youths pose special problems in respect to diversion. Police generally prefer to break up gangs rather than to try to coopt them through group work methods. This often means filing petitions on suspected gang leaders to get them sent to State institutions. Here the reverse of normalization can occur—something like "abnormalization"—in which a youth with no very serious record is stigmatized as a "troublemaker" or "young hood" and referred to court.

It is also true that police have dealt with youthful disturbances in some places by more or less sweeping large numbers of them into detention for curfew violations—called "weekenders." In other situations, where large numbers of youths flood into resort towns, police may have no way to contact parents or to get information that might avoid a court referral. Attempts have been made to organize extensive police surveillance of such youth masses but part-time police may have to be activated to get the manpower; their use of discretion may be poor and cause more rather than fewer court referrals.[51]

While a large percentage of children and youthful offenders running athwart the police can be safely dismissed out-of-hand or after an interview or hearing, there are others whose problems are such that they may need kinds of help which police or paraprofessional workers cannot give. Furthermore, it is very doubtful whether certain kinds of problems, now called delinquent tendencies, such as runaways, incorrigibility, and some types of sex problems, should ever be processed by the police at all. A more voluntaristic model which unites public and private welfare agencies or generates new agencies and services may be preferred to the law enforcement model.

IS THERE A BETTER IDEA?

Social scientists probably are at their best as institutional critics; they are more likely to know what does not work and what is unlikely to work than what will. When social invention is essayed, their productions are no less apt to be follies than those of others who struggle to solve the riddles of human problems. Hence it is with a proper measure of humility advised by what has or has not been learned from materials examined in this volume that the following are proposed as minimal considerations for the construction of a diversion model:

1. Diversion should be closely articulated with the workings of the juvenile justice system because that's what it is about.
2. Police should become the chief source of referrals to diversion agencies because that's where most official processing starts.
3. There should be positive gains to police from their making referrals.
4. Diversion agencies in large cities probably are best located near schools but not in them.
5. Serious truancy and cases of aggravated disciplinary problems should be referred routinely to diversion agencies. No school should be allowed to dismiss or suspend a child without finding that provision has been made for his continuing education or employment.
6. In unfit home cases, absence of home care, incorrigibility complaints by parents or school authorities, and moral danger cases, the police, sheriffs' departments, district attorneys, and probation departments should be compelled to find that no agency exists or none is willing to accept the cases before referring them to juvenile court or filing petitions.
7. Diversion agencies should reserve the right to reject cases but should not refer cases to the police or juvenile court.

Stated in more positive terms, the purpose of a diversion agency should be to preempt problems which otherwise would enter the juvenile justice sys-

---

[51] French police have experimented with "control missions" to handle masses of vacationing juveniles. See Jean Susini, Deux essais de prévention de la délinquance juvénile par la police française, *Revue de Science Criminelle et de Droit Pénal Comparé*, 1960, second series, 697–701.

tem. Its purpose should *not* be case finding; nor should it be the coordination of services. Rather it should be problem solving, conflict resolution, or the provision of services germane to the specific nature of the deviance and the imminence of official action. Special attention should be given to "making the victim whole" or satisfying complainants that "something is being done" about the problem. Mediation, arbitration, and restitution should be freely used. Finally, public relations techniques are recommended to dissipate spurious moral indignation, which often complicates nonofficial handling of delinquency.

Much of what has been suggested here pertains to jurisdictional matters and procedures and neglects to say what kind of an organization design is necessary for diversion. Yet this is a logical consequence of the kinds of questions asked throughout this monograph: What kinds of problems of children and youth should be officially recognized and what happens when they are? These are operational questions, not questions as to what can be done for or to minors. Therefore, the form of diversion agencies may not be too important so long as they are operationally oriented.

It may be most profitable to conceive of diversion as an integral part of a system—in this case, of the juvenile justice system. This poses a question as to what the juvenile justice system is and how cases flow into and out of it. Some believe that it can be defined by research:

> . . . there is need for a large scale program of action research involving person-nel at all levels focusing on connections between agencies, developing common information sources and data banks, predicting and testing ultimate goal oriented changes in each component as it affects the others.[52]

There are others who are less sanguine about the possibilities of "systems research" or who believe it is a snare or delusion. The debate is unsettled.

Meanwhile, it seems safest to hold that diversion of children and youth from the official court system is a state of mind; once it is established as a predominant social value, the question of adaptation of means to the end should be more easily answered.

---

[52] A. W. McEachern, A systems approach to juvenile delinquency, April 1969, Public Systems Research Institute, University of Southern California, manuscript.

9
THE ORGANIZATIONAL BUILDING UP
OF STIGMATIZING LABELS*

Kenneth Polk and Solomon Kobrin

The following paper is taken from a larger publication which was, in effect, a position statement for a federal agency. It places considerable emphasis on the socializing institutions which provide *legitimate* identities for youth. It is not sufficient merely to divert—to avoid stigmatizing experiences. One must also engage youth more successfully in positive identities by means of employment, educational, familial, and other community institutions. Obviously, a major implication of such an approach is the need to bring about significant changes within these socializing institutions.

* From *Delinquency Prevention Through Youth Development,* Youth Development and Delinquency Prevention Administration, U.S. Department of Health, Education and Welfare [Washington, D.C.: U.S. Government Printing Office, Publication No. (SRS) 72-26013, 1972], pp. 15–18. Reprinted by permission of the authors.

. . . There is a further complication, one which brings us to the juvenile justice-correctional system. Our institutions have come to serve as an analogue to radar, identifying potential or real deviants, "locking on" to them, and then progressively intensifying the process of negative labeling, especially (but not only) in the justice-corrections process. Thus, over the years records are accumulated and "files" built up. In many cases, these records pile up well before contact is made with police or court. School records especially, but also those of mental health, welfare, and other service agencies, are likely to have accumulated for "difficult" youngsters.

The point is that *even before* the young person encounters the court, there is likely to have been created grounds for questioning the individual's claims to legitimate status. Once such questions have been raised, there is a heightened likelihood that in his exposure to the justice-corrections system, a label denoting *official illegitimacy* will be applied.

What we encounter here is the possibility of what Lemert terms "secondary deviance," whereby the "helping" process actually becomes part of the problem. Using as an illustration the case of the juvenile court, Lemert observed:

One of the great paradoxes of organized society is that agencies of social control may exacerbate or perpetuate the very problems they seek to ameliorate. In so doing they foster conditions of secondary deviance. Such deviance evolves out of adaptations and attempted adaptations to the problems created by official reactions to original deviance. From this point of view the sanctions, dispositions, or "treatment" imposed by the juvenile court personnel too often simply add another series of problems to original problems of parents and children, then further stigmatize the failures to cope with the new problems. The specifics of this process lie in the reactions made to special status which sets wards apart and special conduct standards which hold them accountable in ways not expected of other children. Probation exemplifies this process, wherein a youth is forbidden to associate with persons he regards as his friends, a girl is barred from seeing her boyfriend, or a child is ordered not to see an "unfit" parent.[1]

Expanding on Lemert's ideas, there are two major problems that contribute to secondary deviation. First, the process itself frequently creates a new and additional set of rules which apply only to those in the deviant category, but which serve principally to expand the grounds whereby his behavior may be termed deviant:

> A teenager placed in a foster home is expected to obey orders of people who are strangers; the boy placed in a ranch school must tread a narrow path hedged with rules, many of which are drawn up with his potential deviance in mind. A youth may violate rules with perfectly good motives—to show loyalty to friends, to visit with a parent, or to look for employment. In other cases a boy may take leave from a ranch school because of problems beyond his power to solve. Yet the court typically defines such actions as "failures" or disobedience of its orders, which become legal justification for more severe measures whose effect is to move a minor farther along the road to correctional school.[2]

Second, each escalation of the record may add further stigma, entangling the deviant and the persons surrounding him in a web of rigidity and self-fulfilling prophecy which may become increasingly difficult to escape.

THE CONCERN FOR DIVERSION

It is in the court and correctional setting that there has been the greatest recognition of the negative consequences of this labeling process, and the resultant search for diversion mechanisms. Three factors have contributed to the move toward diversion. First, there is the disappointing lack of success of existing correctional practices. As Arthur Pearl puts it, it appears that "the more we do, the worse they get." Recidivism is high in traditional institutional programs, and even where experiments have been tried in institutional settings, the results have been disappointing.[3]

Second, evolving out of concern about what Lemert terms secondary deviance, there is a growing awareness that the stigma of the court for correctional experience may very well be counterproductive for correction. If the treatment serves to aggravate rather than correct, the wisdom of its use must be questioned.

Third, there is growing awareness that the factors which forge legitimate identities lie *outside* the correctional system. It is the community arenas in experience such as found in school, work, politics, and family life that one builds a commitment to conformity. If correctional activities are to be designed to contribute to the development of legitimate identity, access must

---

[1] Edwin W. Lemert, *Instead of Court: Diversion in Juvenile Justice*, NIMH, Center for Crime and Delinquency, Washington, D.C., U.S. Government Printing Office, 1971, p. 13.

[2] *Ibid.*

[3] Don C. Gibbons, *Society, Crime, and Criminal Careers*, Englewood Cliffs, N.J., Prentice-Hall, 1968, pp. 515–30.

be gained, and programs developed, in such institutional arenas. Historically, of course, correctional programs have done just the opposite, physically segregating the offender and through legal sanctions and stigma, imposing significant social barriers to reentry into community life (as seen, for illustration, in the difficulties of finding a job for the ex-convict, or in reenrolling in school on release from the juvenile correctional facilities).

What can be differentiated, then, are two kinds of institutions: those which control access to *legitimate* identities (schools, work, politics, etc.), and those which control access to *illegitimate* identities (police, courts, welfare, etc.). The two are not the same. While they do interlock (and that is what is meant by the organizational accumulation of stigma), they will have different bureaucratic logics. Creation of a legitimate person requires addressing what it is that schools, work, politics, or families do to establish legitimacy. Illegitimacy is what comes out of the "official" processes of the police, courts, and related institutions.

Most "diversion" programs initiated within the justice-correction system are premised on the notion that *not* processing the individual into an illegitimate identity (arrest, court referral, institutional disposition, etc.) avoids stigma and contributes to a correcting experience.

The problem is that by the time the person reaches the justice-correctional system, many of the features of an illegitimate identity may have already been established. Overlapping records from schools, welfare, mental health, and other service agencies may give eloquent testimony to the person's "toughness."

When this has happened, the problem for the correctional system is that its effort to avoid a hardening of the person's illegitimate role does not automatically mean that it has thereby provided him with access to legitimacy. Quite the opposite, in fact. If the individual has been fixed by school, work, welfare, and other institutional experiences into a marginal identity, the institutional pressures toward illegitimacy remain.

Not doing something negative does not in this instance mean that something positive will result. The positive part of the equation will follow only when at the same time there is movement away from illegitimacy, and experiences are provided that build up a legitimate identity and thus provide a new stake in conformity.

For the diversion program, what this means is that, as steps are taken to alter procedures relating to illegitimacy which fall *within* the domain of justice and correctional agencies, at the same time ways must be found to modify institutional practices in the educational, work, and political arenas that lie well outside the more limited justice-correctional system. Diversion programs, in other words, should link up with those program arenas that can provide the experience with competence, belongingness, usefulness, and power that are features of legitimate identity.

10

PERCEPTIONS OF STIGMA
FOLLOWING PUBLIC INTERVENTION
FOR DELINQUENT BEHAVIOR*

Jack Donald Foster, Simon Dinitz,
and Walter C. Reckless

The next article is one of the very few empirical attempts to assess level of labeling from the viewpoint of the labeled individual. The results show very little impact as a result of police or court processing. They suggest that the youngster's self-image is already established by the time of the incident and that official processing is merely a confirmation of the self-image or is rationalized away. While youth perceptions are just one facet of the issue, and one can raise questions about the context in which these perceptions were obtained, there is a potential lesson here. One arrest or one court appearance may generally be insufficient to yield a label-related change in self-image. The die, whether in positive or negative direction, may already have been cast.

* From "Perceptions of Stigma Following Public Intervention for Delinquent Behavior," *Social Problems*, 20, 2 (1972), pp. 202–209. Reprinted by permission of the authors and publisher. The research reported here was supported by grants from the Office of Research of the Ohio State University and the Research Council of Youngstown State University.

There has been much discussion in recent years about the stigmatizing effects of identifying juveniles as "delinquent" by police and court personnel.[1] This emphasis has come to be referred to as the "labeling hypothesis," which maintains, among other things, that public designation of deviance produces a "spoiled" public identity, which, in many cases, reinforces the deviance rather than inhibits it. The position of the labeling theorists seems to be that public intervention in instances of deviant behavior has the potential effect of reinforcing the deviance, because public assignment to a deviant status negatively affects the deviant's interpersonal relationships with others (e.g., family, peers, neighbors, etc.). This makes it difficult for the stigmatized person to resume or continue conventional roles. It tends to place the person in a milieu of suspicion and social opprobrium.

A critical issue in labeling theory is how the deviant perceives what has happened as a result of the public disclosure of his law-violating behavior. Much of the literature on this subject assumes that a deviant perceives the

[1] Cf. Frank Tannenbaum, *Crime and Community* (New York: Columbia University Press, 1938); Edwin M. Lemert, *Social Pathology* (New York: McGraw-Hill Book Company, 1951); John I. Kitsuse, "Societal reactions to deviant behavior: problems of theory and method," *Social Problems* 9 (Winter 1962), 247–256; Kai Erikson, "Notes on the sociology of deviance," *Social Problems* 9 (Spring 1962), 307–314; Howard S. Becker, *Outsiders: Studies in the Sociology of Deviance* (New York: The Free Press, 1963); Stanton Wheeler and Leonard S. Cottrell, *Juvenile Delinquency: Its Prevention and Control* (New York: Russell Sage Foundation, 1966); Edwin M. Schur, *Labeling Deviant Behavior* (New York: Harper & Row, Publishers, 1971).

extent to which his public identity has been spoiled by the actions of the legal authorities. The delinquent boy is supposed to realize that it is no longer possible for him to maintain a public image of being a "good boy," since now it is a matter of public record that he is not.

The general focus of this analysis is upon the delinquent youth's awareness of the social consequences of being publicly identified as "delinquent." The specific areas of perceived social liability examined here are: (1) loss of the esteem of various significant others, and (2) social structural liabilities such as difficulties in completing school or obtaining desired employment.

A study of self-perceptions of being stigmatized encounters a number of important methodological problems. Police and court intervention is not equally disastrous for all, since previous experience with law enforcement agencies, the nature of the offense, the amount of public exposure given to the intervention, and the type of disposition enter into the situation as variables. Also, it cannot be assumed that a delinquent boy accurately perceives the full nature and extent of the liability he has incurred, since the effects of legal stigma are somewhat diffuse and subtle in nature; and the full extent of the damage might not be immediately apparent. Furthermore, involvement in certain types of delinquent activity could be more damaging to some children than to others, because social liability is relative to certain persons and situations. Finally, a stigma is not stable over time, since the eventual amount of liability that may flow from a single event can be altered by subsequent behavior (good or bad). Therefore, the actual long-range consequences might not be consistent with what they appear to be at the moment.

It is very difficult to control effectively all of these variables in a single study. Nonetheless, there has been a serious attempt to control the following variables: previous contact with a law enforcement agency, age, type of disposition, ethnicity, and the nature of the offense. Variables that are not effectively controlled are the amount of public exposure given to the intervention, the degree of esteem that existed between the subject and certain significant others both before and after the intervention took place, and the actual liability incurred. Undoubtedly, the availability of this information would have enhanced the results, but limitations of the project did not permit such measurement. A longitudinal study will follow this one to examine the effect time has upon the responses reported here.

THE SAMPLE

The study on which this article is based was conducted in an urban community of 300,000 population. The study group consisted of 195 boys involved in activities definable as crimes under adult statutes. Cases were gathered consecutively over a period of three months from both the police department and juvenile court simultaneously. All subjects were interviewed within a week to ten days but no more than twenty days after disposition of their cases. The study group consisted of 80 cases disposed of by the police (excluding referrals to Juvenile Court) and 115 cases disposed of by the

Juvenile Court. The racial composition was 44 percent white and 56 percent nonwhite. The average age was 14.9 years. Slightly less than one-half (41 percent) of the boys had a record of previous arrests and/or referrals to Juvenile Court.

The subjects were interviewed in their homes by a trained female adult interviewer after final disposition. In each case, the consent of the parent was obtained; in the great majority of instances the parent sat in on the interview. There were only a few cases in which a parent attempted in any way to influence the subject's responses; on the other hand, they often volunteered some insightful information that was helpful in interpreting the boy's responses. A combination of direct and "open-ended" questions was used by the interviewer.

Responses of juveniles made to an adult interviewer in the presence of parents are certainly subject to damaging biases which cannot be controlled. Alternative methods were considered, such as direct observations of behavior or indirect techniques, perhaps involving responses to hypothetical situations. However, the former was beyond the resources available. Indirect techniques are difficult to use in this type of situation, since the life experiences and ages of the subjects are so different. Responses to hypothetical situations are often contrived by the subject out of imagination rather than experience. In this instance, the decision was made to permit the subjects to respond in the context of their own experience at the calculated risk that in some cases the subjects might not give fully honest answers. The gains were judged to outweigh the risks involved.

THE PERCEPTION OF SOCIAL LIABILITY

Generally, it was found that the youths interviewed did not feel their contact with a law enforcement agency had resulted in any significant social liability in terms of interpersonal relationships. They did not perceive any negative effect whatever upon the attitudes of their friends toward them; and there were only few mentions of slight negative effects upon family relationships. Seventy-three percent of the boys who responded to questions concerning changes in parental attitudes believed there was no change at all. The type of disposition (e.g., advised and released, placed on probation, or institutionalized), the age, or the ethnicity of the subjects did not significantly alter these responses.

The boys' perception of little change in parental attitudes toward them appears to be valid. The boys seem to feel that their parents have relatively fixed opinions of them that were developed *prior* to their being in "trouble," and this "brush" with the law has not significantly changed these opinions. This impression appears to be confirmed by information volunteered by nearly all of the parents who were present at the interviews. Parents who regard their sons as troublesome express no surprise at the police arrest or juvenile court referral, so their opinion is correctly reported as not changed. These parents appear to expect their boys to get into trouble. Likewise, the parents who consider their children basically good continue to believe so despite what happened with the police. They express confidence that their children will turn out well, even though they have been in some trouble with the police.

The interviewed subjects were asked if they thought what had happened would "create any special difficulty in completing school." Twenty-three of the 195 subjects had already been expelled or had quit, so the question was not relevant to them. Of the remaining 172 interviewed boys, 159 (92 percent) felt that getting into trouble with the law would not create any special problems at school. The main exception was found among the few cases where the boys were having school problems *before* their encounter with the police. They obviously saw this new event as not improving the situation. When the boys who were doing well in school were asked why they believed it would not create any special difficulty in completing school, the two most common responses were: "What I did has nothing to do with school," and "The teachers don't know about it, so it won't matter."

The boys seemed to think that secrecy and role separation would protect them against social liability in completing school. They perceived the school and "the street" as two distinctly different and separate social settings; they did not see how what happens in one social world can influence what happens in the other. The following responses were typical of the confidence in secrecy:

> Teachers don't know—just the principal knows.
>
> They don't know about it. Nothing is wrong in school.
>
> Only one teacher knows and he is OK and won't pick on me in any way.

The following responses were typical of the notion of separation of roles:

> It had nothing to do with school.
>
> Their job is to teach me and not worry about what I do in my spare time.
>
> That (stoning of the police cruiser) wasn't even part of school.

The boys interviewed seem to take the position that, as long as one performs the roles expected at school, what happens elsewhere will not interfere with completing school.

The only significant spheres of social liability perceived by the interviewed boys are in the area of contact with the police and future employers. The boys were asked: "Do you think the police will continue to hold this against you?" Of the 181 boys who responded to this question, 54 percent expected the police to keep an eye on them, once they had been in trouble. As one boy put it, "They'll keep us in mind." The more serious the disposition of the case, the more prevalent this opinion. The data revealed no statistically significant difference between the white and nonwhite boys who responded to this question. It is worth noting at this point that the comments made by the boys indicate they perceive an increased susceptibility to future intervention by the police, but they also believe this can be overcome if they are able to prove to the police that they do not intend to violate the law again.

Each boy in the sample interviewed was asked: "Do you think future employers will hold this against you?" Of the 193 subjects interviewed who responded to this question, 40 percent felt that future employers would hold the incident against them. The proportion of boys who perceive employment liability increases as the severity of disposition increases (see Table 1). However, the type of disposition a boy receives is closely associated with the existence of a previous record. "Previous record" is defined here as any previous police or court contact of sufficient significance that the agency recorded the incident. There is no difference between employment responses of white and nonwhite subjects when the existence of a previous record is controlled as a variable. The responses of these boys do not seem to be influenced by perceptions of limited employment opportunity due to race.

TABLE 1

Perceptions of Attitudes of Employers

Type of Disposition	"Do you think future employers will hold this against you?"					Total
	No		Maybe or Yes		NA	
	Number	Percentage	Number	Percentage	Number	
Police						
Advise and Release	29	78	8	22	0	37
Police probation	31	72	12	28	0	43
Subtotal	60		20		0	80
Juvenile Court						
Advise and release	33	57	25	43	0	58
Probation	13	50	13	50	0	26
Commitment	7	27	19	73	0	26
Other	3	60	0	0	2	5
Subtotal	56		57		2	115

$\chi^2 = 24.55$, $p < .001$, excluding NA column.

Differences in perceptions of liability at the different levels of disposition could be attributed to a growing offense record rather than the type of disposition received. When the responses are grouped according to the existence of a previous record, we find 37 percent of the 114 boys without previous records expressing concern that employers might hold the incident against them compared to 44 percent of the 79 boys with a record of previous incidents (see Table 2). While the statistical significance of difference is somewhat reduced for both groups of boys, there is no clear indication as to the exact effect previous record has on their responses. It seems plausible to speculate some type of interaction effect exists between the type of disposition received and the existence of a prior law violating record, but the size of the sample from which these data are drawn prohibits any clear inference on statistical grounds.

TABLE 2

Perceptions of Attitudes of Employers Held by Boys with and without Previous Records

	No Previous Record [a]		Previous Record [b]		Total
	"Do you think future employers will hold this against you?"		"Do you think future employers will hold this against you?"		
Type of Disposition	No	Maybe or Yes	No	Maybe or Yes	
Police					
Advise and release	26	8	3	0	37
Police probation	18	7	13	5	43
Subtotal	44	15	16	5	80
Juvenile Court					
Advise and release	24	20	9	5	58
Probation	3	6	10	7	26
Commitment	1	1	6	18	26
Other	0	0	3	0	5
Subtotal	28	27	28	30	113 [c]

[a] $\chi^2 = 8.38$ N.S.
[b] $\chi^2 = 16.33, p < .01$.
[c] Excludes two no response cases.

In the discussion earlier concerning problems in completing school, it was noted that many of the interviewed boys did not feel that being in "trouble" would interfere with their progress in school. They did not believe the teachers knew about the trouble, or the trouble was considered irrelevant to their school performance. However, when the issue of employment was raised, they seemed to feel that secrecy would be much more problematic. The subjects of this study expressed considerable concern about the possibility that employers might check their records. Some boys interviewed in this study seemed to believe that employers are much more concerned about one's "record" than are public school personnel. Perhaps this reflects their experience in seeking employment or, more likely, what they have been told about job applications.

But some boys deny any employment liability on the grounds that the social consequences of their misconduct will be minimal if they do not get into any more trouble with the police. Although these boys are aware of the possible liability of a "record" with the police and future employers, they are hoping that time will erase the errors of youth. Other boys who deny any employment liability do so on the grounds that their particular police or court record consists of minor offenses that are inconsequential for employment purposes.

The data support the following conclusions: *at the time of the disposition of their case* (1) only a relatively small proportion of youths perceive any significant change in interpersonal relationships with friends or family; (2) only a relatively small proportion anticipates any difficulties in completing school as a direct consequence of the public intervention; (3) slightly more than one-half of the youths expect increased police surveillance as a consequence (social liability) of public intervention; and (4) slightly less than one-half of the youths perceive that they may have endangered their chances of obtaining desired employment.

The data also indicate that perceptions of changes in interpersonal relationships remain unaltered by recidivism, but the awareness of increased liability in terms of completing school and obtaining desired employment increases with recidivism and severity of disposition. Finally, the data indicate that a substantial proportion of juveniles count on certain factors such as age at time of offense, subsequent good conduct, and secrecy of juvenile records to minimize the social impact of their contact with the police or court.

DISCUSSION

The results of this study indicate that, according to the perceptions of the officially acted-upon boys, the extent of perceived stigmatization and social liability that follows police or court intervention seems to be overestimated in the labeling hypothesis. Only a small proportion of the boys studied felt that they were seriously handicapped by having a record with the police or court. This, of course, does not deny the existence of public stigma, nor its consequences in terms of the actual liabilities the delinquent may encounter in certain future situations.

The labeling perspective presumes that a "deviant" is concerned about his public identity, and that a feeling of having incurred a "spoiled identity" as a consequence of public disclosure of deviance reinforces the deviance rather than controls it. A key point in this "vicious circle" notion is the extent to which a deviant exposed to public intervention actually perceives he has incurred a "spoiled" identity as a consequence. W. I. Thomas noted that behavior can only be understood when it is studied within its whole context—the situation not only as it exists in verifiable, objective form, but also as it seems to exist to the person himself. If he believes that his misdeeds are "really nothing at all" or that people will soon forget about it, then the tragic nature of the incident is lost from the deviant's perspective regardless of the real existence of social liability.

The major significance of the findings reported above, so far as labeling theory is concerned, lies in the fact that little empirical evidence can be found to support the notion delinquent boys who have encountered public intervention actually *perceive at the time of intervention* the negative effects attributed to stigma, either in terms of interpersonal relationships with family, friends or teachers, or social structural limitations in terms of education or employment. Although there seems to be some indication that boys with previous records perceive more stigma than boys without previous records, it remains unclear at this point whether this perception of social liability is attributable to experience after the first intervention (which would support labeling theory) or to the *cumulative effects* of a growing "record" of public intervention. It is worth noting, however, that only 43 percent of the

81 boys with previous records perceive any significant social liability; and this is primarily in the area of employment, where they believe "records" are most damaging. Clearly a significant number of boys with previous records are not caught up in the "vicious circle" phenomenon due to perceived stigma described by the labeling theorists. To the extent that a "vicious circle" phenomenon exists, it must depend upon more than *perceived* effects of stigma.

On the basis of the evidence presented above, it would appear that sociologists who advocate the labeling hypothesis have not sufficiently considered the extent to which juveniles who are subjected to public intervention for law-violating behavior actually perceive that they have incurred social liability by being labeled "delinquent." As theorists, sociologists seem to have assumed that their own perceptions of stigmatized status are shared by persons who have been acted upon officially by authorized agents of the criminal justice system.

On the contrary, it appears that most of the subjects do not perceive that their contact with the juvenile justice system has substantially affected or will substantially affect their lives. This perception or misperception of the acted-upon boys may simply be a function of their inability to project a stigmatized status into the future. It may also reflect a time dimension: namely, that awareness of stigma grows with the passage of time. Finally, it is possible that this group of predominantly lower-class boys has accepted and internalized conceptions of limited economic and social opportunities which social stigma would hardly decrease. In other words, the boys may have already neutralized the unfavorable consequences which result from stigma.

11
THE LABELING PROCESS: REINFORCEMENT AND DETERRENT?*

Bernard A. Thorsell and Lloyd W. Klemke

This article moves us farther away from labeling as a creator of deviance by suggesting the role of labels as deterrents. Labeling theorists seldom manifest much interest in this possibility, yet much of society's formal and informal control mechanisms assume this deterrent role. Obviously, an issue requiring very careful consideration in diversion programs is whether (and how) we can tell *before* acting if diversion for label-avoidance purposes is detrimental because it misses an opportunity for deterrence via labeling.

* From *Law and Society Review*, 6, 3 (1972): pp. 393–403. Reprinted by permission of the authors and publisher. This is a revised version of a paper presented at the Annual Meetings of the American Sociological Association, Washington, D.C., August 31–September 3, 1970.

The labeling-theory approach to the analysis of deviance depicts stable patterns of deviant behavior as products or outcomes of the process of being apprehended in a deviant act and publicly branded as a deviant person. The involvement of an individual in this process is viewed as depending much less upon what he does or what he is than upon what others do to him as a consequence of his actions. Deviant persons are regarded as having undergone a degradation ceremony with the result that they have been relegated to membership in a deviant group. In the process, they are thought to have come to acquire an inferior social status and to have developed a deviant view of the world and all the knowledges, skills, and attitudes associated with that status.

Labeling analysts make a basic distinction between primary and secondary deviance. This distinction has been clearly formulated by Lemert.[1] In his view, primary deviance is simply any behavior which might cause an individual to be labeled as a deviant person, whereas secondary deviance is behavior which is generated when an individual is placed in a deviant social role as a result of having been labeled and processed as a deviant person. Labeling analysts attach much greater significance to secondary deviance than to primary deviance, except insofar as other persons react to an act which might be labeled as deviant. They view deviance as a product or outcome of the interaction between the individual who performs the deviant act and those who respond to it by labeling the individual as a deviant person.

Thus, the labeling-theory approach to the analysis of deviant behavior typically stresses the importance of the impact of societal reaction on the deviant person rather than focusing upon his psychological or sociological characteristics. Apropos of this, the central issue to which labeling analysts have consistently addressed their inquiries is the consequences of having

[1] Edwin Lemert, *Human Deviance, Social Problems and Social Control* (Englewood Cliffs, N.J.: Prentice-Hall, 1967), p. 17; *idem, Social Pathology* (New York: McGraw-Hill, 1951), p. 75.

become the target of a label as a deviant person. The labeling process is depicted as resulting characteristically in the reinforcement and crystallization of deviant behavior as a life style. This *negative* result is attributed to what are considered to be typical sequelae of the labeling process, namely, the isolation of the deviant from nondeviant social relationships and a resultant acceptance of a definition of self as a deviant person.[2]

While readily acknowledging the highly significant contributions that this approach has made to our understanding of deviant behavior, this paper takes special note of the fact that a possibly highly important alternative consequence of the labeling process, namely its *positive* effect on future behavior,[3] has been virtually ignored in the work of labeling analysts. Indeed, the treatment of this issue has been limited almost entirely to a concern for the *negative* effect of the labeling process on future behavior. While labeling analysts have demonstrated that the labeling process appears to reinforce and solidify deviant behavior in many cases, they apparently have not seriously considered the possibility that in other cases it might serve to terminate on-going deviance and to deter future deviant behavior. It is somewhat difficult, at first glance, to understand why labeling analysts have failed to examine, to any appreciable extent, the possibility that the labeling process may have positive or deterrent effects on behavior. It does not appear to be for lack of evidence in the literature or in personal experience. For example, depictions by social scientists of social control techniques often point to labeling as a negative sanction and behavioral deterrent. A good case in point is the Bank Wiring Room experiment in the Western Electric Hawthorne Works studies.[4] In that experiment, deviants were sanctioned by their work group by being labeled "rate busters," "speed kings," and so forth, when their work output exceeded the group norm defining "a fair day's work." This treatment by their fellow group members was, on the whole, quite successful in pressuring the deviants to conform to the group norm. Moreover, one's own everyday experiences and observations and common sense all lend support to the general contention that labeling by friends, peers, colleagues, and other associates often does result in a cessation of deviant behavior and can serve to deter future deviance.

The ultimate reasons for the failure of labeling analysts to attend to this dimension of the problem are probably many and varied. Although the determination of these reasons is not the central concern of this paper, it seems appropriate to note in passing that at least one of the roots of the

[2] See especially Howard S. Becker, *Outsiders: Studies in the Sociology of Deviance* (London: Free Press, 1963); Kai Erickson, "The Sociology of Deviance," *Social Problems* 9 (1962): 307; John Kitsuse, "Societal Reaction to Deviant Behavior: Problems of Method and Theory," *Social Problems* 9 (1962): 247; and Lemert, *Social Pathology;* also Lemert, *Human Deviance;* and Thomas J. Scheff, *Being Mentally Ill: A Sociological Theory* (Chicago: Aldine, 1966).

[3] The terms "positive" and "negative," as used in this context, are utilized only to indicate that deviant behavior is usually regarded negatively by the larger society, whereas a reduction in its frequency or its termination is normally regarded positively. There is no intention of implying that conformity to the norms of the larger society is necessarily better or more desirable than deviance from them. The question as to whether deviance should be discouraged or promoted, while a legitimate and interesting issue, is not at stake here.

[4] Fritz J. Roethlisberger and William J. Dickson, *Management and the Worker* (Cambridge, Mass.: Harvard University Press, 1939).

labeling-theory approach to the analysis of deviance would seem to lie in a larger perspective on the phenomenon which was established by earlier analysts of deviant behavior, most of whom were criminologists.[5] These analysts sought to identify the social and cultural, as contrasted to the individual and psychological, sources of deviance, particularly crime. Very importantly, they found that the established societal channels for dealing with criminal deviance yielded, on the whole, essentially negative results. The societal agencies and processes involved in apprehension, adjudication, and rehabilitation of the criminal deviant were shown to be largely ineffective in stopping ongoing criminal behavior and deterring future crime. Moreover, these agencies and processes were shown to have characteristics which not only failed to rehabilitate the criminal and to deter new criminal behavior, but which actually helped establish and support criminal careers.

This criminological tradition seems to have focused attention almost exclusively on deviance and the labeling process as they take place in an urban, secondary-group-dominated setting, where opportunities for personalized observations about behavior are vastly outnumbered by (and thus take second place to) those which are based upon typifications. As a result, it would seem that contemporary labeling analysts, as heirs of this tradition in the study of deviance, have come to center their attention almost exclusively upon the negative outcomes of the labeling process as they typically occur in a mass society setting. Thus, the perspective of contemporary labeling analysts appears to be a carryover from work within this larger criminological tradition which has been directed at the negative outcomes of the inept and ineffective social control measures characteristic of an urban society.

This approach to deviance and the analytical and empirical results it has produced are highly significant as far as they go. However, it is important to call attention to the fact that it has failed to take into consideration the possibility that the impact of the labeling process may not be uniform in all social settings and across all forms of deviant behavior. For example, there is reason to believe that the effect of the labeling process in a primary group situation may be quite different from that found in a mass society setting. Primary group settings characteristically provide the labeled person much greater exposure to personalized observations by others which may help neutralize the negative stereotypic aspects of the label. Further, as illustrated in the Western Electric Bank Wiring Room research,[6] the effect of labeling in a primary group setting seems to be just the opposite of that observed by labeling analysts in secondary group settings. That is, the labeling process seems to work, for the most part, as a deterrent in the former, in sharp contrast to its apparent reinforcing effect upon deviant behavior in the latter. In sum, there is evidence to suggest that the labeling process apparently can function either as a negative, socially disintegrative force or as a positive, socially integrative force, depending upon the social setting and the interpersonal circumstances.

[5] The work of pioneering analysts, such as Clemmer, Lemert, Reckless, Sutherland, Taft, Tannenbaum, and others whose work falls within the framework of this general tradition, comes to mind here.

[6] Roethlisberger and Dickson, op. cit. –

The validity of the currently accepted hypothesis concerning the outcome of the labeling process, therefore, has not to date been completely established. The empirical evidence which lends support to the contention that the labeling process typically results in negative outcomes for future behavior, while significant, is actually very selective in nature and, therefore, satisfies only part of the requirement for the establishment of the validity of this hypothesis. While the data for crime, for example, tend, on the whole, to support the current formulation, it has not been demonstrated that comparably significant data could not be marshalled in support of the converse of the hypothesis with regard to other types of deviant behavior and alternative social settings. Thus, while few, if any, social scientists would contest the idea that the labeling process does in many cases result in negative consequences, it is important to realize that positive outcomes may also be part of the social reality of this phenomenon. The issue is not simply whether the labeling process reinforces or deters future deviance. Rather it is that an examination of the current state of the art in labeling theory forces an increased recognition that both reinforcement *and* deterrence may be outcomes of the labeling process.

At this time, there is no indication that there has been a systematic effort on the part of labeling analysts to evaluate these issues. Moreover, there have been few efforts to undertake the empirical exploration of the implications of labeling theory. In view of this, it seems fair to say that, at this time, the validity of the currently accepted hypothesis that the labeling process typically reinforces deviant behavior seems to rest more upon its repeated assertion by labeling analysts than upon a substantial body of empirical evidence and carefully reasoned conclusions. If this is the case, it seems incumbent upon labeling analysts to entertain the possibility of a systematic empirical exploration of all the possible outcomes of the labeling process.

It is the contention of this paper that the determination of whether the labeling process will result in positive or negative outcomes for future behavior turns upon several conditions of the labeling process which, to date, have received little or no attention from labeling analysts. Several observations regarding these conditions will be examined with the intention of suggesting directions which future research in this area might take.

Observation 1. The labeling process seems to have different effects at various stages in a deviant career. Given Lemert's distinction between primary and secondary deviance,[7] it seems likely that labeling will have fewer effects, positive or negative, after the person has moved into the stage of secondary deviance. The primary deviant seems to be more vulnerable to the direct influence of the labeling process inasmuch as he is still "corruptible." At this stage, the label will either tend to end his deviance or it will serve to push him closer to secondary deviance. Tannenbaum[8] has emphasized how the youthful troublemaker may be propelled into a delinquent career by being so labeled. On the other hand, Cameron[9] found that the labeling of the novice pilferer as "shoplifter" usually terminated this activity in her

---

[7] Lemert, *Social Pathology; idem, Human Deviance*.

[8] Frank Tannenbaum, *Crime and the Community* (Boston: Ginn, 1938).

[9] Mary O. Cameron, *The Booster and the Snitch* (London: Free Press, 1964), p. 165.

subjects. She points out that the novice pilferer does not think of himself before his arrest as a thief and has no peer group support for such a role. Therefore, being apprehended and labeled as such results in his rejection of that role. In this case, the labeling process serves to terminate the ongoing deviant behavior and apparently deters further deviance of this type.

In a recent study[10] of students who had been officially labeled academic failures by having been dropped for poor scholarship from a large state university, it was found that those attending a local community college did not seem to be caught in a self-fulfilling prophecy of failure. Instead, those who had been stigmatized as failures were found to be earning better grades and to have more favorable attitudes toward their academic work than did the nonfailure students. This finding runs counter to the labeling analyst's expectation of a negative outcome in this case and indicates again that there is a need to examine all possible outcomes of the labeling process. Thus, while the primary deviant is still "corruptible," he is also still susceptible to the sanctions of the larger society.

Observation 2. When a label is assigned confidentially, and the person so labeled is a nonprofessional deviant, there appears to be a greater chance that future deviance will be avoided. There is a vast difference between the impact of labeling which is carried out in a limited, confidential manner, as, for example, behind the closed doors of a department store manager's office, and that which takes place before a public audience, such as in a court of law. If labeling is done publicly, the processes of alienation and differential treatment, as discussed by Tannenbaum,[11] tend to be set in motion. This outcome would seem to be even more likely if opportunities for acceptance by a deviant subculture were also available. Such acceptance would certainly enhance the probability that the labeled person might move into secondary deviance. However, it must be noted that even when labeling is carried out publicly, it is not inevitable that the labeled person continues or intensifies his deviant behavior. Indeed, most persons so labeled probably do not. Thus, the majority of young males repeatedly labeled in the manner discussed by Tannenbaum do not turn out to be professional criminals. Moreover, in contemporary mass society such public labeling "ceremonies" are increasingly easier to keep secret, and thereby additional negative reactions from others are avoided.

Observation 3. When the deviant person has some commitment to and is, therefore, sensitive to the evaluation of the labeler, the effect of the labeling process appears more likely to be positive than negative. Cameron's research,[12] noted earlier, points out that the labeling techniques utilized in handling shoplifting cases worked well to discourage the amateur pilferer but had little success with experienced shoplifters. This points up the importance of subcultural supports which encourage renunciation of the legiti-

[10] Lloyd W. Klemke, "Higher Education Failures Coming to a Community College and Labeling Theory" (Presented at the 1971 Annual Meeting of the Pacific Sociological Association in Honolulu, Hawaii).

[11] Tannenbaum, *op. cit.*

[12] Cameron, *op. cit.*

macy of conventional morality. The "techniques of neutralization" provided by the subculture to nullify conventional morality seem to abrogate any effect, positive or negative, that the labeling process might have on the labeled person. This, in turn, suggests that when the labeler is not a member of the "target's" in-group, his evaluation may not carry the same effect as if he were a member. This observation is borne out empirically in the Western Electric Bank Wiring Room experiment noted earlier.[13] In that study, labels applied by members of one's own work group were more effective in controlling deviation from group norms than was labeling carried out by management representatives with respect to formal orders contradicting the group norms concerning daily output. Similarly, it has become an increasingly common observation in treatment and correctional settings, such as Synanon and Alcoholics Anonymous, that labeling by one's peers or significant others seems to be more successful in stopping deviant behavior and rehabilitating the deviant than that carried out by nonpeers, such as counselors, psychiatrists, or prison guards applying the same labels.

Observation 4. If a label can be easily removed, then the probability that the stigmatized person is likely to move toward conforming behavior is greater. In their research on occupational opportunities, Schwartz and Skolnick[14] found that the revelation of an arrest record, irrespective of conviction or acquittal, markedly reduces the number of job opportunities for the individual, particularly for the lower-class person. In an effort to cope with this problem, some legal authorities for some time have pressed for the expungement of the records of persons placed on probation or parole. In the United States, this has been limited, for the most part, to juvenile records in cases where the community views the young person as deserving of a "second chance." In Sweden, however, the present policy in this regard is so advanced that it is a cardinal principle of Swedish penal policy to protect and maintain the anonymity of released offenders, especially released murderers.[15] The released offender is advised to change his name and to take up residence in a community or part of the country different from the one in which his crime was committed. A job and, if necessary, living accommodations are found for him there. The only member of his new community aware of his true identity is his employer, who is sworn to secrecy. In short, the released offender has the opportunity to embark on a new life completely free of any evidence from the past that might stigmatize him. Swedish penal officials report that for decades there have been no cases of homicide offenders who have been released under this program repeating their crimes. These results suggest that by making the realistic removal of such labels feasible, it is possible, in many cases, to initiate and to sustain movement away from deviant behavior.

Observation 5. The nature of the societal reaction which follows or ac-

[13] Roethlisberger and Dickson, *op. cit.*

[14] Richard D. Schwartz and Jerome H. Skolnick, "Two Studies of Legal Stigma," *Social Problems* 10 (1962): 133.

[15] Giles Playfair and Derrick Sington, *The Offenders: Society and the Atrocious Crime* (London: Secker and Warburg, 1957).

companies the application of a label is of central importance in determining whether the outcome of the process will be positive or negative. In the area of mental illness, the difficulties of the person who has been labeled as "sick" once again becoming perceived as "normal" or "well," has been of interest to labeling analysts.[16] An examination of the ways in which the Hutterites deal with persons exhibiting abnormal behavior was carried out by Eaton and Weil.[17] They found that persons so identified became the objects of extensive efforts on the part of friends and the community in general to aid and support the labeled person in becoming reintegrated into the community. This contrasts sharply with the larger societal reaction to the mentally "sick" person in the United States. In American society, the person so labeled characteristically is regarded as someone to be avoided, rejected, and isolated. Viewed from this perspective, the labeling process is essentially a stimulus which can set off a wide range of societal reactions, varying from negative, isolative, and socially disintegrative responses to highly positive, supportive, and socially integrative actions. Where societal reactions are positive, supportive, and socially integrative, the labeling process seems to generate a positive atmosphere in which the effect on future behavior is to move it in the direction of greater conformity.

It is important to distinguish between official, institutionalized reactions to deviant acts and the informal reactions of one's significant others. In the study of academic failures mentioned earlier,[18] it was found that official expulsion from the university was countered by positive, supportive reactions from the student's significant others. These positive reactions were instrumental in encouraging the students to reenter college and try again to succeed academically. They also were significant in maximizing the chances for academic success once the student decided to enter the community college for another try. This finding adds still another dimension to the labeling process and its outcomes which has not been adequately examined by labeling analysts.

Observation 6.   A liberal assignment of positive labels, within realistic limits, seems to stimulate and increase the prevalence of desirable behavior. In their apparent preoccupation with the negative effects of the labeling process, labeling analysts have paid little attention to the possibility that an increase in desirable behavior might result from the application of positive labels. That positive labeling can function as a stimulus to desirable behavior is shown in the work of Rosenthal and Jacobson.[19] In their study, teachers in an elementary school were led to believe at the beginning of the school year that certain pupils could be expected to show considerable academic improvement during the coming year. The teachers were told that these predictions were based upon intelligence tests which had been administered at the end of the preceding academic year. The children so designated were labeled "spurters" by the investigators in their conversations with the

[16] See, for example, Scheff, *op. cit.*

[17] Joseph Eaton and Robert J. Weil, *Culture and Mental Disorders* (Glencoe: Free Press, 1953).

[18] Klemke, *op. cit.*, p. 16.

[19] Robert Rosenthal and Lenore F. Jacobson, "Teacher Expectations for the Disadvantaged," *Scientific American* 218 (1968): 19.

teachers. In reality, the children designated as "spurters" were chosen at random from the roster of students enrolled at the school by using a table of random numbers. After the school year was in progress, standard intelligence tests were given to all pupils during the year at predetermined intervals. The results indicated clearly that the randomly chosen children labeled as "spurters" improved scholastically considerably more than the rest of the children who were not so designated. Moreover, in addition to depicting the "spurters" as intellectually more alive and autonomous than the other children, their teachers described them as being happier, more interesting, more appealing, and more affectionate, as well as being better adjusted and less in need of social approval. In this case, the application of a positive label clearly generated socially desirable behavior both as perceived by others and as measured by standardized psychological tests.

On the basis of these six observations, it is possible to construct six hypotheses that seem to be amenable to systematic empirical evaluation by the labeling analyst. While there seems to be little doubt that continued observation and reflection could yield additional hypotheses, those suggested here seem sufficient to point the way to a systematic investigation of the converse of the currently accepted hypothesis concerning the outcome of the labeling process. This is the primary purpose of this paper. In order to express the hypotheses as formal statements, it seems to be most convenient to summarize them as follows.

The labeling process is more likely to terminate existing deviant behavior and to deter future deviance:

1. If the labeled person is a primary rather than a secondary deviant.

2. If the labeling is carried out in a confidential setting with the understanding that future deviance will result in public exposure.

3. If the labeling has been carried out by an in-group member or significant other.

4. The more easily the label is removable when the deviant behavior has ceased.

5. The more the labeling results in efforts to reintegrate the deviant into the community.

6. If the label is favorable rather than derogatory.

Empirical evaluation of these hypotheses will do much to expand our knowledge concerning the possible positive effects of the labeling process on both on-going deviance and future conduct. Hopefully, in time it will be possible to amass sufficient empirical evidence so that an objective evaluation of the converse of the currently accepted labeling hypothesis will be possible. All of this will do a great deal to enhance our understanding of the labeling process itself as well as its consequences for future behavior. Moreover, research such as this can begin to provide an objective basis for a systematic evaluation of labeling theory as a general theory of deviant behavior.

SECTION 3

POLICE DISCRETION

The topic of discretion—its origin, validity, use, and overuse—has always been a lively one within the criminal justice system. Every agent in the system has some amount of discretion legally available—everyone from the uniformed patrol officer to the trial judge, parole board, and the Governor of the state. Although a number of people in the system tend publicly to minimize the amount of discretion available to them, its existence certainly cannot be denied. This is particularly true in the juvenile area and is epitomized by diversion decisions. The papers in this section provide both proof of and viewpoints about police discretion with juvenile offenders.

There is a particular context within which we would like the reader to consider the topic of discretion, the context of professionalism. The literature on the professions is voluminous and requires no extensive coverage here. However, a few particularly relevant points should be made. For instance, no one can truly attain the *ideal* of professionalism. Consider this characterization (actually, a caricature), offered some years ago in a release from the U.S. Office of Education:

> Their main driving force is professional spirit rather than the desire for gain; the true measure of their success is the quality of the service they render, not the financial gains they amass. . . . The professional man is sustained by the satisfaction which he obtains from rendering a service well, from gaining the esteem of his fellow professionals, from living up to the solidly established tradition of the little society or professional group of which he is a member, from discharging faithfully the high professional obligation in which he has been indoctrinated [sic!]. . . . A truly professional man is a dedicated man; he espouses the high ideal of service to his fellow man; he is devoted to his art. . . . Obviously in this matter the professions stand in contrast with industry and commerce, where the main driving force is the desire for profit. . . .[1]

This overstatement separates the good guys from the bad guys; unfortunately, it makes it almost impossible to be a good guy. From this and other statements on the professions, we can nevertheless distill the "flavor of professionalism." We can characterize as a profession any discipline that is

[1] Blauch, Lloyd E. (ed.), *Education for the Professions*, Washington, D.C.: U.S. Government Printing Office, 1955.

formalized, service-oriented, based upon a body of demonstrated knowledge and techniques, oriented toward equally applied (universalistic) normative standards, and fosters the exercise of individual judgment and self-regulation.

Modern, urban police have placed more emphasis on some of these factors than on others. They have stressed formal organization, advanced techniques, the application of universalistic standards, and self-regulation. They have, to put it in more familiar terms, turned their back on the old "beat cop" who knew his area, his residents, and relied heavily on his own judgment in carrying out his role.

At the same time, the body of knowledge pertinent to successful police work has expanded inordinately, forcing the profession toward more formalized educational and training enterprises. This has created problems. The knowledge and skills within each profession are shared more closely by those within the profession than by outsiders. Indeed, it is this very specificity of an area of knowledge and coordinated skills and argot that most easily permits the outsider to differentiate among the various professional groupings. It is the presence of these knowledge areas which necessitates professional training, which in turn not only helps separate profession from nonprofession, but also one profession from another. This is not to say that inclusive areas of knowledge (and skills) are limited to the professions—this is obviously not the case—but rather that the professions, again on an institutional level, place more emphasis on their exclusive areas of competence and presumably derive more of their overt practices from an accumulated body of knowledge. The sheer amount of information available varies widely from group to group, as does its demonstrable scientific validity and the extent to which it is indispensable to the use of professional skills and practices and the welfare of the appropriate client populations. In addition, the knowledge tends to be somewhat conceptual in nature, above the level of simple technical or experiential content. For the police, who depend so heavily upon citizen support, this has resulted in increased estrangement from their support base in the community.

In addition, the prestige of a profession is often correlated with the "availability" of its special knowledge. As the mystique of an area increases, there is less tendency for the lay public to assume its own expertise, and more willingness to accept independent decision making and advice from the profession in question. Education and the clergy have perennially found this a sore point, for the general public has assumed the level of its own knowledge in these areas to be quite high, and has denigrated the technical skills of the professional practitioners. For that matter, many medical malpractice suits can be attributed in part to this same tendency. It is no wonder that, along with the knowledge and skills and necessary technical language, there is often found among professional groups an esoteric jargon often incomprehensible to the outsider. Its purpose is as much defensive as communicative.

On the institutional level, it must be clear that the emphasis on formal training and apprenticeship, and the accumulation of valid knowledge and technical skills, perforce make a professional field one in which judgments are expected to be superior to random actions or the actions of the untrained laity. *One can legitimately view much of the process of professionalization as the preparation for independent exercise of judgment and discretion* within a defined area of competence. Thus, as police become more professional, we should find them using *more* judgment, maximizing their knowledge, skills, and training. We go to a lawyer for his judgment. We go to a physician for his judgment. Should not the same be true of the law officer who must make decisions about arrested juveniles? Judgment here is synonymous with discretion, the judgment about the most appropriate action to take and the responsibility to exercise that judgment.

We make this point strongly here because a significant error is being made in the modern "professionalization" of many police departments. In moving toward bureaucratization, increased legalism, and uniformity of action, many police forces are decreasing, rather than increasing, the discretion available to individual officers. They are training officers more to exercise judgment less.

Diversion programs can be seen as a contrary development, for they ask an officer to make a new or additional judgment about the disposition of a case. The recent expansion of police diversion programs would in fact suggest that our analysis of the antidiscretion developments noted above is in error. Yet when one looks closely at the *operation* of police diversion programs, one of their most striking characteristics is the restrictive guidelines developed for them. A large portion of the available community agencies are found unsuitable for referrals. The majority of young offenders are found—are, in fact *declared*—unsuited for referral: they are too young (or too old), their offense is too minor (or too serious), this was only their first offense (or they have too many prior offenses), they are already on probation (or probation would be harmful to them), and so on.

So an important question becomes: How can diversion programs develop the same *legitimated* level of discretion that has been available in other aspects of juvenile police operations? The papers in Section 3 make it clear that there has traditionally been a great deal of discretion available in the police handling of juveniles. One reason for this, as stated in the paper by Ferster et al., is the vagueness of the statutes regarding juvenile matters. Vagueness leads to alternative interpretations and actions.

Similarly, the paper by Piliavin and Briar illustrates how a wide variety of factors impinge upon the decisions to arrest and release juveniles. These are factors in which the officers' training, work situations, and personal predispositions are inextricably tied up. All the bureaucratization and legalisms in the world could not totally erase them as partial determinants of the officers' judgments and decisions.

The paper by Kobetz, as an expression of semiofficial police positions, and the paper from the National Council on Crime and Delinquency, as an expression of semiofficial welfare and correctional positions, provide an interesting contrast. Both deal with guidelines and procedures that hopefully will mold and modify individual discretion. They are far from identical in specifics or in spirit. Each is designed to shape the directions for discretion. Because they differ substantially, taken together they provide an illustration of the flexibility (or ambiguity) that underlies professional judgment and discretion. The Kobetz article elaborates a number of reasons that discretion is often denied, but it and the other articles in this section amply illustrate the need for the trained use of discretion in disposing of juvenile cases.

12
JUVENILE DETENTION: PROTECTION, PREVENTION, OR PUNISHMENT?*
Elyce Zenoff Ferster, Edith Nash Snethen, and Thomas F. Courtless

Although the following paper is concerned with detention rather than directly with police diversion and referral, it is included here for several reasons. Detention is one form of insertion into the system, and therefore the other side of the release coin. The discretion involved in the decision to detain is similar to that in the decision to release and/or refer. Also, detention presumably epitomizes a major danger of insertion, that is, contamination by committed offenders. This is one of the factors often cited in label acceptance. Finally, the material cited on the wide variations in detention rates provides an operational documentation of discretion at work. Parenthetically, the reader might make note of the many references to the inadequate data available to the authors—for example, the fact that twenty-two states do not maintain detention statistics!

* From *Fordham Law Review*, 37, 2(1969); pp. 161–96. Reprinted (with editorial adaptations) by permission of the authors and publisher. Copyright 1970 by Fordham University Press.

More than 400,000 juveniles, approximately two-thirds of all those apprehended by the police, were placed in jails or detention homes in 1965.[1] This high rate of detention is contrary to the articulated philosophy of the juvenile court that usually a juvenile is to be released to his parents to await court action. It is also considerably in excess of the National Council on Crime and Delinquency (NCCD) recommendation that the detention rate "should not normally exceed ten per cent of the total number of juvenile offenders apprehended. . . ."[2] In fact, no supporters of a high detention rate are found in the literature.[3] Instead, one finds not only complaints about the detention rate but also objections to almost every aspect of juvenile detention.

The following statement, made forty years ago, is similar to comments made today:

[1] National Council on Crime and Delinquency (hereinafter cited as NCCD), Juvenile Detention, in Correction in the United States, 13 Crime and Delinq. 11, 15 (1967) (hereinafter cited as Juvenile Detention); President's Commission on Law Enforcement and the Administration of Justice, Task Force Report: Juvenile Delinquency and Youth Crime 37 (1967) (hereinafter cited as Juv. Delinq. and Youth Crime).

[2] NCCD, Standards and Guides for the Detention of Children and Youth 18 (2nd ed., 1961) (hereinafter cited as Detention Standards).

[3] See D. Freed and P. Wald, Bail in the United States: 1964 (1964); S. Norman and A. Barstis, The Controlled Use of Detention (1963); Dorsen and Rezneck, In re Gault and the Future of Juvenile Law, 1 Fam. L.Q., No. 4, at 1 (1967) (hereinafter cited as Dorsen and Rezneck); Downey, State Responsibility for Child Detention Facilities, 14 Juv. Ct. Judges J., No. 4, at 3 (1964).

From the data here submitted it becomes evident that children are still commonly detained in jails all over the country; that there is an absence of adequate facilities for detention in many jurisdictions; that detention homes are sometimes little better than jails; that all too commonly, policies of intake and discharge of children are inadequate; that the wrong kind of children are detained; that children are confined for too long periods; in short, that which is technically known among social workers as "good casework standards" are too often lacking in the treatment of these children.[4]

The marked difference between juvenile detention practice and policy for so many years raises some serious questions: Is a high juvenile detention rate necessary because of the seriousness of the offense and/or the deviancy of the offender? Or are the practices simply a result of society's failure to implement a nonpunitive system of juvenile justice? Is detention another example of juveniles receiving "the worst of both possible worlds"? In other words, is it detention policy or practice which needs to change?

This article, the second in a series[5] reporting the findings of a three-year study on "The Juvenile Offender and the Law," attempts to answer these questions.[6] It is based on an analysis of statutes and cases, a review of the literature including statistical and field reports, and a field study of "Affluent County"[7] conducted by the Juvenile Offender and the Law Project (hereinafter called the Juvenile Study).

I. DETENTION

Detention is usually defined as "the temporary care of children who require secure custody of their own or the community's protection in physically restricting facilities pending court disposition."[8]

Unfortunately, detention statistics, like statistics on arrests of juveniles,

---

[4] Detention Standards, *supra* note 2, at xxii.

[5] The first article dealt with juvenile arrest, search and seizure, fingerprinting, and police records. See Ferster and Courtless, The Beginning of Juvenile Justice, Police Practices, and the Juvenile Offender, 22 Vand. L. Rev. 567 (1969).

[6] The study was financed by Public Health Service Grant MH-14500 from the National Institute of Mental Health.

[7] Affluent County has the highest median family income of any county in the United States .An estimate for 1968 indicates that 34,000 families earned between $10,000 and $15,000, with an additional 47,600 families with incomes between $15,000 and $25,000, and 18,000 families earning over $25,000. These three groups of families comprised 78% of all families in the county. Department of Community Development, Population and Social Characteristics 2, 3 (1968).

[8] W. Sheridan, Standards for Juvenile and Family Courts 23 (U.S. Children's Bur. Pub. No. 437, 1966) (hereinafter cited as Children's Bureau Standards). Similar definitions are used by the NCCD in its Detention Standards, *supra* note 2, and Guides for the Detention of Children and Youth (1961) and the nine states which explicitly define the term by statute. Colo. Rev. Stat. Ann. § 22-1-3(12) (Supp. 1967); Idaho Code Ann. § 16-1802 (1969); Ill. Ann. Stat. ch. 37, § 701-9 (Smith-Hurd 1969); Iowa Code Ann. § 232.2(6) (1969); Md. Ann. Code art. 26, § 70-1(m) (Supp. 1969); Miss. Code Ann. § 7187-02(i) (Supp. 1968); S.D. Comp. Laws Ann. § 26-8-1(7) (Supp. 1969); Utah Code Ann. § 55-10-64(5) (Supp. 1969); Vt. Stat. Ann. tit. 33, § 632(5) (Supp. 1969).

are both difficult to obtain and difficult to interpret.[9] Twenty-two jurisdictions do not keep any detention statistics at all.[10] Of the twenty-nine that do, most of the statistics are so incomplete[11] that it is almost impossible to assemble comparable statistical information on such items as rate of detention, length of detention, and disposition of juveniles after detention.

In spite of these difficulties, enough information on detention rates has been obtained to show that there is a very large variation in the use of detention from one jurisdiction to another. For example, a recent study of detention in eleven counties in California showed that the detention rates among the counties ranged from 19 to 66 percent.[12] Substantial variations in detention rates have also been found by other studies.[13] Since there is little comparative detention information available, the Juvenile Study obtained detention information from ten communities. The Study indicated a considerable variation in detention rates from jurisdiction to jurisdiction.[14] Although it might be thought that this variation is due to a difference in the number of serious offenses under the various penal statutes, the California study found that this is not so.[15]

The Juvenile Study's analysis of statistics obtained from communities in eleven states found similar results.[16] As well as a large variation in detention rates between communities, the Study indicates that the highest detention rates are not always related to the most serious offenses.[17] The "Affluent County" field study also confirms these results.[18]

A. Purpose of Detention

Although there is supposedly agreement about which children should be detained,[19] communities actually use different criteria or different interpre-

[9] Ferster and Courtless, *supra* note 5, at 569–73.

[10] Juvenile Detention, *supra* note 1, at 33.

[11] *Id.*

[12] NCCD, Locking Them Up: A Study of Initial Juvenile Detention Decisions in Selected California Counties 118 (1968) (hereinafter cited as California Study). The Study analyzed detention practices in 11 California counties.

[13] D. Freed and P. Wald, *supra* note 3, at 97. "In some places, all children referred to juvenile court are detained. In others, only two or three out of every 100 are held. A 50% ratio is not uncommon. . . ." See also Juvenile Detention, *supra* note 1, at 31; California Study at 120–21.

[14] See App. A. The project wrote to detention facilities serving ten of the largest cities in the United States requesting detention statistics: Atlanta (Fulton County), Baltimore, Boston, Chicago (Cook County), District of Columbia, Los Angeles, New York City, Philadelphia, St. Louis, and Oklahoma City. Useful statistics were obtained from Baltimore (NCCD study), Chicago (Police Annual Report), District of Columbia (Receiving Home Annual Report), Los Angeles County (Probation Department Report), and New York. In addition Children's Bureau studies of four communities (Volusia County, Florida; Sangamon County, Illinois; Trumbull County, Ohio; Tarrant County, Texas) were obtained for contrasting population size and geographical differences.

[15] California Study, *supra* note 12, at 120–21.

[16] See App. B.

[17]*Id.*

[18] Only 5 (9.9%) of the detained juveniles were alleged to have committed dangerous offenses such as attempted robbery and assault.

[19] D. Freed and P. Wald, *supra* note 3, at 95–96.

tations of the same criteria.[20] The reasons for detaining a child are most often described as follows: children who will run away during the period the court is studying their case, or children who must be held for another jurisdiction (e.g., runaways from institutions to which they were committed by a court)[21]; children who will commit an offense dangerous to themselves or the community before court disposition.

1. Runaways. All authorities state that a juvenile should be detained if such action is necessary to assure his presence in court.[22] They differ, however, in how they determine when a particular child might run away. The NCCD recommends that a child is to be detained only if it is "almost certain" that he will run away.[23] The child should be a runaway at the time of detention or have some history of absconding to justify detention under this standard.[24] None of the eight states, however, whose statutes authorize detention to assure presence in court, use the language recommended by the NCCD.[25] The wording ranges from authorizing detention if the child "may abscond"[26] to requiring a "substantial probability"[27] that he will not appear in court.[28]

Only one case, *People* v. *Poland*,[29] deals specifically with the issue. The detained juvenile was found "in need of supervision" because she violated her probation by late hours, truancy, and difficult behavior at home. She was placed in detention while the possibility of placement with family friends was evaluated. In a habeas corpus petition the court held that the past history of truancy and difficult behavior justified the Family Court's decision that there was a substantial probability that she would not appear at the scheduled hearing.[30] It is noteworthy that in this jurisdiction the only other grounds for detention is serious risk that the juvenile will commit a criminal act. Although it is necessary to know why a child is detained before high detention rates can be analyzed, most detention statistics do not report the number of children detained for the various reasons. In one of the jurisdic-

[20] *Id.* at 96.

[21] *Id.*

[22] NCCD Standard Fam. Ct. Act § 17, Comment (1959); NCCD Standard Juv. Ct. Act § 17, Comment (1968); Uniform Juv. Ct. Act § 14; Juv. Delinq. and Youth Crime, *supra* note 1, at 37; Detention Standards, *supra* note 2, at 15; S. Norman and A. Barstis, *supra* note 3, at 5; Downey, *supra* note 3, at 3.

[23] Detention Standards, *supra* note 2, at 15.

[24] Juvenile Detention, *supra* note 1, at 29.

[25] California, Illinois, Maryland, Michigan, Mississippi, Nebraska, New York, North Dakota.

[26] N.D. Cent. Code § 27-20-14 (Supp. 1969).

[27] N.Y. Fam. Ct. Act § 739 (1963).

[28] In the other six states, four allow detention if the minor is likely to flee the jurisdiction, Cal. Welfare and Institutions Code § 628(e) (West Supp. 1969); Ill. Ann. Stat. ch. 37, § 703-6(2) (Smith-Hurd 1969); Md. Ann. Code art. 26, § 70-11(2) (Supp. 1969); Neb. Rev. Stat. § 43-205.03 (1968); one is restricted to those who have run away, Mich. Stat. Ann. § 27.3178(598.15)(b) (1962); and the other allows detention if it is "necessary" to assure court attendance, Miss. Code Ann. § 7187-06 (Supp. 1968).

[29] 44 Misc. 2d 968, 255 N.Y.S.2d 455 (1964).

[30] *Id.* at 969, 255 N.Y.S.2d at 456.

tions, which does give such information, 35 percent[31] of the children detained were held because they were "potential runaways."[32] A second study[33] showed that 14 percent of the detained children were held because they were runaways,[34] and a third showed that 6 percent of them were detained on that ground.[35] In "Affluent County," 30 percent of the children detained during the period of the field study had run away from their homes or institutions.[36]

There is even less information about the number of children who do not appear in court. The one study found which contained information on this subject said that judges and court personnel in low-detention counties reported that children "rarely" fail to appear in court.[37] "Affluent County" court records also indicate that only a small number of juveniles failed to appear at their court hearings.[38]

2. Danger to community. The likelihood that a child's actions will be a danger to the community is almost as widely accepted a reason for detention actions as doubt about the child's appearance in court. Virtually all authorities approve of detaining a child because of danger to the community,[39] and twelve states specifically authorize detention for this reason by statute.[40] The danger referred to is the likelihood of the child's committing new offenses. The NCCD recommends that only children who are "almost cer-

---

[31] See Marion County, Oregon Juvenile Court Center, Joseph B. Fleton Home, Annual Report, A Broken Promise 37 (1968) (hereinafter cited as Oregon Study).

[32] The applicable statute states that the child shall be released to the custody of his parents except "[w]here it appears to the court that the welfare of the child or of others may be immediately endangered by the release of the child." Ore. Rev. Stat. § 419.573(3)(b) (Replacement 1967).

[33] California Study, *supra* note 12, at 122.

[34] The statute in this jurisdiction authorizes detention if a minor is likely to flee the jurisdiction of the court. Cal. Welfare and Institutions Code § 628(e) (West Supp. 1969). It was not clear from the study if the children classified as "runaways" included children "likely to flee" or was limited to those who had already run away from home.

[35] See D. Borden, Report of Youth Aid Division 35 (1967) (hereinafter cited as D.C. Study). This unpublished 1967 study for the Committee on the Administration of Justice analyzed the District of Columbia's policemen of the Juvenile System, the Youth Aid Division. All cases of police detention during one week were studied.

[36] Affluent County, *supra* note 7.

[37] Juvenile Detention, *supra* note 1, at 31. This study of juvenile detention was undertaken by the NCCD for the President's Commission on Law Enforcement and Administration of Justice.

[38] Affluent County, *supra* note 7.

[39] See Detention Standards, *supra* note 2, at 15; Children's Bureau Standards, *supra* note 8, at 62–63.

[40] Alaska Stat. § 47.10.140(a) (1962); Cal. Welfare and Institutions Code § 628(d) (West Supp. 1969); Colo. Rev. Stat. Ann. § 22-2-2 (Supp. 1967); Ill. Ann. Stat. ch. 37, § 703-6(2) (Smith-Hurd 1969); Ind. Ann. Stat. § 9-3212 (Replacement 1956); Md. Ann. Code art. 26, § 70-11(a)(1) (Supp. 1969); Mich. Stat. Ann. § 27.3178(598.15)(c) (1962); Neb. Rev. Stat. § 43-205.03 (1968); N.Y. Fam. Ct. Act § 739(b) (1963); N.D. Cent. Code § 27-20-14 (Supp. 1969); Utah Code Ann. § 55-10-91(1) (Supp. 1969); Vt. Stat. Ann. tit. 33, § 643(a) (Supp. 1969). See also Uniform Juv. Ct. Act § 14; Model Rules for Juv. Cts. rule 17, Comment (1969).

tain" to commit dangerous offenses be detained.[41] None of the statutes uses the "almost certain" qualification, nor do any of them define a dangerous offense.[42]

The first problem in interpreting these statutes is deciding what evidence is relevant to a determination that the child will commit another offense. A 1965 Alabama Work Conference on Juvenile Court Judges suggested that detention is proper when the child's attitude suggests that he would go home and immediately repeat the offense.[43] This criterion places maximum credence upon the child's appearance of repentance, a highly subjective factor.[44] The Advisory Council of Judges suggests that children with strained family relationships and serious problems are likely to get into further trouble and, consequently, should be detained.[45] This criterion seems too vague to be helpful without definition of the terms "problems" and "strained family relationships."

In some communities, the juvenile who has been apprehended or adjudicated in the past is judged to be likely to commit a new offense. A recent study found that children who have been detained previously and those who are on probation are more likely to be detained than those who have not.[46] Although prior delinquent behavior may seem to be the logical way to predict future offenses, it has not yet been verified by empirical data. The one empirical study which attempted to validate this hypothesis was carried out with adult criminals. It found that neither the seriousness of the crime charged nor the offender's past record provides a reliable basis to predict adult pretrial behavior.[47] Unfortunately, there has been no similar study for juveniles.[48]

Even assuming that the kinds of evidence which will justify a prediction that a juvenile is "likely" or "almost certain" to commit a dangerous offense are known, the term "dangerous" still needs to be defined. Detention statistics from most communities do not contain this information. However, one study found that if the juvenile was accused of rape, arson, or an offense with

[41] Detention Standards, *supra* note 2, at 15. New York and Michigan isolate the danger the child presents to the public. Michigan sees it in "those whose offenses are so serious" whereas New York sees it as a "serious risk that he may do a (criminal) act."

[42] The remaining standards are vague. Alaska specifies detention must "be necessary" to protect the community. Four states require the necessity to be "immediate," "urgent," or both. See California, Colorado, Illinois, and Nebraska. Maryland and North Dakota allow detention if "required" to protect the community; Vermont does if "reasonably required." Indiana permits release "without danger" to the public whereas Utah allows detention unless "unsafe to the public."

[43] D. Ottman, Proceedings of the Ala. Work Conference for Juvenile Court Judges 21 (1965).

[44] Adverse police reaction to provocative behavior has long been noted and warned against. See Paulsen Fairness to the Juvenile Offender, 41 Minn. L. Rev. 547, 552 (1957).

[45] NCCD, Guides for Juv. Ct. Judges 46 (1963).

[46] California Study, *supra* note 12, at 162.

[47] Report of the President's Commission on Crime in the District of Columbia, Minority Views of Patricia M. Wald, 930-36 (1966) (hereinafter cited as the D.C. Crime Commission Study).

[48] Although the Gluecks have done numerous prediction studies of juveniles, they have not studied the activities of juveniles awaiting adjudication. See, e.g., S. and E. Glueck, Unraveling Juvenile Delinquency (1950).

a gun, detention was automatic. Otherwise, the kind of offense was weighed with his age and the number and recency of prior police contacts.[49]

Another study said that police tend to detain all juveniles who commit sexual offenses and acts which would be felonies if committed by adults.[50] If the investigating officer finds the child to have a "reliable" family, however, and there is little likelihood that he will not appear in court, there is less tendency to detain the child. The Juvenile Study collected and analyzed data on the offenses allegedly committed by detained juveniles in eleven communities in order to obtain some information on the seriousness of offenses. If "dangerous" is defined as including only offenses against persons, then in only two localities were more than 10 percent of the juveniles detained because they were "dangerous."[51]

An attempt was made to find out the specific offenses with which the juveniles were charged because "offenses against the person" encompasses a variety of acts from simple assault to homicide. Unfortunately, the data were available for only five of the eleven communities. The results[52] indicate that under any reasonable definition of "dangerous," danger to the community is not the reason for holding the majority of the detained children in any of the five jurisdictions. In fact, if burglary is not included in the definition "dangerous offense," three-fourths of the detained children are held for some reason other than dangerousness.

In addition to authorizing detention for children who will run away before adjudication and those who will commit an offense dangerous to the community,[53] the NCCD also recommends that children "almost certain to commit an offense dangerous to themselves" be detained.[54] The only relevant statutory provisions are even more vague than the Council's statement. Typically they allow detention in order to protect the minor or the community.[55] Unfortunately, defining which acts committed by a juvenile are sufficiently dangerous to him to justify detention is even more difficult than defining those acts dangerous to the community.

Certain acts which would seem to fit the definition are specifically excluded by the Council. Thus, school truancy is not considered a reason to detain.[56]

Girls who stay out late at night and are suspected of being promiscuous and juveniles who are charged with alcohol and drug offenses are described as those who might commit acts dangerous to themselves prior to adjudica-

---

[49] D.C. Study, *supra* note 35, at 38.

[50] U.S. Children's Bureau, A Study of Services for Delinquent Children in Trumbull County, Ohio, pt. III, at 31 (1967) (hereinafter cited as Trumbull County Study).

[51] See App. B.

[52] See App. C.

[53] See pp. 164–70.

[54] Detention Standards, *supra* note 2, at 15.

[55] Alaska Stat. § 47.10.140(a) (1962); Ind. Ann. Stat. § 9-3212 (Replacement 1956); Neb. Rev. Stat. § 43-205.03 (1968).

[56] Detention Standards, *supra* note 2, at 17. The NCCD takes the position that "[t]ruancy is a school problem which should be handled in the school system through social services and special classes or schools when necessary." *Id.*

tion. The question is whether there is sufficient danger that they will seriously injure themselves to justify detention. The fact that these children are usually returned to the community even if they are adjudicated delinquent should be considered in any decision about detention.

Another difficult question is whether juveniles who have been apprehended for participation in civil rights protests need detention for their own protection. A Maryland court answered this question affirmatively. In *Ex Parte Cromwell*[57] the Maryland Court of Appeals justified detention of two fifteen-year-old juveniles who had participated in peaceful protests against segregation. The town was under virtual military occupation at the time and the court thought it would be reasonable to remove the children "from the scene of danger, where they would be safe from the physical injuries they might suffer if they remained at home and persisted in their past course of action."[58] The court also pointed out that the parents might be unfit because they were either indifferent to the children's activities or encouraged them.[59] It is of interest that the court in a subsequent decision in the same case reversed the adjudication of delinquency of these children because their conduct was "not so fundamentally wrong as to require permanent treatment, as distinguished from temporary custodial care."[60]

Although the Maryland court believed that detention of juvenile civil rights demonstrators is for their protection, there are others who think such detention is frequently used as a punishment. The Civil Rights Commission reports that many juvenile demonstrators were detained for long periods of time without bail or hearing.[61] A judge in one community explained that "[i]f one is bad enough to keep locked up, they're not entitled to bail; and if they're not bad enough, there's no use to make them make bond."[62] In another community, one fourteen-year-old girl demonstrator was detained in jail for eighty-seven days without a hearing of the charges against her.[63]

In contrast with the many states whose statutes state specific reasons which justify detention, at least ten states merely authorize detention when release would be "inexpedient," "impracticable" or "inadvisable."[64] Although it seems as if any alleged delinquent could be detained under this language, in *Baldwin* v. *Lewis*,[65] the court ordered a child released "unless

---

[57] Ex Parte Cromwell, 232 Md. 305, 192 A.2d 775 (1963).

[58] *Id.* at 309, 192 A.2d at 778.

[59] *Id.* at 310, 192 A.2d at 778.

[60] In the Matter of Cromwell, 232 Md. 409, 414, 194 A.2d 88, 90 (1963).

[61] United States Commission on Civil Rights, Law Enforcement: A Report on Equal Protection in the South at 81 (1965). See also Starr, Southern Juvenile Courts, A Study of Irony, Civil Rights, and Judicial Practice, 13 Crime and Delinq. 289 (1967).

[62] United States Commission on Civil Rights, Law Enforcement: A Report on Equal Protection in the South 81 (1965).

[63] *Id.* at 82.

[64] "Inexpedient": Ala. Code tit. 13, § 352(4) (1959). "Impracticable": D.C. Code Ann. § 16-2306(a) (1967); N.J. Rev. Stat. § 2A:4-32 (1952); Ohio Rev. Code Ann. § 2151.31 (Page 1968); R.I. Gen. Laws Ann. § 14-1-20 (1956). "Impracticable and undesirable": Mo. Ann. Stat. § 211.141(1) (1962); Wis. Stat. Ann. § 48.29(1) (1957); "Impracticable or inadvisable": Nev. Rev. Stat. § 62.170(1) (1967); Okla. Stat. Ann. tit. 10, § 1107(a) (Supp. 1969-70).

[65] 300 F. Supp. 1220 (E.D. Wis. 1969).

there is a finding that because of the circumstances, including the gravity of the alleged crime, the nature of the juvenile's home life, and the juvenile's previous contacts with the court, the parents or guardian of the juvenile are incapable under the circumstances to care for him."[66]

II. DETENTION PROCEDURES

To find out who is making detention decisions which do not conform to juvenile court philosophy and why they are doing so, the procedures for these decisions must be examined. Detention decisions are made at three different levels by people with different professional backgrounds and duties.

A. Police

The initial decision to detain or release a juvenile is made by the police.[67] The police can: (1) release; (2) release accompanied by an official report describing the encounter with the juvenile; (3) officially "reprimand" with release to parent or guardian; (4) refer to other agencies when it is believed that some rehabilitative program should be set up after more investigation; (5) supervise when it is felt that an officer and parent can assist a child cooperatively; (6) refer to the juvenile court without detention; and, (7) refer to the juvenile court with detention.[68]

Most statutory references to the police suggest a preference for release. A typical provision directs the officer to release the child to the custody of his parents or other responsible adult upon his promise to return the child to court for a hearing.[69] However, the policeman's duty to release is far from

---

[66] *Id.* at 1233.

[67] Juvenile Detention, *supra* note 1, at 29.

[68] Piliavin and Briar, Police Encounters with Juveniles, 70 Am. J. Sociol. 206, 208 (1964).

[69] See Cal. Welfare and Institutions Code § 626(b) (West 1966) which allows release without a promise; Colo. Rev. Stat. Ann. § 22-2-3(4) (Supp. 1967); Del. Code Ann. tit. 10, § 975(a)(1) (Supp. 1968); D.C. Code Encycl. Ann. § 16-2306(a) (1966); Fla. Stat. Ann. § 39.03(2) (1961); Hawaii Rev. Stat. § 571-31 (1968); Idaho Code Ann. § 16-1811.1(c) (Supp. 1969); Ind. Ann. Stat. § 9-3212 (Supp. 1968); Iowa Code Ann. § 232.16 (1969); Ky. Rev. Stat. § 208.110(3) (1962); Md. Ann. Code art. 26, § 70-10(a) (Supp. 1969); Mass. Ann. Laws Ann. ch. 119, § 67 (1965); Mich. Comp. Laws Ann. § 712A.14 (1968); Minn. Stat. Ann. § 260.171(1) (Supp. 1969); Miss. Code Ann. § 7187-06 (Supp. 1968); Mo. Rev. Stat. § 211.141(1) (1959); Nev. Rev. Stat. § 62.170 (1967); Mont. Rev. Codes Ann. § 10-608.1(2) (Supp. 1969); N.J. Stat. Ann. § 2A:4-32 (1952); N.M. Stat. Ann. § 13-8-42 (1953); N.Y. Fam. Ct. Act § 724(b)(i) (Supp. 1969); N.C. Gen. Stat. § 110-27 (1966); N.D. Cent. Code § 27-20-15(1)(a) (Supp. 1969); Ohio Rev. Code Ann. § 2151.31 (Page 1968); P.R. Laws Ann. tit. 34, App. I, Rule 3.2 (Supp. 1968); S.C. Code Ann. § 15-1095.17(a) (Supp. 1969); S.D. Comp. Laws Ann. § 26-8-39 (1967); Tex. Rev. Civ. Stat. art. 2338-1, § 11 (1964); Utah Code Ann. § 55-10-90 (Supp. 1969); Wyo. Stat. Ann. § 14-102(b) (1957). See also Uniform Juv. Ct. Act § 15(a)(1); NCCD Standard Fam. Ct. Act § 16 (1959) and NCCD Standard Juv. Ct. Act § 16 (1968), which allow the officer to request a written promise if he thinks it desirable. Some statutes direct that the officer "in determining which disposition of the minor he will make . . . shall prefer the alternative which least restricts the minor's freedom and movement." See Cal. Welfare and Institutions Code § 626(b) (West 1966) and Neb. Rev. Stat. § 43-205.02(3) (1968). References to statutory provisions in this section are, unless otherwise indicated, to the above provisions.

mandatory. The statutes often provide that he need not release the juvenile if such action would be "undesirable,"[70] "impracticable,"[71] or not in the best interests of the child or community.[72] Only a few statutes, such as Georgia's, express a preference for detaining rather than releasing a juvenile.[73]

Despite this statutory preference for release, police often detain rather than release a child. A 1964 study reported that although detention rates vary widely, it was not uncommon for over 50 percent of children referred to court to be detained.[74] Recent studies show similar results. For example, one study of several counties revealed that 66 percent of those referred to court were detained,[75] while a study of a community in another state showed a detention rate of 62 percent.[76]

Most jurisdictions have some statutory limitations on police detention. The most severe one is a requirement that the police take the child before a juvenile court "immediately," "forthwith," or "without delay."[77]

In jurisdictions with these statutory limitations, the police do not have the authority to detain, but can only recommend detention to the judge or the probation officer. In practice, however, the police make detention decisions even in these jurisdictions. For example, in California, a jurisdiction with this limitation on police detention, a recent study of several counties showed that "police officers make the initial detention decision with the endorsement of both the judge and the probation department."[78]

Equally startling to the study team was "police belief that law enforcement agencies are responsible for, and in fact [are], determining local detention policies. If police respondents perceived this issue correctly, then law enforcement agencies are doing the work of the courts and probation departments."[79]

Despite the fact that California police do not have the power to detain, the statutory procedure "has not been sufficient to relieve California of the ignoble distinction of having one of the highest detention rates in the country."[80] The reasons for the high detention rates and perhaps the prominent police involvement in them are described in a recent article.

> Most minors are arrested at night or on the weekends. The Attorney General has ruled that the obligation to immediately investigate is satisfied if the probation officer begins the investigation at 8 A.M. on the next judicial day. . . .

[70] See Missouri.

[71] See the District of Columbia, Florida, Indiana, Missouri, Nevada, and New Jersey.

[72] See Idaho, Minnesota, South Dakota, Utah, and Virginia.

[73] Ga. Code Ann. § 24-2416 (Supp. 1968): "It shall be the [duty] of the officer taking the juvenile offender into custody to place him in such detention home. . . ."

[74] For release and detention figures taken from Detroit, Indianapolis, San Diego, and Washington D.C. police reports, see D. Freed and P. Wald, *supra* note 3, at 97.

[75] California Study, *supra* note 12, at 66.

[76] Seattle Police Department, Annual Report for 1967 at 24.

[77] See California, Florida, and Vermont, Vt. Stat. Ann. tit. 33, § 640 (Supp. 1969).

[78] California Study, *supra* note 12, at 40.

[79] *Id.* at 62.

[80] Boches, Juvenile Justice In California: A Re-Evaluation, 19 Hastings L.J. 47, 73 (1967).

The probation officer can detain the minor for 48 hours, *nonjudicial days excepted,* without filing a petition, and the detention hearing is not held until the following day. As a practical matter this may stretch the period of detention to 6 days.[81]

Other statutory schemes for limiting police authorized detention, such as requiring a court order for detention,[82] notifying the judge or intake that a juvenile is in detention,[83] filing of a petition alleging delinquency within a specified time,[84] and/or requiring court review of the decision to detain within a specified number of days,[85] have also proved ineffective.

Because the police department is the only agency which is available twenty-four hours a day, seven days a week,[86] it is frequently called on to

---

[81] *Id.* at 73–74.

[82] See pp. 180–86 *infra* on Judicial Review. Those jurisdictions requiring a court order or authorization for detention are: Alabama, Ala. Code tit. 13, § 352(4) (1958); Connecticut, Conn. Gen. Stat. Rev. § 17-63 (1960); District of Columbia, D.C. Code Encycl. Ann. § 16-2306(b) (1967); Florida, Fla. Stat. Ann. § 39.03(3) (1961); Georgia, Ga. Code Ann. § 24-2416 (Supp. 1968); Idaho, Idaho Code Ann. § 16-1811(4) (Supp. 1969); Iowa, Iowa Code Ann. § 232.17 (1969); Kentucky, Ky. Rev. Stat. § 208.110(4) (1962); Mississippi, Miss. Code Ann. § 7187-06 (Supp. 1968); Missouri, Mo. Rev. Stat. § 211.141(2) (1959); Nebraska, Neb. Rev. Stat. § 43.206.04 (1968); New Mexico, N.M. Stat. Ann. § 13-8-43(2) (Replacement 1968); Oregon, Ore. Rev. Stat. § 419.577(3) (1968); Pennsylvania, Pa. Stat. Ann. tit. 11, § 248 (1965); Puerto Rico, P.R. Laws Ann. tit. 34, § 2007(b) (Supp. 1968); South Carolina, S.C. Code Ann. § 15-1095.17(b) (Supp. 1968); Vermont, Vt. Stat. Ann. tit. 33, § 641(a) (Supp. 1969); Washington, Wash. Rev. Code Ann. § 13.04.053 (Supp. 1968); Wisconsin, Wis. Stat. § 48.29 (1963); NCCD Standard Fam. Ct. Act § 17(1) (1959); NCCD Standard Juv. Ct. Act § 17(1) (1968). All references to detention statutes in this section are to the statutory provisions cited in this footnote.

[83] See Alaska Stat. § 47.10.140(b) (1962); D.C. Code Encycl. Ann. § 16-2306(a) (1966); Fla. Stat. Ann. § 39.03 (1961); Hawaii Rev. Stat. § 571-32 (1968); Iowa Code Ann. § 232.17 (1969); Mass. Ann. Laws ch. 119, § 67 (1965); Minn. Stat. Ann. § 260.171(2) (Supp. 1969); Miss. Code Ann. § 7187-06 (Supp. 1968); Mont. Rev. Codes Ann. § 10-608.1(4) (Supp. 1969); Nev. Rev. Stat. § 62.170(1) (1967); N.H. Rev. Stat. Ann. § 169.6 (Replacement 1964); N.J. Rev. Stat. § 2A:4-32 (1952); N.M. Stat. Ann. § 13-8-43 (Replacement 1968); Ore. Rev. Stat. § 419.577(1)(b) (1968); R.I. Gen. Laws Ann. § 14-1-20 (1956); S.D. Comp. Laws Ann. § 26-8-19.4 (Supp. 1969); Utah Code Ann. § 55-10-90 (Supp. 1969); Wash. Rev. Code Ann. § 13.04.120 (1962); Wyo. Stat. Ann. § 14-102 (1957).

[84] Within forty-eight hours, excluding noncourt days, see Cal. Welf. and Institutions Code § 631 (West 1966); Colo. Rev. Stat. Ann. § 22-2-3(3) (Supp. 1967); Iowa Code Ann. § 232.17 (1969); Neb. Rev. Stat. § 43-205.04 (1968); S.D. Comp. Laws Ann. § 26-8-23.1 (Supp. 1969). Within twenty-four hours see Idaho Code Ann. § 16-1811(4) (Supp. 1969). Within seventy-two hours, see Wash. Rev. Code Ann. § 13.04.053 (Supp. 1968). The Uniform Juv. Ct. Act § 17(b) merely requires the petition to be made "promptly." The typical period is forty-eight hours, excluding the noncourt days, long enough to allow short-term punitive detention. The success of this limitation has been noted in one city where the court requires a petition to be filed within forty-eight hours of detention. The embarrassment of commencing cases that cannot be successfully prosecuted is considered an effective sanction against unnecessary detention. See Note, Juvenile Delinquents: The Police, State Courts, and Individualized Justice, 79 Harv. L. Rev. 775, 792 (1966) (hereinafter cited as Harvard Study).

[85] Although many statutes require a court order for detention, the extent of actual judicial review contemplated by such provisions is uncertain. Only Idaho seems to require the child actually to be brought before the court within twenty-four hours when the court must hand down its order. This encourages the court to independently assess the need for detention, rather than to perfunctorily approve a police officer's report.

[86] Juv. Delinq. and Youth Crime, *supra* note 1, at 13.

detain juveniles. Although juveniles can be detained at any time,[87] procedures for release must fit into the more relaxed eight-hour day, five-days-a-week schedules of courts and probation departments.[88]

Several suggestions have been made to alleviate this problem: (1) An intake officer should be on duty after regular court hours[89]; (2) a juvenile should not be detained for a period of longer than twenty-four hours without the filing of a petition (this rule should operate continuously irrespective of Sundays or holidays)[90]; (3) police should be required to furnish a complete report at the time of detention, describing the reasons for their recommendations.[91]

III. LENGTH AND PLACE OF DETENTION

A large number of children are detained longer than one would expect from the phrase "temporary detention." Only a few states effectively limit the period of detention by requiring the fact finding hearing to be held within a specified period of time after detention.[92] A few others merely give priority

[87] That a higher proportion of juveniles are detained after court hours has long been suspected. Recent California statistics confirm this pattern in nine out of eleven counties studied. In three counties virtually all children apprehended after work hours are automatically detained. California Study, *supra* note 12, at 71–72.

[88] For example, in one county where petitions are routinely filed before detention, when a child is apprehended after 3:00 P.M., the required paper work cannot be completed in time to take children to the detention home that day. These children are held in special juvenile quarters, until the next day when they are transferred to the detention home. Nat'l Council of Juv. Ct. Judges, Study of Peoria County, Illinois 6 (1965). In one Ohio county, it is reported that police can "cool" a child by apprehending and detaining him after court hours, thereby avoiding court intake screening until the next court day. Trumbull County Study, *supra* note 50, at 31.

[89] Sheridan suggests that in larger communities, intake staff coverage regarding need for detention should be provided at least until midnight, after which consultation should be available by telephone. Sheridan, Juvenile Court Intake, 2 J. Fam. Law 139, 152 (1962). One smaller community has succeeded in vastly reducing its detention rate by limiting detention authorization on weekends and after 5:00 P.M. to the county Probation Director whose phone number is listed with law enforcement officials. See Panel Discussion: "State Responsibility for Regional Detention: A Means of Getting Out of Jails," 19 Juv. Ct. Judges J. 67 (1968) (Statement by Carl J. Constantino). See also S. Norman and A. Barstis, *supra* note 3, at 8.

[90] The Children's Bureau requires the petition to be filed within twenty-four hours, not exempting weekends or holidays. See Children's Bureau Standards, *supra* note 8, at 61.

[91] Many jurisdictions now require such a report. See Colo. Rev. Stat. Ann. § 22-2-2(4) (Supp. 1967); D.C. Code Encycl. Ann. § 16-2306 (1966); Ga. Code Ann. § 24-2416 (Supp. 1968); Hawaii Rev. Stat. § 571-32 (1968); Ky. Rev. Stat. § 208.110(4) (1962); Miss. Code Ann. § 7187-06 (Supp. 1969); Mont. Rev. Codes Ann. § 10-608.1(4) (Supp. 1969); N.M. Stat. Ann. § 13-8-43 (Replacement 1968); N.D. Cent. Code § 27-20-15(1)(b) (Supp. 1969); Ohio Rev. Code Ann. § 2151.31 (Page 1968); S.C. Code Ann. § 15-1095.17(b) (Supp. 1968); Utah Code Ann. § 55-10-90 (Supp. 1969); Uniform Juv. Ct. Act § 15(a)(2); Model Rules for Juv. Cts. rule 12. Detention Standards, *supra* note 2, at 24–25 suggests a copy of the report should go to the probation department immediately.

[92] See Cal. Welfare and Institutions Code §§ 638, 657 (West Supp. 1969) (hearing within fifteen days with continuances only on day to day basis at respondent's request); Ill. Ann. Stat. ch. 37, § 704-2 (Smith-Hurd Supp. 1969) (hearing within ten days, or later if necessary to serve the summons or give statutory notice); New York Fam. Ct. Act §§ 747, 748 (Supp. 1969) (hearing within three days of petition's filing, but less severe, yet meaningful restrictions on adjournment). One New York case condemned the granting of a motion to adjourn where the detained child's attorney had opposed it. *People* v. *Poland,* 44 Misc. 2d 769, 225 N.Y.S.2d 5 (Sup. Ct. 1964).

to detained juveniles when scheduling adjudicatory hearings.[93] Some states limit how long the court may detain a child but they also allow the court to renew its order.[94]

Unfortunately, substantial numbers of children are detained for periods much longer than the two-week period recommended by the NCCD.[95] Complete statistics on length of detention are difficult to obtain, as are most detention statistics. However, some information on the subject was obtained by the NCCD in its survey for the President's Commission on Law Enforcement and the Administration of Justice. The survey found that in jails and detention homes, the period of detention ranged from one to sixty-eight days.[96] Fifty percent of the children, as tabulated in their sample counties, stayed more than sixteen days.[97]

NCCD concluded that the long stays result from the misconceptions shared by many judges

. . . that these facilities are all-purpose institutions for: (a) meeting health or mental needs; (b) punishment or "treatment" in lieu of a training school commitment; (c) retarded children until a state institution can receive them; (d) pregnant girls until they can be placed prior to delivery; (e) brain-injured children involved in delinquency; (f) protection from irate parents who might harm the child; (g) a material witness in an adult case; (h) giving the delinquent "short sharp shock" treatment: (i) educational purposes ("[h]e'll have to go to school in detention"); (j) therapy; (k) "ethical and moral" training; (l) lodging until an appropriate foster home or institution turns up.[98]

The Juvenile Study also obtained recent data on length of detention and found that large numbers of children are detained for longer than two weeks.[99] The most alarming figures were those for the District of Columbia.[100] This decision to detain a juvenile is a most significant one. He will be removed from his home, his friends, and his school for a considerable period of time. Yet in 1965, approximately 88,000 children were held in jails throughout the United States.[101]

Jail has been described as the "weakest link of the entire correction system."[102] "Even when a competent sheriff maintains good internal discipline, proper segregation of inmates, and satisfactory housekeeping condi-

[93] E.g., N.D. Cent. Code § 27-20-29(5) (Supp. 1969).

[94] Alaska Rules of Ct. Proc. and Administration, Rules of Juv. Proc. 7(a) (Supp. 1966) limits the order to thirty days, allowing renewal upon written findings and approval of a superior court. Wash. Rev. Code Ann. § 13.04.053 (1968) allows thirty days' detention under a court order, with no apparent limits on renewals.

[95] Detention Standards, *supra* note 2, at 30.

[96] Juvenile Detention, *supra* note 1, at 34.

[97] *Id.* at 35.

[98] *Id.*

[99] See App. D.

[100] District of Columbia Receiving Home, Weekly Master Population Sheet 1 (Sept. 28, 1969). See App. E.

[101] Juvenile Detention, *supra* note 1, at 14–15.

[102] Eaton, Detention Facilities in Non-metropolitan Counties, 17 Juv. Ct. Judges J. 9, 10 (1966).

tions, the usual absence of a rehabilitation program, detrimental to adult prisoners, is even worse for juveniles."[103]

Abuses in juvenile jail detentions were highlighted in a Washington newspaper account of disciplinary practices in a suburban jail, where juveniles were sent because of overcrowding in the regular juvenile detention facilities. At least one "misbehaving" juvenile had been placed in solitary confinement on a bread and water diet; a regime without parallel in other Washington, D.C., suburbs, according to the newspaper account.[104] The story noted that solitary confinement is used in all jurisdictions for juveniles but without dietary restrictions.[105]

Jail "atrocities" are not confined to the Washington metropolitan area. A witness before a Senate Judiciary Subcommittee reported that in the Cook County jail juveniles fourteen years old or older were sexually molested, tortured, beaten, and murdered by other prisoners.[106] Other examples have been noted. Although there have been no court decisions on the suitability of a jail as a place of detention, two recent cases challenged the suitability of detention homes in the District of Columbia. Detention facilities, since they are intended to be used for very short periods, do not have, and are not intended to have, programs comparable to those in the facilities for adjudicated juveniles, nor can they realistically duplicate a home environment. The kind of care that they must provide has not been established as yet.

In the first case attacking the suitability of detention facilities, *Creek* v. *Stone*,[107] the juvenile alleged that the D.C. receiving home had no provision for the psychiatric assistance he needed. Despite his repeated requests, the juvenile court refused to hold a hearing regarding the suitability of the receiving home as a place of detention.[108] Although the appeal was dismissed as moot, the United States Court of Appeals for the District of Columbia pointed out that the juvenile code establishes a legal right to custody not inconsistent with the *parens patriae* premise of the law.[109] The court also said that when a juvenile court is presented with a substantial complaint that needed treatment is not provided, it should make an appropriate inquiry to ensure that the statutory criteria as applied to juveniles is being met.[110]

Wilson v. *Stone*[111] also raised the question of the suitability of a detention facility. The juvenile alleged that the receiving home annex did not have a proper education, recreation, or therapy program. The court ordered the detention facility to conduct classes for the same number of hours per day as the public schools.[112] It is worth noting that although Wilson was detained

[103] *Id.*
[104] Washington Post, Feb. 13, 1969, § F at 1, col. 2.
[105] *Id.*
[106] Washington Post, Mar. 7, 1969, § A at 11, col. 1.
[107] 379 F.2d 106 (D.C. Cir. 1967).
[108] *Id.* at 108.
[109] *Id.* at 111.
[110] *Id.*
[111] No. 69-3250-J (D.C. Juv. Ct. Sept. 10, 1969).
[112] *Id.*

for more than three months, waiting for a hearing because he could not be trusted in the community, the hearing resulted in his return to the community.[113]

IV. THE NEED FOR DETENTION

The *Wilson* case was not an isolated incident of a detained juvenile being returned to the community after his adjudication hearing. In fact, the NCCD study showed that of 409,218 children detained, approximately 167,000 were neither committed to an institution nor placed on probation.[114] Either the court found that these children were not delinquent when the hearing finally occurred, or no delinquency petition was filed. Justification for detention in these cases seems completely lacking.

The Juvenile Study obtained statistics from five communities in order to get more detailed and recent statistics on the disposition of detained children. The results showed that the vast majority of detained children remained in the community after adjudication. In Massachusetts only 25.9 percent of all children held in detention homes were removed from the community.[115] In Sangamon County, Illinois,[116] Trumbull County, Ohio,[117] and Tarrant County, Texas,[118] only 22 percent, 19.5 percent, and 9.7 percent of the detained population were removed from the community.

A more complete picture of dispositions of detained juveniles can be obtained by taking a comprehensive look at the detention picture in one jurisdiction. Of the 284 juveniles in the "Affluent County" sample, fifty-five, or 19.4 percent, were detained. This rate of detention compares favorably with the "standard" rate established by the NCCD, as determined by the rate of police referrals to juvenile courts.[119]

Eighteen (32.7 percent) of the fifty-five children were released by the intake department of Affluent County Juvenile Court. An additional eleven (20.0 percent) were released from detention following a detention hearing. Thus, the court decided that thirty-four (61.8 percent) juveniles detained by the police did not require continued detention.

More than three-fourths of the detained children remained in the community after court action on their case was completed. In fact, no petition at all was filed for one-fourth of the children.

The detention of forty-five of these fifty-five children is, at best, highly questionable.

---

[113] *Id.*

[114] Juvenile Detention, *supra* note 1, at 36.

[115] Massachusetts Study, *supra* note 74.

[116] U.S. Children's Bureau, A Study of Services for Delinquent Children in Sangamon County, Illinois. pt. III, at 5 (1967).

[117] Trumbull County Study, *supra* note 50, pt. II, at 5.

[118] Texas Study, *supra* note 75, pt. II, at 8.

[119] Detention Standards, *supra* note 2, at 19.

V. CONCLUSION

This article began as an inquiry into factors that cause the high rate of juvenile detention. The rate has been criticized by innumerable commentators, as has almost every other aspect of juvenile detention.

Very few communities, however, have adopted suggested solutions. One must assume that there are valid reasons why reforms have not been adopted.

One possibility is that the generally accepted policy of releasing most juveniles to their homes to await court action is wrong. If this is the case, the fact that the detention rate remains high is to be expected. On the other hand, if the policy is correct, it is most important to find out why the criticisms and recommendations are ignored time after time.

The available evidence clearly indicates that the policy is not wrong. Large numbers of juveniles are detained and then released to the community, either without any delinquency petition, or after the adjudication decision. Therefore, it seems unlikely that their detention was necessary.

It is possible, of course, that information not currently available would show that a larger number of persons need to be detained than the experts have stated. Such information might also show that disputed criteria are more justifiable than they seem at present.

Unfortunately, the absence of useful information occurs for the same reason as the high detention rates. The fact that twenty-two states do not even bother to keep any detention statistics documents the broad indifference to the problem. The statistics in other states are usually so incomplete that they are useless for planning personnel, facilities, or anything else. The absence of data, crucial for making any changes in the present detention system, is a major block to solving the problem.

The most important, but least available, data is the reason why each detained child has been held. Without this information, it is impossible to tell if the detention is unjustified under existing criteria.

How many children are being held in detention because they need shelter care, foster parents, or treatment in a mental hospital? Until the number of detained children who need this care is known and communicated to the public, there is little hope that the necessary facilities will be established.

The variation in detention practices among the police, the intake worker, and the judge shows an indifference to the plight of juveniles. It does not seem impossible for these departments of the judicial system to coordinate their work. Nor does it seem unreasonable to expect more judges to exercise the legal control that they have over detention. Some of them already do so.

The courts, of course, are to some extent limited by the facilities available to them. Public complaints about the criminal acts committed by juveniles also puts pressure on judges to detain alleged delinquents. It is probably true that large numbers of juveniles who are alleged to have committed delinquent offenses, in fact, have done so. It is also true that the community feels that more attention should be paid to protecting its rights and safety. It is doubtful, however, that present detention practices protect the community.

Indifference on the part of the public, the legislatures, the police, and the juvenile court has created detention procedures and practices in many communities which do not protect the rights of the public or the juvenile and which also fail to meet the needs of neglected and dependent children. This state of affairs will continue until indifference is replaced by concerned supporters, creative solutions, and the funds to carry them out.

APPENDIX A

Rates of Detention in Selected Jurisdictions (1968)

Locality[a]	Percent of All Apprehended Juveniles Detained[b]	Percent of All Court Referrals Detained
A	11.0	N/A[c]
B	14.4	N/A
C	18.0	N/A
D	18.0	55.3
E	22.0	39.7
F	29.0	47.9
G	32.3	59.8
H	33.0	N/A
I	N/A	74.0

[a] See note 14 *supra*. In Trumbull County, Ohio, and Tarrant County, Texas, 1967 statistics were used because they were currently available. Because most of these cities were designated as not for general distribution, we have not identified the specific jurisdictions listed in the table.
[b] NCCD defines rate of detention as follows: "The rate of detaining is the total number of children detained for delinquency divided by the total number apprehended and booked for delinquent acts." Juvenile Detention, *supra* note 1, at 31 (1967). To the best of our knowledge this definition was followed by the communities shown in Table I. NCCD considers the apprehension base more useful than the court referral base. *Id.*
[c] N/A, not available.

APPENDIX B

Percentage of Detention by Offense[a]

Offenses	A	B	C	D	E	F	G	H	I	J	K
Against persons	24.9	8.8	17.6	8.1	N/A[b]	5.2	1.6	1.0	3.0	6.1	3.0
Against property	45.5	19.1	31.1	20.0	N/A	22.3	15.1	24.0	36.7	32.9	32.0
Conduct[c]	9.9	15.0	6.9	N/A	N/A	N/A	8.2	8.1	9.5	12.2	15.0
Status[d]	16.5	32.3	23.0	64.2	21.8	54.3	68.5	65.2	32.5	38.6	45.0
Traffic	N/A	0.4	0.8	N/A	N/A	N/A	N/A	1.0	1.7	1.4	3.0
All others	3.3	24.4	20.7	7.6	N/A	18.2	6.6	0.8	16.6	8.8	2.0

[a] The data were obtained in the same manner as the data for App. A. See note 14 *supra*. For App. B usable data were obtained from Baltimore, Chicago, District of Columbia, Los Angeles, New York City, and Seattle; statistics were also obtained from Marion County (Oregon), Sangamon County (Illinois), Tarrant County (Texas), Trumbull County (Ohio), and Volusia County (Florida).
[b] N/A, not available.
[c] Some localities differentiate the category "conduct offenses" as not fitting within the crimes against persons or property categories. Examples of such conduct offenses include drunk and disorderly, escapee, disturbing the peace, and mischief, among others.
[d] Status offenses are those classified as delinquencies only if committed by juveniles, and include truancy, running away, and ungovernableness.

APPENDIX C

Percentage of Detained Children
Charged with Dangerous Offenses

Locality	Percent of All Detained	
	Column I[a]	Column II[b]
C	25.2	41.3
D	18.6	32.7
F	6.7	15.2
G	1.6	5.8
H	1.2	9.8

[a] Homicide, aggravated assault, rape and other sex offenses, robbery, arson, and possession of dangerous weapons are defined as dangerous offenses in Column I.
[b] All of the above, plus burglary, are considered dangerous offenses in Column II.

APPENDIX D

Length of Stay in Detention

Location	Under 2 Weeks	2 Weeks to 1 Month	1–2 Months	Over 2 Months
Affluent County[a]	70.9	14.5	9.9	4.7
State of Massachusetts[b]	57.3	24.8	12.8	5.1
Trumbull County, Ohio[c]	96.6	3.4	0	0
District of Columbia[d]	32.9	20.6	16.2	30.3
Sangamon County, Ill.[e]	94.9	4.4	0.7	0

[a] The percentages for Affluent County are based on our field study. We selected random samples of juveniles handled formally and informally by Affluent County Juvenile Court during 1968 and the first five months of 1969. The samples consisted of 166 informal cases and 126 formals. Of these 292 juveniles, 55 were detained, 19 of the informals and 36 of the formals.
[b] Massachusetts Study, *supra* note 74, pt. III, at 31–34.
[c] Trumbull County Study, *supra* note 50, pt. II, at 5.
[d] District of Columbia Receiving Home, Weekly Master Population Sheet 1 (Sept. 28, 1969).
[e] U.S. Children's Bureau, A Study of Services for Delinquent Children in Sangamon County, Illinois, pt. II, at 14 (1967). Sangamon County includes the city of Springfield, and had a population of 150,000 at the time of the study.

APPENDIX E

Period of Detention in District of Columbia

Time Detained	No. of Children	Percent of All Detained
More than 2 weeks	157	67.1
More than 6 weeks	83	35.4
More than 10 weeks	59	25.2
More than 14 weeks	39	16.7
More than 18 weeks	18	7.7
More than 20 weeks	12	5.1

13
POLICE ENCOUNTERS WITH JUVENILES*
Irving Piliavin and Scott Briar

This is one of the most commonly cited and reprinted papers in the criminological literature of the past decade, probably because it demonstrates the distinctly *human* (nonuniversalistic) nature of discretion. The decision to arrest and/or detain is very much a function of the social interaction between officer and offender. While in this case we are dealing with discretion on the street, there is no reason to assume that the situation in the station is all that different. Nor is it the case that social and legal factors act in opposition to each other, i.e., decisions being based *either* on demeanor *or* on the nature of the offense. The Piliavin and Briar data show an *interaction* effect, such that demeanor is most important in first offenses and declines with subsequent offenses.

---

* From *American Journal of Sociology*, 70, 2(1964): pp. 206–14. Reprinted by permission of the authors and publisher. This study was supported by Grant MH-06328-02, National Institute of Mental Health, United States Public Health Service.

As the first of a series of decisions made in the channeling of youthful offenders through the agencies concerned with juvenile justice and corrections, the disposition decisions made by police officers have potentially profound consequences for apprehended juveniles. Thus arrest, the most severe of the dispositions available to police, may not only lead to confinement of the suspected offender but also bring him loss of social status, restriction of educational and employment opportunities, and future harassment by law enforcement personnel.[1] According to some criminologists, the stigmatization resulting from police apprehension, arrest, and detention actually reinforces deviant behavior.[2] Other authorities have suggested, in fact, that this stigmatization serves as the catalytic agent initiating delinquent careers.[3] Despite their presumed significance, however, little empirical analysis has been reported regarding the factors influencing, or consequences resulting from, police actions with juvenile offenders. Furthermore, while some studies of police encounters with adult offenders have been reported, the extent to which the findings of these

---

[1] Richard D. Schwartz and Jerome H. Skolnick, "Two Studies of Legal Stigma," *Social Problems* 10 (April 1962): 133–42; Sol Rubin, *Crime and Juvenile Delinquency* (New York: Oceana Publications, Inc., 1958); B. F. McSally, "Finding Jobs for Released Offenders," *Federal Probation* 24 (June 1960): 12–17; Harold D. Lasswell and Richard C. Donnelly, "The Continuing Debate over Responsibility: An Introduction To Isolating the Condemnation Sanction," *Yale Law Journal* 68 (April 1959): 869–99.

[2] Richard A. Cloward and Lloyd E. Ohlin, *Delinquency and Opportunity* (New York: The Free Press, 1960), pp. 124–30.

[3] Frank Tannenbaum, *Crime and the Community* (New York: Columbia University Press, 1936), pp. 17–20; Howard S. Becker, *Outsiders: Studies in the Sociology of Deviance* (New York: The Free Press, 1963), chaps. 1 and 2.

investigations pertain to law enforcement practices with youthful offenders is not known.[4]

The above considerations have led the writers to undertake a longitudinal study of the conditions influencing, and consequences flowing from, police actions with juveniles. In the present paper findings will be presented indicating the influence of certain factors on police actions. Research data consist primarily of notes and records based on nine months' observation of all juvenile officers in one police department.[5] The officers were observed in the course of their regular tours of duty.[6] While these data do not lend themselves to quantitative assessments of reliability and validity, the candor shown by the officers in their interviews with the investigators and their use of officially frowned-upon practices while under observation provide some assurance that the materials presented below accurately reflect the typical operations and attitudes of the law enforcement personnel studied.

The setting for the research, a metropolitan police department serving an industrial city with approximately 450,000 inhabitants, was noted within the community it served and among law enforcement officials elsewhere for the honesty and superior quality of its personnel. Incidents involving criminal activity or brutality by members of the department had been extremely rare during the ten years preceding this study; personnel standards were comparatively high; and an extensive training program was provided to both new and experienced personnel. Juvenile Bureau members, the primary subjects of this investigation, differed somewhat from other members of the department in that they were responsible for delinquency prevention as well as law enforcement, that is, juvenile officers were expected to be knowledgeable about conditions leading to crime and delinquency and to be able to work with community agencies serving known or potential juvenile offenders. Accordingly, in the assignment of personnel to the Juvenile Bureau, consideration was given not only to an officer's devotion to and reliability in law enforcement but also to his commitment to delinquency prevention. Assignment to the Bureau was of advantage to policemen seeking promotions. Consequently, many officers requested transfer to this unit, and its personnel comprised a highly select group of officers.

In the field, juvenile officers operated essentially as patrol officers. They cruised assigned beats and, although concerned primarily with juvenile offenders, frequently had occasion to apprehend and arrest adults. Con-

---

[4] For a detailed accounting of police discretionary practices, see Joseph Goldstein, "Police Discretion Not To Invoke the Criminal Process: Low Visibility Decisions in the Administration of Justice," *Yale Law Journal* 69 (1960): 543–94; Wayne R. LaFave, "The Police and Non-enforcement of the Law: Part I," *Wisconsin Law Review*, January 1962, 104–37; S. H. Kadish, "Legal Norms and Discretion in the Police and Sentencing Processes," *Harvard Law Review* 75 (March 1962): 904–31.

[5] Approximately thirty officers were assigned to the Juvenile Bureau in the department studied. While we had an opportunity to observe all officers in the Bureau during the study, our observations were concentrated on those who had been working in the Bureau for one or two years at least. Although two of the officers in the Juvenile Bureau were Negro, we observed these officers on only a few occasions.

[6] Although observations were not confined to specific days or work shifts, more observations were made during evenings and weekends because police activity was greatest during these periods.

frontations between the officers and juveniles occurred in one of the following three ways, in order of increasing frequency: (1) encounters resulting from officers' spotting officially "wanted" youths; (2) encounters taking place at or near the scene of offenses reported to police headquarters; and (3) encounters occurring as the result of officers' directly observing youths either committing offenses or in "suspicious circumstances." However, the probability that a confrontation would take place between officer and juvenile, or that a particular disposition of an identified offender would be made, was only in part determined by the knowledge that an offense had occurred or that a particular juvenile had committed an offense. The bases for and utilization of nonoffenses related criteria by police in accosting and disposing of juveniles are the focuses of the following discussion.

SANCTIONS FOR DISCRETION

In each encounter with juveniles, with the minor exception of officially "wanted" youths,[7] a central task confronting the officer was to decide what official action to take against the boys involved. In making these disposition decisions, officers could select any one of five discrete alternatives:

1. Outright release.
2. Release and submission of a "field interrogation report" briefly describing the circumstances initiating the police-juvenile confrontation.
3. "Official reprimand" and release to parents or guardian.
4. Citation to juvenile court.
5. Arrest and confinement in juvenile hall.

Dispositions 3, 4, and 5 differed from the others in two basic respects. First, with rare exceptions, when an officer chose to reprimand, cite, or arrest a boy, he took the youth to the police station. Second, the reprimanded, cited, or arrested boy acquired an official police "record"; that is, his name was officially recorded in Bureau files as a juvenile violator.

Analysis of the distribution of police disposition decisions about juveniles revealed that in virtually every category of offense the full range of official disposition alternatives available to officers was employed. This wide range of discretion resulted primarily from two conditions. First, it reflected the reluctance of officers to expose certain youths to the stigmatization presumed to be associated with official police action. Few juvenile officers believed that correctional agencies serving the community could effectively help delinquents. For some officers this attitude reflected a lack of confidence in rehabilitation techniques; for others, a belief that high case loads and lack of professional training among correctional workers vitiated their efforts at treatment. All officers were agreed, however, that juvenile justice and correctional processes were essentially concerned with apprehension and punishment rather than treatment. Furthermore, all officers believed

---

[7] "Wanted" juveniles usually were placed under arrest or in protective custody, a practice which in effect relieved officers of the responsibility for deciding what to do with these youths.

that some aspects of these processes (e.g., judicial definition of youths as delinquents and removal of delinquents from the community), as well as some of the possible consequences of these processes (e.g., intimate insitutional contact with "hard-core" delinquents, as well as parental, school, and conventional peer disapproval or rejection), could reinforce what previously might have been only a tentative proclivity toward delinquent values and behavior. Consequently, when officers found reason to doubt that a youth being confronted was highly committed toward deviance, they were inclined to treat him with leniency.

Second, and more important, the practice of discretion was sanctioned by police-department policy. Training manuals and departmental bulletins stressed that the disposition of each juvenile offender was not to be based solely on the type of infraction he committed. Thus, while it was departmental policy to "arrest and confine all juveniles who have committed a felony or misdemeanor involving theft, sex offense, battery, possession of dangerous weapons, prowling, peeping, intoxication, incorrigibility, and disturbance of the peace," it was acknowledged that "such considerations as age, attitude and prior criminal record might indicate that a different disposition would be more appropriate."[8] The official justification for discretion in processing juvenile offenders, based on the preventive aims of the Juvenile Bureau, was that each juvenile violator should be dealt with solely on the basis of what was best for him.[9] Unofficially, administrative legitimation of discretion was further justified on the grounds that strict enforcement practices would overcrowd court calendars and detention facilities, as well as dramatically increase juvenile crime rates—consequences to be avoided because they would expose the police department to community criticism.[10]

In practice, the official policy justifying use of discretion served as a demand that discretion be exercised. As such, it posed three problems for juvenile officers. First, it represented a departure from the traditional police practice with which the juvenile officers themselves were identified, in the sense that they were expected to justify their juvenile disposition decisions not simply by evidence proving a youth had committed a crime—grounds on which police were officially expected to base their dispositions of nonjuvenile offenders[11]—but in the *character* of the youth. Second, in disposing of juvenile offenders, officers were expected, in effect, to make judicial rather than ministerial decisions.[12] Third, the shift from the offense to the offender as the basis for determining the appropriate disposition substantially increased the uncertainty and ambiguity for officers in the situation of apprehension because no explicit rules existed for determining which dis-

---

[8] Quoted from a training manual issued by the police department studied in this research.

[9] Presumably this also implied that police action with juveniles was to be determined partly by the offenders' need for correctional services.

[10] This was reported by beat officers as well as supervisory and administrative personnel of the juvenile bureau.

[11] In actual practice, of course, disposition decisions regarding adult offenders also were influenced by many factors extraneous to the offense per se.

[12] For example, in dealing with adult violators, officers had no disposition alternative comparable to the reprimand-and-release category, a disposition which contained elements of punishment but did not involve mediation by the court.

position different types of youths should receive. Despite these problems, officers were constrained to base disposition decisions on the character of the apprehended youth, not only because they wanted to be fair, but because persistent failure to do so could result in judicial criticism, departmental censure, and, they believed, loss of authority with juveniles.[13]

DISPOSITION CRITERIA

Assessing the character of apprehended offenders posed relatively few difficulties for officers in the case of youths who had committed serious crimes, such as robbery, homicide, aggravated assault, grand theft, auto theft, rape, and arson. Officials generally regarded these juveniles as confirmed delinquents simply by virtue of their involvement in offenses of this magnitude.[14] However, the infraction committed did not always suffice to determine the appropriate disposition for some serious offenders[15]; and, in the case of minor offenders, who comprised over 90 percent of the youths against whom police took action, the violation per se generally played an insignificant role in the choice of disposition. While a number of minor offenders were seen as serious delinquents deserving arrest, many others were perceived either as "good" boys whose offenses were atypical of their customary behavior, as pawns of undesirable associates, or, in any case, as boys for whom arrest was regarded as an unwarranted and possibly harmful punishment. Thus, for nearly all minor violators and for some serious delinquents, the assessment of character—the distinction between serious delinquents, "good" boys, misguided youths, and so on—and the dispositions which followed from these assessments were based on youths' personal characteristics and not their offenses.

Despite this dependence of disposition decisions on the personal characteristics of these youths, however, police officers actually had access only to very limited information about boys at the time they had to decide what to do with them. In the field, officers typically had no data concerning the past offense records, school performance, family situation, or personal adjustment of apprehended youths.[16] Furthermore, files at police headquarters provided data only about each boy's prior offense record. Thus both the decision made in the field—whether or not to bring the boy in—and the

---

[13] The concern of officers over possible loss of authority stemmed from their belief that court failure to support arrests by appropriate action would cause policemen to "lose face" in the eyes of juveniles.

[14] It is also likely that the possibility of negative publicity resulting from the failure to arrest such violators—particularly if they became involved in further serious crime—brought about strong administrative pressure for their arrest.

[15] For example, in the year preceding this research, over 30 percent of the juveniles involved in burglaries and 12 percent of the juveniles committing auto theft received dispositions other than arrest.

[16] On occasion, officers apprehended youths whom they personally knew to be prior offenders. This did not occur frequently, however, for several reasons. First, approximately 75 percent of apprehended youths had no prior official records; second, officers periodically exchanged patrol areas, thus limiting their exposure to, and knowledge about, these areas; and third, patrolmen seldom spent more than three or four years in the juvenile division.

decision made at the station—which disposition to invoke—were based largely on cues which emerged from the interaction between the officer and the youth, cues from which the officer inferred the youth's character. These cues included the youth's group affiliations, age, race, grooming, dress, and demeanor. Older juveniles, members of known delinquent gangs, Negroes, youths with well-oiled hair, black jackets, and soiled denims or jeans (the presumed uniform of "tough" boys), and boys who in their interactions with officers did not manifest what were considered to be appropriate signs of respect tended to receive the more severe dispositions.

Other than prior record, the most important of the above clues was a youth's *demeanor*. In the opinion of juvenile patrolmen themselves, the demeanor of apprehended juveniles was a major determinant of their decisions for 50–60 percent of the juvenile cases they processed.[17] A less subjective indication of the association between a youth's demeanor and police disposition is provided by Table 1, which presents the police dispositions for sixty-six youths whose encounters with police were observed in the course of this study.[18] For purposes of this analysis, each youth's demeanor in the encounter was classified as either cooperative or uncooperative.[19] The results clearly reveal a marked association between youth demeanor and the severity of police dispositions.

TABLE 1

Severity of Police Disposition by Youth's Demeanor

Severity of Police Disposition	Youth's Demeanor		Total
	Cooperative	Uncooperative	
Arrest (most severe)	2	14	16
Citation or official reprimand	4	5	9
Informal reprimand	15	1	16
Admonish and release (least severe)	24	1	25
Total	45	21	66

The cues used by police to assess demeanor were fairly simple. Juveniles who were contrite about their infractions, respectful to officers, and fearful

[17] While reliable subgroup estimates were impossible to obtain through observation because of the relatively small number of incidents observed, the importance of demeanor in disposition decisions appeared to be much less significant with known prior offenders.

[18] Systematic data were collected on police encounters with seventy-six juveniles. In ten of these encounters the police concluded that their suspicions were groundless, and consequently the juveniles involved were exonerated; these ten cases were eliminated from this analysis of demeanor. (The total number of encounters observed was considerably more than seventy-six, but systematic data-collection procedures were not instituted until several months after observations began.)

[19] The data used for the classification of demeanor were the written records of observations made by the authors. The classifications were made by an independent judge not associated with this study. In classifying a youth's demeanor as cooperative or uncooperative, particular attention was paid to: (1) the youth's responses to police officers' questions and requests; (2) the respect and deference—or lack of these qualities—shown by the youth toward police officers; and (3) police officers' assessments of the youth's demeanor.

of the sanctions that might be employed against them tended to be viewed by patrolmen as basically law-abiding or at least "salvageable." For these youths it was usually assumed that informal or formal reprimand would suffice to guarantee their future conformity. In contrast, youthful offenders who were fractious, obdurate, or who appeared nonchalant in their encounters with patrolmen were likely to be viewed as "would-be tough guys" or "punks" who fully deserved the most severe sanction: arrest. The following excerpts from observation notes illustrate the importance attached to demeanor by police in making disposition decisions.

1.   The interrogation of "A" (an eighteen-year-old upper-lower-class white male accused of statutory rape) was assigned to a police sergeant with long experience on the force. As I sat in his office while we waited for the youth to arrive for questioning, the sergeant expressed his uncertainty as to what he should do with this young man. On the one hand, he could not ignore the fact that an offense had been committed; he had been informed, in fact, that the youth was prepared to confess to the offense. Nor could he overlook the continued pressure from the girl's father (an important political figure) for the police to take severe action against the youth. On the other hand, the sergeant had formed a low opinion of the girl's moral character, and he considered it unfair to charge "A" with statutory rape when the girl was a willing partner to the offense and might even have been the instigator of it. However, his sense of injustice concerning "A" was tempered by his image of the youth as a "punk," based, he explained, on information he had received that the youth belonged to a certain gang, the members of which were well known to, and disliked by, the police. Nevertheless, as we prepared to leave his office to interview "A," the sergeant was still in doubt as to what he should do with him.

As we walked down the corridor to the interrogation room, the sergeant was stopped by a reporter from the local newspaper. In an excited tone of voice, the reporter explained that his editor was pressing him to get further information about this case. The newspaper had printed some of the facts about the girl's disappearance, and as a consequence the girl's father was threatening suit against the paper for defamation of the girl's character. It would strengthen the newspaper's position, the reporter explained, if the police had information indicating that the girl's associates, particularly the youth the sergeant was about to interrogate, were persons of disreputable character. This stimulus seemed to resolve the sergeant's uncertainty. He told the reporter, "unofficially," that the youth was known to be an undesirable person, citing as evidence his membership in the delinquent gang. Furthermore, the sergeant added that he had evidence that this youth had been intimate with the girl over a period of many months. When the reporter asked if the police were planning to do anything to the youth, the sergeant answered that he intended to charge the youth with statutory rape.

In the interrogation, however, three points quickly emerged which profoundly affected the sergeant's judgment of the youth. First, the youth was polite and cooperative; he consistently addressed the officer as "sir," answered all questions quietly, and signed a statement implicating himself in numerous counts of statutory rape. Second, the youth's intentions toward the girl appeared to have been honorable; for example, he said that he wanted to marry her eventually. Third, the youth was not in fact a member of the gang in question. The sergeant's attitude became increasingly sympathetic, and after we left the interrogation room he announced his intention to "get 'A' off the hook," meaning that he wanted to have the charges against "A" reduced or, if possible, dropped.

2. Officers "X" and "Y" brought into the police station a seventeen-year-old white boy who, along with two older companions, had been found in a home having sex relations with a fifteen-year-old girl. The boy responded to police officers' queries slowly and with obvious disregard. It was apparent that his lack of deference toward the officers and his failure to evidence concern about his situation were irritating his questioners. Finally, one of the officers turned to me and, obviously angry, commented that in his view the boy was simply a "stud" interested only in sex, eating, and sleeping. The policemen conjectured that the boy "probably already had knocked up half a dozen girls." The boy ignored these remarks, except for an occasional impassive stare at the patrolmen. Turning to the boy, the officer remarked, "What the hell am I going to do with you?" And again the boy simply returned the officer's gaze. The latter then said, "Well, I guess we'll just have to put you away for a while." An arrest report was then made out and the boy was taken to Juvenile Hall.

Although anger and disgust frequently characterized officers' attitudes toward recalcitrant and impassive juvenile offenders, their manner while processing these youths was typically routine, restrained, and without rancor. While the officers' restraint may have been due in part to their desire to avoid accusation and censure, it also seemed to reflect their inurement to a frequent experience. By and large, only their occasional "needling" or insulting of a boy gave any hint of the underlying resentment and dislike they felt toward many of these youths.[20]

PREJUDICE IN APPREHENSION AND DISPOSITION DECISIONS

Compared to other youths, Negroes and boys whose appearance matched the delinquent stereotype were more frequently stopped and interrogated by patrolmen—often even in the absence of evidence that an offense had been committed[21]—and usually were given more severe dispositions for the same violations. Our data suggest, however, that these selective apprehension and disposition practices resulted not only from the intrusion of long-held prejudices of individual police officers but also from certain job-related experiences of law enforcement personnel. First, the tendency for police to give more severe dispositions to Negroes and to youths whose appearance

[20] Officers' animosity toward recalcitrant or aloof offenders appeared to stem from two sources: moral indignation that these juveniles were self-righteous and indifferent about their transgressions, and resentment that these youths failed to accord police the respect they believed they deserved. Since the patrolmen perceived themselves as honestly and impartially performing a vital community function warranting respect and deference from the community at large, they attributed the lack of respect shown them by these juveniles to the latters' immorality.

[21] The clearest evidence for this assertion is provided by the overrepresentation of Negroes among "innocent" juveniles accosted by the police. As noted, of the seventy-six juveniles on whom systematic data were collected, ten were exonerated and released without suspicion. Seven, or two-thirds, of these ten "innocent" juveniles were Negro, in contrast to the allegedly "guilty" youths, less than one-third of whom were Negro. The following incident illustrates the operation of this bias: One officer, observing a youth walking along the street, commented that the youth "looks suspicious" and promptly stopped and questioned him. Asked later to explain what aroused his suspicion, the officer explained, "He was a Negro wearing dark glasses at midnight."

corresponded to that which police associated with delinquents partly reflected the fact, observed in this study, that these youths also were much more likely than were other types of boys to exhibit the sort of recalcitrant demeanor which police construed as a sign of the confirmed delinquent. Further, officers assumed, partly on the basis of departmental statistics, that Negroes and juveniles who "look tough" (e.g., who wear chinos, leather jackets, boots, etc.) commit crimes more frequently than do other types of youths.[22] In this sense, the police justified their selective treatment of these youths along epidemiological lines: that is, they were concentrating their attention on those youths whom they believed were most likely to commit delinquent acts. In the words of one highly placed official in the department:

> If you know that the bulk of your delinquent problem comes from kids who, say, are from 12 to 14 years of age, when you're out on patrol you are much more likely to be sensitive to the activities of juveniles in this age bracket than older or younger groups. This would be good law enforcement practice. The logic in our case is the same except that our delinquency problem is largely found in the Negro community and it is these youths toward whom we are sensitized.

As regards prejudice per se, eighteen of twenty-seven officers interviewed openly admitted a dislike for Negroes. However, they attributed their dislike to experiences they had, as policemen, with youths from this minority group. The officers reported that Negro boys were much more likely than non-Negroes to "give us a hard time," be uncooperative, and show no remorse for their transgressions. Recurrent exposure to such attitudes among Negro youth, the officers claimed, generated their antipathy toward Negroes. The following excerpt is typical of the views expressed by these officers:

> They (Negroes) have no regard for the law or for the police. They just don't seem to give a damn. Few of them are interested in school or getting ahead. The girls start having illegitimate kids before they are 16 years old and the boys are always "out for kicks." Furthermore, many of these kids try to run you down. They say the damnedest things to you and they seem to have absolutely no respect for you as an adult. I admit I am prejudiced now, but frankly I don't think I was when I began police work.

IMPLICATIONS

It is apparent from the findings presented above that the police officers studied in this research were permitted and even encouraged to exercise immense latitude in disposing of the juveniles they encountered. That is, it was within the officers' discretionary authority, except in extreme limiting cases, to decide which juveniles were to come to the attention of the courts and correctional agencies and thereby be identified officially as delinquents. In exercising this discretion policemen were strongly guided by the de-

[22] While police statistics did not permit an analysis of crime rates by appearance, they strongly supported officers' contentions concerning the delinquency rate among Negroes. Of all male juveniles processed by the police department in 1961, for example, 40.2 percent were Negro and 33.9 percent were white. These two groups comprised at that time, respectively, about 22.7 percent and 73.6 percent of the population in the community studied.

meanor of those who were apprehended, a practice which ultimately led, as seen above, to certain youths (particularly Negroes[23] and boys dressed in the style of "toughs") being treated more severely than other juveniles for comparable offenses.

But the relevance of demeanor was not limited only to police disposition practices. Thus, for example, in conjunction with police crime statistics, the criterion of demeanor led police to concentrate their surveillance activities in areas frequented or inhabited by Negroes. Furthermore, these youths were accosted more often than others by officers on patrol simply because their skin color identified them as potential troublemakers. These discriminatory practices—and it is important to note that they are discriminatory, even if based on accurate statistical information—may well have self-fulfilling consequences. Thus it is not unlikely that frequent encounters with police, particularly those involving youths innocent of wrongdoing, will increase the hostility of these juveniles toward law enforcement personnel. It is also not unlikely that the frequency of such encounters will in time reduce their significance in the eyes of apprehended juveniles, thereby leading these youths to regard them as "routine." Such responses to police encounters, however, are those which law enforcement personnel perceive as indicators of the serious delinquent. They thus serve to vindicate and reinforce officers' prejudices, leading to closer surveillance of Negro districts, more frequent encounters with Negro youths, and so on in a vicious circle. Moreover, the consequences of this chain of events are reflected in police statistics showing a disproportionately high percentage of Negroes among juvenile offenders, thereby providing "objective" justification for concentrating police attention on Negro youths.

To a substantial extent, as we have implied earlier, the discretion practiced by juvenile officers is simply an extension of the juvenile court philosophy, which holds that in making legal decisions regarding juveniles, more weight should be given to the juvenile's character and life situation than to his actual offending behavior. The juvenile officer's disposition decisions—and the information he uses as a basis for them—are more akin to the discriminations made by probation officers and other correctional workers than they are to decisions of police officers dealing with non-juvenile offenders. The problem is that such clinical-type decisions are not restrained by mechanisms comparable to the principles of due process and the rules of procedure governing police decisions regarding adult offenders. Consequently, prejudicial practices by police officers can escape notice more easily in their dealings with juveniles than with adults.

The observations made in this study serve to underscore the fact that the official delinquent, as distinguished from the juvenile who simply commits a delinquent act, is the product of a social judgment, in this case a judgment made by the police. He is a delinquent because someone in authority has defined him as one, often on the basis of the public face he has presented to officials rather than of the kind of offense he has committed.

---

[23] An uncooperative demeanor was presented by more than one-third of the Negro youths but by only one-sixth of the white youths encountered by the police in the course of our observations.

14

POLICE DISCRETION:
THE NEED FOR GUIDELINES*

Richard W. Kobetz

This material is taken from a book published by the International Association of Chiefs of Police. It is, not surprisingly, written from an enforcement point of view and presents, in cookbook fashion, the preferable do's and don't's for exercise of discretion. These guidelines are somewhat more restrictive than those found or implicit in most of the papers in this volume. They are more restrictive with respect to referral resources and also with respect to allowing others to do the work of the police, as in screening. This latter point is unique to this paper, and should not be; the matter of screening and who should do it is an integral part of the overall decision process.

* From *The Police Role and Juvenile Delinquency* (Gaithersburg, Md.: International Association of Chiefs of Police, 1971), pp. 111–122. Reprinted by permission of the author and publisher.

Because the philosophy of the juvenile justice system requires that the "best interest of the child" be the prime concern of all agencies working with children, this poses special problems for the police officer. What is in the "best interest of the child" as far as the police department is concerned? To answer this question, each officer coming into contact with juveniles must use his own discretion, following departmental policy guidelines.

The power of discretion allows each officer to act in certain situations in accordance with his own judgment and conscience when the course of action is not completely clear. Discretion is not simply the decision to arrest or not to arrest. Looking at discretion in a broader view, it is the choice between two or more possible means of disposing of a situation confronting the police officer.

This definition was chosen for its emphasis on choice and its deemphasis on judgment. The advantage to the police administrator of using a definition based on choice is that it helps him to recognize situations where discretion exists, and to delineate all the available choices. It should be distinguished from an operational definition, one that is used by the department to define the discretion exercised by the officer in the performance of his duties.[1] The latter definition would allow only for the use of authorized choices, and would exclude alternatives that are proscribed by the department or prohibited by law.

It is recognized that judgment is an element of all discretionary decisions. But judgment can be, and often is, removed from the beat officer and

[1] For example, the Chicago, Illinois, Police Department defines discretion: "The police must necessarily exercise discretion in the enforcement of the laws because of the limited resources available to them, because of the inherent ambiguity of some laws, and because there are often a number of acceptable and more effective ways of accomplishing the purpose of the law." From *On This We Stand,* Chicago Police Department, 1963. This may imply a somewhat narrow view: that discretion is simply the decision not to enforce the law to the letter.

exercised by personnel at other levels of command, such as the supervising sergeant, commanding officer, and the chief of police. The practical effect of the removal of judgment is to limit the choices available to the beat officer in a given situation. The exercise or control of judgment by the chief of police and his staff is the essence of centralized control. It involves the recognition and examination of situations where discretion exists, the elimination of choices which are clearly illegal or against the interests of the department, and the establishment of means of control over the selection of valid choices.

The use of discretion by juvenile officers is more difficult to define. When dealing with adults, the police officer has his role spelled out for him: The path of criminal justice is well laid out and standardized and the officer has little latitude. However, the predictable response accompanying the adult arrest does not always exist in juvenile cases. Here more than anywhere else in police work, the officer is given wide latitude to make his own judgments because of the concept that the juvenile justice system exists to "protect" the child.

The exercise of discretion can never be completely eliminated where human beings are involved. If police are not considered to possess the competence and understanding to make selective judgments in dealing with youngsters on the streets—who will?

But police discretion does not mean arbitrary decisions made on the spot without following some guidelines. Discretionary action is correct only when it follows procedures set by departmental policies for the purpose of guiding individual judgment in situations where the course of action is not completely clear.[2] The officer must act within well-defined departmental policies and keep in mind that he is not a representative of the judicial branch of government.

It is necessary then for police supervisors to clearly define guidelines for the exercise of discretion in juvenile cases to limit and govern choice of action and establish a justification for the choices which are made. Commanding officers are ultimately responsible for the beat officer's actions.

Centralized control of discretion fulfills two basic needs of the department: (1) the need for uniformity; and (2) the need for centralized formulation and dissemination of policy. However, where the juvenile is concerned a departmental policy rarely covers every aspect of every situation which an officer meets. Although the departmental policies set the general guidelines for dealing with juveniles, the beat officer, when confronted with situations not specifically defined in departmental policies, must base his decision on the "spirit" of the policy, his training, experience, and the guidance of his superiors. When in doubt, he must consult with his superiors before taking action.

Clearly defined departmental policy guidelines on the use of discretion are needed to offset any criticisms that may arise. Some law enforcement agencies will not acknowledge that their officers use discretion: They fear that this would leave them open to accusations because of problems sur

[2] Albert Hamann, *Law Enforcement and Juvenile Justice in Wisconsin*, Madison: The University of Wisconsin, University Extension, Institute of Governmental Affairs, 1965, p. 12.

rounding the use of discretion. For example, the International City Managers Association cites three major problem areas:[3]

1. A policy of discretion would apparently contradict a police goal of impartiality. The use of discretion indicates that laws are not uniformly administered. This may invoke distrust of the police agency.

2. It is difficult to prepare a criterion for uniform action in the exercise of discretion. To prepare a written modification of a law in effect abrogates that law and obviates the role of the legislative body—a presumptuous role for a police administrator to play. Additionally, a police officer could not be forced to exercise discretion since his oath of office requires that he enforce all laws impartially.

3. Some police administrators believe that discretion serves as a breeding ground for corruption of individual officers. The integrity of a police officer can more readily be observed if there is an exact scale against which his actions can be measured. The exercise of police discretion would make this measurement difficult and hence increase the problem of detecting evidences of corruption within the department.

The most significant misuse of discretion by juvenile officers occurs when the officers assume judicial functions—setting discretionary policy permitting informal police probation activities in cases which they believe merit some attention but do not require formal referral to a social agency or the juvenile court. It is easy to assume duties that are not a legitimate police function when working with juveniles, but the police officer must remember that his role is to *prevent and suppress crime, not the supervision of either adult or juvenile offenders.*

STATION ADJUSTMENT

All juveniles taken into police custody do not end up in court. The question of whether or not alleged juvenile lawbreakers are fed into the juvenile justice system will significantly be determined by the decision of the police officer. Experts at all levels of the juvenile justice system are in sound agreement that it is entirely unfair and unnecessary for the police to bring to the court's attention every juvenile who falls within police custody, and strongly recommend that departments increase pre-judicial disposition and recognize it as a valid aspect of the police function.[4]

The President's Commission on Law Enforcement and the Administration of Justice, recognizing the need for station adjustments, said:

Informal and discretionary pre-judicial dispositions already are a formally recognized part of the process to a far greater extent in the juvenile than in the criminal justice system. The primacy of the rehabilitative goal in dealing with juveniles, the limited effectiveness of the formal processes of the juvenile justice system, the labeling inherent in adjudicating children delinquents, the inability of the formal

[3] George Eastman, ed., *Municipal Police Administration,* Washington, D.C.: International City Managers Association, 1969, pp. 13–14.

[4] Thomas M. Frost, *The Juvenile Officer's Role: A Law Enforcement and Corrections Dilemma—Where Does It Fit,* unpublished ms., Chicago Police Dept., 1970.

system to reach the influences—family, school, labor market, recreational opportunities—that shape the life of a youngster, the limited disposition options available to the juvenile judge, the limitations of personnel and diagnostic and treatment facilities, the lack of community support—all of these factors give pre-judicial dispositions an especially important role with respect to juveniles.[5]

The widespread use of police discretionary powers in juvenile cases can be attributed in part to the overburdened court system and the shortage of court personnel. The lack of sufficient court personnel has led many judges to increase the power of the police indirectly by condoning or encouraging the settlement of complaints without referral to courts.[6]

In addition, the police themselves accept the philosophy that juveniles have a great potential for rehabilitation if they are given proper guidance in time.[7]

Police use their discretionary powers in a wide variety of offenses committed by juveniles, from felonies to misdemeanors. In some jurisdictions, offenses such as involuntary manslaughter, rape, serious assault and battery, armed robbery, burglary, and many other felonies are adjusted by the police at the station and the juveniles, often first offenders, are never sent to court.

Original contact with the juvenile is usually made by the patrolman on the beat. The patrolman has two courses of action which he can follow: (1) He can talk to the juvenile at the place of initial contact, decide whether the juvenile is to be brought into the station or released, and take no further action; or (2) bring the juvenile to the station and turn him over to a juvenile officer for further action.

If the child is brought to the station for further action, the next step for him probably will be an informal hearing conducted by officers handling juvenile cases. This hearing will determine whether the case will be referred to juvenile court or whether it will be terminated at the police station. The purpose of the hearing is not to adjudicate guilt, but to decide what is in the best interest of the child and the community.

Although the police have no legal authority to compel either the juvenile or his parents to attend a hearing or accept any eventual restrictions on the juvenile's freedom, the police do have the necessary leverage. This leverage is often the key to obtaining parental consent to the hearing: The alternative to the police hearing is direct referral to juvenile court and the creation of a permanent police and/or court record. In most cases, both the parents and the juvenile would rather take their chances at an informal police hearing rather than face the formality of court referral.

The hearing enables police to "counsel" the juvenile so that, hopefully, he will stay out of trouble. The hearing itself, held at the police station, is

---

[5] The President's Commission on Law Enforcement and the Administration of Justice, *The Challenge of Crime in a Free Society*, Washington, D.C.: U.S. Government Printing Office, 1967, p. 82.

[6] David R. Barrett, William J. T. Brown, and John M. Cramer, "Juvenile Delinquents: The Police, State Courts and Individualized Justice," *Harvard Law Review*, Vol. 79, No. 4, February 1966, p. 777.

[7] There is a widespread belief that "the early discovery of the pre-delinquent or potential delinquent is the key to the preventive program." John E. Winters, Deputy Chief, "The Youth Aid Division," Metropolitan Police Department, Washington, D.C., 1964, p. 11.

quasi-judicial in order to magnify the apparent authority of the hearing officer and therefore solemnify the interview with the juvenile and increase the chances of obtaining an admission of guilt.

Because police often hope to obtain admissions of guilt for serious violations of law at the hearing, it is necessary to inform the child of his rights under *Miranda* and *Gault*, and, where possible, have his parents or another adult relative or friend present. The rationale for the emphasis placed on obtaining admissions is that the juvenile cannot be rehabilitated until he recognizes his own guilt in a moral sense; if the juvenile persistently denies his guilt when available evidence proves him guilty, then the police hearing officers usually conclude that the juvenile would not be helped by a station adjustment and needs to be referred to court.

Many policemen feel that there is no place for an attorney at the informal hearing, that an attorney would instruct the juvenile to remain silent and refrain from answering questions. However, if the juvenile wishes to have an attorney present during the hearing, his right to counsel must be respected. Both the *Miranda* and *Gault* decisions entitle him to counsel at this stage, although the Supreme Court has never ruled specifically on this issue as far as juveniles are concerned.

Police officers conducting the hearing have six dispositional alternatives available to them (see Figure 1):

1. Release.
2. Release, accompanied by an official report describing the encounter with the juvenile.
3. Release to parent or guardian accompanied by an official reprimand.
4. Referral to social agencies for further rehabilitation.
5. Referral to the juvenile court without detention.
6. Referral to the juvenile court with detention.

How do police decide which alternative best suits each juvenile? It is a difficult task. The hearing officer is guided by departmental policies, his own judgments and experience, and several factors surrounding both the nature of the offense and the juvenile himself. The officer must consider:

1. The age of the child.
2. The nature and severity of the offense.
3. The juvenile's prior contact with the police.
4. The juvenile's attitude toward accepting and cooperating with efforts to help rehabilitate him.
5. The juvenile's need for professional assistance as determined by his physical and mental characteristics.
6. The ability of the child's parents to acknowledge their awareness of the seriousness of their child's involvement with the police and to control and discipline their child.
7. The rights of the complainant—injustice is not done to the victim/complainant through overemphasis on the juvenile offender; and the social tranquility of the community is not sacrificed because police fail to deal with delinquents in a positive manner.

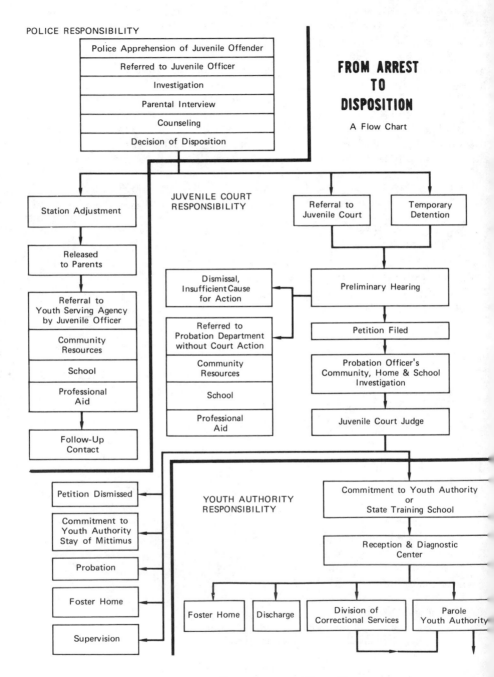

POLICE RESPONSIBILITY

Police Apprehension of Juvenile Offender

Referred to Juvenile Officer

Investigation

Parental Interview

Counseling

Decision of Disposition

**FROM ARREST
TO
DISPOSITION**

A Flow Chart

Station Adjustment

JUVENILE COURT
RESPONSIBILITY

Referral to
Juvenile Court

Temporary
Detention

Released
to Parents

Referral to
Youth Serving Agency
by Juvenile Officer

Community
Resources

School

Professional
Aid

Follow-Up
Contact

Dismissal,
Insufficient Cause
for Action

Referred to
Probation Department
without Court Action

Community
Resources

School

Professional
Aid

Preliminary Hearing

Petition Filed

Probation Officer's
Community, Home & School
Investigation

Juvenile Court Judge

Petition Dismissed

Commitment to
Youth Authority
Stay of Mittimus

Probation

Foster Home

Supervision

YOUTH AUTHORITY
RESPONSIBILITY

Commitment to Youth Authority
or
State Training School

Reception & Diagnostic
Center

Foster Home

Discharge

Division of
Correctional Services

Parole
Youth Authority

Figure 1   From Arrest to Disposition

212

Moreover, the officer is subject to other pressures in the community: the press, the people present at the scene of the offense, attitudes of police coworkers, personal experience, and attitudes of supervisors.

But the most important factor influencing the officer's dispositional attitude should be the possibility of recidivism on the part of the juvenile. Will he return to illegal activity? Thus, any decision to make a station adjustment on the part of the hearing officer involves a certain amount of risk taking because there is no way to guarantee that the station adjustment will serve its purpose and deter the juvenile from future crimes.

The hearing officer will generally release the child to his parents if the case investigation reveals a preponderance of positive factors. If the child is to be released to his parents, an emotionally healthy atmosphere should exist among the members of the juvenile's family. The parents should be aware of and meet the child's emotional needs to a satisfactory degree. In addition, the parents should have a constructive attitude toward the child's delinquency. Do they blame his friends, the neighborhood or society for his illegal behavior or are they willing to accept their responsibility for his behavior?

In some cases, the child has not committed an offense serious enough to warrant referral to juvenile court, yet the juvenile officer feels there is a high risk of recidivism if he is released to his parents. Either the youth has a history of previous minor offenses or his home environment is not conducive to offering him proper guidance. In cases such as this the juvenile officer often refers the child to a private or public social agency which should be able to provide needed professional services to both the child and his family.

Before he refers the child to a specific social agency, the officer must know the aims and capabilities of the agency and should give the family all the information needed to familiarize them with the agency. In addition, it is often necessary for the juvenile officer to follow through to make sure the family and the juvenile are being helped by the agency.

Even though a large percentage of juvenile cases are disposed of by station adjustments, it is often necessary to refer a child to juvenile court rather than settle his problem informally with a hearing at the police station.

Perhaps the child is involved in a felony or serious offense, another offense in a series of minor offenses, or any combination of factors. Or, on the other hand, the officer may fear an unwillingness or inability of the child to control his own behavior. Perhaps the parents are incapable of providing necessary supervision and control over the child. Circumstances such as these may warrant referral to the juvenile court for a hearing at a later date, with temporary release into the custody of parents.

Juvenile officers will usually refer a child to court when:

1. The offense is serious in nature.

2. The offense itself is not intrinsically serious, but the total circumstances surrounding the commission of the act seem to indicate that the child needs some type of protective action.

3. The child has a record of delinquencies committed over a period of time, even though he may not have been referred to court for any of these offenses.

4. The child and/or his parents are unwilling to cooperate either with the police or with social agencies.

5. Voluntary agency casework with the child has failed in the past because the child was not willing to cooperate with a nonauthoritarian agency.

6. The protective services needed by the child can best be obtained through the court and its services.

7. The juvenile denies that he committed the offense but the police have obtained sufficient evidence for a court referral and believe that a judicial determination is necessary.

8. Because of his attitude when he was apprehended, the juvenile has been placed in a detention center by a police officer. When the juvenile has been placed in detention, court referral is usually mandatory no matter how insignificant the offense.

9. The juvenile is on formal or informal probation for a previous offense.

10. The degree of criminal sophistication shown in the offense, such as the use of burglar tools, criminal jargon, premeditation, a weapon or strong-arm methods, generally indicates a need for immediate court referral.

11. Juvenile offenders apprehended in a group will generally be treated on an all-or-none basis. If one of the juveniles warrants immediate court referral, the others will usually be referred, too.

12. The juvenile officer's attitude toward specific offenses, such as sex crimes, arson, or assault, may influence the officer's decision to refer the juvenile to court.

Once the officer refers the child to juvenile court, it is the officer's duty to file a written report with the court explaining all the facts in the case. This report should include a description of the offense—date, time, circumstances, place, and nature of the act. The report must indicate that the person involved is actually a juvenile and that the offense he committed is covered under the statutory jurisdiction of the juvenile court.

Most important, the officer must include information proving that the child committed the act, or is reasonably believed to have committed it. If a confession was obtained from the child or if evidence was obtained by search and seizure, then the police officer must prove that the child knowingly waived his constitutional rights under *Gault* and *Miranda*.

In addition, the report should identify the complainant or victim and accurately describe the extent of injuries or damages. If a child has had previous contact with the police, this should also be included in the report so that the court can make a disposition which is best suited for the child. Agency referrals should also be explained in the report, and, when the officer believes it is significant, he should describe home conditions and any other factors which he thinks would help the court reach the proper decision.

THE BALANCE OF INDIVIDUAL RIGHTS

There is a great need to train policemen to be alert to one of the major objectives of criminal law—that of imposing upon all persons officially recognized minimum standards of human behavior. The police of today are alert to the inherent need for making value judgments and for exercising discretion based upon professional competence. It is the police officer who is faced nightly with the problem of making decisions based upon the information which he has available to him. These "night decisions" based upon "night information" are all too quickly criticized by those who, several hours or days later, enjoy the luxury of a case review based upon an accumulation of information.

The magnitude of the problem and the nature of the situation is such that the greatest improvement in the juvenile justice system can be gained by directing efforts toward improving the quality of discretionary decisions made by police officers screening juvenile cases.

But the police must continue to use their discretionary powers. The introduction of an intermediary agency to perform this screening function or the overburdening of the judicial machinery with a crushing load of cases involving the full range of juvenile misconduct is unrealistic.

The new legalistic approach to delinquency fails to take into consideration the question of how we presently construe the criminal justice system. The new emphasis is placed upon the alleged offenders and not upon the victim or society at large. Society has a right to demand an immediate trial for offenders to protect itself from future trespasses if the accused offender is in fact guilty.

On the other hand, the individual has a right to an immediate trial as well: This is guaranteed by the Sixth Amendment to the United States Constitution.[8] But with the backlog of cases flooding the American court system, immediate trials have become a myth. Both the accused and society wait months and even years for a case to come to trial. What has happened to the concept spelled out in the Constitution that every individual has a right to an immediate trial?

No one knows exactly what kind of criminal justice system the Founding Fathers desired when they attached the Bill of Rights to the Constitution. As a result, as the needs of society change, the Supreme Court finds that it has to continuously reinterpret the Bill of Rights to meet the new needs of society. Because these changes will always be taking place as the needs of our society shift, the police officer finds himself in a position similar to that of a tightrope walker. If he leans too far out in one direction on the high wire, he trespasses upon the rights of society; on the other hand, if he leans too far out in the opposite direction, he violates the rights of the accused. The police officer's role requires fine balance between the rights of the individual and the rights of society—a very precarious position.

From all apparent views, our system of justice has come a long way from its original Judeo-Christian concept of right and wrong and appears to be no longer concerned with the innocence or guilt of the accused. The only concern seems to be that the *state prove the case.* Many "guilty" offenders often go

---

[8] "In all criminal prosecutions, the accused shall enjoy the right to a speedy and public trial, by an impartial jury of the State and district wherein the crime shall have been committed, which district shall have been previously ascertained by law, and to be informed of the nature and cause of the accusation; to be confronted with the witnesses against him; to have compulsory process for obtaining witnesses in his favor, and to have the Assistance of Counsel for his defense." United States Constitution, Amendment Six.

free because they have obtained the services of a lawyer who then finds some technical loophole in the law or can show that the police in some way violated one of the offender's constitutional rights. But what about the victim and the rights of society?

We must question if our adult criminal justice system is the best system for the child. Will our adult systems of justice help the child to rehabilitate himself if he knows that he can get away with being guilty if the state cannot prove it?

The court is, and should, remain the last resort in the juvenile justice system. As police officers, we must find suitable community alternatives to court action and try to stop delinquency before the child becomes a hardened young criminal.

15
GUIDES FOR LAW ENFORCEMENT AND PROBATION OFFICERS*

National Council
on Crime and Delinquency

This paper, the last in the section, is very brief and is of most interest as a contrast to the Kobetz paper. Both are concerned with guidelines, but from very different viewpoints. The present paper is far more oriented to the release of juveniles, and much closer to the position of civil libertarians. Notice, as well, that it seems almost devoid of concerns for the criminal law or the law enforcement establishment. Diversion, it should be remembered, takes place within a partially adversary system, and one in which the clash between juvenile welfare and juvenile rights is heard with increasing frequency. Diversion is, in fact, caught right smack in the middle, advocated by many for almost opposite reasons.

* From *The Youth Service Bureau* (Paramus, N.J.: National Council on Crime and Delinquency, 1972), pp. 170–172. Reprinted by permission of the National Council on Crime and Delinquency.

REFERRAL GUIDE FOR LAW ENFORCEMENT OFFICERS

When a child is apprehended by a police officer, a number of police dispositions are possible, including referral to the Youth Service Bureau if there is one in the community. The following guide indicates the police officer's alternatives and the circumstances under which each is appropriate.

Disposition	*Situation*
1. Outright release.	Cases in which juvenile was clearly not involved in law violation.
2. Referral to another jurisdiction.	Cases which do not fall within jurisdiction of family court but appear to be serious enough for court action.
3. Release with warning.	Cases in which child was only incidentally involved in offense (e.g., riding in a stolen car without knowing it was stolen) or in which child committed minor offense but there is no indication that he or his parents might need assistance.
4. Referral to Youth Service Bureau.	All cases in which (a) law violation is not serious enough to demand court intervention, (b) parties involved do not insist on hearing before judge, and (c) child or parents appear to need counseling or help from some community resource.
5. Release and referral to court intake.	Cases which are serious enough for court action but do not require temporary shelter care.
6. Emergency shelter care and referral to court intake or YSB.	Cases where child is in critical danger in own home or otherwise in need of immediate protection.
7. Physical referral to intake.	Cases which are serious enough for court action and might require shelter or detention. (Child is taken to court intake or, if after court hours, to court-designated person authorized to release or to place in shelter or detention according to judicially determined policy.)
8. Detention (secure custody) and referral to court intake.	Rare: should be used by police only in most serious cases when failure to detain in secure custody would present an immediate danger to other individuals (and probability of danger can be supported at detention hearing).
9. Detention (secure custody) without court referral.	Never! The law should inflict penalties for this.

REFERRAL GUIDE FOR PROBATION OFFICERS

Every juvenile or family court should have an intake service, staffed by qualified probation officers, to determine whether the child is to be handled judicially or nonjudicially and whether he is to be released, sheltered, or detained pending court hearing. A court intake service provides the second screening process after police disposition and enables authoritative intervention if this is thought necessary.

If an immediate decision by the judge is not possible, judicial policy at intake should govern release, shelter or detention, and petitioning procedures.

Action	*Situation*
1. Outright release or release with warning.	Cases which do not call for filing of petition and in which neither child nor parent appears to require assistance of any kind.
2. Referral to another jurisdiction.	Cases in which, because of age or other reasons, child belongs within jurisdiction of court other than juvenile or family court.
3. Referral to YSB or other agency.	Cases where filing of petition is not called for or can be avoided by referral to YSB; cases where child or parent appears to need assistance which can be provided by YSB or other community resources.
4. Informal supervision by probation officer, who may reserve judgment regarding necessity for filing of petition.	Cases where child appears unlikely to cooperate voluntarily with YSB and where need for authoritative intervention is uncertain.
5. Petition to be filed but child released to parents.	Guide for Filing Petitions [omitted].
6. Petition filed, or to be filed, and child placed in shelter care.	Shelter care[1] should be used in lieu of detention where facilities are available and secure custody is not mandatory. (Where possible, separate facility should be provided for dependent and neglected children.)
7. Petition filed, or to be filed, and child placed in detention.	Detention[2] should be used only when there is *serious risk* that child will commit offense dangerous to society or there is substantial probability that he will leave jurisdiction if not detained.

---

[1] Shelter is the care of children in "open facilities" such as foster family homes, group homes, etc.

[2] Detention is the care of children in physically restricting facilities with locked doors and detention screens or other devices to deter escape.

SECTION 4

SELECTED PROGRAMS

To the extent that diversion represents a new involvement for police agencies, there is little that can currently be said about police diversion programs. Perhaps we can say little more than that there exists an infinite variety of which only a few types have emerged; that diversion programs have many masters, serving both manifest and latent needs of each; that we really do not know yet which types of programs will have the greatest impact, nor do we know the type of impact they will have.

The programs described in this section have been chosen to represent a variety of possibilities, but they are also among the very few which have as yet been given public attention. They therefore illustrate only some of the issues which seem to be emerging as the diversion explosion continues. Some of these, judging from programs developed in the past few years, are as follows:

1. Should diversion programs be "in-house" or not; i.e., should the referral be to an agent or counselor housed within the police department, to an outside, independent agency, or is a compromise possible between these positions?
2. Should referrals place their major emphasis on individual and/or family counseling, or should they stress a multiservice approach? Other possibilities include jobs and job training, educational aid, medical aid, recreation, and big brother/sister connections.
3. Should the program be funded through and administered by the police department, another municipal or county agency, or a private agency? This resolves basically to an issue of control and accountability.
4. In the case of a community-based referral resource, is it best to limit the clientele to those referred by police and other justice agencies, or is it better to mix these diverted offenders with other youths, such as school referrals and walk-ins?
5. Should the referral resource be the service end point, providing whatever service it can, or should it serve more as a clearinghouse, the source of referrals to a broad range of other community resources?
6. Finally (if repetitively), should these programs concentrate on diverting youngsters who would otherwise *clearly* be inserted farther into the system (e.g., those on whom petitions would be filed) or should they be primarily for youngsters who are *judged likely* to get into trouble again? If diversion means the former, as the Vorenbergs suggest in their article, then many—or most—police depart-

ments are getting credit for diversion where none exists. If the latter, then to what extent is diversion really anything new and worthy of our special interest?

These are some of the manifest issues. Others are more latent but nonetheless important. For example, diversion is a "hot" item in the justice system and a great deal of money is available to justice agencies willing to mount diversion programs. Thus, even if diversion has little impact on the offenders, it does add funds to departmental and agency coffers.

In some cases, this translates into increased staffing or even the establishment of new juvenile or diversion units. In others, it translates into better service for the juvenile clients. In some, both can occur. However, it also means the development of a rhetoric which is used to justify the program and the energies put into it, with the attendant danger that the rhetoric becomes its own justification. We begin to believe our own press clippings.

Some feeling for this rhetoric can be obtained from the first two papers in this section. Both describe programs with countywide mandates. The first comes from an established traditional agency experimenting with change, while the second comes from the new "establishment" initiated under the enormous bureaucracy of the law-and-order 1960s and still seeking its proper place among the other justice establishments. The vigor and imaginativeness underlying both programs is obvious.

The third paper presents yet another and more modest model, one which contrasts in philosophy with the first but could fit under the framework of the second. The fourth provides an overview of program varieties which, by and large, do not include these earlier three models. The latter two require a separate explanation.

As far back as 1967, the President's Commission on Law Enforcement and Administration of Justice strongly recommended the development of Youth Service Bureaus. With the concomitant rise of interest in diversion, it was inevitable that Youth Service Bureaus would become a primary model for diversion programs. These Bureaus have appeared all across the country and are thought by many to be the quintessence of diversion. If they are, then these two papers suggest that we do indeed have a complex and discouraging problem at hand. The Seymour paper lays the problem out very clearly, and the final paper illustrates the rapidity with which the Youth Service Bureaus mushroomed. Perhaps, when the dust settles and our perspectives become more clear, the next book on diversion programs will need to include only one chapter on Youth Service Bureaus. For the present, however, the great popularity of this particular program model requires the comprehensive attention provided by these two papers.

16

LAW ENFORCEMENT SCREENING
FOR DIVERSION*

Peter J. Pitchess

This paper, emanating from a large and prestigious enforcement agency, takes a very strong position on accepting a prevention mandate. A number of enforcement officials might take issue with this mandate. Beyond this, Sheriff Pitchess' discussion is worth careful reading for several reasons: (1) It cites six reasons for police diversion in a comprehensive and thoroughly reasoned argument which employs theoretical, philosophical, and practical rationales; (2) it takes a cautious stance on the appropriate population to be "diverted," namely only 10 percent of the total, half of whom would be released anyway and the other half of whom are "carefully selected" *predelinquents,* and who overwhelmingly come from two-parent families and are status or victimless offenders; (3) it provides a careful statement of agency criteria, yielding quite a narrow or restricted range of appropriate referral resources; and (4) it clearly accepts the commitment to independent follow-up research as one of the project criteria—a very unusual stance for an independent and powerful agency.

* From (California) *Youth Authority Quarterly,* 27, 1(1974): pp. 49–64. Reprinted by permission of the author and publisher. .

Early in 1970, as an outgrowth of informal discussions between the Los Angeles County Sheriff's Department and the Department of Community Services, the Los Angeles County's Delinquency and Crime Commission successfully recommended to the Board of Supervisors that it provide funding for a countywide delinquency prevention effort to be implemented by both departments. After careful examination of numerous prevention strategies, it was determined that a juvenile diversion program would provide the most effective and mutually beneficial prevention effort directly applicable to the highly diversified areas and the 1.75 million people serviced by fifteen sheriff's stations in Los Angeles County.

Since its establishment in 1970, the program has grown to be one of the largest of its kind in the nation. This pilot effort, titled the "Juvenile Referral and Resource Development Program," has succeeded in screening and diverting well over 2,000 youthful offenders to nearly 100 different community-based agencies and organizations.

A key element in the program's success has been the outstanding cooperation between the two separate county departments. The Department of Community Services assists and coordinates the work of community groups, and public and private agencies that specialize in preventing delinquency and crime. The Sheriff's Department's role in the diversion program has been to identify and develop new and significantly improved community resources specifically for the use of law enforcement. The Department of Community Services has provided each of our stations with a regionalized listing of juvenile referral resources which is updated on a bimonthly basis to maintain accuracy and currency.

THEORETICAL BACKGROUND

Diversion of selected offenders to community-based organizations and away from the juvenile justice system is increasingly being suggested as a viable delinquency prevention technique. The President's Commission on Law Enforcement and the Administration of Justice (1967) in its *Task Force Report: Juvenile Delinquency and Youth Crime* developed goals of the prejudicial process and reported:

> First, a great deal of juvenile misbehavior should be dealt with through alternatives to adjudication, in accordance with an explicit policy to divert juvenile offenders away from formal adjudication and authoritative disposition and to nonjudicial institutions for guidance and other services. Employment agencies, schools, welfare agencies, and groups with programs for acting-out youth all are examples of the resources that should be used. The preference for nonjudicial disposition should be enunciated, publicized, and consistently espoused by the several social institutions responsible for controlling and preventing delinquency.[1]

Many law enforcement agencies throughout the country have traditionally treated the concept of delinquency prevention with ambivalence. As an example, almost every agency has included delinquency prevention in its list of departmental objectives; however, few agencies have initiated systematic and specific programs directly aimed at the problem. The lack of accomplishment in this area is due in part to the failure of some agencies to develop an ongoing philosophical and practical commitment to prevention.

PREVENTION PHILOSOPHY

Law enforcement agencies, with their crime control mandate to protect life and property, investigate crime, and arrest violators, have nearly succeeded in separating the areas of control and prevention. Prevention, as the logical extension of control, is clearly the optimum function of law enforcement; and today's society, as a rapidly changing and dynamic force, compels us as law enforcement officials to examine and develop worthwhile prevention strategies.

Because law enforcement is integrally interwoven into the community, the justice system, and the delinquent subculture, it becomes the most logical element to suggest, recommend, and implement programs designed to prevent recidivism. It must function as the catalytic agent for prevention efforts in the community. However, it should be noted that the responsibility lies not only with law enforcement, but rather "prevention is a cooperative

---

[1] The President's Commission on Law Enforcement and Administration of Justice. *Task Force Report: Juvenile Delinquency and Youth Crime*. Washington, D.C., 1967, p. 16.

enterprise among all social agencies. . . . Police do not function in a vacuum; they work within a social context with a web of interlinked, interdependent units working for human improvement."[2]

WHY DIVERSION?

There are numerous reasons for diversion, the first "rationale behind attempting to divert youth out of the justice system is to avoid some of the pitfalls of being processed by the present system."[3] Sociological theories of "labeling" and "self-fulfilling prophecy" have been advanced on evidence that criminal processing does more harm than good and that the farther a juvenile penetrates the system, the greater are his chances of subsequent arrest.[4] Further, the self-fulfilling phenomenon occurs when a youth tends to act as a delinquent after being labeled a delinquent.

As an alternative to justice system processing, diversion of selected offenders to community-based organizations seeks to eliminate these pitfalls and substitute constructive, nonstigmatizing assistance to these youth. These concepts were summarized in a monograph by Judge David L. Bazelon:

> The battle against juvenile crime can't possibly be won in court. . . . the name of the game is Prevention, and that's a job for the institutions in the community that can help children without stigmatizing them, without labeling them delinquents and saddling them with a court record for the rest of their lives."[5]

A second major reason for diversion by law enforcement is illustrated in the changing role of the juvenile court. Courts have made it increasingly more difficult to sustain juvenile court petitions and have evolved from a philosophy of *parens patriae* to an almost adversary system. This evolution to an adversary system has generally slowed the court processes, which has in turn necessitated court calendar restrictions. In fact, recent philosophical changes have induced the courts to seek community-based treatment whenever possible.

The third reason is recent legislative and judicial actions, which have caused authorities to question the fate of section 601 of the California Welfare and Institutions Codes, which delineate noncriminal juvenile offenses such as runaway, truancy, and incorrigibility. It appears that these

[2] Samuel H. Jameson, "Prevention Programs—Our (Police) Responsibility?" (paper read at the California State Juvenile Officers' Association Annual Training Conference, March 1972, Sacramento, California).

[3] California Youth Authority, *Youth Service Bureaus in California: Progress Report Number 3*, State of California, January 1972, p. 4.

[4] Wheeler, Stanton, Cottrell, Leonard S., Jr., and Romasco, Anne. Juvenile Delinquency: Its Prevention and Control. In the President's Commission on Law Enforcement and Administration of Justice, *Task Force Report: Juvenile Delinquency and Youth Crime*. Washington, D.C., 1967, p. 428.

[5] David L. Bazelon, "Beyond Control of the Juvenile Court," *Juvenile Court Journal*, Vol. 21, No. 2, Summer 1970. (Reprinted with permission by U.S. Department of Health, Education and Welfare, Social and Rehabilitation Service, Youth Development and Delinquency Prevention Administration, 1971.)

codes may undergo major revisions or even be abolished entirely in California. When and if this happens, law enforcement agencies will be expected to handle these problems without the aid of the juvenile court. Diversion to community-based organizations provides an effective disposition for youth currently regulated by section 601 W.I.C.

A fourth reason for diversion of offenders is the advantageous cost/benefit ratio inherent in community treatment. While justice system processing of offenders is tremendously expensive, community treatment greatly reduces government expenditures.

The fifth significant reason for diversion is improvement of police-community relations. In combining with the community in a program to prevent delinquency, law enforcement greatly enhances its image as a concerned, helpful agency committed to community improvement and augments the positive features of the law enforcement role. As we work directly with the citizens of the community in a mutual goal of delinquency prevention, we build lasting and viable bridges to that community.

Finally, a sixth major reason addresses the appropriateness of diversion by law enforcement. Because protection of the community is law enforcement's primary responsibility, law enforcement then becomes the most logical element of the justice system to develop diversion programs which are consistent with the charge for community safety. If the community's safety is to receive foremost consideration in regard to crime and delinquency matters, then diversion must be performed by law enforcement in order to ensure rationality within the system.

PREVENTIVE VS. CORRECTIONAL DIVERSION

Diversion as a delinquency prevention technique can be broadly defined as movement away from the official justice system. However, Dr. Robert Carter, Director of the Delinquency Control Institute of the University of Southern California, has more accurately defined it as "justice system oriented and focused upon the development of specific alternatives for the justice system processing of offenders."[6] Thus, the concept of diversion, in the absence of specific guidelines, can be applied to both juvenile and adult offenders and accomplished at any point in the justice system continuum, i.e., after contact with law enforcement, county probation, juvenile or adult court, parole, and local or state institutions.

In that the effectiveness of diversion, as a prevention strategy or rehabilitation strategy, has yet to be empirically tested and evaluated, unbounded and unrestrained application would be administratively unsound. Additionally, without specific guideline criteria, extensive diversion of hardened offenders could constitute a safety hazard to the very community law enforcement is sworn to protect. Consequently, we have chosen to restrict our program model to the area in which we can most significantly realize our prevention aims and simultaneously maintain community safety. Thus we have purposely selected juveniles as the target population.

[6] Robert M. Carter, "Diversion of Offenders" (paper read at Diversion Conference, June 1972, Lawndale, California).

In an effort to maximize the positive aspects of diversion and to formulate a more narrowly defined target population, two distinctively different and separate forms of diversion have been identified: preventive diversion and correctional diversion. It is significant to make a distinction between the two: The former concerns itself with diversion of the juvenile in the predelinquent stage while the latter is typically oriented toward diversion of the more advanced recalcitrant offender.

Preventive diversion is best performed by schools and law enforcement. As the "gatekeepers" to the juvenile justice system, the schools and law enforcement, in that order, represent the first institutions to make official contact with potential delinquents. It should be noted that effective preventive diversion is predicated on early identification of delinquent symptoms—hence, the schools are all-important. However, until the schools are able to develop adequate prevention strategies and programs, the "police become the chief source of referral to diversion agencies because that's where most official processing starts."[7]

While law enforcement is customarily involved in preventive diversion of predelinquent offenders, probation departments and the juvenile courts are typically active in what has been defined as correctional diversion. This type of diversion is characteristically concerned with diverting the more advanced delinquent away from the remainder of the justice system after the youth has penetrated the system via law enforcement referral. In effect, it is an effort to rehabilitate an identified delinquent; whereas preventive diversion, after early identification of potential delinquents, is truly a prevention effort aimed at preventing the development of a delinquent life-style.

Without debating the philosophical differences in the two defined diversion areas, it is obvious that our program is committed to preventive diversion of predelinquent youth and has not concerned itself with correctional or rehabilitative diversion.

JUVENILE ARREST DISPOSITION PATTERN

Having established juveniles as the target population of our department's diversion program, it was necessary to determine what percentage would benefit most from diversion and where this number fits into our total juvenile arrest disposition pattern. Figure 1 represents approximately the departmental juvenile disposition data for a single year. Our department currently takes into custody approximately 26,000 juveniles per year. This total, arranged on a scale of 0 percent to 100 percent, represents: (1) the average percentile breakdown for juvenile case dispositions, and (2) a continuum of case seriousness ranging from the least serious cases (0 percent) to the most serious cases (100 percent).

With these two factors in mind, examination of Figure 1 reveals that our department has traditionally "counseled and released" the least serious 60 percent of all juvenile arrests. Our juvenile officers, after careful investiga-

[7] Edwin M. Lemert, *Instead of Court: Diversion in Juvenile Justice,* one in a series of monographs by The Center for Studies of Crime and Delinquency, National Institute of Mental Health (Washington, D.C.: U.S. Government Printing Office, 1972), p. 94.

tion of each case, have determined that official court action is not warranted.

The next 26 percent, from 60 percent to 86 percent, represent more serious cases, and in the opinion of our investigators these youths should be brought to the attention of the juvenile court. However, in that the juvenile himself represents no overt danger to the community, he is released to the custody of his parents, and a nondetained (released) petition is filed with the probation department requesting a juvenile court hearing.

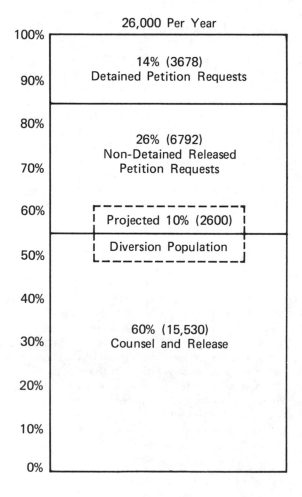

Figure 1

The remaining 14 percent of the cases, from 86 percent to 100 percent, represent the offenders with the most serious offenses, who have been identified as a hazard to themselves, the community, or who fall within certain legal boundaries. These youths are referred to juvenile hall for detention via detained petition requests which are filed with the probation department.

Proper selection and placement of the diversion target population required preliminary research. Information indicated that a significant portion of these youth (midrange of seriousness in Figure 1) appeared to be in a "high-risk" situation in regard to developing delinquency life-styles. Although many of the juveniles in this area would not be termed delinquent, our records indicate that they are most likely of all those in the nondelinquent category to have further contacts with law enforcement and thus create the "cycle of failure" which ultimately leads to a delinquent and criminal life-style.

In an effort to break the "cycle of failure" and prevent the development of delinquency patterns, we utilized this information to strategically select the 10 percent target population of our diversion program. By diverting these carefully selected youth to community-based organizations with staff trained specifically to provide personal, nonstigmatizing supportive guidance, we are confident that many predelinquents may ultimately be deterred from a life of crime.

DIVERSION MECHANISM

The opportunity to help the youth and to realize the tremendous potential of the diversion program occurs during the counseling and processing period at the sheriff's station. Frequently, the officer recognizes that there are serious emotional or situational problems facing the youth and the family. By diverting the youth to the appropriate community agency it is hoped that solutions to these problems can be identified and alleviated, thereby reducing or eliminating any further antisocial behavior.

Our program is designed to aid the juvenile investigator in obtaining the proper disposition of a case by providing him with an additional option for handling arrested juveniles. Basically, the program operates as follows:

1.   The juvenile officer has contact with an arrested youth.

2.   After investigating the case and talking with the juvenile and his parents, the investigator determines which option is most appropriate (i.e., counsel and release, detained or nondetained petition to probation, or diversion to a community agency).

3.   If it appears that the youth would benefit more from treatment by a nonauthoritative agency than the other alternatives, the investigator consults a master directory of resource agencies within the community and selects the resource providing the appropriate type of service (i.e., drug counseling, employment, etc.).

4.   When an appropriate agency is selected, and the youth's parents agree to the referral and the resource agency, the agency is contacted by phone and an intake appointment is determined.

5. An appointment card is given to the parents, and the youth is instructed as to the time and date of the appointment.

6. He is then released to the custody of his parents.

An integral part of the referral system and program evaluation is feedback to the diverting investigator and the central coordinating unit. This is facilitated by a referral form initiated by the officer and completed and returned by the resource agency. The officer fills in data about the youth, his parents, and the incident (i.e., names, ages, addresses, offense, etc.), and the resource agency completes information regarding the intake appointment and specified program. The resource agency, after completing the form, returns it to the investigating officer, who makes a copy for his records and reroutes it to the central unit, where a master file of all referrals is maintained.

In an effort to enhance the successful disposition of each case, we emphasize the need to make complete referrals as opposed to merely "forwarding problems." An appropriate referral must lead to service rendered to the juvenile and, if need be, to his family. An inappropriate referral or a mere "forwarding of problems" often leads to frustration and additional trauma which the juvenile and his parents need to avoid if they are to develop an increased ability to cope with deviant behavior. In short, an adequate referral by a juvenile investigator must be developed through:

1. Extensive knowledge of community resources.

2. Careful choice of community agency.

3. Communication with agency personnel to familiarize them with problems at hand.

4. Preparation of juvenile and parents to accept the agency.

5. Follow-up after referral to see that beginning contact has been made.

REFERRAL PATTERNS

Recognizing the need for the examination of discernible diversion patterns, several postdiversion surveys have been conducted. One study, utilizing a sample base of 454 diverted youth, was aimed at examining several aspects about youth "typically" selected for diversion. These data are compiled in Figure 2.

Although juvenile arrests in California are not classified with "felony or misdemeanor" labels, it is significant to note that our juvenile investigators diverted 100 of the group of juveniles surveyed that had committed felony offenses by adult standards. Close investigation of these apparently serious offenses revealed that the cases often contained mitigating circumstances which established the specific offenses as secondary to their underlying causes. In that these juveniles represented no danger to the community, community-based assistance was recommended as a method to alleviate the core problems.

Figure 2 also reveals that the bulk of the youth diverted are between the ages of fourteen and sixteen. It is not surprising that a program aimed at

Figure 2

Total diverted	454
Felony arrests	100
Misdemeanor arrests	159
Noncriminal contacts (truancy,	195
incorrigible, runaway, etc.)	
	454
Age	
11 and under	27
12	14
13	31
14	98
15	106
16	109
17	69
	454
Sex	
Male	269
Female	185
	454
Family status	
2-parent family	392
1-parent family	55
0-parent family	7
	454

identifying and assisting the potential delinquent would be weighed heavily in this area; it is a well-documented fact that with peer group pressures, identification problems, etc., these years represent a critical period in the young person's life.

The predominant pattern in the sample group studied is the overwhelming number of diversions of juveniles coming from two-parent homes. While this is undoubtedly due in part to the fact that the majority of families have both parents living together, there is also present a very definite selectivity pattern. Although often unconsciously, the juvenile officers in an attempt to maximize the positive reinforcement to the predelinquent youth, have selectively diverted those juveniles who come from a relatively stable family background as they would appear to represent the group most likely to succeed in a community treatment program.

Another survey utilizing a different and larger sample base was conducted to more accurately delineate the types of juvenile offenses typically diverted by our juvenile investigators. Examination of this offense data, which is grouped into general categories for simplicity, is depicted in Figure 3.

From the sample group of 565 juveniles studied, diversions for crimes against persons and property represent only 25.3 percent. Conversely, the victimless offenses (narcotics, runaway, truancy, incorrigibility) constitute 72.6 percent of all referrals made. It is apparent that our juvenile officers have actively selected youth who demonstrate no overt safety hazard to the community, but have concentrated on juveniles who have clearly displayed self-destructive tendencies.

Figure 3
Juvenile Referrals by Offense

	% of Total	
162 drug and alcohol	28.7 ⎫	
151 runaway	26.7 ⎬	72.6
97 truancy–incorrigible	17.2 ⎭	
95 crimes against property	16.8	
48 crimes against person	8.5	
12 other (victims, etc.)	2.1	
565 Total	100.0	

A closer inspection of the pattern of diversion by offense reveals that: (1) our juvenile officers have utilized this program to provide a constructive alternative for those youth falling under the now-threatened section of the California Welfare and Institutions Code covering runaway, truancy, and incorrigibility; and (2) a major portion of the community agencies receiving diversions from law enforcement should be programmatically oriented toward combating the types of offenses most often referred by law enforcement (i.e., narcotics, runaway, truancy, and incorrigibility).

COMMUNITY RESOURCES

The key component underlying the effectivensss of diversion is the quality and quantity of community resources. Regardless of how well law enforcement agencies select and divert juveniles, without positive community agency follow-through the program would undoubtedly be ineffective as a prevention tool. To establish an effective and coordinated resource network, the Department of Community Services and the Sheriff's Department identified four major objectives:

1. Produce a regionalized listing of juvenile referral resources to be updated on a bimonthly basis.
2. Develop a coordinated "system" of juvenile referral resources.
3. Engage the community in education, study, and planning of referral resources.
4. Assist and coordinate the development of new or significantly improved community resources.

However, to accomplish these objectives it was necessary to develop criteria for evaluating an agency's worth to our department's diversion program.

RESOURCE EVALUATION GUIDELINES

Evaluation of a resource agency is accomplished via an on-site interview with the agency director, and is generally performed by one or more staff of both the Department of Community Services and the Sheriff's Department.

During the interview the agency is rated according to the following generalized guidelines:

1. Attitude: Does the resource agency support the rule of law—neither condones nor supports delinquent or criminal conduct?
2. Ability: Does the resource have competent personnel, effective management, adequate facilities, and a variety of services?
3. Adaptability: Does the staff demonstrate unbiased attitudes in accepting clients, and express a willingness to use new techniques?
4. Accessibility: Does the resource have a provision for walk-in application, can the resource be reached outside of regular hours in crisis situations, is it located in an area that is accessible to a particular station's referrals, and is the cost of services reasonable?

In addition to these general guidelines, there are several specific criteria to be considered. Among these are:

1. The resource must provide direct services for youth under eighteen that have had law enforcement contact.
2. The initial intake interview should be within three days with the onset of services commencing within ten days.
3. The resource agrees to participate in follow-up research and share nonconfidential information with a responsible research organization.
4. The resource must be a nonprofit organization and must meet appropriate zoning, licensing, certification, and other legal requirements.
5. New agencies must demonstrate probability of continuity of service.
6. A substantial amount of free or reduced-fee service must be provided.
7. Agencies must be staffed year round, be open at least five days a week, and maintain a stable intake system.

Of the criteria listed above, the first two are worthy of more elaborate explanation. The concept of "direct services" to the youth is critically important to the referral process. While it is expected that an agency would not provide 100 percent direct services to all of the referred youth, the balance between direct and indirect services is important.

Indirect services agencies, or umbrella agencies, are those that provide little or no counseling, employment, or other services directly to the referred juveniles; rather, they specialize in referring youth to other agencies which provide direct service. Although the umbrella agencies are often very experienced in rereferring to direct service agencies, we have found that the re-referral process often proves to be unsuccessful. One possible reason for this is that it may be too time-consuming—thus causing the motivation engendered by the officer's interview to dwindle to such a point that the youth and/or the parent fails to contact the direct service agency. Another possible reason may be that the parent or youth feels "rebuffed and runaround" and hence rejects another referral. Although experience has demonstrated the apparent superiority of direct service programs over those specializing in re-referral, there are instances when, after careful analysis, a secondary referral should be made to a more appropriate agency.

Another criterion critically important to the establishment of a successful referral contact is agency follow-up and reach-out. Because motivation of the youth and parent is greatest at the time of the officer's interview, the agency intake should be performed at the earliest possible time. If several weeks are allowed to pass, it becomes very difficult to regenerate the enthusiasm for behavioral change that was apparent immediately after the incident. Also we have found that agencies with aggressive reach-out services are generally more successful in establishing ongoing programs. Often by contacting the referred juvenile and his parents, these agencies are able to solicit intake and subsequent appointments that would not have been kept otherwise.

CONCLUSION

This article has examined numerous aspects of diversion and outlined the diversion model currently operational in the Los Angeles County Sheriff's Department. While our model may be conceptualized as a series of Sheriff's Stations, each surrounded by a network of community agencies, there is one other basic model which some law enforcement agencies have adopted.

Briefly, this model is best described as a law enforcement–staffed counseling center, physically located either in the community or in the station. As an extension of the juvenile bureau, this counseling center is readily available as a referral source. Although this model has some real benefits (i.e., ease in referring, good communication, accountability), it is in essence creating a secondary probation department, attached to the policing agency. Rather than providing an alternative to justice system processing, this model duplicates and confuses the already fragmented and overlapping juvenile justice system. In addition, because law enforcement personnel would provide long-term counseling and ongoing assistance to referred youth, this model clearly extends the organizational boundaries of a law enforcement agency into the social work field. Law enforcement administrators would be cautioned to examine carefully the ramifications of movement in this direction.

After analysis of the two basic models, we opted for the community treatment model, for various reasons. Our model:

1.   Provides a direct bridge between law enforcement and the community, and establishes mutual understanding through common endeavors and goals.

2.   Provides a broad selection of specific juvenile services in various geographical locations.

3.   Reduces the input into the already overburdened juvenile justice system.

4.   Provides a clear alternative to justice-system processing without stigmatizing or labeling the predelinquent as a delinquent.

5.   Provides an opportunity for concerned citizens to participate in a relevant, worthwhile program of community improvement.

6.   Reduces county government costs through community-based treatment.

7.   Generates tremendous police-community relations benefits.

While community-based treatment appears to have tremendous potential as a prevention technique, community agencies have long been the victims of financial problems. State and federal grant monies have been predominantly responsible for the funding of these community programs, but unfortunately the programs have suffered when the grant money ceases. One particularly viable method of supporting diversion resource agencies would utilize the "purchase of service" concept.

This concept would allow law enforcement agencies to purchase services from resource agencies based on a performance basis. Thus, when a youth is diverted to a community agency for counseling, guidance, etc., the law enforcement agency could subsidize the agency for its services. Providing the youth is receiving ongoing service and has demonstrated behavioral improvement (to be based on specified criteria, i.e., recidivism, school, family, etc.), the resource agency would continue to receive subsidy money. However, should the youth not demonstrate improvement or terminate the program, the money would be discontinued.

Law enforcement agencies would become the recipients of state or federal block grant money to be utilized in this purchase of service prevention effort; the resource agencies would receive the financial support they desperately need to administer effective programs; and the entire law enforcement–community resource network could be upgraded.

Finally, the need for testing and evaluation of diversion is clearly present. Although the prevention aspects of diversion appear to be potentially great, diversion should not be viewed as a delinquency panacea. There is no one program that can totally prevent delinquency, and a multifaceted approach is undoubtedly warranted. However, until we are able to gather enough empirical data to critically evaluate its effectiveness, diversion to community agencies may be the single most effective delinquency prevention effort to date.

17
PLANNING FOR DIVERSION:
A CASE EXAMPLE*
Donald Graham and Rebecca Wurzburger

Here is a paper describing not one project but a whole regional approach to diversion. The existence of such a grand plan is indication enough of the acceptance of diversion by government bureaucracies. Two points should be noted additionally. First is the change in style from funding many new programs to making better use of existing resources. Second is the acknowledgement of dependence of the regional plan on reliable and up-to-date information, specifically deviance or arrest rates and available community resources. This provides a good example of research for "mapping the system" mentioned in the last section of this volume.

* Unpublished manuscript, School of Public Administration, University of Southern California, Los Angeles, 1974. Printed by permission of the authors. The views expressed in this manuscript do not necessarily reflect those of the Los Angeles Regional Criminal Justice Planning Board.

The concept of criminal justice planning was established as an important function of the justice system, with the passage of the Omnibus Crime Control and Safe Streets Act in 1968. Dramatically, the Act mandated a planning effort charged with the coordination of the numerous disparate components of a "system" which is actually a complex intergovernmental network. The purpose of this paper is to demonstrate how diversion, a program area which affects all justice-system components, can be utilized as a focus for interagency planning and cooperation. The implementation of a diversion system by the Los Angeles Regional Criminal Justice Planning Board, which operates as an administrative arm of the California Office of Criminal Justice Planning, will be used as a case example.

The following discussion will describe the rationale for the diversion program currently being developed by the Regional Planning Board, its basic elements, the proposed methodology for its implementation, and the anticipated results of such implementation.

RATIONALE FOR DEVELOPING DIVERSION SYSTEM

The Regional Planning Board is charged with developing the local allocation plan for LEAA categorical grant funds. In an effort to obtain maximum impact of these funds, a number of factors led to the development of diversion as a program area for the Regional Planning Board. The first was the Board's recognition that much effort of the justice system is directed toward individuals who can probably be rehabilitated more effectively outside the formal criminal justice system. In particular, the "revolving door" process that occurs with juvenile delinquents, alcoholics, and drug users was identified. Second, the Board recognized the need to avoid processing offenders of minor crimes through the present justice system since such processing simply contributes to the labeling phenomenon and to acute recidivism rates. Third, the Board adopted diversion as an acceptable alternative to more intensive involvement in the justice system because it was anticipated that diversion could not only result in improved rehabilitation of offenders but also in a reduced workload for the justice agencies.

Having accepted the value of diversion, from 1970 through 1972, the Board funded over thirty community-based direct service programs for juvenile delinquents, adult alcoholics, and drug offenders. However, the creation of additional community resources was found to be a limited response to diversion programming. It became apparent that continuously funding programs to fill gaps in service was not creating a better system, but was simply providing new specialized services to selected and limited populations. In many parts of Los Angeles County, the need for coordination of existing community resources was found to be more critical than was the creation of additional resources.

As a result, in 1973, the Board developed a new policy which limited the funding of grant projects to those which enhanced system coordination through interagency cooperation and planning, as opposed to additional service development. This policy, it was believed, would create a more effective diversion program which would coordinate not only community service agencies but also the primary diverting agencies—law enforcement and schools.

The Proposed Diversion Program

The Regional Diversion Program was designed to bridge the prevention and treatment capabilities of existing social agencies with the postapprehension processing of the criminal justice system. This linkage would be accomplished by the creation of a series of multijurisdictional planning and coordinating agencies at the community level, consisting of management representatives from law enforcement, probation, court, schools, social services, health, and mental health agencies, under the leadership of elected officials (Figure 1). The objectives of such a coordinated program included the following:

1.   To identify existing resources available outside the criminal justice system for diversion of offenders.
2.   To identify and redirect appropriate individuals to resources outside the Los Angeles County criminal justice system.
3.   To establish diversion planning and coordination projects over a five-year period in every city in Los Angeles County.
4.   To develop a research program to determine the most effective diversion methods for target populations.
5.   To develop evaluation methods that accurately measure diversion program effectiveness.

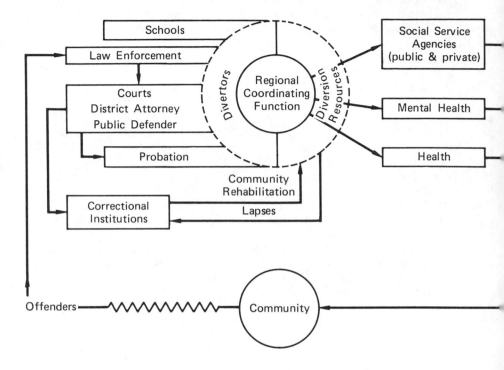

Figure 1   Regional Diversion System

In establishing the above objectives, the Regional Board formulated the following policies:

1.   To utilize existing resources as much as possible.
2.   To base decisions regarding funding on a detailed analysis of current needs.
3.   To utilize grant funds as a catalyst for implementing diversion planning.
4.   To fund new additional treatment programs only when no appropriate resources exist.
5.   To utilize purchase of service as a possible means for developing public and private cooperation.

METHODOLOGY FOR IMPLEMENTATION

The size and complexity of Los Angeles County has required that a multiyear implementation strategy be developed for the establishment of the diversion program countrywide. The Regional Board's allocation of grant funds totals approximately $10 million, which, if not utilized strategically, will have little impact on the $450 million public justice system in the Los Angeles region, which services over 4,000 square miles, 7 million people, and 78 local governments.

The multiyear strategy called first for dividing the region into twelve reasonably distinct geographic areas. These twelve areas were arranged in priority order on three separate lists—one for each target population (i.e., drug offenders, alcoholics, and juvenile delinquents). Priority was established according to frequency and rate of offense per target population and the availability of community resources which serve these populations. The goal of this ranking process was to establish an order by which to proceed with the implementation of the diversion program. Priority was given to geographic areas with high crime rates and moderate numbers of community resources to serve the target populations. These criteria were used on the assumption that it would do little good to develop a coordinated network of available services if there were only a few services in the area. To ensure that geographic areas with high crime and moderate levels of service would be ranked near the top of the list, crime rates were assigned a weighting factor twice that of availability of resources.

Second, the Board allocated available regional diversion funds to the geographic areas in priority order. The Board developed broad funding parameters for the primary target areas for each population based on information concerning the costs of existing diversion projects and community-based treatment programs obtained from both public and private agencies. Since major legislation was being considered and health program services were being provided for drug addicts and alcoholics at the time the allocation was made, it was decided to emphasize delinquency diversion projects during the first year. Greater emphasis could be placed on the other populations in later years when the changing roles and responsibilities of the health, social service, and justice system were defined in greater detail.

The next step in implementing the diversion program was the development of planning and coordinating projects within the identified geographic areas. The Planning Board utilized a Request for Proposal (RFP) process by which potential proponents in the target areas were given specific guidelines and instructions on the kinds of projects to be considered for funding and incorporated in the Regional Plan. The basic project design called for a policy board of elected officials representing each participating jurisdiction, an advisory board of top-level management from public and private agencies and the community, a small number of staff, and a "purchase of service" component to support a program development process. The intent was to have the elected officials take charge of planning for diversion while the operating agencies would both coordinate these services through the advisory board and provide professional advice to the policy board. Further, the purchase of service component would foster the development of a working relationship between the public and private sector.

The RFPs were sent to all justice-system agencies, school districts, and concerned individual agencies serving the identified geographic areas. As a result of the RFP process, nine proposals were received. Five projects were approved for funding covering the first two target areas, encompassing twenty-five cities.

As these five projects were being implemented, the second-year planning cycle was initiated. The same basic process was followed as in the first year, including a reassessment of the first year's direction. A committee of the Regional Board, operating with suggestions from an advisory panel consisting of representatives from the Sheriff, Probation, California Youth Authority, County Community Services Department, and the Office of the Mayor of Los Angeles, made recommendations to the Board on priorities, allocations, and RFP design. Once approved by the Board, the RFP process was implemented with "technical assistance" provided by field staff of the advisory panel departments, Community Services, Sheriff, and Mayor's Office.

As a result of the second RFP process, planning and coordination projects were funded in eight new areas, encompassing a total of thirty-six additional cities. The remaining geographic areas were handled in priority order in a contingency plan should funds unexpectedly become available.

ANTICIPATED RESULTS

The anticipated results of the implementation process will be the phased-in development, countywide, of formal planning and service delivery networks for intake–referral–treatment and aftercare services for selected offender populations. Direct impact on the justice system will result, since it is projected that the diversion rate for each selected population should be increased by 10 percent per year in each target area. In addition, implementation should result in improved selection criteria for divertable populations, in more uniform application of the law by law enforcement agencies, in a better working relationship between public and private agencies, in improved treatment methods, and in a verification of the value of diversion as a legitimate justice system activity. Improved interjurisdiction program planning may also result as agencies and different local governments build more effective communication. Finally, and perhaps most importantly, grant funds will be utilized in a systematic, planned manner which focuses on more than mere isolated project development, resulting in greater potential improvement of criminal justice operations.

EXPERIENCE TO DATE

As indicated earlier, the Planning Board has implemented several projects, one for alcoholics and four for juveniles. Proposals for an additional eight juvenile projects have been recommended for funding. These projects will encompass sixty-one cities by the spring of 1975. Experience to date indicates that there is a general acceptance of the diversion concept among community agencies with anticipation that each project will more than meet its original objectives. As additional information becomes available, as program feedback is received from projects, and as other agencies recognize the value of diversion, the modification and expansion of the program to other target populations appears likely.

In conclusion, it should be noted that a potential weakness of the diversion concept is that it implies "output" from one subsystem and "input" to another. The shifting of case responsibility to alternative processing subsystems represents a true value to the community only to the extent that it results in less expensive and/or more effective treatment or rehabilitation of the target populations. The concept is of little value, except to justice-system agencies, if it results in expensive "revolving-door" processing of individuals by social service or health systems. Experience to date in Los Angeles has not answered the questions as to whether this potential transfer will occur. Past experience does indicate, however, that if the simple transfer of workload to the social service sector is to be avoided, it will be accomplished only through a formal cooperative interjurisdictional planning process such as has been created by the Los Angeles Regional Criminal Justice Planning Board.

18
POLICE HELP YOUTH*

Patricia Ann Hunsicker

Here, perhaps, we have a description of the ultimate in "in-house" diversion. Counselors are given full police academy training, sworn in as officers, and then relieved of all duties as peace officers and returned to counselor status. This is the social work involvement which Sheriff Pitchess specifically warned against. One can be sure that many social workers would also look askance at this wolf-in-sheep's-clothing approach. Neither concern makes the program wrong, just controversial. The reader might also note here a considerable amount of interagency crossing and mixing of mandates. This is presumably better for treatment, but it may also be seen as endangering civil rights in an adversary system.

---

* From "Police Help Youth," *Delinquency Prevention Reporter*, Youth Development and Delinquency Prevention Administration, U.S. Department of Health, Education, and Welfare (Washington, D.C.: U.S. Government Printing Office, March–April, 1972), pp. 3–7. Reprinted by permission of the author.

In the early 1800s English courts sentenced *children* to hang for stealing. New Jersey hanged a *twelve-year-old boy* convicted of murder in 1828.

The United States criminal justice system has come a long way in recognizing that treatment is more effective than punitive measures, and that diversion from the juvenile justice system affords youth a better chance for rehabilitation.

Montclair, California's Police Chief R. L. McLean heads up a force of thirty-five sworn personnel in a city of 22,560 people. Residents have an average age of twenty-three and fall in the lower-middle-class tax brackets. Incorporated in 1956, Montclair lies 1.5 miles south of the San Gabriel Mountains in San Bernardino County. It is the county's most densely populated city and covers 4.5 square miles. In the center of the city there is a large shopping plaza with major department stores and small shops. Considered a bedroom community, most of the working people travel outside the city limits to their jobs.

Three years ago McLean proposed to the city council the hiring of a delinquency prevention officer who would establish and coordinate prevention and community relations programs. He would effect dispositions and referrals on police juvenile arrests and provide counsel and assistance to both parents and juveniles.

McLean felt police should play a *major* role in the control of delinquency and protection of children because they observe firsthand where, when, and why delinquency develops in a community. The police officer is also the first one to observe problem family situations and is in a position to investigate relationships as trouble occurs.

In most police departments a juvenile officer is a police specialist skilled in police methods, but generally *lacking* the specialized education, training, and insight for implementing a rehabilitative or treatment philosophy within the scope of a police program. By having a youth specialist, other officers can request guidance on disposition of children's cases and close contact is established with courts, schools, probation, and community agencies.

What makes Montclair unique is that Chief McLean recruited people from *outside* law enforcement to create and supervise a juvenile diversion program which is implemented by all officers. Fred Drury, Youth Services Coordinator, was hired in November 1969 and has a degree in psychology and extensive experience working with young people representing both sides of the law. Because of program growth, Bruce Bess was hired eleven months later. Bess has similar background and experience.

Drury and Bess were put through the police academy and are full-fledged officers in plain clothes. By exposing them to police philosophy and problems, McLean and the city council felt that two somewhat divergent schools of thought would be amalgamated. They were given full exposure to the police perspective and the problems involved in fulfilling the police responsibility to uphold the law. But after finishing the police training they were *not* given the responsibilities of making arrests, clearing cases, and responding to day-to-day investigative needs. *They are expected to devote their entire effort toward developing preventive and rehabilitative programs.*

Drury and his assistant have full authority to dispose of all juvenile arrests not immediately referred to the probation department. One out of nine arrests goes to the juvenile hall—not for punitive reasons but for psychological evaluations or because the home environment requires removal of the child. The remaining eight are diverted to one or more of several programs or agencies within Montclair and surrounding areas.

Many regular officers were critical of becoming "social workers" and cynical about how effective they could be. Gradually, through in-service training and exposure to children in an educational program at the junior and senior high schools, ride-along programs with youth in police cars, and participating in counseling sessions, they learned that they now have *alternatives to arrest*. The officer is learning how to be concerned with the individual and can make a discretionary decision based on the juvenile and his circumstances—not entirely upon the offense.

Police reports are reflecting this change. Instead of stating the offense and recommending juvenile court action, the report might say that the father is an alcoholic who beats his family and the youth needs help. The officers are recognizing that time spent incarcerated in juvenile hall is not the answer. The answer is to get the child or the family into a treatment program as soon as possible.

The Youth Coordinator schedules counseling sessions as necessary. He reviews the background of arrested subjects and, when appropriate, calls the juvenile and his parents into the office to discuss the disposition of the matter.

Most juveniles and parents expect a long-winded lecture and are uncertain about what will happen after that. Instead the atmosphere is relaxed and they are met with a patient listener who waits to be told what the problem is. All are involved in seeking the solution. When alternatives are placed before the juvenile, the responsibility and decision rests with him. Diagnosis and treatment plans are formulated on an individual basis.

One seventeen-year-old boy had been caught taking a tape deck out of a car and was booked for burglary. He had no previous police record. In talking with him and his mother the Youth Coordinator felt there were emotional problems which ought to be dealt with. While the arrest was solid and the chances would be good for sustaining the juvenile court petition, it was unlikely that court action would lead to any sort of treatment program. The young man was not so seriously disturbed that he needed professional therapy; yet it was clear that he could benefit from a counseling relationship and that he ought to be impressed with the seriousness of his act.

The Youth Coordinator discussed the seriousness of the consequences which might follow from court action and indicated that some action had to be taken to clear the case. He left the young man with a choice to either take his chances in court or to cooperate in a program of voluntary or informal probation. It was explained to him that such a program was not a legal probation, but simply a way of settling the matter outside of court.

The conditions of his acceptance would be that he report to the officer twice a week for four weeks and that he cooperate with his mother. After four weeks there would be another conference with his mother and the officer. If the mother and the officer were satisfied with his cooperation in the four-week program, the case would be closed. The program would be implemented only with the mother's approval. He agreed.

The mother was then called in, apart from her son. She was greatly relieved to hear of the proposal as she felt that her son needed some guidance from an older male. She offered the officer much information about her son's background which she felt would be helpful in the counseling program. The arrangement was agreed to and the Youth Coordinator gained an opportunity to make a more complete diagnosis and begin a treatment program.

The officer focuses on specific short-term goals and the opening up of communications between the parents and the youth. After two to six weeks of counseling he is in a better position to suggest other resources for resolving problems and has established a rapport and trust with the youth and the parents.

Sometimes the youth or the parents request that the counseling appointments continue. Then the officer can become involved in longer-term counseling relationships within the limits of his training and time available.

PROBATION

Police and probation use a team approach with those on formal probation. The probation officer serving Montclair works in close contact with the Youth Coordinator.

Probation officers often have such heavy caseloads that close supervision for all clients is impossible. The probation officer selects clients from Montclair who can benefit from a closer relationship and requests secondary supervision from the police. The Youth Coordinator meets with the client biweekly for a month or more and then recommends for or against continued involvement.

Several results are achieved. The probation officer's caseload is reduced; local, intensive care is given to the probationer; and the Youth Coordinator and the probation officer develop a team approach.

For example, a probationer may not be capable of accepting one person to act as an authority figure as well as a friend. The Youth Coordinator is not in on the case as a "cop," but as a helping person who is free of responsibility for disposing of the case. The probation officer has the power to return the case to court and can assume the authority position.

This arrangement has proven so successful that an interagency policy has been developed to expedite new cases. To cut down on the time lapse before treatment begins caused by court hearings, paperwork, schedules, and availability, the Youth Coordinator makes contact with the youth, who has been referred for Juvenile Court action when he is released from custody and makes a determination as to whether he is a candidate for the dual supervision program. If he is, a recommendation is made to the investigating probation officer and a relationship is started immediately with the client.

In this way a service is provided to the probation department by assisting in the investigation. All investigating probation officers are instructed to contact the Youth Coordinator when they receive an application for petition from Montclair. Sometimes the minor is already known to the Youth Coordinator, and diagnostic information relevant to the investigation can be made available.

SCHOOLS

The educational and research consultant to the REAL project (Responsibilities to Enforcement and Attitudes Concerning Laws) said, "Agencies and schools have been alienated too long and it is the kid you're trying to serve who falls in the cracks. The attitudes of all concerned were 'you stay on your turf and I'll stay on mine'."

He felt that educators, police, and social workers need to get "out of their box," as no single agency can expect to fulfill a child's total need. "Society has been specialized too long, and agencies need to work together."

Montclair police are breaking down the barriers. A *trilogy* between police, schools, and probation has been formed, with the philosophy that realistic awareness accomplishes far more than public relations programs designed to impress people.

In early 1970 a pilot group counseling program was established at Montclair High School to reduce misconceptions or vague understandings of the function and purpose of laws.

The first group consisted of students who cut classes regularly, disrupted classes, had academic problems, or were on formal probation. These youths were the potential dropouts.

The group met once a week for an entire semester with a representative from the police department, high school, and probation department. Some of the students were on the verge of expulsion and the group was offered as an alternative. This assured attendance but it caused a stigma to be attached. Some students began to challenge the authority of the agencies involved to force them to come, and it was admitted that there was none.

As the group continued meeting it became apparent that the authority figures were not siding with the parents. The students began to enjoy the opportunity to express their feelings about parents, school, and police and be supported by authorities when they presented critical attitudes. The free, honest rap sessions allowed the participants to point out each other's unreasonable attitudes. As the students began to understand the roles played by probation, police, and school they also could see these agency representatives as human beings with strengths and weaknesses.

The groups have provided an opportunity for the ventilation and discussion of feelings and attitudes held by students, parents, police officers, probation officers, and school officials. Given this opportunity to express themselves, to be taken seriously, and to get an immediate response from the other generation, some of the teenagers involved have been able to act more responsibly toward authority (80 percent stayed in school). The group program also forces authority to be more responsive to the youth.

The pressure for individual change comes from the group process itself. The group atmosphere is one in which all have equal rights. The authority figures do not sit in judgment. As important issues are discussed, the group itself responds to individual positions and a process of social reality testing comes into effect.

Another program has been developed within the school that coexists with the group program. The same trilogy is used. It is open to the entire student body at two junior highs and the high school and takes the form of an academic class.

The class includes lectures, field trips, ride-along outings in squad cars, and guest speakers, but the schedule is entirely flexible. The class may discuss any issue (laws, rights, sex, disease, news events). Scheduled lectures frequently turn into a discussion that resembles the group counseling program. At least one class period per week is set aside for a rap or group counseling session.

Each class is composed of one-third "pro-police" youth who dream of being "cops," one-third "anti-police" rebels, and one-third of students whose attitudes range somewhere between these two extremes. The purpose of the class is not to convert anybody to the police position, but to afford a reality-testing experience.

The class functions as a corrective to misconceptions, false information, and overgeneralizations. Honesty is the cardinal rule, and this applies to the students as it does to the police officer-teacher. Students are repeatedly asked to identify how the issues they voice relate to them as individuals and an effort is made to help everyone think about how they will cope with the hypothetical or real situations they pose. If a student expresses hostility toward police, he will be held responsible for identifying the reasons for his attitudes and discussion follows.

A continual effort is made to raise the question of what responsibilities or attitudes are necessary for good citizenship and good police work in today's society. The classroom atmosphere provides a daily confrontation in which police officers and youth encounter each other in a responsible manner.

A young junior high girl remarked, "I thought that cops were out to get you into trouble, but now I know that cops are there to help."

One encouraging sign of better communication developing because of the course is that school and probation now work in close conjunction with each other. The school counselors go to probation facilities to get acquainted with a court ward before he returns to regular school.

One of the officer-teachers who has been with the Montclair Police Department for three years feels a noticeable change has taken place in the class as a group. Now when he's driving in his patrol car the kids yell "hi" instead of making lewd gestures and calling out "pig."

He found out through his classroom experiences that the youth could see right through him and that only honesty could make the class successful. His teaching experience has increased his own self-confidence and he likes being accepted as a human being. Before his involvement with the school program he never went out of his way to talk to young people. Now he realizes that the way he treats a young person may help the youth get "squared away." He acknowledges that he's becoming more socially aware and feels that police attitudes toward suspects are the key to suspects' reactions.

COMMUNITY SERVICES CENTER

An unused firehouse was put to use in the past year as a multipurpose meeting place for teenagers and young adults. The atmosphere is low-key and nonbureaucratic, with the emphasis on confidentiality.

A visitor might find a group of youth playing chess while they and the onlookers rap about a recent death in a boy's family, favorite TV shows, or "cops." Other drop-ins are looking for employment with the job referral service, while still others are there to see the volunteer doctor at the free clinic.

One room has tie-dyed sheets for curtains and the walls are decorated in brightly colored pencil drawings with messages scrawled from ceiling to floor. The family conference room is more sedate and furnished with couches, chairs, and orange and yellow bamboo curtains. A kitchen provides a never-empty coffee pot and the old engine room is partitioned in one corner into two fully equipped medical examining rooms. The rest of the space has old sofas for follow-up talks with the nurses. At other times this area is used for larger group counseling sessions and craft projects.

The center's philosophy is natural, simple, and pleasant. Staff believes that people are loving, caring, intelligent, and worthy. Therefore, all visitors deserve and need appreciation, respect, concern, and attention. The most important service staff offers to people is human responsiveness to human needs. Whether or not they are able to find someone a job or treat a specific ailment, the staff is committed to a policy of respect and trust.

The center's codirectors have degrees in psychology and extensive experience in group and drug counseling. Both are in their twenties and one is working toward a Ph.D. in social and community psychology.

They were hired for twenty hours a week by the city and are supervised by the Youth Coordinator, but they are putting in around thirty-five hours apiece instead.

"I love the kids," said one director, "and there's so much to do that I can't stay away."

The community center was designed to provide services to meet a variety of needs. Once an individual need is recognized, the staff secures the necessary resource to fulfill that need. The idea is to provide a place for people to come for any reason whatsoever, not to set up a preplanned operation that is rigid in design.

The original concept included four areas of service: counseling, employment, education, and medical treatment. After beginning the renovation of the building, the next step was the organization of a volunteer professional counseling staff. Psychiatric social workers, clinical psychologists, and marriage, family, and child counselors were asked to donate a few hours per week to see clients at the center. The Youth Coordinator began identifying people who wanted professional assistance in dealing with family or personal problems but who were unable to afford it. Appointments were arranged with volunteer counselors. If a family or individual could afford private counseling they were sent to their private physician for referrals to practitioners in the counseling field.

Another program developed at the center was an employment program called *Rent-a-Kid*. There is a full-time coordinator hired by the city, also under the Youth Coordinator's supervision, who devotes his time to seeking job opportunities and referring teenagers and adults to these resources.

Housewives can telephone for yardwork, baby-sitting, car washing, window cleaning, and businessmen can refer to Rent-a-Kid for part- or full-time employees. The applicants and job orders are matched by the employment coordinator.

The coordinator also acts as a counselor. A youth might never tell that he has a problem, but he won't hesitate to say that he needs a job. After once playing the vocational helper the coordinator places himself in a position to offer help in other areas.

One young lady came in seeking a job. During the informal counseling she revealed that she was fearful of being pregnant and having VD. The employment counselor suggested she use the free clinic to find out the facts. The outcome was that she did have VD but was not pregnant. The clinic treated her and provided follow-up counseling so that she would not find herself in a similar situation again. She also found a job.

The center and clinic is an information center providing: crisis telephone counseling; pregnancy counseling and abortion referral; individual problem counseling; referrals to volunteer psychologists; draft counseling; informal discussion groups for juvenile probationers; and a meeting place for groups.

The juvenile probation officer, who is part of the trilogy school program, uses the center to meet the youth on his caseload. The free atmosphere allows for an open, less "uptight" verbal exchange than one would find in a probation office. The probationers realize that they can come in and talk to the probation officer without having to arrange or structure an appointment. By meeting at the center the probationers also become acquainted with the other services that the center provides. They can become involved in art workshops, help with minor carpentry jobs, or get involved in group counseling. The center is also used by youth who need to get away for awhile from serious home problems and meet with others who recognize their individual worth.

The probation officer arranged for textbooks to be donated. He is now helping to set up a study center at the firehouse which provides tutorial services from students at a nearby university.

A student volunteer who helps out at the center as part of his academic training at the University of California, Riverside, sees the center as nondemanding. The client decides what is needed from the center without having the center impose itself upon the client. It is run in an informal way. There are no set rules or bureaucratic codes.

The professional volunteer counselors are developing a trained group of selected teenagers who can help other teenagers with their problems through informal discussions at the center. Interested adult lay counselors are also screened by the professional staff and will become trained cotherapists under the supervision of the professional.

The center not only provides services that are immediately available, but refers people to other existing agencies throughout Southern California, such as county health, welfare, the state employment system, and existing community programs.

The West End Drug Abuse Control Coordinating Council, Inc. (WEDAC), which combines many different programs from communities on the western end of San Bernardino County, has supplied the funds for an employee to coordinate and run the free clinic at the firehouse.

The clinic is open one night a week from 7 to 10 P.M. and is staffed by volunteer doctors and nurses who dress in regular clothing instead of uniforms. Patients come from the surrounding area and from as far as sixty miles away for VD check, abortion referrals, pregnancy counseling, and run-of-the-mill ailments. The clinic attends to the needs of the individual and the need of the community by safeguarding the health of both.

The clinic has been accepted as a provisional member of the Southern California Council of Free Clinics and has initiated the licensing procedure with the state public health department. A million dollar malpractice and liability insurance policy has been secured.

Some comments to the question "How comfortable were you with the services you received here?" were: "cool place," "far out," "the atmosphere eases the hassle of things," "sure is nice to have a place to go and have people care what happens to young people," and "a good place for people to come for help that don't know where else to go." Most of the written remarks dropped in the comment box are accompanied by heartfelt *thanks*.

Referrals to the center come from the police, parents, teachers, service groups, friends, street contacts, probation, doctors, and students. Those referred may need employment, group counseling, loosely structured play therapy (art workshop), or medical attention.

Chief McLean sees all these programs as "breaking down traditional boundaries." "We're not isolating ourselves from other agencies and communities," he said. "Sixty percent of all arrests are people from outside our city limits, but our programs are for all.

"It used to be that people had to be dragged into a police station. Now young men and women, boys, and girls come to the station for help because they know there is someone here who cares about them."

19

EARLY DIVERSION
FROM THE CRIMINAL JUSTICE SYSTEM:
PRACTICE IN SEARCH OF A THEORY*

Elizabeth W. Vorenberg and James Vorenberg

At a time when few program descriptions are available, this next article is extremely valuable for its depiction of the variety of program formats fitting under the rubric of diversion. The article also contains the most explicit statement we have seen about distinguishing "new" diversion from practices already extant; i.e., the Vorenbergs make it clear that they consider diversion to refer only to programs which *increase* the proportion of released offenders. Also commendable are the authors' comments on evaluation. They note its virtual nonexistence, agency reluctance to engage in it, and both federal and state failures to demand it.

---

* From *Prisoners in America*, edited by Lloyd E. Ohlin (Englewood Cliffs, N.J.: Prentice-Hall, Inc., 1973), pp. 151–158, 166–172, and 177–183. Reprinted by permission of the authors and publisher.

In the years since the President's Crime Commission began its work and reform of the criminal justice system became a major national goal, certain words and phrases have become the shorthand for improvements that all "reformers" in the field are deemed to accept. A few examples are "professionalization" and "community service" as applied to the police; "business management techniques" as applied to the courts; and "community treatment" and "collaborative model" as applied to corrections. In hundreds of the criminal justice plans required of the states by the block-grant formulation of the Law Enforcement Assistance Act and in the individual grant applications submitted pursuant to such plans, these and other slogans appear thousands of times, thereby wrapping a particular proposal in the flag of the Crime Commission and the massive subsequent literature. But no word has had quite the power of "diversion" (or, if real specificity is desired, "early diversion") which offers the promise of the best of all worlds: cost savings, rehabilitation, and more humane treatment.

The purpose of this chapter is to explore what we mean by diversion in the criminal justice system, what we have and have not learned from programs or approaches that can fairly use the label, and what the issues are that must be considered in reacting to the concept of diversion generally and to its application to particular situations.

"Diversion"—or "early diversion"—has no real meaning in relationship to the criminal justice system in the absence of a context that tells us (1) what the process is by which diversion takes place; (2) what the person is diverted from—i.e., what is diversion instead of?; and (3) what he is diverted to. Thus, if we take the Perry Mason image of the criminal process by which every person apprehended in a criminal act is arrested, charged, tried, and, if

248

convicted, sentenced to prison, any disposition short of serving the full prison term could fairly be regarded as early diversion. This would include a decision of a policeman to let a traffic violation offender go with a tongue-lashing; a district attorney to drop a shoplifting case against a first offender because the store fails to prosecute; a judge to give a convicted person probation or a suspended sentence; or a parole board to release a prisoner at his first parole hearing. These are all diversions from a more serious burden that would have been imposed but for the action taken.

But these early exits from the system are familiar and of long standing and may fairly be regarded as part of the system itself and will generally be so regarded in this chapter. What is usually meant by current calls for early diversion is, to put it simply, something that is new. This may consist of (1) recognition that some categories of offenders, such as drunks, addicts, and the mentally ill, are special candidates for diversion; (2) new procedures or incentives to raise the number, the percentage, or the seriousness-of-offense level of the offenders who leave the system early; (3) new screening devices to select those who will leave; or (4) new places, programs, or opportunities for those who do leave. Many of the most important new programs are built on well-recognized early exit points in the system. Thus the California probation subsidy program is basically a financial and political device to get judges to put more offenders on probation, and the Manhattan Court Employment Project is an elaborate administrative mechanism to encourage and improve a practice long in use in many places—the suspension of prosecution on condition that the offender show the court he can and will hold down a job.

We will try not to agonize over what does and does not qualify as an early diversion program; the chapter will try to focus on issues raised by relatively recent programs.

Although this chapter is part of a book on corrections, it necessarily looks at diversion at earlier stages of the system. For one of the principal purposes of diversion is to offer an offender the kind of treatment which under certain correctional programs he would receive only after conviction, but without the delays, the pressure on the offender, or the costs of full processing through the system. Thus, in one sense, diversion is simply a way of starting correctional treatment sooner. More broadly, it has become clear that for many purposes the criminal justice system should be seen not as a line but as a closed loop that has as its starting point the offender at the time of the offense and as its closing point and its goal the return of the offender to responsibility for his own life. As discussed below, there are strong arguments that for many offenders the trip around the circle is meaningless and damaging and costly—and that therefore we should consider whether and under what circumstances we should and can leave offenders where we find them.

Early diversion may be seen as a means of implementing a number of theories that underlie current efforts at correctional reform. Two of these deserve brief mention. Perhaps the most important for our purposes—and central to the Crime Commission's recommendations in the corrections area—is that every effort should be made to avoid relieving an offender of the responsibility and burdens of making decisions and managing his own life, since the goal is to return him to society better able to cope on his own. One manifestation of this theory is that if he must be institutionalized, the offender should have the privilege/burden of participating in decisions affecting him—thus the proposal for "collaborative institutions" that was at the heart of the commission's recommendations about prisons. Another manifestation was that the absence from society—necessitating under the best of circumstances a break in the sequence of responsibility—should be as slight as possible.

Also underlying early diversion is the so-called "labeling" theory. This theory hypothesizes that society's label may be accepted in part by the individual himself. Therefore, imposing the status and label of a convicted criminal makes recidivism more likely. Closely related is the recognition that the label limits or precludes opportunities an offender may have to be reintegrated into lawful society.

It is beyond the scope of this chapter to consider in depth the relation of early diversion to theories of corrections or crime causation, and therefore we have dealt only briefly with those issues. However, in addition to whatever theories may have contributed to the movement for diversion, we have a strong sense that perhaps most important of all is the recognition that the system is hopelessly overloaded with cases; is brutal, corrupt, and ineffective; and that therefore every case removed is a gain.

Hundreds of projects have been undertaken around the country which have early diversion as a component. Because of the fragmentation of the criminal justice operations among counties, cities, states, and the federal system, it is impossible to make even a rough quantitative assessment of the extent to which offenders are being diverted out of the system. The nation's sources of information about the operation of the conventional parts of the criminal justice system are limited. And since, as will be discussed below, early diversion takes place in many forms and involves many agencies which we normally do not consider to be part of the criminal justice system, we simply must accept that we do not know, except impressionistically, how much real change the movement toward diversion has made. It may be that notwithstanding all the money and all the writing about diversion, only a relatively few offenders are being treated differently than a decade earlier. (One example of how easy it is to be misled on the extent of actual change was the finding by a study at the Harvard Center for Criminal Justice that more than two years after the Crime Commission had recommended community residential facilities and at a time when much was being written and said about them, less than 2 percent of adult offenders in state custody were in residential facilities outside the walls of traditional prisons.)

Unfortunately, the slipshod handling of evaluation and reporting under the Law Enforcement Assistance Act makes it unlikely that even several years from now we will know what the extent of the shift toward early diversion has been or what impact it has had on crime, criminal justice costs, efficiency, morale, or rehabilitation. Despite the lack of any real quantitative information on the scope of early diversion or probing evaluation of its effects, it may be useful to describe briefly as a basis for discussion and analysis some of the major types of diversion projects—both by the points in the system at which diversion takes place (second part of this chapter) and by the type of offender for whom they are designed (third part). Much of the description of these projects draws on or paraphrases secondary literature.

DIVERSION PROJECTS: EXIT POINTS

There are hundreds of new diversion programs being undertaken in the United States. They result in the offender's leaving the traditional criminal justice system at various points from before arrest until after conviction. The way the offender's case is disposed of depends on where and by whom in the system diversion is considered, and the fact of diversion, in turn, has an impact on the various agencies in the system. To try to illuminate some of these issues, this second part of the chapter will consider examples of diversion projects at different points in the system. It needs emphasis that the projects listed here and in the third part are not necessarily the most important or the best of their kind. They are simply among those about which we have been able to obtain enough information to raise issues for consideration. It is also worth noting that the fact that the Vera Institute of Justice of New York City appears repeatedly in this paper is no accident. Vera has carried the concept of early diversion into practice at various stages of the criminal justice system. Because of its pragmatic approach and its record of success in setting up projects, it has provided an important incentive for the development of such projects nationally.

Diversion by Police

In most jurisdictions, the statutory authority of the police to arrest is mandatory not discretionary. Nonetheless, the police everywhere have always exercised broad discretion to decide whether or not to arrest. Of course, if serious crimes or highly dangerous conduct is involved, the police will arrest and participate in an offender's prosecution. But crime connected with family arguments, such misdemeanors as public drunkenness, loitering and disorderly conduct, mildly destructive behavior by juveniles, and minor crimes generally will often lead to a decision not to arrest or take into custody. Thus at a pre-arrest stage of the process large numbers of potential offenders have already been diverted in the sense that they have been dropped from the system.

Even after an offender is brought into the station, police power (if not legal authority) to handle a case informally continues. In some cities substantial numbers of cases are dropped at the stationhouse in a completely invisible, informal, and nonlegal procedure. A case may be dropped unconditionally or on condition that the offender stay out of trouble or make restitution.

On the other hand, in some cities there are well-structured hearing procedures for juveniles which are similar to intake hearings of juvenile courts. There are formal notices to parents and minors setting the time and place for a meeting with a "hearing officer." The police officer in charge of the hearing seeks to make a common-sense judgment on whether the juvenile should be sent to court. He takes into account such factors as the juvenile's prior record and his reputation with the police and the community as a troublemaker, the likelihood that the family will cooperate in keeping the juvenile out of trouble, and the extent to which the police may be criticized for being too lenient if the offense was serious or if there is further trouble. While the participation of the juvenile and his parents is voluntary in the sense they can opt for a court appearance, there is in fact great pressure to cooperate in order to stay out of court. Often the police will use this pressure and the juvenile's desire to avoid a police record to get a confession for their files that will enable them to treat the case as closed and which may have an *in terrorem* effect on the future misconduct of the juvenile.

Police referral. A much broader role for the police is involved in proposals that the police become a referral agency to effect noncriminal disposition of arrested persons. Vera Institute's Manhattan Bowery project for handling drunks is one example, although the police role is a limited one. The New York City Police Department announced in the fall of 1972 that addicts arrested for offenses or misdemeanors will be offered an opportunity to be sent to a drug treatment program with submission of their cases for prosecution held in abeyance. Addicts who agree to treatment and who are accepted by a treatment center would be paroled, with the court's approval, in the custody of the center. One possible role for the community service officer recommended by the President's Crime Commission would be to screen persons arrested for relatively minor crimes and dismiss or refer to social or health agencies those without a serious criminal record.

There is no way of knowing how many police departments are now engaged in such dismissal-referral programs. What is clear is that to the extent they become visible and acknowledged, such programs have an important bearing on the continuing debate about police participation in a social service role. That debate is usually in terms of how police resources should be allocated. But police responsibility for early diversion raises deeper questions as to whether it is inherently inappropriate for the police to make corrections-type decisions and whether the whole post-arrest situation is simply too pressured to ensure that a suspect's decision to accept a particular form of treatment (such as participation in a methadone program) is truly voluntary. At least until more is known of the extent and content of diversion by the police in this country, one should probably be cautious about taking a general position about the appropriateness of police agencies undertaking this responsibility. There are undoubtedly some situations— particularly where the decision is not onerous—in which a police role would be generally acceptable. There are others where, without strong protections for the suspect including providing him with a lawyer, there would be general agreement that the police should not take responsibility for diversion. There is one point on which we believe there should be no disagreement. To the extent the police are making arrangements for the conditional dropping of cases, the practice should be openly acknowledged rather than hidden as it so often is.

British practice.   In considering formalized diversion by the police, the British experience may provide some guidance. Great Britain has proceeded further than the United States in formalizing police diversion practices by establishing in 1968 the Juvenile Bureaus within the Metropolitan Police in London. Up to that time the practice of the London police was to arrest and charge juvenile offenders in much the same way as adults. The changes included amending police procedure so that many young offenders would be brought in on a summons instead of a formal charge. But the heart of the new system is use of the "caution" by the police as a substitute for court proceedings.

Police Juvenile Bureau personnel are responsible for gathering information from the Children's Departments, Probation and Education Services, and other relevant agencies about a young person brought to the station for an alleged offense. In most cases an officer will visit the juvenile's home. A background report is prepared which, together with the evidence relating to the offense, is considered by the chief inspector in charge of the Bureau who decides whether or not the young offender should be prosecuted. The cautioning procedure, which in 1970 was used for 39 percent of juveniles who committed offenses, is based on the following criteria:

1.   The offender must admit the offense.
2.   The parents must agree that the child be cautioned.
3.   The person victimized must be willing to leave the matter to the police.

The caution is given under formal circumstances at the police station by a chief inspector in uniform. While a juvenile's record is relevant to whether he will have the benefit of the cautioning procedure, the fact that he has been cautioned previously does not necessarily mean that he will be prosecuted if he commits a subsequent offense.

At the outset, other social agencies responsible for juveniles were concerned that the police would not be adequately trained, that they would tend to pass judgment on the character of the juvenile, and that they might abuse confidential information. Representatives of the London Police say that care has been taken in the choice and training of personnel so as to eliminate grounds for such concern.

"SPECIAL POPULATION" DIVERSION PROGRAMS

The second part of this chapter examined the criminal justice system chronologically with examples of diversion projects at particular points in the suspect's or offender's movement through the system. Another approach is to consider certain types of offenders whose personal difficulties or youth make them candidates for less punitive and more therapeutic treatment. This third part will consider briefly some examples of diversion programs for juveniles, drunks, narcotic addicts, and those in need of psychiatric treatment.

Juveniles

In the earlier discussion of diversion at various stages of the criminal process, several programs involving juveniles were outlined. This section will analyze in greater depth some of the special issues relating to juvenile diversion programs, particularly those raised by the President's Crime Commission's recommended Youth Services Bureaus.

The creation of the juvenile court system in the United States was an attempt to treat the juvenile offender in a noncriminal, more therapeutic way. But over time most juvenile courts have become in essence criminal courts with criminal-type dispositions. One consequence has been the United States Supreme Court's imposition on juvenile courts of many of the due process protections required of adult courts. Another is the search for new means of meeting the original goals envisioned for the juvenile courts.

One of the most important recommendations of the 1967 report of the Crime Commission was that communities should establish new agencies as a means of diverting juveniles from the criminal system, including keeping them out of the juvenile court.

The commission suggested that such agencies—which it labeled Youth Services Bureaus—should be available for (1) youths who have not committed criminal acts but whose problems at home, in school, or in the community may lead them to do so if they do not receive help, and (2) delinquents whose misconduct is rooted in similar problems. The Commission report states:

> Such an agency ideally would be located in a comprehensive community center and would serve both delinquent and nondelinquent youths. While some referrals to the Youth Services Bureau would normally originate with parents, schools, and other sources, the bulk of the referrals could be expected to come from the police and the juvenile court intake staff, and police and court referrals should have special status in that the Youth Services Bureau would be required to accept them all. . . . These agencies would act as central coordinators of all community services for young people and would also provide services lacking in the community or neighborhood, especially ones designed for less seriously delinquent juveniles.

Because of the commission's recommendation and the availability of massive funding from the Law Enforcement Assistance Administration, there came into being agencies with an enormous number of programs bearing the Youth Services Bureau label but with widely differing forms and objectives. A seminar held at the University of Chicago Criminal Research Center in 1971 to collect and exchange information on the development of Youth Services Bureaus revealed how varied and conflicting the rationales of existing bureaus are. Some of those responsible for the new agencies sought to work with existing community agencies, while others wanted to have minimal contact with the existing system. Some found it difficult to distinguish between the limited aim of diverting children from the criminal justice system and the more general aim of delinquency prevention. Some believed bureaus should provide direct service; others believed that they should rely on mobilizing existing community resources. In one instance a teenage drop-in center called itself a Youth Services Bureau in order to obtain support. The general impression that emerged was that many local agencies had absorbed the name and the federal funds but felt no obligation to accept the commission's goals of creating comprehensive local diversion agencies.

The situation nationally was summarized by a request of the California Youth Authority for funds to conduct a national survey of Youth Services Bureaus in which it stated:

> Nationally we have no information regarding the total numbers of children served. . . . We do not even know where or how many Youth Services Bureaus exist. We lack information on the relative cost of the services provided. We lack information about the effectiveness of various types of models used for the delivery of services, and we lack specific information regarding whether or not justice agencies and youths themselves are using these new alternatives to the criminal justice system. In brief, we know little about a strongly supported idea that is commanding more and more federal dollars under the umbrella of prevention.

Massachusetts experience. The differing form these agencies have taken is exemplified by the form in which they have developed in one state—Massachusetts—which has sought to evaluate their operations. The Governor's Committee on Law Enforcement and Administration of Criminal Justice has funded four bureaus (known as Youth Resources Bureaus to distinguish them from the Department of Youth Services, the state's juvenile correctional agency). Each is based on a different model:

1. Brockton Youth Resources Bureau: This bureau sees itself as a clearinghouse for agency activity and information, positioning itself between sources of referrals (police, court, schools) and sources of community services.
2. Waltham Youth Resources Bureau: Its approach is clinical, relying on psychiatric and psychological evaluations, followed by an appropriate treatment plan, minimizing contact work with outside agencies.
3. Cambridge Youth Resources Bureau: It has concentrated on a detached worker model of delinquency prevention.
4. New Bedford Youth Resources Bureau: It is a broad juvenile delinquency prevention program based on maximum participation of community residents who are being trained by the program as apprentice social workers.

The fact that the bureaus have taken diverse forms is not necessarily bad. However, there is something peculiar about a decision-making and funding process that does not look beyond the label of an agency in deciding that it has merit. Furthermore, it is simply not clear yet whether the commission's recommendation of Youth Services Bureaus has succeeded in a major shift toward early diversion of juvenile offenders, or whether the concept has been distorted and the label misused to provide a means for funding a miscellaneous collection of preexisting and newly devised programs for juveniles.

Vera program. Even where they have sought to follow the Crime Commission's model, it appears that few of the bureaus have succeeded in producing an agency that will "go to bat" for delinquent and predelinquent youth who now tend to lose out in their access to needed services. The Neighborhood Youth Diversion Program, begun early in 1971 by the Vera Institute of Justice in New York City, appears to come close to meeting the Youth Services Bureau goals in design and execution. As described by Vera,

> Its aim is to divert young people in trouble with the law from the conventional police–probation–Family Court processes to a community-based program of assistance and mediation. It is designed to do so by drawing on and, where necessary, constructing new community resources that can help resolve the problems of troubled youths. . . . It is based on a concept that perceives of rising delinquency in terms of unstable social conditions and of cultural patterns rather than merely of disturbed personalities.

The program operates in a limited section of the Bronx, New York, an area that in a little more than five years moved from a predominantly Jewish community to one overwhelmingly black and Puerto Rican. Many religious and social organizations moved to other locations or dissolved, with the result that the schools and other public agencies were unable to meet the needs of the residents.

The program works with young persons between the ages of twelve and fifteen and is run by people living in the community. Of all the program's elements, the most innovative is a device called the Forum, a series of panels of community residents who receive training as mediators and conciliators. Forum members work out the problems surrounding minor offenses committed by neighborhood juveniles and deal with crises between parents and children which had often resulted in sending young people to the state training schools.

Cases are referred to the program from three sources—the Office of Probation, the Police Department's Youth Aid Division, and Family Court. Referrals from agencies not involved in the juvenile justice system are not sought. (While this varies from the commission's Youth Services Bureau format, it may be the only way to ensure that those most in need of services do not come at the end of the line.)

Each case is assigned to an advocate, a person generally under thirty who also resides in the community. He acts as a counselor and a link to family, friends, and schools, and provides assistance to outside referrals—especially for finding temporary homes, useful jobs, and education. All referrals are followed carefully to determine what is being done for the youth. The project has referral arrangements with more than 150 agencies, including boys' clubs, health centers, child welfare agencies, and drug programs. As described by Vera,

> Almost all cases go to a Forum hearing at some point during their participation in the program, usually early. Each Forum consists of three volunteer judges who live in the community and who agree to mediate. Usually two or three hearings are required. The Forum's task is not to make judgments and rulings, but to attempt

to bring the disputing parties together to resolve their differences without reference to the formal criminal justice system. . . . During the first four months of the program, 21 cases were presented to Forums. All but one resolved the problems sufficiently to eliminate the necessity of Formal Court proceedings. One case was returned to Family Court.

An evaluation reported that the recidivism rate of those in the project was half that of a comparison group. It was also reported that between February and October 1971 the program was able to divert 36 percent of the delinquency cases and 21 percent of PINS (Persons in Need of Supervision) cases appearing in probation intake. The evaluation also indicated that the youths referred were not necessarily the more pliable and easy to work with. It was further reported that the program has had difficulty delivering services because (1) it lacked funds to purchase services, (2) there are few services in the area, and (3) the indigenous staff is not part of the professional network that controls most of the social services in the city.

Sacramento county project. Because so many serious criminal careers begin with truancy, running away from home, and other conduct not criminal for adults, the 601 Diversion Project of the Sacramento County Probation Department is worth noting. The project is testing whether juveniles charged with a 601 offense (a predelinquent offense) can be handled better through short-term family crisis therapy administered at intake by specially trained probation officers than through the traditional procedures of the juvenile court. Youths beyond control of their parents, runaways, truants, and others falling within section 601 of the Welfare and Institutions Code constitute over one-third of all juvenile court cases in Sacramento County.

In October of 1970, the project began receiving referrals on 601 matters from police, schools, parents, and other sources. Family sessions are held to discuss the problem, the first session usually within the first hour or two after referral. The counselor tries to have the family as a whole take responsibility for the problem. Locking up the youth is discouraged; what is sought is a return home with a commitment to work through the problem. If this seems impossible, an attempt is made to find a temporary place for the youth to stay. This is a voluntary procedure which requires the consent of both the parents and the youth.

Families are encouraged to return for subsequent discussions, although after the first session all sessions are essentially voluntary. Normally the maximum number of sessions is five, based on recent evidence that crisis counseling and short-term casework are one of the most effective ways of dealing with problems arising out of family situations and that extended casework is much more expensive and seems no more successful. In many cases counselors are in contact with the family by phone whether there is a follow-up session or not. All members of the family are encouraged to contact the counselor in the event of a continuing or additional problem.

During its first nine months the project handled 803 referrals involving opportunities for diversion, but filed only eighteen court petitions. Court processing was thus necessary in only 2.2 percent of these referrals compared to 30.4 percent brought in on 601 charges in a three-month preproject period and 21.3 percent of the referrals handled in the normal manner in a control group. Youths handled during the first four months were followed for a period of seven months after the initial contact. During this period, 45.5 percent of the control group had been rebooked for a 601 or 602 offense (a 602 offense involves criminal conduct), while the comparable figure for the project group was 35 percent. This is an improvement of over 23 percent in the rate of repeat offenses. For 602 offenses, the rate for the control group was 23.4 percent and 15.3 percent for the project group—a drop in the rate of repeated offenses of 34.6 percent.

Data indicated that project youths required overnight detention in less than 10 percent of the cases while the figure for control cases is over 60 percent.

Foreign experience.   While comparisons are difficult, it appears that many foreign countries without our experience with juvenile courts have gone further on diversion of youths than we have. Juvenile courts have never existed in Sweden. In that country no one less than fifteen years old can be prosecuted or put into prison for a criminal act. Child Welfare Councils, of which there are more than a thousand, have absolute jurisdiction over children below the age of fifteen. Youths fifteen to twenty-one may be diverted from courts to the Child Welfare Councils at the discretion of the public prosecutor. Each council consists of five members, one a pastor of the Lutheran State Church, one a public school teacher, and at least two "chosen for their special interest in and dedication to the care of children and youth." Many cases that in this country would be treated as involving delinquency are seen as welfare problems and are handled as cases of neglect and dependency. Dissatisfaction with the juvenile court system in Great Britain led to the "caution" system used by some British police departments and described earlier in this chapter. We know that other countries deal with juvenile offenders in ways aimed at avoiding institutionalization. For example, a study supported by the Harvard Center for Criminal Justice showed that juvenile court judges in Israel use institutions as a last resort, having as alternative forms of treatment daytime rehabilitation centers, army workshops, assignments to kibbutzim, hostels, and group homes.

ISSUES RELATING TO EARLY DIVERSION

The first part of this chapter outlined briefly some of the reasons for the attempts to divert offenders from the criminal justice system. The second and third parts sought by examples to give an impressionistic picture of what some of these attempts have been and the experience with them. By way of conclusion, this fourth part will suggest, in a necessarily superficial and summary form, what we believe to be the major problems and issues that must be taken account of in deciding what the scope and form of diversion programs should be.

Effect of Deterrence

It is probably fair to say that deterrence—the discouragement of potential offenders through the imposition of punishment on one who is caught—is the most important theoretical goal of criminal sanctions. To the extent diversion projects result in a less onerous imposition on offenders than they would have received had they been kept in the traditional criminal justice system, there is the possibility of dilution of deterrence. Of course, many of the diversion programs include obligations or limitations that most people would find undesirable. And many represent a fairer and more rational technique for providing relatively lenient treatment for classes of offenders, some of whose cases might previously have been dropped altogether on an invisible and haphazard basis. (With respect to this latter point, however, some would argue that invisibility and informality may be the best of both worlds—that one can get the deterrent effect of the formal system of penal sanctions while still dropping cases on a bootleg basis.) In any event, it is clearly important before drawing any conclusion as to the likely effect of a particular project to consider its impact on the whole class of potential offenders from whom it draws its population and on potential offenders generally.

Most important, one must be enormously tentative about the effects of deterrence, because so little is known about the extent and method by which the deterrent message is communicated and how effective it is in its impact on any particular group under particular circumstances. The development of the many new diversion projects provides opportunities to begin to seek answers to such questions. But little research of this sort is under way.

Failure to Restrain

Another stated goal of criminal sanctions is taking dangerous persons out of circulation. Proponents of early diversion are met with the argument that they are increasing the general risk to the public by putting offenders back into the community at a relatively early stage. This argument is plausible, but it fails to take account of the possibility that the impact of whatever treatment program follows diversion may make the offender less dangerous than the treatment that follows conventional disposition. To measure the net effect on the offender's dangerousness, we would have to weigh (1) the virtual guarantee that the community will be safe from crime by the offender during incarceration offset by the volume of crime during the offender's lifetime following release from prison, against (2) the volume of crime during the offender's lifetime if a diversion alternative is followed. While there are some data (notably from the California Treatment Project) suggesting that recidivism may be lower for persons who have been diverted to treatment in the community, we lack the data that would permit even rudimentary comparisons of the sort suggested. The development of such data may be the most important research need facing criminal justice administration, since it would permit resolution of what is probably the most politically volatile issue in the field. For the present, we have to settle for reminders to those who say diversion programs are endangering public safety that they *may* be wrong—that aggregate exposure to the risk of crime may be decreased rather than increased by diversion away from incarceration. At the same time, those who by reason of hunch or idealism are committed to diversion and de-institutionalization must be prepared to acknowledge that they may be wrong—that perhaps they are fostering a more dangerous society.

Diversion to What?

Early diversion has become a fashionable concept. Unfortunately, this has led to the widespread and promiscuous use of the diversion label to apply to all sorts of activities. In many instances existing programs have been re-named Youth Services Bureaus or given other diversion-like labels to qualify for funding from Law Enforcement Assistance Administration funds or just to appear to be up to date.

One of the most disturbing aspects of this process has been the preoccupa-tion of administrators and funding agencies with the fact and mechanics of diversion, without much consideration of the adequacy of what the offender is diverted to. Many of the reasons for this tendency are obvious. Much of the incentive to develop diversion programs is the reduction of the caseload for jails, courts, and correctional programs and facilities, and the fact of diver-sion accomplishes this purpose—at least temporarily—even if the offender is being diverted to nothing.

Many of the kinds of services the diverted offenders need are in short supply or are costly and the offender group is likely to be harder to service than others. For example, agencies responsible for job training or placement recognize that their success record will be lower and their headaches greater when they try to help offenders. It is not surprising therefore that with limited resources and enormous demands these agencies respond poorly to offenders unless there is some special pressure or incentive to do so. Indeed, it was in recognition of this problem that the President's Crime Commission proposed the development of youth-serving agencies at the local level with specific responsibility for providing or acquiring services for juveniles di-verted from the juvenile court. And it was for similar reasons that the commission and others have proposed service-purchase arrangements under which probation officers or others who represent offenders would have funds with which to buy the services that their clients need.

Of course, to be dropped from the system outright, with no attempt to provide supervision or services, often serves the interests of both the of-fender and society, but it would be a mistake to allow ourselves to be fooled by the diversion label into believing that we are doing something we are not. This is similar to what commonly happens now when a judge's decision to sentence a person to prison is based in whole or in part on an assumption that it will rehabilitate him, when, in fact, the evidence is to the contrary. Being honest with ourselves will not reform criminal justice administration, but it is an absolutely necessary condition to any reform. One danger of the diver-sion concept is that it will simply become another method of self-deception.

Who Makes the Decision?

By definition early diversion involves a decision outside the framework of a conventional court or correctional adjudication. Both the decision to divert and the choice of program offered the offender is likely to reflect the discretionary judgment of someone other than a judge or correctional official. In many instances this will be the prosecutor. In some, it will be a police official. In some, it will be a person with presumed expertise in the kind of service being offered.

Two related concerns about such decisions are: (1) they involve broad, unreviewable discretion by the decision maker that may impose unfair burdens on the offenders; and (2) they are made by persons other than those who now have responsibility for correctional decision making and therefore may not fairly reflect the interests of society and the rehabilitation needs of the offender.

In evaluating the first of these concerns it is important to bear in mind that in most jurisdictions sentencing decisions by judges and release decisions by parole officials are as a practical matter unreviewable. Nonetheless, the emergence of a new set of "correctional" decision makers is a realistic basis for concern that offenders may be unfairly imposed upon. While strongly supporting the concept of early diversion, the President's Crime Commission expressed its concern about possible abuse in these terms:

> Experience with civil procedures for the commitment of the mentally ill, for so-called sexual psychopaths, and for similar groups demonstrates that there are dangers of such programs developing in ways potentially more oppressive than those foreclosed by the careful traditional protections of the criminal law. When the alternative noncriminal disposition involves institutionalization or prolonged or intrusive supervision of the offender in the community, the disposition should be reviewed by the court.

More recently Tentative Draft No. 5 of the American Law Institute's Model Code of Pre-Arraignment Procedure has proposed a formal screening conference in the prosecutor's office to make early dispositional decisions. The draft has also provided for both substantive and procedural guidelines for the prosecutor's exercise of discretion.

There would be even greater basis for concern about diversion programs imposing unfairly on their clients if we should discover that such programs include people who would be left alone altogether but for the availability of the diversion alternative. For example, it may be that some types of drug offenders who previously would have been ignored by the system are being arrested and brought to court with the aim of diverting them to methadone maintenance or some other treatment program.

The concern that officials who are not expert in correctional decision making may be making decisions that fail to reflect society's interest seems to have little substance. In the first place, great dispositional power already resides in prosecutors in connection with plea bargaining and in making sentence recommendations, as well as in their power to dismiss cases. There is no reason to believe that well-designed diversion programs—particularly if they include provision for full information about the offender and the alternatives available—will result in less wise judgments. Nor does it seem likely that the people who would have dispositional authority under diversion programs would be less sensitive to the interests of society than prosecutors are now.

Furthermore, one has to be at least a bit skeptical about how much "expertise" with regard to the rehabilitation needs of the offender would be lost by relieving judges and traditional correctional officials of some of their dispositional power. How much evidence do we have that they operate with the kind of knowledge, consistency, or concern for following up the results of their decisions that would make the introduction of new decision-making processes unwise? In addition, many of the new diversion projects involve substantive programs for offenders with which judges and correctional officials have had little or no experience.

Lack of Evaluation

It is striking that the emphasis on early diversion of offenders has grown with so little data as to its effect on crime, on the operation of the criminal justice system, and on the quality of treatment afforded. Professor Ward's chapter discusses research and evaluation in the corrections field generally and documents how little we know even about those correctional programs which have been available for evaluation for many years. It should be no surprise that even less is known about the vast number of recently established early diversion projects. As discussed earlier, strong arguments can be made for early diversion in terms of immediate cost savings for the criminal justice system and humane treatment of offenders. It does not seem irrational to seek these benefits, even at a time when the case that diversion reduces crime (or at least does not materially increase it) can be made only in theoretical rather than empirical terms. Perhaps this view is simply a reflection of the sad fact that almost everything we do in the criminal justice field is on the basis of faith, and that there is generally no more empirical support for continuing what is being done than there is for changing.

What is far more disturbing is that so little groundwork is being laid that would permit judgments about the worth of various diversion programs three, five, and ten years from now. The two principal reasons are (1) lack of research funds and (2) chronic reluctance of operating agencies to subject themselves to intensive and possibly critical evaluation. In the late 1960s when the federal government first began providing funds for state and local criminal justice operations, the President's Crime Commission urged that federal support of intensive research be given high priority. Except for the relatively meager funds of the Justice Department's National Institute of Law Enforcement and Criminal Justice and research supported by the Department of Labor on the court employment projects which it finances, the only potential source of funding for research on diversion programs has been the evaluation funds of the state planning agencies which receive and dispense federal funds under the Law Enforcement Assistance Administration program. These agencies have been strikingly unambitious and unsuccessful in developing in-depth research or evaluation of diversion projects—or projects in any other area—and the Law Enforcement Assistance Administration seems to have done little to press for such evaluation.

It thus seems a fair guess that for many years the case for—or against —diversion will continue to be made on the basis of theory, the pressure of backlog in the system, rather superficial cost figures, and views as to the humaneness of more or less coercive treatment.

This paper has not sought to argue the case for early diversion, but rather to provide a basis for consideration and discussion of issues and problems. However, in concluding, it may be worthwhile to suggest that arguments for and against diversion in terms of leniency or toughness may miss the most important issue.

In effect, diversion seeks to offer the offender a set of social controls in lieu of the criminal justice system, our most drastic and overpowering form of social control. The assumption is that many who violate criminal laws are people whose lives will always be difficult and who need continuing support and that supervision and supplemental services may be more promising than the combination of a stigma and a cage. Diversion, with its gentler, less debilitating controls, may offer the best hope of developing in such people a lasting capacity to deal with a complex and difficult society.

20
THE CURRENT STATUS
OF YOUTH SERVICES BUREAUS*

J. A. Seymour

Readers should find this next article quite unique. As a lawyer and a citizen of another country, Seymour's perspective is less committed to our recent entrenchments in diversion. Youth Services Bureaus supposedly represent *one* model of diversion programs, yet note the diversity which emerges from this description. The author is very insightful about this diversity and also about many issues which are more implicit than explicit. He reports not only on the difficulties inherent in the model, but also on the difficulties of people attempting to assess the model. It would be an interesting exercise to take each issue, each merit, and each danger identified by Seymour and study a wide sample of Youth Services Bureaus to see how often each occurs.

* Unpublished manuscript, Center for Studies in Criminal Justice, the Law School, University of Chicago. See also J. A. Seymour, "Youth Services Bureaus," *Law and Society Review*, Winter 1972. Reprinted by permission of the author. The author acknowledges the help given by Margaret K. Rosenheim, Norval Morris, and Hans W. Mattick.

The following is a report and commentary on the seminar on youth services bureaus held in Chicago on January 24 and 25, 1971, jointly sponsored by the Center for the Study of Welfare Policy and the Center for Studies in Criminal Justice, University of Chicago.

The basic purpose of the seminar was to collect and to facilitate the exchange of information on the developments which have occurred since the youth services bureau idea was first outlined by the President's Crime Commission. In particular, the organizers hoped to learn something about the form bureaus have taken, and about the major types of difficulties encountered.

Present at the seminar were administrators, working within the juvenile field, from Illinois, Minnesota, New York, Michigan, and Florida; youth services bureau directors from Washington State, Virginia, Rhode Island, North Carolina, Connecticut, California, and Massachusetts; and scholars with a particular interest in the subject. Also present was a Canadian Juvenile Court Judge.

The seminar took the form of three wide-ranging sessions which overlapped to a considerable extent. This report, which was compiled from tapes of the proceedings, is an attempt to reflect the main topics considered. These topics were widely diverse, and it has not proved possible to achieve overall continuity.

ANOTHER PERSPECTIVE

In the report which follows, the writer has adopted, as his point of reference, the existing organizational framework of youth services. Many of the comments and criticisms made regarding the seminar discussions flow from this fact: As will become apparent, one of the writer's particular concerns was to analyze the seminar's discussion of the place of youth services bureaus within the existing judicial/child welfare system and their relationship to it.

However, underlying the debate as to bureau function, which this report underlines, is what appears to be a fundamental challenge to the juvenile justice system which provides the point of departure for the ensuing commentary. At no point did any of the seminar participants make this challenge explicit.

Yet, implicit in the comments of some speakers was the view that entanglement with, or participation in, the existing system should be minimized. Here, then, we are confronted by what seems to be a radical challenge based on the view that any remodeling of the present system might amount to no more than tinkering with dysfunctional establishment structures. The question then becomes: *Where do we locate the problem?* Is our object of concern the child, or the institutions which society has produced for dealing with the child? Do we wish to adjust the child to society, or society to the child?

Though at no stage during the seminar was the issue clearly articulated, there lay beneath the surface of the discussions of bureaus' roles two profoundly different world views. Some saw the bureaus, basically, as cooperating, conforming institutions, working with existing agencies, while others held a more nonconformist view. Those who subscribed to this latter view wanted to have minimal contact with the existing system—which, no doubt, they saw as part of the problem—and were determined to redefine their relationship with it. Hence their approach embodied an unspoken challenge to the establishment, a desire to be as independent as possible of existing agencies of control. They were apparently engaged in a search for a new organizational structure, and for new definitions of behavior.

The following report does not reflect this broader perspective, for the writer's aim has been no more than to consider the issues directly raised by the seminar participants. Nevertheless, it is important to bear in mind the deeper level of analysis which can be applied to any consideration of this report.[1]

THE ROLE OF YOUTH SERVICES BUREAUS

The seminar discussions of the functions of youth services bureaus were most disappointing. Admittedly some of the difficulty lies in the nature of the bureau concept itself: It would be unrealistic to demand a definitive statement as to what constitutes a youth services bureau, for the idea is capable of implementation in a variety of forms. It must be conceded, at the outset, that diversity of form and function is inevitable. Several speakers rightly emphasized that no *one* model for a bureau could be devised; a wide variety of approaches was revealed by practitioners and planners. Clearly the forms these agencies will take will vary greatly across the country, and even within a single state.

Nevertheless, a consciousness of this diversity should not be allowed to stand in the way of an attempt to analyze the rationale and functions of youth services bureaus in general. In fact, these deeper issues were not adequately explored.

Two opposing views of the purpose of a bureau were put forward, but these proved difficult to disentangle. First, the source of the confusion must be examined, and then each view must be considered.

The youth services bureaus' potential for diverting children from the juvenile justice system was discussed in general terms, but this discussion failed to bring the concept of diversion into sharp focus. Much of the difficulty stemmed from an initial failure, by some speakers, to distinguish between the limited aim of diverting children with existing problems from the criminal justice system (by providing a different sort of service within a fundamentally different context), and the more general aim of delinquency prevention. This is not to say that there is only one way of defining diversion: Indeed, in the broadest sense, it can be argued that preventive strategies contribute to diversion, for their aim is to ameliorate those conditions which lead children into difficulties. However, in the interests of clarity, it does seem helpful to distinguish between the two aims of general community change, on the one hand, and, on the other, the provision of genuine alternative responses for certain groups of children at risk or in trouble. In time the distinction did emerge, but not before considerable confusion had been generated.

Some interesting comments were made on the subject of diversion. Several speakers saw the bureau as performing the specific function of diverting

[1] I am very grateful to Hans W. Mattick for his guidance on this issue of the "hidden ideologies" at work in the seminar.

children from the official criminal justice system. To do this, it should provide services for those already on the threshold of that system—for example, minor offenders or children in harmful situations who have come to the attention of the police or school authorities. This aim is reasonably clear, but it presupposes that society can in fact make available alternative resources. In practical terms, what does this mean? Many bureaus, for example, seem to use the services of probation officers. If our aim is diversion from the court system, how do these officers fit in? Is it enough to say that they are not serving in their regular capacity?

One speaker raised some fundamental points about the nature of the services which bureaus will provide in their attempt to channel juveniles away from the official system. Those who plan and operate these new agencies should be able to answer two questions: What services can bureaus provide which cannot be provided by existing agencies? Why can the bureaus provide these services when existing agencies cannot? It was suggested that there is a danger of undermining existing agencies and setting up some new apparatus which, in the long run, will be just another bureaucracy on a par with other bureaucracies in the community. This, in the speaker's words, "seems a major challenge to anybody who would defend a youth services bureau." The challenge went unanswered.

A related matter is the hope that the bureau handling will not result in harmful labeling of children. Yet bureau processing might result in some form of stigmatization, and hence the question must be faced: Would it not, perhaps, be better to develop existing services, rather than risking a possible bureau labeling effect?

The same speaker raised the possibility that "diversion for diversion's sake" might be valuable. Perhaps some children are better off the less we do for them, and therefore it might be well to set up a social institution which will enable the community to do less for some children. The key problem here is, of course, the diagnostic one. How do we identify the children for whom minimal intervention is desirable?

The speaker's final point was that talk of diversion can mask assumptions. We must ask whether youth services bureaus will inevitably deal with children who would have been fed into the criminal justice system, or whether one result of the creation of these agencies might be the imposition of controls on children upon whom such controls might not otherwise have been imposed.

Of course, in one sense, this is to put the question a little unfairly, for one of the purposes of bureaus—however conceived—is to offer assistance to children not at present receiving it, to fill gaps in existing child welfare facilities. But we must beware of the rhetoric of benevolence—it is important to be reminded of the fact that a helping service might in fact amount to one which imposes controls. It should be noted that the aim of providing services for children at present unreached by official agencies can be seen as part of a diversionary strategy, in that some of these children might drift from problem to problem, until, by default, they end up being dealt with by law enforcement agencies.

Another aspect of the diversion aim concerns the economic bias operating in the juvenile justice system. One speaker saw it as a function of youth services bureaus to provide in low-income neighborhoods the kinds of opportunities to avoid contact with the official justice system which at present exist in more affluent communities. Thus the bureaus can be viewed as one possible means of reducing the emphasis on low-income families, which is a feature of the operation of the criminal justice system.

Next let us consider the alternative view of the function of youth services bureaus—that they should pursue the much broader aim of primary prevention. One speaker labeled diversion as a by-product, stating that the fundamental purpose of the bureaus should be community change. Those who agreed with him saw the bureau as a very general and broad-ranging preventive agency, concerned with social and attitudinal change, directing its efforts toward eliminating conditions which produce delinquency. The logical outcome of this definition of function is that a bureau should concern itself with many aspects of community life and should in no way be limited to the cases referred to it. The objection was raised that this function is beyond the competence of a specific agency such as a youth services bureau. This objection was not adequately answered, nor was it made clear why bureaus should not be distinct from general community change organizations, such as those which work to change the pattern of life in a ghetto.

At issue, then, was the question of the *focus* of bureau activities. If specific types of youth problems are tackled by endeavoring to stimulate community involvement and a sense of responsibility, clearly one result might be community change. Also if bureau staff work with children in trouble, they will, to some extent, become involved in the solution of community problems. Nevertheless, analysis in terms such as these does not throw light on the *identity* of youth services bureaus, and objections can be raised for this reason. Yet one speaker put forward the argument that specificity as to goals was not desirable on the grounds that too constricting an approach should be avoided. He saw the bureau as a general umbrella under which professionals and volunteers should come together to work for change in the community.

Thus the difference of opinion on bureau function was fundamental —some saw the task in terms of broad community change, while others ascribed to the bureau the more limited role of an agency whose purpose is to provide new alternatives for children in trouble, a purpose which it should perform by dealing with individual cases which come to the notice of bureau staff.

What can be said of this difference of approach? The major defect in the lengthy discussions of the function of youth services bureaus was the disturbing failure to view them in the context of an overall strategy for dealing with problems of youth. Too often, it seemed, the bureaus were conceived of as independent agencies whose task was no more, and no less, than to provide an ill-defined range of services for any young people for whom they seemed appropriate. It is submitted that for this vague humanitarianism there must be substituted a rigorous analysis of the structure and—more important —the interrelationships of youth-serving agencies. The seminar did not effectively come to terms with the key issue of the bureaus' place in the pattern of organizations for helping youth. Indeed, there was little to indicate any awareness of a total pattern.

Some discussion took place as to whether a youth services bureau was to be seen as part of the criminal justice system. Clearly this is a point of some importance, for two of the benefits sought from youth services bureau handling are informality and avoidance of stigma, both of which, it is hoped, will flow from unofficial procedures. However, at a more fundamental level, to argue whether the bureaus are part of the criminal justice system is to play with words and miss the more important point that clearly the bureaus *must* be seen as part of—in the sense of related to—the criminal justice and child welfare systems, and must, therefore, be seen as part of an overall pattern, part of a total system for dealing with a broad range of youth problems. The pattern must be identified, and then the bureau's place within it must be determined. No attempt can be made to bring the role of the youth services bureaus into sharp focus until these underlying questions have been tackled.

It is surprising that the seminar discussions contained so few references to the Presidential Crime Commission's *Task Force Report: Juvenile Delinquency and Youth Crime*. This gives a clear indication of the rationale and function of bureaus; what is provided, though not a blueprint, is, at least, a point of departure.

The seminar's failure to view bureaus as part of a total system was particularly marked with regard to the juvenile court. Certainly there was some discussion as to whether juvenile court judges were showing support for bureaus, but the deeper issue of the bureaus' role with regard to the court was not satisfactorily explored. The development of youth services bureaus must be seen against a background of mounting criticism of the rationale and jurisdiction of juvenile courts, criticism which was most clearly expressed in the *Gault* decision. The basic problem was aptly summed up by one commentator: "We see the court being misused, we see legal gates being opened in order to get into the field of social chaos, we see rather frivolous charges being laid in order to get into disturbed homes."

The youth services bureau concept does not, and cannot, exist in a vacuum, and yet the seminar failed to come to terms with the key question of the bureaus' relevance to the jurisdiction of the juvenile court. As one speaker put it, the youth services bureau concept embodies a departure from the assumption, which originally underlay the juvenile court, that criminal and troublesome children were to be identically handled in a nonpunitive manner.[2] Yet this question—the youth services bureau's place in a new pattern of juvenile services, a pattern dependent on the identification of a more limited role for the court—was not adequately examined. Early in the seminar the need to probe this matter was made clear: it was pointed out that we must beware lest "we are presiding over the liquidation of the juvenile

[2] Further historical perspective was provided by another speaker. It was pointed out that, early in the century, it might have been appropriate for the juvenile court to assume responsibility for a multiplicity of youth problems, simply because there were no other welfare services. Today we must ask whether there is any reason for the court to retain jurisdiction over such cases as truants and incorrigibles. Thus the development of the bureau can be seen as part of a changing pattern of integrated services for juveniles.

court concept before we have a better model." The same speaker asked whether the bureau *is* part of a better model. Yet the question was not taken up. Society has criticized the court because it did not provide the answers, but will the bureaus provide better solutions? Of course, it could legitimately be objected that it is premature to ask such questions; bureaus are only just beginning to take shape, and they are still at the trial-and-error stage.

It would, however, be inaccurate to state that there was no discussion of the relationship between bureaus and existing agencies. Thus one speaker suggested that bureaus might not be very different from court intake, but that bureaus, as new agencies, might bring about real change and might attract federal funds, whereas reform of juvenile court intake would not get this money or produce the same change. Also some parallels were drawn between youth bureau activities and the functions performed by consent decrees and child advocates. The child advocate was described by one speaker as having the task of coordinating services for youth—he was likened to an ombudsman with special responsibility for children.

Relations with police and the juvenile court were the subject of some comment; as was to be expected, in view of the diversity of bureaus, it soon became plain that there was no characteristic or typical relationship between bureaus and these two agencies. At least one speaker expressed concern about lack of law enforcement referrals, but, predictably, the discussion revealed great variations in the degree of police support for the youth services bureau idea. In California, for example, referrals by law enforcement personnel have ranged from 0 to 75 percent of the total cases dealt with by different bureaus.[3] One speaker expressed the fear that police might regard bureaus merely as somewhere to "dump" troublesome juvenile cases; the need for a clear-cut referral system was stressed. Also, it was pointed out that it helps the police image in the community if officers are seen to cooperate with the bureaus. At the policy-making level it is clearly valuable to have the local police chief on the board which directs a bureau.

Similarly, the presence of a juvenile court judge on the board seems desirable, as does the inclusion of a senior probation officer. A good relationship with the local court is most important. The problem facing developing bureaus was seen as one of building credibility with, and acceptance by, existing agencies. However, as was pointed out, if one cannot gain credibility with *everybody*, difficult choices must be made. When a new organization emerges, conflicts and tension are inevitable, and, as one speaker reminded the meeting, if an innovation upsets no one, the chances are that it is not achieving anything of significance.

The same speaker dealt with the need for bureaus to make an active effort to integrate themselves, to reach consensus with existing agencies as to a new division of labor, and to define their role in the political hierarchy so that they are not accused, from above, of being subversive, or, from below, of

---

[3] The seminar discussions revealed interesting variations in referral sources. Thus one practitioner stated that the larger part of referrals to his bureau came from schools and neighborhood organizations. In another bureau 70 percent of referrals have come from parents. Yet there were some examples given of lack of cooperation—in one area the local high school refused to make referrals to the bureau. And one bureau—whose aim was general prevention—took the extreme position of not accepting any referrals.

being preemptive. Some friction with other agencies is to be expected, although the view was expressed that an awareness among professional staff that poor use is being made of existing resources leads to cooperation with bureau workers. Conversely, of course, there is the possibility that staff of existing agencies will see bureaus as a threat, bent on pointing out gaps in their programs and making inroads into their territory. Some practitioners did complain about lack of cooperation and suspicion on the part of other organizations in the field. One speaker particularly stressed the need to involve staff of all related agencies at the planning stage—if people are initially left out, they will be alienated.

Thus, though there was some consideration of bureau relationships with existing agencies, this concentrated on the politics of coexistence,[4] rather than on the more fundamental issue of the bureaus' place in the total pattern of services for youth. The seminar did not really come to grips with the question, posed by one commentator, as to whether there exists, among those who plan and operate bureaus, a common understanding as to the function of bureaus with regard to the juvenile justice system. As another speaker put it, the bureau concept has been only superficially defined. Much that has been done has been done on an intuitive basis without the preliminary research necessary to sound planning and to clear specification of goals and function.

THE PROBLEM OF CHANGE

One general theme which was touched upon was the difficulty of producing *real* change in a complex, interlocking system such as criminal justice, a system which has an unlimited capacity to absorb and neutralize innovation. A speaker pointed to the danger that the introduction of youth services bureaus might achieve nothing more than a reshuffling of existing resources. For example, although the specific aim might be to reduce the number of children being dealt with by the court, a bureau's operations might produce an effect only on the exercise of police discretion. This could occur if the police continued to refer the same proportion of children to the court, and merely exercised the option of bureau referral within the group which would previously have been dealt with by station adjustment. In this situation, although the bureau would seem to be performing its function, it would in fact have no impact on the court.

Another speaker gave an example, from his own experience, of such a process. He had been involved in a street-work project, one of the aims of which was to divert children from the juvenile court. The local police department cooperated and referred a large number of children to the new

---

[4] During the seminar there were lengthy analyses of the development of relationships with other agencies. One speaker pointed to the importance of careful evaluation of these relationships, to the need to record how links were forged, the difficulties encountered, and the nature of the planning and development process. He thus underlined the importance of description of organizational relationships.

agency. The effect of this was to free police energy, and the police had more time to scrutinize marginal cases, many of whom would previously have been dealt with by station adjustment. The result was that they referred *more* of these cases to court after the inception of the new program.

Thus the introduction of a new agency into the system might have no effect, or it might have a distorting effect. We must not underestimate the difficulties of achieving diversion from the juvenile justice system.

Another suggested effect of the development of bureaus which should be scrutinized is the financial one. It has been assumed that bureau handling will result in the diversion of children from the cumbersome, costly juvenile court procedure to a simpler, and hence cheaper, system. However, it was pointed out that this might be a naive assumption. The view was expressed that whatever services are provided will be fully used. It might prove to be the case that the major impact of the growth of bureaus will be the uncovering of extra cases not previously dealt with, and thus the overall cost of the system will not be significantly reduced. Perhaps, by some variation of Parkinson's Law, caseloads will expand to utilize the facilities provided.

If planners do not recognize this possibility, and do not take into account the fact that *additional* funds might be needed, the result might be a dilution of existing services by the addition of cases without making financial provision for them.

Another relevant point raised by a bureau coordinator is that youth services bureaus might, in some cases, provide more intensive and prolonged work with clients, whereas the probation department might close these cases after one contact. The resulting services might be better, but they will certainly be more expensive than handling within the official system.

One or two speakers raised some fundamental questions in their discussion of the change represented by the youth services bureau movement. It was suggested that more is at issue than simply the creation of a new agency. Perhaps the bureau idea masks a struggle for social change, in that what is sought is a redefinition of certain types of troublesome behavior: a redefinition in the sense that this behavior will come to be viewed as no longer the concern of our criminal justice system. Unfortunately, this matter was not pursued, although clearly the youth services bureau concept could be viewed as the precursor of profound changes in attitude in our society. It should be noted that a fundamental attitudinal change is at issue: Is there a possibility of merely changing the labels?

It is, however, profoundly important that we should scrutinize the assumptions underlying any suggested redefinition of behavior. In particular we should beware of the perspective which leads us automatically to assume that a troublesome child suffers from a pathological condition. This point was clearly emphasized by one speaker who, in effect, asked: Should we redefine conduct in this way? The danger, it was suggested, is that the bureau philosophy of early, noncoercive, supportive intervention might lead us to regard all cases as problems of individual pathology. We must not overlook the fact that in many cases delinquency is part of growing up, and that every community must accept responsibility for the minor misconduct of its children. Juvenile misbehavior must not be automatically equated with individual maladjustment, and our approach to it within the context of the youth services bureau must not preclude consideration of delinquency as a social phenomenon.

COMMUNITY INVOLVEMENT

The seminar revealed widespread agreement on the need to involve the community in coping with children's problems. It was made plain that this should be done at all levels—from policy making and control (by including residents on managing boards) to a variety of forms of voluntary help in the field. One difficulty to which attention was drawn was the role of the professional in a community organization. Should he act merely as a consultant? Should he, on occasions, attempt to dominate residents?

Talk about community participation should not, however, lead us to overlook the fact that this might not be easy to obtain. As one speaker pointed out, the areas where the greatest needs exist might be precisely those areas where there is least sense of community, and least willingness, leisure, or ability among residents to involve themselves in social problems.

Also the difficulties of getting local people involved, and keeping them involved, should not be underestimated. Simply putting them on a committee is not enough. Clearly the vision of a youth services bureau as a mode of fostering community responses to community problems will not be an easy one to realize.

As one speaker put it, it is easy to fall victim to a kind of nostalgia for the idea of rediscovering the community. How realistic is it to expect, in the anonymous world of a large, turbulent city, a genuine sense of community which will produce involvement in, and an acceptance of responsibility for, youth problems?

Further, there is a danger that community control might produce such a degree of conflict with the wider society as to threaten that society's basic values. It is not likely that society as a whole will readily surrender the right to impose certain minimal standards.

CONTROL

Mention has been made of the importance of including local residents on managing boards of bureaus. This raises the question of just where ultimate control should lie. Should agency officials hold the purse strings? General discussion of community participation should not be allowed to mask the basic issue as to who has the balance of power. To consider this is, of course, to view the bureaus in their political context. At the most fundamental level, are these agencies to be a means of transferring authority from a centralized system (the justice system) back to local communities?

One participant was adamant about community control. He stated that the community must decide what to do with its young people, and that the youth services bureau role was to give them the technical assistance they need to do the job. Those from outside the community, he said, should not attempt to impose solutions.

When we speak of the community, which segments do we mean? Do we wish to give control to the parents, to the youth, to the poor, to the minority groups?

AVOIDANCE OF STIGMA

There was little discussion of the problem of stigma, and little indication was given as to whether it was realistic to regard bureau handling as nonstigmatizing. The one exception was the emphatic comment by one participant that involvement with a bureau does not result in any kind of stigma. He contrasted this with the situation of a child on probation who, he said, was definitely stigmatized and was seen to be "in the system." In his view the bureau is not identified with the system.

The most interesting comment on stigma was the suggestion that bureau stigma might be *greater* precisely because the organization is community-based. The child's situation will be known to members of the local community, and more stigma could result than in the case of a child dealt with by a more remote, official agency. Also it was pointed out that before we can talk about stigma, we need to know the views of those in the community. For example, how do minority groups regard a juvenile court appearance? It must be remembered that stigma cannot only deprive a person of status; it can also confer status, depending on the audience.

PARTICIPATION BY YOUTH

One matter on which the practitioners contributed forceful and convincing comments was the need to involve youth in bureau work; there was much emphasis on what youth could contribute to these agencies. The need to have youth representation on the controlling boards was stressed, and there was some consideration as to what proportion youths would be allowed on the boards. In one bureau, it was reported, the advisory committee is made up predominantly of youth. Several speakers argued strongly that a considerable degree of control should be given to youth; there was recognition of the fact that such a policy might bring opposition from conservative adult groups, who saw control as their perogative. The practitioners' argument was, of course, that, in our rapidly changing society, only young people can really understand the problems of youth. Hence, it was felt, youth should be involved at all levels—as leaders, policy makers, counselors, and as street workers. To be effective, the bureaus need credibility with the young, and the involvement of youth is one obvious way to seek it.

LEGAL ASPECTS

Legal aspects were touched on by only one speaker, who made the point that, although we must be conscious of the legal rights of a child who is dealt with by the youth services bureau, respectable arguments can be adduced in support of the view that lesser constitutional protections are needed here than in a court, as lesser powers are being claimed. The same speaker asked the seminar to consider whether a consent decree backed up by a threat of court referral is genuinely consensual, and he also asked how important the jurisdictional facts are (for example, did the child commit the act; is he neglected, deprived, or a truant?) if bureau intervention is being contemplated. Unfortunately, the practitioners present did not explore these issues.

FUNDING

There was some discussion of long-term funding problems. Concern was expressed as to future financial support for bureaus once the initial federal grants have run dry. Will further funds come from both state and community agencies? It was pointed out that bureau staff should take care to underline the value and purpose of the services they are providing, and be able to show that they are making a distinct contribution if they wish to support their claims for continued funding. It must be plain that bureaus are fulfilling a real need and have been firmly built into the system.

EVALUATION

There was widespread agreement on the need for evaluation of bureau results. As has been seen, however, there was a wide divergence among participants as to the goals that should be pursued, and so no searching analysis of evaluative techniques was possible, as clearly any attempt to analyze success presupposes precise specification of the objectives sought. Once those objectives have been determined, a research design should be built into each project from the outset.

For those who accept diversion as the basic aim of youth services bureaus, the task must be to view bureaus in the context of the criminal justice system, in an endeavor to determine the impact on arrest and court figures. The coordinator of one bureau—that in Pacifica, California—claimed that his agency had achieved a significant change in referral patterns, and a reduction in arrest and delinquency rates. Needless to say, we must bear in mind the fact that many variables operate in a social control system, and that it is extremely difficult to isolate the effect of a bureau. Also to be considered is the possibility that what will in fact be achieved is a redistribution of resources which we have no means of assessing. One speaker expressed deep skepticism as to the possibility of demonstrating—with methodological rigor—bureau success either in preventing delinquency or in better handling of delinquent children.

CONCLUSION

The major disappointment of the seminar was the absence of really penetrating analysis into the function and identity of youth services bureaus. Of the existing bureaus, it seems that few have acquired a distinctive role and image, and there is clearly a need for much greater awareness of the bureaus' place in a larger pattern of law enforcement, judicial, correctional, and child welfare agencies. The bureau movement has some vitality but lacks a firm theoretical basis.

The overall impression was that bureaus have grown rather haphazardly. There is a danger that the concept might be abused; some might see it merely as a general device for getting more money into services for youth: "an excellent flag to fly when you want to get more resources," as one speaker put it.

It must, however, be reiterated that it is unrealistic to expect a clear blueprint as to the form bureaus should take. The concept can accommodate a diversity of agencies serving different purposes. Research is needed in each area to determine local needs, and each bureau must develop services appropriate to the needs and conditions of the community it serves. An illustration of the fact that rigid preconceptions cannot always be adhered to is provided by the California experience. Although the emphasis in the empowering legislation is on coordination, in fact, as the bureaus have developed, the focus has been on filling gaps in services. How many bureaus have no other aim in view than to do what other agencies do not do?

There was little discussion of the types of cases for which bureau services are suitable, a surprising fact in view of the obvious relevance of this topic to the question of defining the nature of youth services bureaus. Clearly it is important to ask: What precisely are the problems that we expect bureaus to resolve? What are the needs that we expect to meet? These matters must be rigorously analyzed and the most logical way of bringing some focus to this analysis is to think in terms of the types of cases which at present constitute an inappropriate burden on the criminal justice system. What, specifically, has the youth services bureau to offer to the truant, the incorrigible, the child in need of supervision, the minor first offender?

This might, however, be too destructive a view to take. One speaker urged a more modest approach: he reminded the seminar that we should not—in our present state of knowledge—overestimate our capacity to solve children's problems. Should our goal be no more than to try to divert children from a system that might make them worse? Certainly in our zeal for the youth services bureau idea we should not expect too much; the bureaus can have no more than a relatively small impact on the problem of juvenile misbehavior.

21
THE CHALLENGE
OF YOUTH SERVICE BUREAUS*
Youth Development
and Delinquency Prevention Administration

Following the somewhat chaotic situation described by Seymour in the last paper, the next article presents a picture of greater reason and direction by means of cataloguing what was taking place in the early 1970s. However, it is now very clear, with the examples provided in this paper, that a great variety of models does exist. Readers can take their choice among these, based on their views of the issues raised in prior chapters. For the researcher, a serious problem remains: How can we ever empirically validate the utility of such multifarious organizations?

---

* From *The Challenge of Youth Service Bureaus,* Youth Development and Delinquency Prevention Administration, U.S. Department of Health, Education and Welfare (Washington, D.C.: U.S. Government Printing Office, Publication No. (SRS) 73-26024, 1973], pp. 1–28.

I. INTRODUCTION

The Crime Commission's recommendation for youth service bureaus set forth general purposes but was not specific in regard to operation or definition. References to youth service bureaus in the original Commission report have been called both too general and too limiting, and interpretations as to the purpose and organizational structure of youth service bureaus continue to be a matter of debate.

In the original Commission report it is difficult to determine whether the youth service bureau was meant to be independent or a part of some larger agency, or both. In some references, the Commission report urged the establishment of a single agency with a broad range of services. Yet, in other sections of the report it is implied that such an agency should be located in a comprehensive community center and be a part of some other agency. This report is also ambiguous in the sense that it defines permissive programs for nondelinquents, as well as emphasizing programs that must be offered to delinquent youth within what appears to be a modified justice agency structure, i.e., which in fact shares an agency responsibility for some of the jurisdiction and services traditionally offered by the juvenile court.

There is also a subtleness about the text of the Commission report that creates problems. "Thought in the United States has concentrated on creating *alternatives* to adjudication for an increasing number of cases, rather than on providing substitutes for adjudication."[1] Alternative and substitute,

---

[1] U.S. Government, Task Force on Juvenile Delinquency. *The Task Force Report: Juvenile Delinquency and Youth Crime, Report on Juvenile Justice and Consultants' Papers.* President's Commission on Law Enforcement and Administration of Justice. Washington, D.C.: U.S. Government Printing Office, 1967, p. 20.

although frequently used as synonyms, are not; the former provides additional choices, while the latter replaces. A very careful reading of all pertinent parts of the Commission text relating to youth service bureaus suggests that youth service bureaus provide needed services to youth *as a substitute* (a replacement) for court services and *not an alternative* (additional choices). This includes delivering services to youth who are in jeopardy of committing public offenses or engaging in conduct which is not considered acceptable in the general community. Emphasis is clearly on a process that does not stigmatize nor involve youth exhibiting problem behavior in the criminal justice system any further than is absolutely necessary.

The Commission report implies that the youth service bureau is something more than just a new service agency providing alternatives to the juvenile court. Some have argued that the Commission's recommendation for youth service bureaus went too far, yet others, not far enough. The bureau concept could have been expanded by providing operational models; it was not! In effect, the President's Crime Commission's reports do not offer a clear definition regarding what a youth service bureau is or should be. The various reports mixed ideas and concepts, while at the same time providing fragments of program prescriptions.

It was for this reason that staff of the National Youth Service Bureau Study elected to consider for possible inclusion in the study any program identified by Governors, state planning agents, or regional staff of national private and governmental organizations as a youth service bureau. Less than 200 survived the initial national census of youth service bureaus conducted by project staff.

II. RATIONALE FOR YOUTH SERVICE BUREAU

The recommendation for the establishment of a new community agency to be known as a youth service bureau was an attempt by staff of the President's Crime Commission to come to grips with the failure of the juvenile court to achieve its goals. Diversion from the criminal justice system through a substitute agency, whether planned or stated, was the primary and underlying reason for the advancement of the concept of youth service bureaus.

More and more questions are being asked as to whether the justice system is the most effective method for preventing further delinquency among the bulk of juveniles who get into trouble. Disillusionment with the effect of the juvenile justice system stems from ambiguous definitions of delinquency, dispositions based on idiosyncratic decisions, adverse consequences resulting from the justice system processing, and consistent understaffing of manpower and resources required to carry out the objectives of the juvenile court system.

Because of the ambiguities of the law regarding juvenile behavior and the opportunity for minor law infractions, the massive volume of officially labeled delinquents represents only a fraction of the young people who could be labeled.

Given the broad mandate of the juvenile court and the catchall character of the statutes which define delinquency, there are virtually no nondelinquents.

Juveniles have committed and commit acts daily which, if detected, could result in adjudication. Consequently, from the standpoint of social control, it is necessary to question the utility of legal norms about which there is such ambiguity.[2]

If the system of criminal justice did not operate selectively, we would literally have all been in jail at one time or another and many of us would still be there. This is not because crime is rampant but because opportunities for running afoul of one prohibition or another are so abundant.[3]

The catchall character of delinquency creates an uneven response to delinquency by the community, the police, and the court—even in defining and reporting of delinquency and in apprehending, detaining, and referring the young person for further processing by the system. Ideally, this processing would be through a system of procedures by which illegal behavior by juveniles would be handled through stages of decision and action according to some deliberate plan. In reality, the system by which we process children in trouble is faulty.

At each decision point within the juvenile or criminal justice system, there is a selective reduction of young people who penetrate the next step. For example, estimates indicate that during 1970 almost 4 million juveniles had a police contact. Two million of the contacts resulted in arrest, and over 1 million of the arrests resulted in referral to the juvenile court. Of the 1 million national arrests referred to court, only 500,000 resulted in a court appearance.[4] Although some of these cases were closed for lack of evidence, a large part of this reduction in cases is based on the overreferral for service; i.e., many more young people are referred to court by police, parents, schools, and others than can realistically be processed by the juvenile system at the present time.

Discretion throughout the various parts of the justice process permits the police, probation departments, or courts to eliminate many referrals from further processing. The absence of clear-cut criteria for selective reduction from the juvenile justice system processing encourages screening based on idiosyncratic choice. Currently, law enforcement and court personnel are tacitly encouraged ". . . to develop their own policy, for good or evil, and perhaps discover policy by looking backward to determine what has been done."[5]

Studies have reported a variety of bases for decision making at each step of juvenile justice system processing. Decisions are heavily weighted by individual discretion and are often based on factors which may be irrelevant

[2] LaMar T. Empey and Steven G. Lubeck, *Delinquency Prevention Strategies,* Department of Health, Education and Welfare, Youth Development and Delinquency Prevention Administration, 1970.

[3] Robert D. Vinter, *Justice for the Juvenile: Myth or Reality?* Lecture presented at the University of Delaware under the auspices of E. Paul DuPont Endowment for the Study of Crime and Delinquency in Corrections, Newark, Del., Mar. 26, 1969.

[4] Robert J. Gemignani, "Youth Services Systems," in *Delinquency Prevention Reporter,* Department of Health, Education and Welfare, Youth Development and Delinquency Prevention Administration, July–August 1972.

[5] Ted Rubin, "Law as an Agent of Delinquency Prevention," paper prepared for the Delinquency Prevention Strategy Conference, California Youth Authority and California Council on Criminal Justice, Santa Barbara, February 1970.

to preserving public safety in the community. For example, one study pointed to the youth's demeanor, style of dress, and ethnic group as factors used in making an arrest decision.[6]

Another study of police-juvenile interaction showed that decisions to arrest juveniles are greatly affected by the presence and preference of a complainant, with arrest more frequent when the complainant is present and when he urges strong action.[7] Thus, police attitudes and the attitudes of the community residents toward youth are significant factors affecting whether they will be processed further by the justice system.

These examples are in part manifestations of the social and economic inequities in the present system of discretion and decision making exercised in response to criminal and delinquent behavior. More specifically:

> The power of a group determines its ability to keep its people out of trouble with the law even in instances where they have actually violated it. . . . When a group's general capacity to influence is high, the official delinquency rates of its children and youth tend to be low.[8]

The same writer points out that competent communities have long been reducing official delinquency by meeting the problem through unofficial means, utilizing the community's—*not* an individual's—sustained, organized, recognized, and utilized power. In this way, community conditions and organizational arrangements significantly contribute to and differentiate who is to be or not to be a delinquent. Other experts have cited individual economic power to buy services for one's child as another method of selective reduction from justice system processing.[9]

The juvenile court has been called ". . . the marketplace wherein the community reputation and social identities of youth in trouble are transacted.[10] For all too many youth it becomes a marketplace wherein a negative community reputation is unwillingly purchased, consumer protection is minimal, and all sales are final.

Once a juvenile is identified as a delinquent, labeling and differential handling allow him few opportunities for positive participation in the normal or more acceptable institutions within his community. There are many examples of how the stigma resulting from a delinquency record can produce multiple handicaps: increased police surveillance, neighborhood isolation, lowered receptivity and tolerance by school officials, and rejection by prospective employers.[11]

[6] Irving Piliavin and Scott Briar, "Police Encounters with Juveniles," *American Journal of Sociology*, September 1964.

[7] Edwin M. Lemert, *Instead of Court: Diversion in Juvenile Justice*, National Institute of Mental Health, Center for Studies of Crime and Delinquency, Chevy Chase, Md., 1971.

[8] John M. Martin, *Toward a Political Definition of Delinquency Prevention*, Department of Health, Education and Welfare, Youth Development and Delinquency Prevention Administration, 1970.

[9] Margaret K. Rosenheim, "Youth Service Bureaus: a Concept in Search and Definition," *Juvenile Court Judges Journal*, 20(2), 69–74, 1969.

[10] Vinter, *op. cit.*

[11] Lemert, *op. cit.*

Disadvantages arising from the present practice of enmeshing juveniles in the justice system are many. There is excessive referral to the justice system of youth committing acts based on the ambiguous catchall character of current delinquency statutes and the community's attitudes toward defining and responding to delinquency. There is differential selection for further processing determined by idiosyncratic dispositional choices, but on a more profound level, based on the community's political power or the family's economic power. Officially labeling a young person a delinquent, thereby stigmatizing him, only compounds the inequities generated by his initial selection from an amorphous pool of would-be delinquents.

Programs need to focus on problem behavior rather than labeling. For example, the child or youth who suffers from a reading handicap is not permanently or negatively labeled if the reading deficiency is overcome; the ex-student labeled a "dropout" is. Acting-out behavior that is dealt with on a behavioral level, rather than a legal level, avoids the unnecessary noun label of psychotic or delinquent, depending on what type of agency is doing the labeling. Noun labels present society with an easy opportunity to organize their thoughts about the person or the offense on a permanent basis; hence, we have ex-offenders, ex-delinquents, or ex-psychotics. A definition of issues in terms of behavior changes the approach to care, control, or treatment, and limits society's ability to permanently label behavior—hence, label the individual.

People tend to support systems and enterprises in which they have a vested and real stake.[12] The virtue of the youth service bureau movement is that it gives the local citizen an opportunity to gain a share in the design, building, and operation of a community institution serving local children and youth. No matter how positive in its approach, a public agency, because of a myriad of formal rules and regulations governing behavior, is unable to relate directly or personally with the individuals of the community it attempts to serve. Most public agencies have restrictions, even prohibitions, against positive participation by the clientele. The youth service bureau, at least in part, begins to address the issue by offering the community a program in which the children and the adults of given communities can participate, can give of themselves, can have a stake in their own enterprise.

III. METHODOLOGY

In the fields of youth development and delinquency prevention, where facts are hard to establish, one obvious "fact" is that people are not all alike —communities are not all alike—and youth service bureaus are not all alike.

Although goals and objectives of different programs may be similar, the reasons for these objectives and means for achieving them may be quite different. The national study of youth service bureaus did not arbitrarily hypothesize what a youth service bureau should be and then seek out programs that met the definition. Instead, the study sought out programs that others identified as youth service bureaus—programs with similar prob-

---

[12] Robert Sutermeister, *People and Productivity*, McGraw-Hill, 2d edition, 1969.

lems, goals, and procedures along with influences that were significant in shaping the nature of bureaus in different communities. The project sought to locate and describe youth service bureaus in whatever form and by whatever name others identified them. The national study of youth service bureaus utilized what Dr. John M. Martin called the classic "butterfly collector's" survey method.[13] In the style of the experienced collector who had a good idea of what a butterfly looks like and how, for example, a butterfly differs from a sparrow or an American eagle, project staff searched nationally for projects believed by informants to be youth service bureaus. If a Governor, State planning agency, Federal bureaucrat, or public agency thought a particular program was a youth service bureau, staff attempted to catch up with it, examine it, and match it with other youth service bureaus (butterflies) with similar characteristics. In the process, a few doves and hawks were eliminated because they really were not butterflies at all. No effort was made to identify "the typical or the best form of youth service bureau." Instead, project staff grouped programs with similar problems, goals, procedures, and operations for serving youth either directly or indirectly as a way of trying to describe and classify the elusive youth service bureaus of the President's Crime Commission.

Locating Youth Service Bureaus

The study identified a significant number of youth service bureau programs throughout the United States which have funding from Federal sources. A number of other programs which existed prior to, or independent of, Federal funding were also located and described.

The study began in late September 1971, with a national census. Officials and agencies in the fifty States and six territories were contacted through 300 inquiries sent out to Governors, State planning agencies, regional offices of the Federal Government, and State or local juvenile correctional agencies.

There was response from every State and territory with over 300 programs recommended as likely prospects for study. After screening out duplicates and other obvious nonprograms (i.e., Boy Scouts, Little League, general YMCA programs, etc.) from the preliminary census, questionnaires were sent out. The questionnaires were sent directly to the administrators of programs identified by others as youth service bureaus. Information accumulated gave an indication as to: (1) number and location; (2) auspices; (3) functions; (4) services; (5) types of cases served; (6) nature of services provided; (7) number of staff; (8) involvement of volunteers; (9) organizational structure; and (10) basis of financial support.

The Sorting Task

Questionnaires were mailed to 272 possible youth service bureaus. Ten of these programs were later found to be duplicates. The adjusted total for questionnaires mailed was 262. The net response was 222 out of 262, or 85

---

[13] This analogy was contributed by Professor John Martin, Fordham University, at the first meeting of the National Advisory Committee in Playa Ponce, P.R., Dec. 16, 1971.

percent. Of the 222 responses, 198 questionnaires were completed with sufficient information for analysis. The remaining 24 acknowledged the questionnaire, indicating that it was inappropriate to their program or that they were no longer in operation. Two specialty programs from Washington, D.C., with funding in excess of $2 million, dealt with employment and truancy. These programs were not included in the comparative figures, although a few of the services provided did coincide with youth service bureau programs in other places. Both indicated that they did not categorize themselves as youth service bureaus because they were highly specialized. The questionnaire response from the Los Angeles County School District was in regard to a general counseling program for all youth in the school district. This program was also deleted for comparison purposes.

The remaining 195 programs were analyzed. Although there were many shades of program, approximately 170 appeared to be significantly related to the youth service bureau *concept*. Some of the definitional problems encountered follow.

Seven programs, mostly in Florida, with one in the Virgin Islands, were residential treatment programs for adjudicated delinquents and/or dependent children. In most cases they were group homes and served traditional correctional agency needs for residential care. One additional program, in North Carolina, was identified as a juvenile hall.

The New York programs offered the next dilemma. Questionnaires were mailed to thirty-seven programs. There were returns from twenty-six, and, of these, twenty-four operated under the auspices of the New York Division of Youth Services and were known as youth boards. The programs from the eleven locations not responding were also youth boards. Of the twenty-four youth board programs, seventeen responded that they considered themselves youth service bureaus, four responded that they were uncertain, and three responded that they were not.

The New York youth board program makes recommendations as to youth programs in the community with funds from the State of New York. These funds amount to less than $1 per year for each youth under the age of eighteen years. The twenty-four programs responding represented a minimum of $7 million and involved three-quarters of 1 million youth. All twenty-four responses listed coordination as a significant objective or function, and service rendered was usually to other agencies involved in youth development or delinquency prevention. The most frequently sponsored service is recreation, although some boards emphasize information and referral services which try to put a youth in touch with a specific agency that can benefit his particular need: employment referral, drug information, etc., which may be very much like youth service bureaus represented in other areas.

There were three school-based programs, which ranged from general counseling to those which specifically addressed themselves to school truancy and behavior problems. Several programs concentrated on indirect rather than direct service. In essence, they worked with groups who worked with groups.

There were about five such programs, and these too varied in purpose from general welfare of youth to specific diversion from the juvenile justice system. Another group of programs were housed within police departments or were police administered. There were seven such programs. Four considered that they were youth service bureaus, two considered that they were not, and one was uncertain. There were also ten to twelve programs which created definitional problems. In these programs the main or principal interest was in such matters as supplementary probation supervision, recreation, employment, drug counseling, and other specialties.

One hundred and thirty-six programs had similar characteristics insofar as having similar objectives (i.e., diversion from the juvenile justice system, delinquency prevention, youth and community development); target population (i.e., primarily youth between ten and eighteen and with special consideration to those in jeopardy of becoming involved in the juvenile justice system); and a variety of services, (i.e., counseling, referral, individual casework, cultural enrichment activities). Even here, there was a great variation among the programs, depending on the size and political nature of the community: different emphasis as to methods of delivering service, staff providing service, and the leadership of each program.

Program Selection

On December 15, 16, and 17, 1971, the National Advisory Committee, two representatives of the Youth Development and Delinquency Prevention Administration, Professor John Martin of Fordham University (Consultant to the Playa Ponce Youth Service Bureau), the project director, and associate project director met to select fifty-five youth service bureaus. Staff of the project and the National Advisory Committee used the following criteria in selecting projects for on-site visits:

1. *Geography:* To the extent possible, programs operating throughout the West, Midwest, East, North, and South were selected. Within these geographic areas, programs representing metropolitan, rural, and suburban areas were also included.
2. *Community Involvement:* To what extent did public and private agencies, along with private citizens, support the identified program and to what extent were groups and individuals involved in planning and implementing the services offered?
3. *Program:* What were the services offered and what rationale existed for the specific services that had been developed for the given youth service bureau identified?
4. *Uniqueness of Target Area:* Was there something special about the target area? Did it represent some special problem, group, or issue that was easily identified?
5. *Visibility:* Was the program itself identified as an operating organization, or was it simply a smaller part of some larger existing program? Did it have special organizational identity and the ability to command its own financial support?

IV. GENERAL FINDINGS

Responses to mail-out questionnaires and other written material provided general reference information as to different types of programs identified as youth service bureaus. Some of the residential treatment programs, youth board programs, and specialty programs were like, or had many elements of, programs similar to general youth service bureau programs; others did not. Emphasis of this section is in regard to the more typical programs.

Number of Youth Served

It is estimated that for twelve months in 1971–1972, approximately 50,000 youth, who were in immediate jeopardy of the juvenile justice system, received direct services from approximately 140 youth service bureaus. At least an additional 150,000 youth, who were from the respective target areas, but not in immediate jeopardy of the juvenile justice system, were also participants in the programs.

Typical Program

It is impossible to isolate the "average man." He can be described, discussed, and counted, but he is not exactly like anyone else. As a composite, he is unique as well as imaginary. The same may be said of the "average" youth service bureau. The following composite description is drawn from an analysis of 195 written responses to questionnaires and/or other information.

Typical programs had five to six full-time staff and either had or were developing programs utilizing the services of from one to fifty volunteers. The annual budget was from $50,000 to $75,000. The objectives were diversion from the juvenile justice system, delinquency prevention, and youth development.

Individual counseling and referral were the most important services for at least 75 percent of the programs responding. Included were referral with general follow-up; family counseling; group counseling; drug treatment; job referral; tutoring and remedial education; recreation programs; medical aid; and legal aid.

At least two-thirds of the programs were located in an urban, core city, or Model City neighborhoods. Socioeconomic conditions for the areas were usually considered lower income with a high crime rate, unemployment, and limited facilities most often noted. The target group was adolescents (fourteen–seventeen years of age).

The ethnic distribution of programs answering questionnaires was: predominantly white, 25 percent; predominantly black, 15 percent; predominantly Latin, 5 percent. In addition, 20 percent of the programs were mixed between whites and blacks; 10 percent between whites and Latins; and 5 percent predominantly Latin and black. Twenty percent of the programs had most ethnic groups represented.

The "typical" program provided intensive services for 350 cases per year;

about 60 percent were male and 40 percent female. The average age was 15.5 years. Primary sources of referral were school, law enforcement, and self. Primary reasons for referral were unacceptable behavior, personal difficulties, or some professional services needs. Drugs and delinquency were the primary reasons for police referral. Approximately 25 percent of the programs were open Monday through Friday for a total of forty hours per week. The remaining 75 percent worked in excess of this, usually forty-one to seventy-two hours throughout the entire week.

The evaluation component for programs ranged from no evaluation to extensive evaluation.

Patterns of Organization

The organization of youth service bureaus ranged from a "one-man operation" with a few volunteers to a sizable unit of government. This range of organizational pattern is due in part to the various interpretations given to the President's Crime Commission report about what constitutes a youth service bureau. However, it also reflects the needs, resources, attitudes, and priorities of the community and different levels of government and funding sources.

The matter of auspices has been a point of considerable discussion regarding youth service bureaus. There are those who argue that it should be a public agency, closely identified with government; others argue for a private agency, independent of government; and still others seem to prefer some compromise between the two absolute extremes. The study showed that the majority of youth service bureaus involve participation by some unit of state or local government.

Complexity of Program Administration

It is difficult not to be amazed at the number of layers of government, organizations, and individuals between those receiving the service and the funding source. For example, some programs received funds from four Federal sources (LEAA, HEW, Model Cities, and the Labor Department)—all with different funding dates. The program may also have several political entities at the local level, as well as the State level, for approval of cash and "in kind" match in order to obtain the Federal funds. This is in addition to advisory groups, organizations, managing boards, and informal influences of groups and of powerful individuals. These various individuals and groups may not have the same objectives as the funding source, let alone the same objectives as the layers of government between them; and, last, but not least, they may not have the same idea of service needs as the people who are the "target population." It becomes clear that those responsible for programs serve many masters.

Funding

A discussion of youth service bureaus is hardly possible without an examination of funding. It is an understatement to comment that funding fluctuates and is uncertain. For the most part, programs are dependent on Federal funds for primary support and local resources for "in-kind" services. Programs are often beholden for funds from sources where the representatives are their severest critics and competitors for available money.

When the Omnibus Crime Control Act and the Juvenile Delinquency Act first made funds available, there was a search for new and innovative programs. The youth service bureau idea captured the imagination of many because it was seen as an immediate solution with high visibility. Although more Federal money has become available, State criminal justice planning agencies now tend to give greater priority to law enforcement and rehabilitation than prevention. Not only have the police and correctional programs become more adept at submitting successful proposals for funding, but procedures have become more institutionalized, favoring traditional agencies over alternative programs which, no matter how subtle, challenge established governmental agencies for money and responsibility.

Of 188 programs responding to the question regarding funding, 155 had some Federal funding, amounting to less than $15 million. The most significant source of funding was from the Law Enforcement Assistance Administration, which invested in 135 of the 155 programs. Hence, the most critical problem facing youth service bureaus throughout the country today can be summed up in a single word, "funding"!

People Providing Service

To a great extent, the *staff* of the youth service bureaus *are* the *programs* of the youth service bureaus. Perhaps no group brings more energy, training, character, and experience to the fledgling youth service bureau programs than the project directors. They are key people and their talents are needed; yet the majority of programs are not only in danger of going out of business but also of losing leadership due to the uncertain funding future, long hours, and hard work.

Youth service bureau employees are atypical of traditional social agency staff. They are people of great contrast who learn from one another. Their manner of dress is neat and casual but with a ring of youth and the times. Their style of talking with people is straightforward and without the language of bureaucracy. They are the people who maintain the principal contact with clientele. They "meet the client where he is."

Program Participants

Clientele, as described by the President's Crime Commission Report, are "a group now handled, for the most part, either inappropriately or not at all, except in time of crisis."[14] Clients interviewed during the course of this study met this criteria. The overall reasons for referral and sources of referral supported the contention that program participants were youth in jeopardy of the juvenile justice system. Yet an important characteristic of the young people who come to youth service bureaus for any reason is their need to contribute to, as well as participate in, the program. The youth service bureau is a place where youth can serve as well as come to be served. Youth

[14] *The Challenge of Crime in a Free Society, op. cit.*, p. 83.

who come to the bureau seeking service frequently become deliverers of service and implementors of the program.

More than half of all referrals to the youth service bureaus contacted (50.9 percent) were for unacceptable behavior, i.e., youth in jeopardy of processing in the juvenile justice system but whose behavior would not have been illegal if engaged in by an adult.

Although law enforcement and schools were the most frequent sources of referral, approximately 18 percent each, no single source was dominant. The number of referrals from unofficial sources approximated 40 percent (i.e., parents, self, friends). More than half the females were self-referrals. Self-referrals appear to be older with a median age of 16.8. The overall pattern of referrals suggests that many of the participants and their families were waiting for the services that youth service bureau programs began to provide.

Primary Objectives of Youth Service Bureaus

Although diversion from the juvenile justice system was reported to be the primary objective by the majority of the directors (63.8 percent), this response diminished the further one moved down to the administrative hierarchy. Staff in general tended to emphasize goals that were broad in focus, such as delinquency prevention and youth development. Program participants tended to see the objectives of the bureaus as practical help to people with problems; help with family problems; individual help; help to keep out of trouble. Overall, participants seemed to view the programs as service agencies for young people.

Diversion

It is not known when the term "diversion" became a part of the vocabulary associated with youth service bureaus, but it was and is as badly defined as the term "bureau" itself. Mixing justice system processes with nonjustice services, the term "diversion" has been applied to almost any discretionary action available to a public or private agency dealing with children and youth. Only recently has the Law Enforcement Assistance Administration attempted to define diversion as an objective and observable program offered in lieu of justice system processing between the period of arrest and adjudication.[15]

V. PROGRAM EXAMPLES

Youth service bureau programs tend to focus on the special problems of youth in the community.[16] The youth service bureaus serve as a bridge

[15] *The Commission on Standards and Goals, Task Force on Corrections,* Chapter on Diversion, currently in preparation: Law Enforcement Assistance Administration, Washington, D.C., December 1972.

[16] Examples taken from: *The National Study of Youth Service Bureaus,* prepared for the Department of Health, Education and Welfare, Social Rehabilitation, Youth Development and Delinquency Prevention Administration, by the Department of the California Youth Authority, Sacramento, Calif., October 1972.

between the needs of youth and the attitudes of the adult community. In communities where both exist, bureaus serve as a bridge between traditional agencies for social service and justice and unorthodox organizations also providing service to youth.

Over all, the youth service bureau movement is permeated by an attitude of concern and dedication to making gentle the lives of the people. To the extent that a bureau's objective is diversion, then the bureaus most capable of diversion are those that have a linkage to the juvenile justice system, maintaining immediate communication, but that are not coopted by the justice system, its traditionally most powerful leaders, or its existing practices.

Coordinated planning such as this presumes that the community and its justice system are characterized by a strong sense of cooperation. For less cohesive communities, diversion may only come about much more painstakingly after the bureau begins operation, using individual and system advocacy to encourage justice agencies to change their way of handling children and youth.

The planning process for a diversionary bureau is illustrated by efforts carried out in Pacifica, Calif. Here the probation department hosted a meeting for administrators from several related agencies to discuss the need, concept, and possible services and direction of a youth service bureau. A smaller community team, with the police and probation departments providing the core leadership, developed the plans in more detail.

The youth services project in San Antonio, Tex., provides an example of how an administrative policy change by the police department is bringing about diversion in that city. The police chief has ordered all officers to deliver juveniles picked up for such offenses as glue or paint sniffing, liquor violations, runaway, ungovernable, and disorderly conduct, truancy, or loitering to one of three project neighborhood centers in the city.

Availability of bureau staff to immediately respond to a case being handled by the police also increases the likelihood that diversion will take place in San Antonio. The youth services project places bilingual intake workers in the juvenile aid bureau of the police department at night and on weekends to guarantee immediate follow-up on a case.

The immediacy of service and the convenient physical location of the bureau saves police a long drive to juvenile hall; i.e., three centers are located in housing projects of the target area. Location is a stimulant to implementing a diversion policy.

Accessibility of the bureau's offices to law enforcement is another asset in encouraging diversion. The Rhode Island Youth Service Bureau's regular work hours are 2 P.M. until 10 P.M., a fact greatly appreciated by the Providence Police Department. Until recently, the Youth Services Bureau of Greensboro, Inc., in North Carolina, was located across the street from the police department. Not only did this permit bureau staff to daily pick up "paper referrals" from the police department, but it also increased understanding between the police department's juvenile officers and the bureau staff during the youth service bureau's developmental stages. A similar effort exists in Seattle, Wash., where the center for youth services and the police department have cooperatively developed a social agency referral project for youth in trouble.

Detaching law enforcement officers from the juvenile division to work full time in the bureau is another method of increasing the confidence of the police department and thereby enhancing diversion. This method is utilized in east San Jose, Calif., with the role of the police officers clearly agreed upon in advance. The police officers are viewed as a part of the youth service bureau program rather than the police establishment. This is done in order to protect the confidential, noncoercive stance of the bureau.

After the youth service bureau was established in 1971 in Dekalb, Ill., each of the eighty-six youth arrested by the police department were referred to the youth service bureau; none were referred to the court system. Only twenty of the eighty-six again came to the attention of the police department. All were again referred to the youth service bureau. Court statistics for youth from Dekalb reflect this policy change.

In many communities where law enforcement has been closely involved with establishing the youth service bureau, the bureau has found it necessary to break down distrust among the young people it serves. Only after a period of providing services have some of the bureaus successfully developed a reputation of providing voluntary and confidential service.

One of the most pervasive areas of controversy in the youth service bureau movement is whether a bureau should develop and provide services itself or should function principally as an information and referral service, following up with individual advocacy or case coordination for the young people it refers.

Most youth service bureaus have focused primarily on developing alternative services to fill the gaps in the community rather than facilitating access to ongoing services. Thus, they provide direct service more often than refer youth to other agencies for service.

The fundamental strength of most bureaus has been in their provision of a variety of innovative services for youth—services that include counseling, tutoring, job referrals and other employment services, crisis intervention, crisis shelter care, and medical services, generally provided at accessible locations and hours in an appealing manner to their clients. Moreover, several of the bureaus that provide direct service also provide referral services—follow-up, individual advocacy, and service brokerage.

Where a youth service bureau's office is the focal point of activities, accessibility has been increased by locating near a school or in a business and commercial area frequented by young people. In rural areas or other communities with widely dispersed populations, some bureaus (such as the Tri-County Youth Services Bureau in Hughesville, Md.) have opened one-day-a-week outreach centers in churches and other locations.

Accessibility has been improved over many traditional agencies by maintaining evening and weekend office hours. Youth service bureaus seeking to assist youth with problems make their services available to young people not only through accessible locations and hours but by instituting hotlines, drop-in centers, and outreach workers.

In some communities, youth service bureaus operate hotlines—

anonymous listener services which young people with problems can call. Examples of hotlines linked to youth service bureaus include those in Peru, Ind.; Palatine, Ill.; Shamokin, Pa., and El Paso, Tex. In these communities, volunteers staff telephones so that young people with personal crises can call in and discuss problems anonymously with a concerned, trained listener. In many instances, the telephone conversation is the only assistance needed. However, the volunteer listener refers the young person to the bureau or another resource if further help is necessary. In Palatine, college students receive credit for volunteering to staff the hotline. Although it does not operate a hotline, the Hughesville, Md., bureau urges young people with problems to call collect, thus overcoming economic and transportation barriers to accessibility. Youth in need of the services of Manteca House in California can receive free transportation from a local cab company.

A more aggressive approach to reaching out to young people is seen in the use of outreach or street workers. Many of the outreach workers go where groups of youth gather—in order to link individual youths to services, to divert the groups into constructive activities, or to attempt to prevent confrontations between young people and the police. Traditionally, outreach workers have worked with gangs in urban areas, but in many of the youth service bureaus located in suburban communities, outreach workers have instead attempted to involve unaffiliated and alienated youth in purposeful activities. In Pacifica, Calif., high school and college age students are employed by the youth service bureau as outreach workers, with a few assigned to each of the young people's gathering places, including the beach in this suburban town. In Fairmount Heights, Md., the roving youth leader program concentrates on an outreach approach. This program sends five part-time teams, each composed of a young adult male and high school student, into the community to provide positive role models and to encourage idle youth to participate in the roving leader's recreation programs and community services.

Although it has been suggested that counseling should not be the primary service of a youth service bureau, it is, in fact, the nucleus of many bureaus. It also appears that many of the activities of the youth service bureaus are inadvertently obscured by the term counseling, since the counseling services for youth also requires bureau staff to deal with problems that are broader than those initially presented by the youth. Solutions to these broader problems sometimes require serving as an advocate for youth with other institutions in the community.

The bureaus in Wayzata and St. Louis Park, Minn., and Boulder, Colo., specialize in counseling "counter culture youth." In Tulsa, Okla., and Santa Rosa, Calif., bureaus emphasize one-to-one counseling and practical assistance through the use of volunteers. In Portland, Ore., professional workers volunteer to offer the specialized skills and knowledge to young people needing this type of practical help. Paraprofessionals are the primary counseling-outreach staff in Brooklyn, N.Y., and New Bedford, Mass.

Counseling of young people, many of them runaways, is a primary program in the Youth Services Bureau of Greensboro, N.C. Accessibility is greatly magnified by the staff's willingness to respond immediately to youth in trouble—regardless of the day or hour. This program is unique in its ability to gain the confidence of youth in trouble while maintaining the respect for other agencies in the community. A demonstration of the confidentiality that exists is that staff do not take any action without the young person's knowledge. Police and staff have agreed that staff, provided they notify the police when they know the whereabouts of a runaway, can continue to work with the runaway and need not turn him or her in.

Family counseling is a frequently provided service in Maricopa County Youth Service Bureau in Arizona, San Diego, and Pacifica, Calif. This is in sharp contrast to Greensboro's services, where the focus of the bureau's counseling is the youth himself and on developing his responsibilities. In Pacifica, the agreement is generally for five counseling sessions. Families in need of long-term treatment are referred to other agencies.

Hughesville, Md., and Tri-County Community Center in Jackson, Miss., offer diagnosis and evaluation prior to counseling. In El Paso, Tex., where court approval is required before any youth under sixteen can drop out of school, the juvenile court requires youngsters to first be counseled by the youth service bureau. The bureau attempts to solve the underlying problems, such as employment, and then makes its recommendation to the court regarding leaving school.

A drop-in center primarily frequented by youth experiencing identity problems characterizes the Glastonbury, Conn., Youth Service Bureau. Individual conjoint family and group counseling are the main services provided.

The Youth Intercept Project of Kansas City, Mo., does not provide traditional casework services. Instead, it helps the child survive and stay in school and helps his family get what they need in order to allow that kind of success.

In the Bronx, the neighborhood youth diversion program and in East Palo Alto, Calif., the community youth responsibility project have developed a program on the premise that indigenous people who know the problems and who have had minimal training in conciliation and arbitration techniques can help resolve interpersonal and interfamily problems without relying on the formal judicial system.

In Los Angeles County, the Bassett Youth Service Bureau focuses on strengthening the community's efforts to meet youth needs. It developed a free clinic in conjunction with other community groups, staffed primarily by volunteers. It includes a counseling and drop-in center in addition to an outpatient medical clinic. Venereal disease, pregnancies, and drug abuse are among the most frequently treated medical problems.

Individually tailored service provided by the bureaus has occasionally been supplemented by purchase of services. For example, the Tucson, Ariz., Youth Service Bureau supplements its range of services by contracting for services for its clients, including remedial reading.

Coordination of services for individual youth is taking place through case conferences, e.g., in Worcester, Mass., and Howard County, Ind., representatives of all agencies involved with the youth meet in an attempt to attain a complete view of the problem and to develop a comprehensive plan to meet the youth's needs. The program in San Angelo, Tex., emphasizes linking-up community resources for youth through conferences and training workshops. Special programs of coordination, counseling, and direct services for blacks are found in Louisville, Ky., and Columbus, Ohio. The program in Bowling Green, Ky., is similar, but serves a racially mixed population with a racially mixed staff known as the Mod Squad. The Youth Services Bureau of Tarrant County (Fort Worth, Tex.) emphasizes its role as a crisis intervention service by attempting to understand each client's problem and make a referral to the most appropriate agency.

Advocacy is another role some bureaus fulfill. The most notable example of this is the youth service bureau in Ponce, P.R., Youth and Community Alerted. Here, twelve young people are trained to act as advocates for youth who have come in contact with the police or the juvenile court, or are in danger of becoming delinquent. In addition, the bureau and its leadership are advocates for community improvements, i.e., better sanitation, drug abuse prevention, and improved educational facilities.

In Bridgeport, Conn., one staff member of the youth service bureau appears in juvenile court each day to "stand up" for young people for whom they feel they can provide service. And in Fairmount Heights, Md., Roving Youth Leaders staff act as a third party with school authorities and juveniles in instances where parents or guardians are unwilling to act.

Meeting the needs for shelter has been a subgoal in several bureaus. The Omaha, Nebr., YMCA Youth Service Bureau operates a group home which is responsive to the runaway problem and emphasizes family reconciliation. Whether a youth stays is his choice, but parental permission is required.

The Youth Crisis Center, Inc., in Jackson, Miss., provides shelter and services up to five days for a few youth at a time who come to it for help. Parents are not contacted unless the youth agrees. Professional volunteers, including medical and legal people, supplement the small staff.

In Scottsdale, Ariz., the youth service bureau is located in a four-bedroom home, with two of the bedrooms used as offices and two for youth to stay if they need overnight accommodations. If the youth is under eighteen, parental consent is required.

The youth service bureau in Boise, Idaho, provides temporary shelter care in lieu of incarceration. In Las Cruces, N. Mex., the Council for Youth operates a group home for boys, most of whom remain there for a few months. The council's outreach program provides aftercare. The Youth Action Commission in Arvada, Colo., operates a group home for girls requiring short-term placement.

The Yuba-Sutter Youth Service Bureau in California developed crisis homes where youth could stay for short periods of time. These crisis homes were private homes volunteered for short-term care. Volunteer homes were paid a nominal sum per day for expenses.

Programs for groups of youth and parents are to be found in many of the youth service bureaus—or organized by the bureaus in several communities. These group programs include new approaches to youth-police relations, education, and parental education.

The El Paso, Tex., Youth Services Bureau bridges gaps in understanding between youth and police by its youth patrol, youth-police dialogues, and youth-police recreation program. The youth patrol permits youth to spend four hours on patrol with a police officer during periods of high activity. The youth-police dialogues involve antiauthority youth and selected police officers in encounter sessions, under the supervision of psychiatrists. The youth-police recreation program pairs an off-duty police officer with a selected youth-police recreation program. The youth patrol permits police to establish communication with young people in a neighborhood and develop constructive programs in cooperation with the neighborhood's residents.

Rap sessions (informal group discussions) take place in several of the bureaus, with Cambridge, Mass., among the bureaus holding them most regularly.

In the Tri-County Youth Services Bureau in Hughesville, Md., staff are joined by correctional camp inmates in leading group counseling for boys who have been referred to the bureau. Inmates are driven to the bureau one evening a week to participate in this program.

The Palama Settlement of Hawaii has a successful ongoing "behavior modification school" program for court referrals and rejects from the regular schools. The youth advocacy program in South Bend, Ind., contracts for a "street academy," an alternative school program for junior high and high school youth who have dropped out of the regular schools. In Ann Arbor, Mich., the Washtenaw Youth Service Bureau, funded through the school system, has set up an alternative school program.

In Kansas City, Mo., the program instituted art classes in several schools to which problem children are referred. A prominent local artist teaches these classes, including discussion of social problems that relate to the content of the art.

One of the first steps of coordinated planning of programs is information gathering and distribution. A thorough and systematic approach to this is seen in the Youth Services Bureau of Wake Forest University, in Winston-Salem, N.C. This bureau does not provide direct services to juveniles. Instead, it has developed a comprehensive, communitywide approach to coordinated planning of youth opportunities. Young people, as well as agency representatives, participated in the planning.

In other efforts to systematically plan and create change in existing institutions, the Youth Services Bureau of Wake Forest University has conducted a study of attitudes and knowledge of drug abuse; a study of drug use; a participant-observation study among black youth on factors preventing their becoming involved in recreation and character development programs; and a survey to determine what recreation or youth opportunities low-income white youth would like to see developed.

The Youth Development Service in Billings, Mont., and the rural America project operating out of Helena, Mont., provide consultant and technical assistance to a variety of other social service agencies in their respective areas. Coordination efforts bring agencies together to agree on community priorities, to eliminate service duplication, and to redirect resources where current projects are inappropriate. Morreltown, Ark., uses a technique referred to as "resource management" to meet the needs of rural youth.

The Washtenaw Youth Service Bureau in Ann Arbor, Mich., emphasizes the initiation of programs for young people who, although troubled and acting out, have not yet had contact with the justice system. It has published a youth services guide, which is to be updated every three months. It conducts demonstration projects, primarily in the schools, and attempts to develop skills and resources within the system.

The youth advocacy program in South Bend, Ind., also attempts to get youth-serving agencies to develop new ways of dealing with young people. Their methods are positive proposals and involvement. Field workers are assigned to five youth-serving agencies—the recreation department, schools, a family and child agency, city government, and Model Cities—with the task of making them more responsive to youth needs.

The program examples cited often effect social change and systems modification as well as provide direct services. For example, the decision structures in the youth service bureau in Winston-Salem, N.C., and the youth advocacy program in South Bend, Ind., both include recipients of the services. While this characteristic does not further interagency coordination by rapidly providing the program with power to coordinate resources, it nonetheless institutes the beginnings of a power base which can ultimately bring about changes in the system of social and judicial services.

This approach requires a sense of security that the program will continue to exist beyond a single funding year. It also requires continually training, developing, and invoking young people in the decision making for the bureau. Only in this way will the youth service bureau evolve to meet the needs of the middle and late 1970s, as today's youth themselves become recognized as established leaders of the adult community.

Youth service bureau programs tend to focus on the special problems of youth in the community. The youth service bureaus serve as a bridge between the needs of youth and the attitudes of the adult community. In communities where both exist, bureaus serve as a bridge between traditional agencies for social service, justice, and unorthodox organizations also providing service to youth.

VI. SUMMARY AND CONCLUSION

Youth service bureaus are as varied and different as the people and the locations in which they are found; yet, they demonstrate certain similar and important characteristics. For example, almost without exception, youth service bureaus are pioneering new organizational models for delivering services to children and youth. They are, in a limited way, transforming traditional bureaucratic models into flexible service systems which freely and directly cater to the differing needs of children and youth throughout America. Within the communities they serve, youth service bureaus deliver practical and direct services to children and youth in need.

Organizational Principles

The national study identified four main influences as having significance in the development, organization, and primary service of youth service bureaus. They were:

1. The nature of the community.
2. The power base.
3. The orientation of staff.
4. The funding sources.

These influences, in turn, suggested a series of principles for those promoting or implementing a youth services bureau:

1. The organization and program must remain flexible in order to respond to the unique needs and unanticipated problems of the community it serves but without undue reliance on traditional bureaucratic responses.
2. The program must be prepared to deal objectively and effectively with the powerful in the community, including those who believe in a punitive and deterrent course of action.
3. Whatever the staff orientation, the program implemented must be a real substitute for other courses of action, particularly if the object is to reduce the likelihood of recurring delinquency, minimize stigmatization, or maintain youth who are in jeopardy of the criminal justice system.
4. The program must be organized in such a manner that the favorable public bias for children and youth is used to full advantage.
5. Research and evaluation must be included as a part of program developments if there is to be systematic organizational change based on fact rather than prejudice and hunch.

Target Area

Community forces affecting youth service bureaus express themselves in many ways. For example, if a college or university is located in the target area, the services offered focus on program, and the types of clientele served will differ from a similar program operating in a ghetto or a "bedroom" community. Population characteristics, social or economic status, physical characteristics of the community, and the auspices under which the program operates are all critical factors affecting the nature of the program offered as well as its success. Who sponsors the youth service bureau is less important than whether or not the sponsoring body has enough power and commitment to see the program carried through.

Funding

Bureaus with some assurances of continuous funding are able to operate effective programs that can be adapted to changing needs and circumstances. The expansion and continued development of youth service bureau models depends upon increased funding, but in the long run, stability of supporting revenues is the most critical issue.

Staff

Staff is the single most important ingredient of the youth service bureau. Enthusiastic and committed people are essential to program, yet this energy will lead to little unless staff are aware of and sensitive to the power structure of the community (and its effect on program). Staff of youth service bureaus are sometimes at a disadvantage in dealing with private and/or governmental hierarchies that influence and control programs. Nevertheless, leaders who have successful youth service bureaus possess the tenacity, energy, sensitivity, and charisma to deal effectively with the most powerful forces in the community, while at the same time being able to relate to the least powerful and socially primitive individuals and groups in that community.

Program Content

Most youth service bureaus provide at least one standard service, e.g., some form of counseling. Unlike traditional case service agencies, counseling in youth service bureaus is geared to action and change. In many cases, an initial counseling problem requires the bureau to become an advocate around a specific community problem that affects more children than the one child presenting the initial problem, e.g., remedial education, improved health services, etc.

Most successful bureaus offer practical programs of assistance to young people such as tutoring, medical treatment, legal aide, temporary housing, and recreation. Some, but not the majority, use referrals to other agencies or purchase of service for those services they cannot provide directly.

Other important services include planning, training, consultation, case conferencing, advocacy, and serving as host for other agency activities such as community fairs, craft displays, open houses, educational rap sessions, and other efforts that bring in a broad cross section of the community for information and participative action.

Conclusion

The effective youth service bureau involves good programming plus operational knowledge by staff about how to effectively use the resources of the community. Successful bureau directors use their knowledge to work through the red tape normally found in governmental bureaucracies.

A good youth service bureau is program plus know-how.

The effective youth service bureau is one where youth can relate. It is a place where youth gains by giving, where youth come because of personal needs and often resolve those needs by serving others. Almost without exception, clientele of youth service bureaus are people who want to belong, want to share, and want to give of themselves. This characteristic of giving and wanting to be a part of something larger than themselves is found in such divergent places as an affluent suburb like Wayzata, Minn., or in the New York inner city.

In 1972, youth service bureaus were primarily models for delivering direct services to children and youth. In this sense, bureaus are a pioneering example of a service delivery component for a broader effort now identified as a comprehensive youth service delivery system (i.e., a total system which brings together and organizes resources for all children and youth in a given target area in ways that increase the effectiveness of the services provided).

Ultimately, every society is forced to examine the services it offers in terms of cost effectiveness. Today in the United States, over $12 billion are spent annually on programs advancing youth services. Because the programs are fragmented with each operating agency requiring its own overhead, staff, policy, and administration, and insisting on dealing with only one part of the child, there is little evidence that the $12 billion is being used effectively. Yet, in spite of this, a few youth service bureaus, greatly underfunded and outside the "real" money, are making a difference.

On the basis of total national resources assigned to the youth service bureau in 1972 (less than $15 million), it is unreasonable to expect youth service bureaus to be able to command either the careful attention or authority that would permit greater coordination of existing youth service agencies now spending billions of dollars. The fact that some bureaus have been able to coordinate and to serve as advocates for youth services is a glowing tribute to the staff and the community in which these few programs exist.

Whether or not the youth service bureau movement survives and transforms itself into what is now called "comprehensive youth service systems" will be determined by time and the commitment of the public and private agencies to consider reordering their priorities for delivering services to children and youth. The youth service bureau has demonstrated very clearly that there are flexible and better alternatives for the traditional ways of providing youth services. Further, it has demonstrated that a small number of commited people (overwhelmingly young), armed with even minimal resources, can begin to effectively address some of the most critical problems facing the new American majority—the Nation's youth.

SECTION 5

EVALUATION
AND EMPIRICAL DATA

It is true of most new social programs that program development moves ahead in direct proportion to its perceived need and the energy of its early proponents. It is equally true—and this is necessarily the case—that program development moves ahead far more rapidly than does its empirical base. In other words, these programs generally proceed and flourish on faith rather than on fact. This is certainly true of diversion programs.

There are two broad types of research with which we must be concerned. Our primary interest in this section is with the broad area of evaluation research. Evaluation is often a dramatic as well as a tension-producing form of research. Done correctly, it is also very difficult. More easily conceived and carried out, and in many ways more critical to program development, is what is generally termed exploratory or descriptive research. In one interesting treatise on research in social programs,[1] the term "mapping the system" is used to refer to the descriptive or exploratory research needed. Mapping the system involves finding—rather carefully—what is now being done, and with what consequences. It involves looking at any existing programs, in the general category of those being considered, to derive good program ideas and to avoid the mistakes others may already have made; we spend too much energy reinventing the wheel every few years. It involves determining beforehand both levels of receptiveness to the idea of the new program and potential sources of resistance.

The article by Klein in this section is an example of "mapping the system" with specific reference to diversion practices in a large and very heterogeneous metropolitan area, Los Angeles County. The example is even more pertinent than it may seem, because this research was done under contract to the agency which was charged with developing a comprehensive plan for the county. Klein's data thus were available to and presumably (or at least hopefully) employed in developing the diversion plan outlined in the article by Graham and Wurzberger in the preceding section of this volume.

Unfortunately, a research endeavor as comprehensive as this is seldom undertaken prior to program development and initiation. We usually settle for haphazard guesswork backed up by selected contacts with individuals

[1] David Twain, Eleanor Harlow, and Donald Merwin, *Research and Human Services: A Guide to Collaboration for Program Development.* New York, Jewish Board of Guardians, 1970.

299

probably sympathetic to our ideas anyway. This throws even more of a burden upon those undertaking evaluation research. Not only must they find ways to assess the impact of the new programs; they must also be able to comment on aspects of the program which might have been arranged differently to yield more satisfactory results. This does not make such researchers popular with program personnel.

Referring again to the Graham and Wurzberger article, it seems fair to suggest that a diversion explosion is taking place in Los Angeles County (as it is elsewhere). Not only is this county alone about to expend close to $5 million in police diversion programs, but a new professional association has emerged—the California Association of Diversion and Youth Service Counselors. A new jargon is appearing, centering around a client population known as "divertees."

Yet with all this activity, it is significant that no reference has been made by the planners to any single instance of evaluation. Indeed, no genuine evaluation has ever been attempted prior to the funding of the projects described by Graham and Wurzberger. One after-the-fact evaluation was carried out by Lincoln (see her report later in this section) as a separate enterprise. The results, casting a negative light on diversion, have been assiduously avoided by county officials charged with diversion planning.

This wholesale immersion in police diversion programs with such a skimpy empirical base must perforce have some undesirable consequences, some of which are already emerging.

First, many of the operations now under way and contemplated are not *diversion* projects at all, but referral programs for minor offenders who would otherwise have been released. This has occurred in part because no evaluation has taken place pointing up the consequences of diversion without referral, diversion with referral, and referral prior to diversion.

Second, most of the new programming has resulted from holding the federal carrot before numerous city horses. The impact of such programs on matters critical to city councils has not been evaluated. Thus, when the federal funds have been exhausted, there is no particular reason to assume continued funding by the cities.

Third, as diversion programs have proliferated, a practical and philosophical dichotomy has appeared between those referring offenders to "in-house" counselors and those referring offenders to outside community agencies. The absence of any attempt to evaluate the implications and consequences of these divergent approaches is causing unnecessary travail in the entire enterprise.

Fourth, the question of the degree to which police departments are accommodating to the diversion programs has not been evaluated, with the result that the likelihood of incorporation of the many new programs is tenuous at best. Our distinct impression from observations in many police settings is that the new programs are like "overlays" which do not involve structural changes or altered departmental commitments. If this is true, diversion will end coterminously with the cessation of federal funding. This would amount to a tragic waste of investment in personal, departmental, and community resources.

Fifth, suppose—just suppose—that an early empirical evaluation of several prototypical police diversion programs would have revealed a resultant *increase* in juvenile offense rates. How will we manage to announce such a finding when it emerges from the programs in sixty-one cities, all of which had devoted their efforts to an unevaluated program idea?

The foregoing comments derive from the first few months of research observations under a grant awarded to one of the editors for the specific purpose of assessing the contextual impact of the current diversion explosion. It represents another kind of research in that it attempts to assess the impact of "natural events" in no way under the researcher's control in order to make guesses about what might have happened had there been research controls. The difficulty in making such guesses is that they are inevitably confounded by two concurrent problems.

The first of these is that the researcher is often limited to the kinds of data normally gathered by the very people who have a stake in the outcome; in this case, officials in police departments and community agencies provide the data for their own evaluation. For the same and obvious reasons that we prefer independent evaluations to in-house evaluations, we should be wary of assessments that rely on in-house data and data-collection decisions. After-the-fact research is limited to data already available, data gathered for other purposes and for specific, selected purposes at that.

The second problem is that, to the extent that we judge the value of diversion programs from the findings of evaluations, we do so on the basis of atypical programs. The evaluated project is very probably different from the unevaluated project. It stands to reason that those willing to be evaluated, and those seeking evaluations, are probably in better shape than those who would prefer to avoid evaluations.

In addition, the very process of being evaluated—especially by an independent organization—leads to differences in the program. Records are more carefully and fully kept. Supervision is tighter and alert to the presumed and stated interests of the evaluator. Staffing on evaluated projects is probably greater on the average, and staff assignments more clearly delineated. Criteria for client selection are more likely to be made explicit; in fact, the researchers often have a hand in determining those criteria. Finally, feedback on client progress is more regular and more comprehensive in evaluated projects.

None of these factors can be genuinely overcome, so that broadly generalizable conclusions can be drawn from our evaluations, unless the evaluations are (1) designed as part of the program itself from the beginning, and (2) designed with built-in experimental controls. The reticence of most program administrators to commit themselves to such stringent conditions for evaluation dooms their programs to that limbo of results with unknown validity.

22

IMPLICATIONS FOR
RESEARCH AND POLICY*

Donald R. Cressey and Robert A. McDermott

Although writing principally about diversion by the court or probation intake officer (post-arrest but pre-judicial diversion), the authors of this statement could just as easily be referring to police diversion. Two emphases in this article should be highlighted. First, note the emphasis on "mapping the system" and the concern with the types and validity of data available within the justice agencies. Second, note the concern not only with juvenile recidivism but also with impact on the professionals and their system. Diversion is an organizational activity or response and must therefore affect the organizations and their personnel.

* From *Diversion from the Juvenile Justice System,* National Assessment of Juvenile Corrections (Ann Arbor: University of Michigan, June 1973), pp. 56–62. Reprinted by permission of the authors and publisher.

Diversion policy, whatever its base in theory, is bound to inhibit and frustrate anyone wanting merely to study diversion programs, let alone anyone who desires evaluation of them. Taking the matter of informal diversion, for example: Agents of the juvenile justice system are asked to avoid official, formal actions in their processing of juveniles in trouble. Stated another way, the agents are asked to use their own judgment, to exercise individual discretion, to take informal and unofficial actions. But when individual discretion is manifested in informal action, there surely has to be a sharp reduction in the formal rules directing the agent's conduct, with a consequent muddling—even in the mind of the agent—of the criteria on which decisions are based. This muddling, in turn, makes accurate record keeping almost impossible, even if such record keeping is desired, paradoxically, by the same people who would make all actions unofficial and, thus, unrecordable. Such a situation clearly complicates the task of the researcher, especially one who seeks statistical and survey data that can be generalized.

Consider again the key diversion position within the juvenile justice system, that of the intake officer. His decisions are generally held to be too sensitive to be bound by specific criteria, and the officer is left free to exercise his discretion, so that the criteria for diverting juveniles vary greatly from officer to officer. Any intake officer's diversion decisions depend principally on his own general correctional philosophy, knowledge of alternative services, informal relations with other probation officers and personnel of outside agencies, and the types of juvenile cases he receives, or thinks he receives. His department's official policy or philosophy establishes only the direction or trends he should try to follow.

It is not surprising, then, to find the stated goals of a diversion policy or program at variance with the actual mode of implementing those goals. Today everybody is for apple pie and "diversion," but opinions vary on how best to make the pie and on how best to divert. To one intake officer, a CWR or placement on informal probation is "diversion." To another, diversion has not occurred unless a referral to an outside agency is made and the case officially dismissed. Rarely, if ever, do even a minority of officers within a unit agree on what diversion is all about. Nearly everyone we talked to asked us to help clarify the definition of diversion. We started out trying to learn something about diversion practices but wound up responding to questions about the form and content of "proper" diversion programs. When the identity of the thing being studied is so obviously up for grabs, the overall statistics showing how it works or whether it is a "success" aren't likely to be very meaningful to the scientifically oriented researcher.

As a case in point, most of the readily available statistics on intake dispositions refer only to the number of bodies processed in certain ways—"30 percent CWR, 20 percent petitioned, 30 percent on informal probation, 20 percent dismissed." Maybe there will be a simple male-female breakdown, maybe not. There will be little else, and almost certainly there will be nothing to help the outsider discover the modal patterns of even officially processed cases, let alone the ones handled "informally."

As a general rule, a social history or "face sheet" is compiled only when a case becomes officially official, i.e., when a petition is filed. These sheets can be used as a source of data on socioeconomic background, race, offense, parental relationships, etc. But most likely there will be no face sheets for the juveniles handled by a disposition short of petition. Moreover, the information on the sheets that can be located is likely to be incomplete—whether a piece of information is recorded depends entirely upon whether obtaining and recording such information was deemed important by the intake officer.

It must be recalled that these difficulties are encountered even when dealing with "officially" processed cases. Coincident with pressure on officers to divert, many cases—such as walk-ins and telephone referrals—are handled without any official paperwork. Even in the Scottville experimental Diversion Unit, phone contacts are merely noted on the listing taped to the wall (name and date), and such notation is frequently forgotten. The Scottville unit was attempting to maintain a running inventory of social data for its experimental cases, but data gaps were prolific and varied for all the above reasons. In not a single instance did we find a probation office maintaining a complete inventory. Although many individual officers said that such an inventory might be very helpful in reviewing their own decisions, they claimed they had no time to invest in the additional work necessary to maintain an inventory. Perhaps such data are unconsciously considered threatening.

With the exception of Scottville, even rates of recidivism are most often mere guesses. "Success" at diverting is customarily equated with avoiding the filing of an official petition and not with degree of positive help given the juvenile. Rarely is a case followed for more than six months or a year; hence whether or not diversion is permanent (i.e., the juvenile never again encounters the juvenile court) is pretty much guesswork. In line with this seemingly narrow definition of success, most diversion personnel feel that, regardless of the permanence of their diversionary action, contact with their service is more beneficial than harmful for the juvenile.

Social data do exist, but digging them out will entail an exhaustive, personal, "raw data" examination of the files of individual agencies. Upon completion of this job the information gathered would still, we think, be very fragmentary, because each officer differs in his approach to recording data.

We are pessimistic, but we do not entirely surrender. A quantitative study of discretionary programs and practices is not impossible. Each probation department maintains a statistical or "research" unit, usually a single clerk or secretary. Some digging in the files of this unit should produce a somewhat accurate listing of all currently active official juvenile cases—those to which a case number has been assigned. A random sample could be pulled, and a social data code could be developed to organize the material in at least a preliminary manner. The files on many "active" cases will be on someone's desk, not in the record office, but this problem is not insurmountable. Important data, such as socioeconomic class, would probably have to be inferred by using a number of methods, depending on what is in the files; in one case, "father's occupation" might be recorded, in another it will be "family income," and in still others it would be necessary to infer class from the area of residence.

Clearly, evaluation of diversion programs based on recorded information will be a time-consuming and expensive process and without the brightest prospects for meaningful results.

When probation personnel were asked what they thought of such an involved quantitative analysis, they usually laughed. One officer said: "Go ahead and do it if you want, but it wouldn't be worth the paper it was printed on, except to help snow the public."

There is a pressing need to study the careers of juveniles who are diversion fodder. Most current concern (including ours) has been for changes in juvenile justice bureaucracies. Evaluation of the correlated change, if any, in the juveniles who have been processed is mostly an uncharted area. The faddist nature of diversion has produced a proliferation of diversion units and programs without generating a close look at whether the juvenile subject to all this attention is receiving a better deal. It is quite possible that participating personnel have revamped terminology and procedures without seriously altering what happens to the juvenile.

So far as we know, no one has shown that the juvenile offender and his family perceive their handling as materially different under the auspices of a diversion unit than under a more traditional juvenile justice agency. The question is rarely formulated, let alone asked. It is probable that the juvenile does not discriminate as readily as the intake officer among such realities as counseling, informal probation, regular probation, and coercion. It seems plausible that if an act of diversion were truly successful in an individual case, the subject of the act would perceive that something positive had entered his life and something negative had gone away. For this reason, it seems crucial that in-depth qualitative and longitudinal studies be the first order of business for subsequent diversion research.

Compilations of official data will be greatly aided by clear narratives explaining what actually happens to juveniles confronted by the juvenile justice system and its programs. Such study would examine the perspective, and the working milieu of the individuals charged with doing the diverting. One finding here may be that explicit or implicit labeling of juvenile justice workers as bad or inefficient will make them bad or inefficient. Our observation is that, thus far, the diversion demands have not had this effect; they have only raised a spectre of self-doubt, perhaps justifiably, perhaps not. One unit supervisor complained:

> True diversion supposedly means referral out of the system, but what if competent community services are not available? What's more, why do planners seem to take for granted that probation personnel are not competent for counseling roles? Our people are all highly trained and probably are *more* competent than most personnel in community service agencies.

When the professional person's career and services are called into question by establishing some organizational alternative to them, the result is likely to be a defensive reaction, not a shift in career or even in orientation. Teachers reacted to the "Free School" movement by noting the "incompetence" of noncertified teachers and the "inadequacy" of cheap buildings and furniture. Juvenile justice workers have reacted to the presumed threat of "diversion" by developing and lauding their own diversion programs —sponsored, developed, and directed by juvenile justice professionals —claiming them to be better than the shoddy facilities and "do-gooder" motifs of the paraprofessionals in community service agencies. Research should be addressed to an understanding of the organizational realities of bureaucratic professionals engaged in the dual process of implementing social ideals and establishing successful professional careers.

The temper of national and local justice agencies seems to indicate that diversion is the watchword of the day. On the adult level we are seeking to empty our prisons by diverting offenders to local control agencies. In Massachusetts state juvenile incarceration facilities have gone by the board, and in California a transfer of the state Youth Authority correctional services to the county level is being considered. Everywhere in the realm of juvenile justice there is the belief that a new day is dawning.

The enduring and often intransigent philosophy of juvenile justice that developed at the beginning of the century is experiencing both attack and revival. The *Gault* decision by the Supreme Court in effect asked that the system for processing juveniles be modeled on the processes used in the criminal courts. The spectre of juveniles being submitted to all the disabilities of the adult model of criminal justice has, however, seemingly stirred juvenile officials to reexamine their services. Diversion has been embraced and lauded as a means of implementing the humanistic elements of juvenile justice philosophy—but without incorporating the more structured humanism of the adult due-process model. Thus, it is maintained that diverted juveniles do not need the legal rights available to adults, for they have been removed from the system to be "helped." After all, isn't diversion really rehabilitation or prevention rather than punishment?

The near future should witness many structural changes in the realm of juvenile justice. It appears that there will be a polarization of attitudes and programs: Lawbreaking juveniles are likely to be procesed along the lines of the adult model and hence will receive more due process and less humanistic consideration—after all, are they not merely small criminals? Juveniles who have been called "predelinquents," because they can't get along at home or in school, will be diverted.

The emphasis on diversion, unfortunately, diverts our attention from the etiology of juvenile offenses. It serves to focus our resources on the problem of secondary deviancy rather than on the problem of preventing juveniles from engaging in *initial* acts of deviancy. As a consequence, the proactive process of delinquency prevention is downgraded in favor of expanding our reactive capabilities. We suggest that opinion leaders and decision makers within juvenile justice systems must worry not only about reform of juvenile courts and correctional programs but also about the conditions in homes, schools, and communities that launch children on the march toward the door of the juvenile court in the first place. After all, the labeling theory and differential association theory underlying diversion programs also suggest better child-rearing practices, better educational techniques, and more respect for the delicate status of juveniles.

If recent attempts to guarantee the civil liberties of minors prove successful, present definitions of what constitutes "predelinquency" will become both inadequate and unconstitutional. Juveniles now defined in negativistic terms as "runaways" or "out of control" probably will be redefined as individuals with a legitimate say about their place of residence and other living conditions, including the nature and degree of control imposed by parents or other adults. At present, when communication within a family breaks down, aggressive actions of the adult members are viewed as unfortunate, while aggressive acts of a minor are typically viewed as "predelinquent," "delinquent," or even criminal. As our laws are reformulated to correct this injustice, they will extend constitutional due-process rights to youngsters, creating a critical need for agencies and programs that are truly helpful and noncoercive.

If the policies and programs of diversion serve to pave the way for a better blend of juvenile justice theory and actual societal responses to the problems of youth, then they deserve to be lauded. If, however, diversion becomes merely a bureaucratic means of diverting attention from needed changes in the environment of youth, it will do great injustice. Diversion in the form of rhetorical gloss or mere bureaucratic manipulation is self-serving for the agencies involved, and perhaps it serves only to perpetuate anachronistic institutions. But if other forms of true diversion receive adequate public and private support, they may mitigate the problem of secondary deviancy, and also serve as models for more effective and responsive youth service agencies.

23

ON THE FRONT END
OF THE JUVENILE JUSTICE SYSTEM*

Malcolm W. Klein

The next paper is useful for at least two purposes. First, it illustrates a research *progression,* with each stage raising new or unanticipated questions to be investigated in subsequent procedures. Second, it provides a picture in one large metropolitan area of "preexplosion" diversion. It describes the kinds of referral operations taking place "normally" and provides a baseline against which to judge the growth in diversion programs.

* Unpublished manuscript, Department of Sociology, University of Southern California, Los Angeles, 1971.

My intent in this presentation[1] is not so much to present new data to you—although I will allude to some—as it is to acquaint you with some conclusions about selected aspects of the juvenile justice system as my colleagues and I have recently experienced them. We have been charged with the responsibility of gathering data pertinent to comprehensive planning in the juvenile justice arena.[2] In defining that responsibility for ourselves and for our funding masters, we have chosen to concentrate on what is here inelegantly called "the front end of the juvenile justice system," namely, the police-community connections.

More specifically, we have been concerned with understanding the processes in the "community absorption"[3] of juvenile offenders or the "diversion" of offenders away from the system. How much diversion and absorption take place? For what kinds of offenders? What factors determine absorption and diversion rates? How do these rates affect other system rates,[4] such as probation intake and release, detentions, and court appearances? How can these concerns be related to recidivism as a practical problem, or to labeling as a theoretical problem?

Our data and our impressions are derived from three waves of data

[1] Edited from a presentation to the Pacific Sociological Association, 1971. Four graduate students—Ronald Bates, Susan Labin, Richard Mitchell, and Richard Sundeen—shared in interviewing, questionnaire construction, data analysis, and idea sharing. They have been valued assistants.

[2] The work reported here was carried out under contract to the Public Systems Research Institute of the University of Southern California from the Los Angeles Regional Planning Board, an arm of the California Council on Criminal Justice. Funds from the Ford Foundation have also facilitated the research.

[3] The first use of the term "community absorption," to my knowledge, was in the work of Robert M. Carter and Joseph D. Lohman at Berkeley.

[4] The conceptual framework for this research, as set in a comprehensive planning context, is reported in Malcolm W. Klein, Solomon Kobrin, A. W. McEachern, and Herbert R. Sigurdson, "System Rates: An Approach to Comprehensive Criminal Justice Planning," *Crime and Delinquency,* October 1971, in press.

collection in the police departments within Los Angeles County. These departments consist of the LAPD (17 divisions), the LASD (14 divisions), and 46 (1970) or 47 (1971) smaller departments in various incorporated cities ranging in size from Long Beach, with a population of about 400,000, to Vernon, with a population of 208.[5] The data waves consisted of the following:

1. Interviews in the spring of 1970 with the officers in charge of juvenile matters in all 77 jurisdictions.[6]

2. Interviews in the spring of 1971 with the chief of police in each of these agencies, with the exception of LAPD and LASD.[7]

3. Questionnaires administered to 130 juvenile officers and some of their supervisors in most of these same agencies.[8]

Additional data are derived from questionnaires distributed to private agencies in Los Angeles County. A disappointing 119 of about 400 were returned after follow-up phone calls.

The discussion to follow will concentrate on two substantive areas: (1) connections between community agencies and the police in the person of the juvenile officer, and (2) dispositions of juvenile offenders by the police.

THE POLICE/COMMUNITY CONNECTION

The system.   It is common to describe the juvenile justice system in terms of the formal governmental agencies legally mandated to process juvenile suspects and offenders, i.e., the police, courts, district attorney, public defender, probation and correctional personnel, and so forth. A more careful analysis would suggest that the juvenile justice system should be conceived as including as well various components of the community—in particular, the schools and the private agencies which can absorb juvenile offenders. In comprehensive criminal justice planning, then, one is required to look not only at the *formal agencies* (police, courts, etc.) and their connections, but also at these agencies as they connect with the community components of the system.

How much.   This is just what we have done. We asked juvenile officers about their referrals of youngsters back into the community (diversion) as an alternative to inserting them farther into the formal system. We asked the community agencies about referrals they receive from the police. The first conclusion we can offer is that the diversion process is, at best, minimal. Of 119 private agencies queried for the year 1969, 3 reported receiving refer-

---

[5] Population estimates for 1969 were provided by the Los Angeles Sheriff's Department.

[6] A few substitutions were necessary, but never involving someone unfamiliar with the department's juvenile staff.

[7] Three of these were acting chiefs; one was a lieutenant substituting for a chief who refused the interview because "It's all written down in our manuals."

[8] Two departments were omitted because no officer was given any specific juvenile responsibilities.

rals from LAPD, 2 from LASD, and 8 from one or more of the other 46 departments. In all, these connections led to 428 referrals. By way of contrast, there were 6,142 referrals to 84 of the 119 agencies from probation, court, and correctional components of the system. Available private agencies are used for rehabilitation, but not for diversion.

This picture, derived from the absorbing agencies, does not change substantially if we take our perspective from police sources. Only nineteen of the smaller cities in the 1970 study reported making direct referrals; i.e., they made the connection by phone or mail. Others mentioned or recommended agencies to the families of the offenders. But 20 percent (1970) and 17 percent (1971) in the small agencies said they did not do even this; i.e., they made *no* referrals. In the LAPD and LASD, 45 percent reported making no referrals.

I might repeat that these data come from personal interviews and questionnaires. Almost none of the police agencies keep a record of referrals to community agencies. The recording necessitated by the FBI and the state's Bureau of Criminal Statistics likewise makes no explicit reference to such referrals. That is, the "System" expresses no interest in, and therefore receives no information about, the workings of its input and diversion module.

Crime commissions, planning agencies, and sociologists are all expounding on the merits of the diversion process. If Southern California may serve as an example, it is clear that the message is not leading to much implementation among police agencies or among the agencies responsible for information processing.

Why. Several reasons for this situation emerge from our interviews.

1.   The supposed merits of diversion have not been well documented to the police officer, who is taught that an offender on the streets is an inherent danger.

2.   Juvenile officers do not seek out, nor are they urged to seek out, suitable referral agencies. By the same token, few private agencies offer themselves as willing absorbers of delinquency. Thus the modal number of private agencies known to our smaller-city juvenile officer respondents in 1970 and 1971 was two! In six cities, the officers in 1970 could not name a single private agency to whom youngsters might be referred. Nor is this "accidental" or temporary ignorance of resources. Exactly half of the 1971 respondents reported belonging to no community organizations in the communities they served. Half did not live in the community served. Yet the median number of police associations for these same officers was two and one-half. The situation was even worse in the LAPD and LASD. In these two agencies, officers in one-fourth of the stations could not name any community resources.

3.   The police officer's perspective on suitable referral cases is typically narrow as well. The preferred case is a girl, a younger child, a first offender, a transgressor of a nonserious statute, or a combination of these.

4.   The police officer's definition of an acceptable referral resource is quite narrow. It typically excludes employment resources, free clinics and similar informal community drug facilities, and agencies with a taste of radicalism or militancy or a high proportion of lay voluntarism.

5.   Of those that *are* seen as appropriate, a number of potential resource agencies

are undermanned, with long waiting lists, or have restricted client criteria, or are not geared for immediate response to police referrals.

6. Police officers—despite their often avowed antipathy toward the treatment process—often expressed to us a strong bias in favor of psychiatrically oriented programs—the more casework, the better. Relatively few agencies can provide much by way of genuine psychiatric treatment for juvenile offenders.

7. In some departments, policy or pressure from the top militates against extensive diversion practices.

Remedial action. That some of these barriers can be overcome and the diversion rate increased substantially has been demonstrated recently by a special project in Los Angeles. The Sheriff's Department and the County Department of Community Services have launched a pilot project at a sheriff's station in East Los Angeles.[9] In 1969, this station had a below-average diversion rate of 38.6 percent, and made only an occasional juvenile referral to a church or to the Salvation Army.

During the pilot project, a sheriff's lieutenant was placed in the station with the explicit mandate to see what might be done to increase the diversion rate. He investigated potential resources in the community and worked closely with the juvenile officers. Within the first forty days of the project, thirty-five youths were diverted to ten agencies, a remarkable change in organizational behavior. Only three of these failed to make the agency connection.

Labeling theory. Theoretically, the situation just described represents a rather nice opportunity for some empirical testing of labeling theory. Labeling is clearly our most widely accepted, untested formulation,[10] and I would hope that someone might rise to the challenge presented by current police practices.

Methodologically, my point is this: Because police diversion is so low at present, and because it can be increased so dramatically, we have an opportunity to study the effects of alternative diversion practices against a stable baseline. Diversion without referral, referral to parents, referral to private agencies of specifiable types, and referral to nonwardship probation may all represent *different types or levels of labeling or stigmatization*. With some control over the types of diversion procedures, a reasonable field experiment on the effects of alternative labeling procedures seems feasible. Our interview experience in the police departments in Los Angeles suggests that many police agencies might be willing to participate in such an experimental operation.

[9] The first progress report on the Police Community Referral Project is available from the Los Angeles Department of Community Services.

[10] Approaches to dealing with labeling using delinquency data include A. W. McEachern, Edward M. Taylor, J. Robert Newman, and Ann E. Ashford, "The Juvenile Probation System: Simulation for Research and Decision-Making," *American Behavioral Scientist*, 11, No. 3 (Jan.–Feb. 1968), pp. 1–43; Gerald G. O'Connor, "The Impact of Initial Detention upon Male Delinquents," *Social Problems*, 18, No. 2 (Fall 1970), pp. 194–199. Neither of these studies lends support to the contention that labeling begets further deviance.

DISPOSITION OF JUVENILE CASES

I'd like to turn now to our great enigma. During the 1970 interviews, we collected annual disposition summaries from each of the police agencies, and from the seventeen individual stations of the LAPD and fourteen stations of the LASD. Taken from FBI or BCS forms, these dispositions fall into five categories:

1. Handled within department and released.
2. Referred to juvenile court or probation department.
3. Referred to welfare agency.
4. Referred to other police agency.
5. Referred to criminal or adult court.

Variability. Only the first two categories are used with any frequency: that is, station release (diversion) and referral to court or probation (system insertion). Concentrating on the diversion rates, we found the average among the forty-six smaller cities to be 54.3 percent. Slightly over half of all arrested juveniles are diverted away from the system at the point of police intake. However, the range of diversion rates went from a low of 2 percent in one department to a high of 82 percent in another.[11] We tried to account for this variation across departments by reference to other available data on department size, structure, and caseload; training of the juvenile officers; available community resources for diversion; demographic status of the community on eleven variables such as population density, proportion of juveniles, ethnicity, and income levels; and finally we investigated offense levels and seriousness. Sad to say, these analyses shed little light and accounted for relatively little of the variance in our data.

If there was any discernible pattern at all through these analyses, it was the slight suggestion that departmental or organizational factors might emerge as the best predictors of the obtained diversion rates.[12] Further, our 1970 interviews hinted, although we had not deliberately set out to investigate this topic, that one additional source of variance might be in the definition of the diversion rate's denominator, that is, the definition of a juvenile arrest.

Diversion factors. To throw light on these two possibilities, we have returned to our suburban departments and completed two of three data

[11] Similar rate variability has been reported in David J. Bordua, "Recent Trends: Deviant Behavior and Social Control," *Annals of the American Academy of Political and Social Science,* 359 (Jan. 1967), pp. 149–166.

[12] Support for such a contention can be found in Don C. Gibbons, *Delinquent Behavior,* Englewood Cliffs, N.J., Prentice-Hall, 1970, p. 89; A. W. McEachern and Riva Bauzer, "Factors Related to Dispositions in Juvenile Police Contacts" in Malcolm W. Klein (ed.), *Juvenile Gangs in Context: Theory, Research, and Action,* Englewood Cliffs, N.J., Prentice-Hall, 1967, pp. 148–160, especially Table 10; James Q. Wilson, "The Police and the Delinquent in Two Cities" in Stanton Wheeler (ed.), *Controlling Delinquents,* New York, John Wiley & Sons, 1968.

collection waves. We have interviewed 46 police chiefs[13] and we have administered questionnaires to 130 juvenile officers and a few of their supervisors.[14]

Uniformly, the chiefs claim to have neither a diversion nor a system insertion policy; 37 of the 46 said theirs was a policy of making individual case decisions. Four said they had no policy, and only 6 claimed one of the directional policies. The pattern among the juvenile officers was the same; 87 percent said each case was judged on its merits, with no overall preference for diversion or system insertion.

Fortunately, we had instructed the interviewers to note their impressions of the chiefs' positions at the end of the interview. This yielded 27 *diversion* policies, 16 *case-decision* policies, and 4 *system-insertion* policies. Unfortunately, these interviewer impressions do not relate directly to high and low diversion rates, so we are still in the dark.

When we asked the chiefs to give us direct help and reported to them the 2 to 82 percent range in rates, their responses were interesting, but not of such uniformity as to provide us with new directions. The most common rate determinant suggested by them was the chief himself; i.e., they suggested that the chief set the policy on diversion and that the departmental rates were determined by that policy. Our analysis suggests that this was not, in fact, happening. The next most common determinant suggested was community pressure and community characteristics. Again, we find no support in our analyses.

Other suggestions emerged—workload, experience of the officers, lack of uniformity in reporting—but I can't honestly say that the chiefs' expertise has yielded much more by way of explanation than had already occurred to us. We have higher hopes for an analysis being performed by Richard Sundeen, who is relating chiefs' policy, levels of policy implementation, and juvenile officers' orientations, such as professionalization and community attachments.

Definitional problems.   As indicated, there are also some definitional problems. Technically, the word "arrest" is not applied to juveniles in California. Juveniles are detained or not detained, and petitions are filed —or not—to insert offenders into the probation and court systems. In practice, however, everyone speaks of juvenile arrests, and the FBI reporting system specifically requests dispositions of "persons arrested under eighteen years of age."

We knew from the 1970 interviews that juvenile officers were not of one mind about the definition or criteria of a juvenile arrest. When we put this issue to the chiefs in 1971, we found a similar situation. A few clearly were puzzled by the question and then did their best to "wing it." Others had a quick and direct answer—eleven different answers, in fact (e.g., arrest equals contact, or restraint, or custody, or station detention, etc.). Twenty-

[13] In addition to the one refusal mentioned earlier, one new department materialized between the 1970 and 1971 research waves.

[14] Much of the questionnaire administration was undertaken by the fifty-second class of U.S.C.'s Delinquency Control Institute as part of their field training. Most of the class members are, have been, or will be juvenile police officers.

one of forty-seven cited booking as the critical point. This number still represents less than 50 percent agreement among the chiefs (no wonder juvenile officers are often unclear on this issue) and makes *no* sense in terms of the actual recording procedures used for the FBI and BCS. If booked youngsters alone were considered arrested, the diversion rates would plummet.

Thus we must go back once more, as we have planned from the outset, to watch the actual recording procedures—to look over the shoulder of the records clerk who may have the final and most vital say in the definition of these rates. As the denominator (number of arrests) is defined operationally, so is the diversion rate. Thus different recording operations may contribute to the diversion rate variability, and remedial actions leading to uniform defining and recording procedures may greatly increase our understanding of departmental differences in diversion practices.

Mention of one other project plan will illustrate the importance of such data. We have received approval to return to the nine cities with the highest diversion rates and the nine with the lowest rates, for the purpose of determining recidivism rates. Although this will be far from a controlled experiment on labeling, it does approach the issue on a different level than is often undertaken and will move us one step closer to defining the labeling problem empirically.

But the critical point here is this: comparing high- and low-diversion-rate departments is defensible only if the denominator of those rates (i.e., number of arrests) is defined with some uniformity. If the arrest definitions used for recording purposes are too disparate, then any analyses employing rates based on these definitions will be next to useless. While the doors to these police stations remain open to us, we must concentrate much of our energies on these very basic methodological issues.

SUMMARY

Let me restate very briefly some of the foregoing material. First, we have learned that the diversion process is at best minimal. The police are not currently connecting many juvenile offenders with resources in the community. The reasons are plentiful and reside both with police practices and with inadequacies in the community. Second, the variability in diversion rates among police departments seems *not* to be explained by reference to our usual sociological and social psychological variables. Finally—and this may be taken as a plea and an open invitation—there is much room in this arena for some useful and, in my view, theoretically exciting research. And especially with respect to labeling theory, the field is in desperate need of careful empirical work.

24
POLICE PROFESSIONALIZATION AND COMMUNITY ATTACHMENTS AND DIVERSION OF JUVENILES FROM THE JUSTICE SYSTEM*

Richard A. Sundeen, Jr.

Following up on the research reported in the previous pages, Sundeen has attempted to account for the wide variation in referral or diversion practices. Significantly, no simple relationships emerge on the major independent variables, the orientations of the referring officers themselves. The few relationships that do emerge are rather complex. Whatever it is that leads one department to be "tough" and another to be "lenient" in the handling of juveniles is not obvious, nor, it seems, is it related to the variables that ordinarily come to mind.

* From *Criminology*, 11, 4(1974): pp. 570–580. Reprinted by permission of the author and publisher, Sage Publications, Inc. I wish to thank Malcolm Klein and Daniel Glaser for helpful comments on an earlier draft of this paper.

This paper reports a study of the association between certain characteristics of police departments and police diversion of juveniles from the justice system.[1] The meaning of diversion used here is the return of the juvenile offender by the police to the community—the family or, possibly, a community agency for guidance or treatment—rather than his referral to an official sanctioning agency, e.g., the probation department and juvenile court.[2]

The significance of the police in this process has been suggested by Lemert[3] when he writes that through arrests and court referrals the police have the "strategic power to determine what proportions and what kinds of youth problems become official and which ones are absorbed back into the community." Besides this gate-keeping function for the justice system and its potential labeling effect on the juvenile, the police may also have their own labeling effect on the juvenile. For instance, Wattenberg and Bufe[4] con-

[1] The study was carried out in conjunction with a larger research project on juvenile system rates. The principal investigator was Malcolm W. Klein (see Klein's study, "On the front end of the juvenile system," presented at the annual meeting of the Pacific Sociological Association, Honolulu, April 8, 1971).

[2] Regarding diversion and community absorption of juveniles, see R. M. Carter, *Middle-Class Delinquency: An Experiment in Community Control* (Berkeley: University of California School of Criminology, 1968); V. Eisner, *The Delinquency Label: The Epidemiology of Juvenile Delinquency* (New York: Random House, 1969); E. M. Lemert, *Instead of Court: Diversion in Juvenile Justice* (Chevy Chase, Md.: National Institute of Mental Health Center for Studies of Crime and Delinquency, 1971).

[3] Lemert, *op. cit.,* p. 54.

[4] W. W. Wattenburg and N. Bufe, "The effectiveness of police youth bureau officers," *Journal of Criminal Law, Criminology, and Police Science* 54 (December 1963): 475.

cluded from their study of initial police-juvenile contacts that "the relatively brief contact between a boy or his family and a police officer may be highly influential on a future 'career' in delinquency." Also, Gold[5] attributed apprehension by police as the factor which explained recidivism among a matched group of juveniles.

A majority of the relatively few studies concerning police diversion of juveniles focus on the relationship between the disposition decision and characteristics of the juveniles and their offenses; but findings have not been wholly conclusive, and McEachern and Bauzer[6] conclude that "dispositions are just as much a function of who the police are as of what the delinquent is like." Goldman,[7] in a study of four communities, found that the more integrated the police were with the community, the greater were the number of arrests of juveniles, but the less frequently their cases were referred to juvenile court. Comparing justice in two cities, Cicourel[8] noted that the professional orientation of police departments "emphasizes social control and an efficient administrative operation . . . [and] does not include the allocation of time for a 'treatment oriented' approach to 'helping' youth." This focus on social control and efficiency increases the size of the "law enforcement net" which determines the proportion of juveniles to be processed as delinquent.

Wilson[9] attributed the difference in diversion rates between a Western and an Eastern police department to whether or not the department had a "fraternal" or a "professional" ethos. The professional department officers had more formal education and police training, more complex attitudes toward delinquency, tended to enforce the law more impartially and impersonally, were more likely to come in contact with juveniles, and, once in contact, to arrest or cite (as opposed to reprimand) than their counterparts in the fraternal department. On the other hand, the fraternal department officers were allowed a wide range of discretion in dealing with juveniles. With regard to community attachments, the fraternal force officers tended to be locals from lower-class backgrounds, while the officers from the professional force came from areas outside the city and had not been exposed as youth to lower-class culture.

RATIONALE AND PROCEDURE

These studies suggest that police diversion of juveniles is a function of the department's professionalization and its community attachments. It was hypothesized that level of professionalization, defined as commitment to police work, is associated with legalism, the detached and universalistic

[5] M. Gold, *Delinquent Behavior in an American City* (Belmont, Calif.: Brooks/Cole, 1970).

[6] A. W. McEachern and R. Bauzer, "Factors related to disposition in juvenile police contacts," in *Juvenile Gangs in Context: Theory, Research, and Action*, ed. M. W. Klein (Englewood Cliffs, N.J.: Prentice-Hall, 1967), p. 151.

[7] N. Goldman, *The Differential Selection of Juvenile Offenders for Court Appearance* (New York: National Council on Crime and Delinquency, 1963).

[8] A. V. Cicourel, *The Social Organization of Juvenile Justice* (New York: Wiley, 1968), pp. 64–65.

[9] J. Wilson, "The police and the delinquent in two cities," in *Controlling Delinquents*, ed. S. Wheeler (New York: Wiley, 1968), pp. 9–30.

treatment of juveniles. It was inferred that professionalism in police service promotes an effort to be impersonal, unbiased, and procedurally correct; and, therefore, highly professionalized police are more likely to refer youths uniformly to juvenile court, rather than to treat them in a particularistic way. This legalistic orientation conceives of "really doing police work" as detection and prosecution rather than crime prevention and social work.[10] In this sense, the professional policeman was hypothesized to be legalistic, in wanting to make "good" arrests and to pass offenders on to the other components of the justice system.

High community attachment was hypothesized to imply a less legalistic orientation. The assumption here is that the more the officers participate in the life of the local community, especially on a voluntary basis, the more their particularistic types of relationships and orientations will be reinforced.[11] Rather than routinely or uniformly applying formal rules, they are likely to treat juveniles on the basis of personal judgments and thus be willing to make exceptions or "give the kid a break" because of his circumstances. Because of their personal knowledge of the youth and the community, they may feel that it is in the best interest of the juvenile to keep him in the community rather than expose him to the possible detrimental influences of detention facilities. Also, of course, these officers may be guided in their decisions by local prejudices and stereotyping that develop within the community regarding juveniles.

VARIABLES

The two independent variables—professionalization and community attachment—were operationalized by using five items for each concept. The professionalization indicators were the following: (1) amount of police professional organization activities of juvenile officers; (2) participation by juvenile officers in training programs in juvenile matters; (3) an estimate by juvenile officers of the proportion of social friends who are police officers; (4) the level of formal education of juvenile officers; and (5) readership of police journals by juvenile officers.[12] The five community attachment indicators included the following: (1) the amount of community organization activities of juvenile officers; (2) local residence of juvenile officers; (3) the number of community events participated in by juvenile officers; (4) an estimate by juvenile officers of the proportion of social friends who are local people; and (5) knowledge of and estimate of use of local referral resources for youth by juvenile officers.[13]

[10] J. L. Walsh, "Professionalism and the police: the cop as a medical student," *American Behavioral Scientist* 13 (May–August 1970): 707.

[11] Regarding relationships in the horizontal pattern of a community system, see R. L. Warren, *The Community in America* (Chicago: Rand McNally, 1963), p. 270.

[12] See Walsh, *op. cit.,* p. 720.

[13] The reliability coefficients of two original community attachment and professionalization scales were lower than would be desired. This points to the difficulty in operationalizing an "ethos" which is composed of a variety of components all more or less related to occupational or community commitment. Because of the low internal consistency of the items, an alternative analysis was employed—more exploratory in nature—using five items to represent each of the two independent variables.

The dependent variable, legalism, is negatively indicated by diversion from the justice system. It was operationalized by use of the 1969 counsel and release rates of the departments under study. This rate is computed by dividing the total number of juveniles arrested into the total number of juveniles counseled and released (technically referred to as "Handled within the Department"). Rates among the departments varied from 19 to 82 percent.

The sample under study included forty-three police department juvenile bureaus and details in Los Angeles County.[14] Chiefs of each department were interviewed and roughly 80 percent ($n = 130$) of all juvenile bureau personnel completed a questionnaire concerning community attachment, professionalization, and departmental policy and structure. Police officers studying at the Delinquency Control Institute at the University of Southern California administered the majority of the instruments, after receiving training in questionnaire administration.

The basic unit of analysis for the study was the juvenile bureau. There were two reasons for this choice: (1) the dependent variable—the counsel and release rate—is a departmental rate; and (2) from direct observation there appears to be a substantial amount of informal interaction among juvenile officers with regard to handling cases, suggesting that disposition decisions are the product of group norms. Therefore, the departmental mean for each item, based on the individuals within each department, was employed. The independent variables were dichotomized, and the counsel and release rate was trichotomized. Statistics used were Somers' d_{yx} and chi-square.[15]

FINDINGS

Based on the rationale, it was expected that the professionalization items would be inversely related to counsel and release rate, while the community attachment items would be positively associated with the diversion indicator.

Tables 1 and 2 present zero-order association coefficients between the ten variables and the counsel and release rate. Also, to add a degree of complexity to the model, the relationships are examined when bureaucratic control, defined as the extent to which the officers' decisions are reviewed by superiors, is held constant.[16] Bureaucratic control was included as a control

[14] This includes all police departments in Los Angeles County—with the exceptions of Los Angeles Police Department and Los Angeles County Sheriff's Department, excluded because of their size—and four smaller departments. Two of them did not have juvenile bureaus, while the other two did not have counsel and release data. Data collection occurred during February and March 1971.

[15] R. H. Somers, "On the measurement of association," *American Sociological Review* 30 (June 1968): 291–292; *idem*, "A new asymmetric measure of association for ordinal variables," *American Sociological Review* 27 (December 1962): 802–811.

[16] Bureaucratic control or decentralized decision making within the juvenile bureau was based on the responses by the officers to the following question: "What kinds of procedures are used to implement the policy [of your department]; that is, must the disposition be approved, reviewed, or evaluated by a supervisor? Explain." The responses to this question were grouped by departments and all answers of a department placed on a separate card. (The departments

variable to determine the effects of orientation (community attachment and professionalization) under the conditions of high and low discretion in decision making. It was expected that under low bureaucratic control, when officers have the greatest discretion, orientations would be most likely to come into play and have a more substantial effect.

First, looking at the magnitude of the associations, regardless of direction, the general trend is that of relatively low coefficients. Further, only eight of the thirty coefficients are statistically significant relationships as measured by chi-square, and three of these are curvilinear relationships.[17] These findings suggest the need for a more comprehensive approach to explain differences in diversion of juveniles by police, which would include consideration not only of characteristics of departments, but also characteristics of the communities and of the juvenile offenders and how the three interact.

However, in spite of the absence of any single variable which apparently explains most of the differences in diversion rates, there is value in examining and comparing the independent variables in their capacity to improve prediction of the dependent variable. For example, one will note that not all of the indicators are associated in the hypothesized direction. Only amount of juvenile training (Table 1), estimate of friends who are local people, and local residence (Table 2) tend to fit the hypothesized relationships.

It appears that with regard to diversion and community attachment, there is a qualitative difference as to the manner by which a department is integrated with the community. For example, it may be that—in contrast to community ties by way of participation in events and organizations—juvenile officers who live in the community or are closely attached because of numerous primary relationships feel that the local community can deal better with juveniles than can the official agents of the justice system. This possible distinction in the way police are integrated with a community has implications for further study with respect to police-juvenile relations, community relations, and the issue of community control of police.

As for the professionalization items, departments with policemen highly trained in juvenile matters appear to be a different breed. The juvenile officers with more training may process juveniles dispassionately and uniformly in a universalistic and legalistic sense (as predicted), or they may be trained to believe that the juvenile justice system is actually most effective in dealing with individuals in a particularistic sense. The latter of these speculations received support as the juvenile-training item was positively associated

---

could not be identified.) Two judges, one of them being this writer, rated each department as to whether the responses indicated a high or low degree of centralized control over the disposition decisions of the juvenile officers. The judges agreed on forty-two out of forty-three cases, and a third judge made the decision on the single case of disagreement.

[17] In these instances of curvilinear relationships, it appears that isolation from departmental controls and important reference groups produced extreme counsel and release rates, i.e., divergent from the average of all departments in the sample. This suggests the following proposition: Under conditions of high discretion in decision making, the greater the identification with the profession or the community, the greater the conformity to the norm for diversion (the moderate or average rates); and conversely, the less identification with the profession or community, the greater the divergence from the norm (higher or lower rates).

TABLE 1

Counsel and Release Rate by Professionalization Indicators: Zero-Order and Specified Associations[a]

	(n)	Formal Education	Juvenile Training	Police Friends	Police Organizations	Police Journals
1. Zero-Order associations with counsel and release rate	(43)	.23	$-.31^{b}$	.23	$.30^{c}$	$-.03^{c}$
2. Specified associations						
High bureaucratic control	(19)	.16	$-.17^{\cdot}$	.34	.33	0.0
Low bureaucratic control	(24)	.24	$-.40^{b}$	.19	.26	$-.05^{d}$

[a] Measure of association is d_{yx}.
[b] $p < .05.$
[c] $x^2: p < .10$ (one tail).
[d] $p < .01.$

TABLE 2

Counsel and Release Rate by Community Attachment Indicators: Zero-Order and Specified Associations[a]

	(n)	No. Comm. Events	Local Friends	Community Organizations	Local Residence	Referral Resources
1. Zero-order association with counsel and release rate	(43)	$-.11$	$.31^{b}$	$-.04$	.11	.15
2. Specified associations						
High bureaucratic control	(19)	$-.38$	.17	0.0	0.0	.19
Low bureaucratic control	(24)	$.07^{c}$	$.41^{b}$	$-.05$	.19	.17

[a] Measure of association is d_{yx}.
[b] $x^2: p < .10$ (one tail).
[c] $p < .05.$

with a ten-item particularistic orientation scale (while the number-of-police-organizations item had a negative association).

In contrast to the image of the "professional" department as portrayed by Wilson,[18] where formal education and police training were both emphasized, among the departments of this sample, level of education and amount of juvenile training had opposite relationships with diversion. This raises important theoretical as well as policy questions regarding differing modes of socialization for juvenile officers, images of professionalism, and their consequences for diversion.

Further analysis regarding the effects of different kinds of training remains to be completed. However, at this point it appears that these findings may have some convergence with those of Wheeler et al.,[19] who found that among judges, those with more training in behavioral sciences and, consequently, with more therapeutically oriented attitudes, were more likely than others to commit juveniles to institutions.

An additional interpretation of the data is that professionalization and community attachment should not be treated as constants in the norms they propagate regarding treatment of juveniles. For example, certain kinds of community attachment by police may be a function of highly professionalized community relations programs which spawn rather impersonal and legalistic attitudes toward the community and its juveniles. Further, some police training programs may stress flexible order maintenance, while others stress stringent law enforcement, as police norms.[20] Such differences might explain the low coefficients and bipolar patterns in the data.

SUMMARY AND CONCLUSIONS

The findings of this study generally lead to the conclusion that police characteristics alone (professionalization and community attachment) do not explain police diversion of juveniles. One possible avenue of inquiry would be to examine the combined effects of police, offender, and community characteristics.

Despite this caveat, the findings suggest there is some utility in comparing the relative strengths of various police characteristics in predicting diversion of juveniles. The amount of juvenile training received by the officers, the estimate of local friendships of the officers, and the officers' residence were the best predictors of diversion rates.

The major problem encountered was developing an adequate conceptual framework concerning police orientations and identifying appropriate indicators of police characteristics and orientations. It was found that a single dimension, such as professionalization-community attachment, has limited

[18] Wilson, *op. cit.*

[19] S. Wheeler, E. Bonacich, M. R. Cramer, and I. K. Zola, "Agents of delinquency control: a comparative analysis," in *Controlling Delinquents,* ed. S. Wheeler (New York: Wiley, 1968), pp. 31–60.

[20] E. Bittner, "The police on skid row: a study of peacekeeping," *American Sociological Review* 32 (October 1967): 699–715; J. Wilson, *Varieties of Police Behavior: The Management of Law and Order in Eight Communities* (Cambridge: Harvard University Press, 1968).

value in characterizing juvenile bureau orientations vis-à-vis diversion of juveniles. (It has been suggested that bipolar constructs, such as local-cosmopolitan, while being logical and tidy, are generally overly simplistic.[21]) Further, the findings also raise critical questions concerning the meaning of professionalization and the indicators often used to measure it when dealing with occupational groups such as the police.[22]

[21] A. J. Grimes and P. K. Berger, "Cosmopolitan-local: evaluation of the construct," *Administrative Science Quarterly* 15 (December 1970): 407–416. The authors regard the use of the bipolar construct "local-cosmopolitan" to be similar conceptually to the professional-fraternal typology. They point out the need for more complex constructs, such as mixed types as opposed to single dimensions, and the difficulty in operationalizing such constructs.

[22] Several writers have commented on this issue and concluded that the police as an occupational group do not constitute a profession as defined by most models of professionalization. See, for example, D. Matza, *Delinquency and Drift* (New York: Wiley, 1964); D. J. Bordua and A. J. Reiss, Jr., "Law enforcement," in *The Uses of Sociology,* eds. Paul Lazarsfeld et al (New York: Basic Books, 1967), pp. 275–303; E. Cumming, *Systems of Social Regulation* (New York: Atherton, 1968).

25

JUVENILE REFERRAL
AND RECIDIVISM*

Suzanne Bugas Lincoln

In the absence of planned experimental controls, the best one can do is to strive for retrospective controls by means of individual matching of (hopefully) similar subjects. Using this approach, Lincoln compares the recidivism rates for referred youngsters in a pilot diversion project with matched youngsters handled in other ways. The findings are discouraging, with no differences in numbers of recidivists and worse records for referred than for nonreferred youngsters among those who do recidivate. Note also Lincoln's comments on referral as an alternative to insertion in the juvenile justice system and as an alternative to outright release.

* Unpublished manuscript, Department of Sociology, University of Southern California, Los Angeles, 1974. Reprinted by permission of the author.

By one estimate, there are now hundreds of diversion projects in operation in the United States, and more being initiated or planned.[1] The terms "referral" and "diversion" are used interchangeably here to mean noncriminal disposition of a case with instructions to the offender to appear at a community service agency for treatment, in lieu of having to appear in court.

[1] Elizabeth W. Vorenberg and James Vorenberg, "Early Diversion from the Criminal Justice System." In Lloyd E. Ohlin (ed.), *Prisoners in America.* Prentice-Hall, Inc., Englewood Cliffs, N.J., 1973.

This paper reports on the pilot period of a referral program for juvenile offenders in one station of a large police agency in a major city of a western state.

Diversion programs seem to represent police practitioners' translations of the labeling theoretical approach in sociology.[2] Labeling theorists point out that social control agencies may help to create deviant behavior by imputing deviant identity to individuals who commit isolated deviant acts. Legal stigmatization may be internalized, making recidivism (repeat offenses) more likely. Police officers and diversion counselors maintain that juvenile diversion programs are aimed at reducing recidivism by diverting juvenile offenders away from the stigmatizing and criminalizing effects of the juvenile justice system.

It is important to attempt to evaluate the empirical validity of these expectations for the diversion movement. Police referral to community agencies might constitute more humane treatment of juvenile delinquents, and if police diversion relieves the courts, it might save the taxpayers' money as well. But the biggest hope of all is that police diversion can reduce recidivism. This paper is concerned with evaluating one police referral project in terms of its effectiveness in reducing repeat offenses among the juveniles involved in the project in its pilot period. The situation discussed also lends itself to a brief empirical statement on labeling theory, to the extent that referral may be regarded as the practitioners' operationalization of labeling theory.

METHODOLOGICAL PROCEDURES

In July and August of 1970, a large police agency in conjunction with a metropolitan planning and coordination agency launched a pilot project to refer juvenile offenders to community agencies for social services. The pilot referral program was headed by a police lieutenant, who screened potential resource agencies on the basis of "willingness to accept referrals, service capability, and organizational stability." During the pilot period, the first forty days of the referral program, thirty youths were diverted from the justice system and referred to ten agencies in the community. The ten participating community agencies provided health care, recreational and social opportunities, employment assistance, and individual and family counseling and protective services.

A preliminary one-month progress report available from the coordinating agency reveals enthusiasm and optimism concerning the effectiveness of the referral program on the basis of the verbal reports of both agency personnel and the juveniles referred to the agencies. Nevertheless, in spring of 1971, an evaluative research effort was solicited to determine if the referral program was having an effect in deterring recidivism. To facilitate this research, police personnel made their records available both at the station level and at a central repository for all county juvenile police rec-

[2] Edwin M. Lemert, *Instead of Court*. National Institute of Mental Health, Rockville, Md., 1972; Edwin M. Schur, *Labeling Deviant Behavior*. Harper & Row, Publishers, New York, 1971.

ords. Data were gathered in late summer and fall of 1971, so that juveniles had exactly one year from the date of the "instant" offense in which to recidivate. The instant offense is the offense for which the juvenile has been apprehended so as to be included in the sample studied.

The independent variable here was conceived to be alternative police handling procedures: referral versus normal insertion of offenders into the juvenile justice system. The dependent variables were features of repeat offense behavior—number of subsequent offenses and average seriousness of subsequent offenses. To determine the effects on recidivism of the referral program most reliably, it would have been desirable to assign offenders randomly to the two experimental conditions of referral and insertion into the justice system in order to control systematically for confounding effects. However, the police were not willing to assign offenders to an untested treatment program on a random basis. Rather, the referral decision was left up to the discretion of individual police officers at the station.

A number of confounding variables are known to be associated with both offenders' recidivism patterns and with police discretionary decisions independently of the effects of community referral. These confounding factors on which it is desirable to try to control are: race, sex, age, whether the juvenile lives in an intact family, seriousness of the offense for which the juvenile was apprehended, and number and seriousness of the juvenile's prior record of offenses. It was clearly necessary to determine whether referred offenders differed in any confounding way from typical offenders as a result of police discretion in selecting offenders for referral, or for any other reason. Toward that end, the referred offenders were compared as a group with a typical comparison group. Then referred offenders were matched with offenders of similar characteristics to adjust for discrepancies between the referred and typical offenders on confounding characteristics.

Data on all referred and nonreferred juveniles were obtained using only existing police records.[3] The referred were compared as a group with a larger group of recent offenders from the same neighborhoods. This typical group of about 250 offenders comprised the entire number of juveniles (for whom records could be located) apprehended in the forty-day period immediately preceding the forty-day referral pilot period. Thus, there were no factors such as police personnel turnover or significant historical changes rendering the referred group and the typical group incomparable.

The referred group was also compared with a second group of offenders, a small group of thirty offenders selected from among the large typical group of offenders on the explicit basis of similarity to the referred juveniles with respect to the above confounding factors affecting police discretion and offender recidivism patterns. In this way it was possible to compare the

---

[3] Files could not be located for about 15 percent of all individuals, leaving about 250 offenders included in the large group which would serve as a baseline against which to compare the referred group of thirty juveniles. In order to facilitate identification of behavioral determinants, it will be essential to develop better public record-keeping procedures and reliable system rates. See Daniel Glaser, *Routinizing Evaluation: Getting Feedback on Effectiveness of Crime and Delinquency Programs.* National Institute of Mental Health; Rockville, Md., 1973; Malcolm W. Klein, Solomon Kobrin, A. W. McEachern, and Herbert R. Sigurdson, "System Rates: An Approach to Comprehensive Criminal Justice Planning." *Crime and Delinquency* (October 1971).

referred group with another baseline—a group of similar offenders who had been handled by the police in the usual way.

Thus, the effects of the pilot referral program upon recidivism patterns were, in effect, isolated from the confounding influences of such variables as race, sex, etc., which are known to be associated with police discretionary decisions and with repeat offense behavior, apart from the effects of referral. Again, matching cases was the only quasi-experimental procedure available, random assignment of cases to referred and nonreferred conditions having been ruled out by authorities.

In summary, this research utilizes recorded police documents in order (1) to characterize the referred juveniles relative to a large baseline group of typical offenders, (2) to compare the recidivism patterns of the referred group with the recidivism patterns of this baseline typical group, and (3) to compare the recidivism patterns of the referred group with the recidivism patterns of the small group of similar but nonreferred offenders selected from among the typical offenders group. The purpose of these comparisons is simply to characterize the referred juveniles as a group relative to a meaningful baseline, and to dramatize the effects of police referral upon recidivism among the referred offenders.

RESEARCH FINDINGS

When the referred group of offenders was compared with the large baseline group, the data revealed that juvenile officers selected offenders for referral who were more likely to be members of the prominant local minority than the typical group and more likely to reside in the area surrounding the station than the typical group. The community-oriented rationale of the referral program probably accounts for both of these discrepancies between the referred group and the typical group, because residents of the area were preferred referrals, and the area surrounding the station is quite homogeneous with regard to this minority ethnicity. Specifically, within the typical group about 71 percent of the apprehended caucasians did not reside within the area, and 87 percent of the apprehended minority members did reside in the area. The vast majority of offenders in both groups were minority members.

The data revealed that there were about 75 percent males and 25 percent females in both the referred group and the typical group. The groups did not differ with regard to age, either. The average age in both groups was about sixteen years. It is important to notice that juvenile officers did not refer predominantly young or female offenders, since younger offenders and female offenders are usually considered less serious offenders.

In both the referred and the typical group much information was missing on the status of offenders' families, whether intact or not. In general, however, the pattern across family categories was similar for both groups. Most juveniles in both groups lived with their mothers and fathers together, or with their mothers alone. Only about one-third of the offenders in both groups lived in intact family units where both parents were present.

Looking at the seriousness of the instant offenses, the data reveal that the average seriousness of the instant offenses is insignificantly lower for the referred group than for the typical group.[4] For the referred group, the instant offense was serious enough to evoke the most severe disposition in about 13 percent of the cases. For the typical group, the instant offense was serious enough to evoke the most severe disposition in about 15 percent of the cases—not a large difference.

The referred group did differ from the typical group with regard to both number and average seriousness of prior offenses. The typical group committed an average of three offenses prior to the instant offense, whereas the referred group committed an average of one offense prior to the instant offense. Prior offenses were serious enough on the average to evoke the most severe disposition in about 48 percent of the cases for the referred group of offenders. Prior offenses were that serious in about 36 percent of the cases for the typical group. On the average, then, the referred offenders had committed fewer but more serious prior offenses.

In summary, the group of offenders selected for referral may be characterized in the following way. Offenders selected for the referral program were more likely to live in the area of the station and thus were more likely to be local minority members. Referred juveniles and typical offenders included about the same proportions of males to females, males predominating. Offenders in both groups were about the same age, sixteen years. The group of offenders selected for referral had been apprehended for offenses similar in seriousness to the offenses for which the typical group of offenders had been apprehended. It appears that the referred and typical offenders differed from each other only with respect to prior record. Officers selected offenders for referral who had committed fewer prior offenses but offenses which were somewhat more serious than the prior offenses committed by the typical group of offenders. [The proportion of first offenders was higher in the referred group (43 percent) than it was in the typical group (33 percent).]

Having compared the characteristics of the referred and typical groups, let us now compare recidivism in the two groups. The referred and typical groups did not differ much with regard to number and average seriousness of subsequent offenses. In both groups, about 54 percent of offenders committed some kind of subsequent offense (46 percent of offenders never came to the attention of police again). Juveniles in both groups committed an average of 1.7 subsequent offenses. In the referred group, 31 percent of the subsequent offenses were serious enough to evoke the most serious police

---

[4] Seriousness of offense is calculated using the McEachern–Bauzer index of offense seriousness. McEachern and Bauzer calculated the seriousness of each type of offense as the proportion of instances in which police decided upon the most serious disposition available to officers in dealing with apprehended juveniles. The more serious an offense, the more likely it is to evoke the harshest police reaction—disposing of the case by sending the offender to be adjudicated at juvenile court, or "requesting that a petition be filed at court in the juvenile's behalf." See A. W. McEachern and Riva Bauzer, "Factors Related to Disposition in Juvenile Police Contacts." In Malcolm W. Klein (ed), *Juvenile Gangs in Context.* Prentice-Hall, Inc., Englewood Cliffs, N.J., 1967; Richard I. Martin and Malcolm W. Klein, "A Comparative Analysis of Four Measures of Delinquency Seriousness." Paper presented at the annual meetings of the Pacific Sociological Assn. April 1965, Salt Lake City.

disposition. In the typical group, 36 percent of the subsequent offenses were that serious. So, although the referred juveniles had committed fewer prior offenses which were somewhat more serious than the prior offenses committed by the typical offenders, the referred juveniles committed the same number of subsequent offenses as the typical juveniles, and these offenses were about as serious as those committed by the typical offenders.

Remembering that the referred group was dissimilar to the typical group in number and seriousness of prior offenses, now let us compare the recidivism patterns of the referred group with the recidivism patterns of the small group of matched, but nonreferred offenders selected from among the typical offenders group. This small group not referred to community service agencies was selected from among the large typical group in such a way as to match them with the referred juveniles with regard to number and average seriousness of offenses committed prior to the instant offense, seriousness of the instant offense, sex, age, residence, ethnicity, and family status. By matching the referred group to a similar nonreferred group, control is exercised over these confounding factors, and it is possible to focus attention solely on the effects of the referral program.

The referred and nonreferred matched groups did not differ significantly in proportion of offenders committing at least one repeat offense. There were sixteen recidivists in the referred group and fourteen in the nonreferred group. Considering the small group sizes, it is appropriate to regard the groups similar to each other and to the typical group in sending about half their numbers on to commit subsequent offenses. Similarly, the two groups do not differ with regard to average seriousness of subsequent offenses. In the referred group, 31 percent of the offenses committed subsequent to the instant offense were serious enough to evoke the most serious police disposition. In the matched group, 36 percent of the subsequent offenses were that serious. The two matched groups do differ, however, on the average number of subsequent offenses. Juveniles in the referred group, as we know, committed an average of 1.7 subsequent offenses. Juveniles in the matched nonreferred group committed an average of 1.1 subsequent offenses—54 percent *fewer* repeat offenses than the referred group committed.

However, notice that the recidivist subgroups within each of the two groups here (referred and matched nonreferred) number about half of the original groups. It is unwise to infer much about the universe of offenders in these neighborhoods based on the records of only about thirty juveniles. Furthermore, scrutiny revealed that removing one very active recidivist's case from the referred group reduced the average number of offenses for the whole referred group to 1.4. The reader should interpret these data with caution.

Recidivism within the two groups tended to differ in that the majority of recidivists in the control group (eight) had committed only one subsequent offense, whereas the majority of recidivists in the referred group (ten) committed three or more offenses. Thus, although the proportion of simple recidivists is similar for both groups, recidivists in the referred group seemed to be chronic (multiple) recidivists rather than one-time repeaters as was the case among the matched group's recidivists. Within the typical group, most (49 percent) recidivists committed three or more subsequent offenses, while 31 percent of recidivists committed only one subsequent offense. Therefore, the referred group must be regarded as typical in its higher proportion of chronic offenders, and the matched group as exceptional in producing repeaters who tended to commit only one subsequent offense.

What sort of dispositions would referred offenders' cases have received if there had been no referral program? Is referral really being used as an alternative to sending offenders to court? We can look to see how the matched group of offenders' cases were disposed of. These offenders may have been treated as referred counterparts *would* have been treated. Interestingly, almost all thirty offenders in the matched group were treated either very leniently or very severely. Five cases were sent to probation or disposition of the case had not been recorded. Of the remaining twenty-five cases, twelve offenders were released from the station with no further action, and thirteen offenders were detained and petitions filed at court in their behalf. ("Detained petition" is regarded as the most severe disposition by police officers and by McEachern and Bauzer in their offense seriousness index.)

The most striking feature of these dispositions is, of course, that about half of the juveniles were released outright. One can infer that the referred counterparts to these matched juveniles would have been *released* rather than inserted into the justice system if there had been no referral program. This is interesting in view of the fact that diversion has been advertised by its proponents as an alternative to insertion into the juvenile justice system, not as an alternative to release. Perhaps diversion is used as an intermediate method of disposing of a case, midway in severity between mere release of an offender and sending the juvenile to court.

This pattern of dispositions may reflect the fact that there is disagreement among officers as to whether referral is best designed for the less serious or the more serious offenders. Some officers feel that referral is appropriate for less serious offenders, juveniles whom officers hate to turn loose again but whose *cases* do not seem to be suitable for full court processing. In this instance, referral is regarded as constructive action taken on cases at the same time that officers avoid involving juveniles further in the criminalizing juvenile justice system. Diversion is seen here as social control, but not as full-fledged punishment.

Another school of thought among officers who refer holds that more serious offenders should be referred because the offenders causing greatest concern are those juveniles who have committed serious offenses. Here, referral is regarded as appropriate if offenders seem to be motivated by internal "adjustment problems" rather than by firmly established criminal habits. Officers recognize that punitive juvenile justice institutions may have failed previously, only engaging offenders more deeply in lawless behavior patterns.

So, to review the information on repeat offense behavior for all three groups, the referred group, the typical group, and the matched nonreferred group, it is apparent that whereas the average seriousness of offenses committed subsequent to the instant offenses remained the same for all three groups, differences appeared in the number of subsequent offenses. Offenders in the matched nonreferred group committed fewer subsequent offenses than offenders in either the referred group or in the large group of typical offenders. Around half of all offenders in all three groups committed repeated offenses. Aggravated (multiple) rather than simple recidivism accounted for the greater average number of subsequent offenses in the referred group compared to the matched nonreferred group.

DISCUSSION AND CONCLUSIONS

The major conclusion to be drawn here is that the referral program produced recidivists who recidivated more frequently in a standard time period than did recidivists among a group of matched counterparts to these individuals. It is *not* likely that this is somehow accounted for by the fact that juveniles were selected for referral who had committed fewer prior offenses but offenses of a more serious nature, because referred offenders were matched with offenders who had *similar* prior records. The implication in these data is that referral tends to *aggravate* rather than to deter recidivism. The lower mean number of repeat offenses and the pattern of one-time recidivism found among the matched group both suggest that officers successfully selected offenders for referral who would have recidivated less frequently than typical offenders if it were not for the aggravating effects of the referral program. Obviously, all this amounts to pessimistic comment on the hopes that diversion programs might reduce recidivism.

It is of great interest that officers as frequently referred juveniles who would have been released outright as they referred offenders who would have been treated severely and sent to court. Ostensibly, referral was designed to substitute for court treatment, but it is as often a substitute for release. So far as referral constitutes the police practitioners' operationalization of labeling theory, it may be that this latter discovery accounts for why referred juveniles became chronic recidivists more often than did their nonreferred counterparts. That is, since referral substituted for outright release in half the cases, treatment via the referral program may have been felt as *stigmatizing* by the referred juveniles, rather than as *escape* from the stigmatization of court handling. It appears that some officers' use of referral as a disposition intermediate in severity between release and court adjudication validates the possibility that referral is stigmatizing. These officers used referral as a form of social control. If this is the case, referral programs may simply constitute extension of juvenile justice systems to include community help agencies.

Although the hints provided here do point in a pessimistic direction, none of the data condemn referral programs definitively and absolutely. It may be that procedures could be revised so that referred offenders might be treated more effectively than was the case in this pilot referral project. Of course, research using larger numbers is essential to understanding the details in the various effects of referral on different types of juvenile offenders.

26

PREVENTING DELINQUENCY
THROUGH DIVERSION*

Roger Baron, Floyd Feeney,
and Warren Thornton

As did the Cressey and McDermott article, this final selection concerns itself with diversion at the point of probation intake. There is a good deal of overlap with many police diversion programs, however. The family crisis treatment involved in the Sacramento 601 project should appeal to the many police officials who find family problems to be one of the root causes of much delinquency. A word of caution is in order regarding the project design: As set forth below, the analysis does not permit us to know how much of the experimental group's improvement is due to crisis treatment, or to nonfiling of petitions, or to an interaction between the two. A pivotal control group is missing from the design.

* From *Federal Probation,* 37, 1(1973): pp. 13–18. Reprinted by permission of the authors and publisher.

Almost from the beginning, the jurisdiction of the juvenile court has gone beyond youths violating the criminal law. Thus, in Illinois, where the first juvenile court law was adopted in 1899, jurisdiction over children in danger of becoming involved in delinquent activities was added to the jurisdiction of the court at the very next legislative session.[1] This kind of jurisdiction was included in the juvenile court acts of other states and is the general pattern for the country as a whole.

Section 601 of the Welfare and Institution Code is the California version of this law.[2] It reads as follows:

> Any person under the age of 18 years who persistently or habitually refuses to obey the reasonable and proper orders or directions of his parents, guardian, custodian or school authorities, or who is beyond the control of such person, or any person who is a habitual truant from school within the meaning of any law of this State, or who from any cause is in danger of leading an idle, dissolute, lewd, or immoral life, is within the jurisdiction of the juvenile court, which may adjudge such person to be a ward of the court.

In practice, section 601 is restricted almost wholly to youths who run away from home, are beyond control of their parents, or who are truants.

In recent years a substantial controversy has developed as to whether this

[1] Revised Laws of Illinois, 1901, pp. 141–142. See also Revised Laws of Illinois, 1899, pp. 131–137.

[2] In *Gonzalez* v. *Mailliard,* U.S. Northern District of California No. 50424 (Feb. 9, 1971), a three-judge federal court held the portion of section 601 bringing within the jurisdiction of the juvenile court a person "who from any cause is in danger of leading an idle, dissolute, lewd, or immoral life" unconstitutionally vague.

jurisdiction of the juvenile court is a good thing or not. Much of the impetus for this questioning derives from a feeling held by many experienced observers that the jurisdiction of the court is too broad and that the process of bringing youths into court is now a part of the problem rather than a part of the solution. One strong statement of this viewpoint was that of the President's Crime Commission, which said:

> Thus, for example, juvenile courts retain expansive grounds of jurisdiction authorizing judicial intervention in relatively minor matters of morals and misbehavior on the ground that subsequent delinquent conduct may be indicated, as if there were reliable ways of predicting delinquency in a given child and reliable ways of redirecting children's lives.[3]

The Commission concluded that:

> The range of conduct for which court intervention is authorized should be narrowed.[4]

And this was one of the major reasons involved in the recommendation of that Commission relative to the creation of youth service bureaus. In California an effort was made in 1970 to repeal section 601 and its grant of jurisdictional authority.[5] While this effort was ultimately defeated, there was substantial support for the idea.

Opponents of this viewpoint have felt that total repeal of jurisdiction over runaway and beyond control behavior goes too far. Among other things they have been concerned that repeal alone does little to deal with the underlying problems which brought about the behavior in the first place.

The purpose of this article is not to resolve this controversy but to report the results of a project which sheds new light on the kinds of problems underlying behavior encompassed by section 601 and some possible methods for dealing with that behavior.

SOME TYPICAL CASES

While there is no typical 601 case, several not uncommon situations are portrayed below:

> Jane R. is a large, quiet 16-year-old girl, brought to Juvenile Hall as first-time runaway. Tomboyish with long blonde hair, she lives with her father, a 47-year-old businessman, her step-mother of 4 years and a 13-year-old sister, Debbie. Her real mother deserted the family when Jane was 12 after several involvements with other men and a series of mental breakdowns. She now lives in another city several hundred miles away. Jane indicates constant concern about the situation involving

---

[3] President's Commission on Law Enforcement and Administration of Justice, *The Challenge of Crime in a Free Society*, p. 81 (1967). See also E. Lemert, *Instead of Court: Diversion in Juvenile Justice*, NIMH Crime and Delinquency Series (1971).

[4] *Ibid.*

[5] See, e.g., California Legislature, Report of the Assembly Interim Committee on Criminal Procedure, Juvenile Court Processes, 1970 Interim Session.

her real mother. She doesn't understand why her mother ran away, and hungers for some kind of contact. Her parents, however, and particularly her step-mother, are fearful that Jane will only be hurt by learning the real character of her mother and seek to seal her off from any contact. They refuse to let Jane visit or write, intercept communications from the mother to Jane, and talk the mother down whenever her name is mentioned. Jane, who has made one feeble attempt at suicide, says little and mopes a great deal in her own room. Her step-mother, concerned that Jane might go crazy like her mother, hovers over, asking questions, reading her diaries and coming into her room when she is alone. Jane, picking up on her parents' concern, increasingly worries that something in fact is wrong with her and withdraws more and more into herself. Because of her quietness virtually all the family attention focuses on Jane, and very little on Debbie who is far more talkative and outgoing. While Jane feels very close to her father and enjoys fishing with him, he has a busy business schedule and is around very little.

Johnny G., a somewhat retarded and chubby 14-year-old with a smile and a winning way, was brought to the Juvenile Hall as being "beyond the control of his parents." This was his fourth time to the Hall for this "offense." Twice previously he had been placed on informal probation and had only recently completed his stint. Johnny's father is a 41-year-old truck driver and his mother a 38-year-old housewife. There are no other children. The father says the problem is that Johnny sometimes steals from his parents, never goes to sleep at a decent hour, rarely gets up in time for school and "just doesn't listen." The father says that he has to go to bed early, usually by 10 P.M. because his work requires him to get up early in the morning. The mother, on the other hand, likes to stay up late and does not get up until after Mr. G. has gone to work and Johnny to school (on those occasions when Johnny does get up in time for school). Mr. G. is critical of Mrs. G. and seems strongly to resent Mrs. G.'s hours. At one point he said, "if you got up, Johnny would." Mrs. G. lashed back with, "there's no reason you couldn't get him out of bed in the morning if you wanted to." Both mother and father indicate that Johnny has no specific bed time and that virtually none of the family rules are consistently enforced with respect to Johnny.

These descriptions are not able to portray a full understanding of the depth of feelings involved but do indicate something of the extent to which the problem in the 601-type case is one of conflict and communication within the family. Judges and probation officers have long recognized this, feeling these to be among their toughest cases and among the least appropriate for handling in juvenile court.

This kind of case is also one of the most frequent for the juvenile court. In California, for example, in 1969, 601 cases constituted about 30 percent of all cases reaching intake and over 40 percent of all juvenile hall admissions.[6] More detailed data for Sacramento County indicate that 601 cases comprised over 32 percent of the cases handled at intake, over 40 percent of the detention petitions filed in juvenile court, over 35 percent of the cases handled by probation supervision, and over 72 percent of all placements involving delinquents.[7]

Even more important, however, than the workload involved in handling

[6] California Bureau of Criminal Statistics, *Crime and Delinquency in California*, pp. 149–180 (1969).

[7] These data are from a special analysis.

these youths are the dismal results of this attempt to deal with incorrigibility through the use of juvenile court. The recidivism figures indicate that a high percentage of all 601 cases come back into the system in a very short time—many as a result of having committed acts that are criminal for adults as well as juveniles (section 602). In Sacramento County nearly 48 percent of all 601 juveniles are charged with a subsequent offense within seven months.

These figures only begin to show the burden these cases place on the juvenile justice system. A detailed analysis of a one-month period showed that during the year after referral each case consumed an average of thirty-two hours of court and probation time. Most of this time is spent in the process of filing petitions and disposing of them in court. Approximately nine hours of court and probation time are required to file and dispose of a petition as opposed to two hours to make the decision whether to file a petition and two hours per month of supervision time where the juvenile is put on probation. The juveniles in this sample spent an average of twenty days a year in juvenile hall, thirty-eight days a year in placement, four days a year in the hospital, fifteen days a year in Sacramento County Boys Ranch, and twelve days a year in the California Youth Authority. The total cost to Sacramento County of handling a 601 case was estimated at $931 per case per year.

It is important to note that over 50 percent (95 of 186 cases) in the sample of section 601 cases had petitions filed necessitating court action and 48.9 percent (91 of 186) had detention petitions filed, necessitating a court detention hearing in addition to a jurisdictional and dispositional hearing.

In analyzing the problem of how to prevent the recurrence of section 601 cases, two factors stand out: (1) The traditional structure of the probation department allows too little time for effective handling of 601 cases, (2) the inappropriateness of legal handling.

In the Sacramento County Probation Department an intake unit handles all cases upon their referral to the probation department. This unit makes the decision whether to file a petition and whether to make an initial detention. During the sample month eight intake officers handled approximately 650 cases. This rate of intake allows the officer very little time to resolve the underlying problems involved in 601 cases, as well as affording little opportunity to seek alternative placement with relatives or friends where the parents do not want the minor returned home or the minor refuses to go home. The tendency must necessarily be to initially detain these juveniles, file petitions on them, and let the court resolve the problems.

A detention hearing before a judge or referee follows within twenty-four hours of the filing of a detention petition. Little more information and time is available to the juvenile court at this time, however, and the hearing normally lasts about fifteen minutes.[8] As a result, most juveniles are detained pending a jurisdictional hearing, which must take place within fifteen judicial days from the date of the detention order.[9] In the interim a probation officer is assigned to the case and spends about two hours investigating it for the jurisdictional and dispositional hearings. Typically, the outcome of

---

[8] California Welfare and Institutions Code section 631 (West Supp. 1971).

[9] California Welfare and Institutions Code section 657 (West Supp. 1971).

these 601 cases is that the juvenile is made a ward of the court and returned home or placed. A probation supervision officer is then assigned to the case and spends one-half to one hour per month visiting with the juvenile or with his family to see what progress is being made. If indications are that the situation is not improved, additional petitions are filed and additional detention ordered in the expectation that detention and court action have a deterring effect. Over 65 percent of the cases in one sample handled in this way had a prior or subsequent record for 601 offenses. Fifty-nine percent had a record of two or more other such offenses, 32 percent had a record of three or more, and over 15 percent four or more such offenses. This rate of continued involvement in the criminal justice process, while indicating some success, nevertheless indicates that a great number of cases fail to respond to this kind of handling.[10]

The second factor that stands out is the inappropriateness of handling these cases through the legal system. Most probation officers feel uncomfortable with the problems posed by 601 cases. These cases usually involve family crisis situations and a long history of lack of communication and understanding between family members. Probation staff rightly feel that this calls for family counseling or family crisis intervention rather than legal treatment.

THE PROJECT

The Sacramento 601 Diversion Project is an experiment designed to test whether juveniles charged with this kind of offense—the 601 offense—can be handled better through short-term family crisis therapy than through the traditional procedures of the juvenile court.

The objective of this project is to demonstrate the validity of the diversion concept of delinquency prevention by showing that:

> Runaway, beyond control and other types of 601 cases can be diverted from the present system of juvenile justice and court adjudication.

> Detention can be avoided in most 601-type situations through counseling and alternative placements that are both temporary and voluntary.

> Those diverted have fewer subsequent brushes with the law and a better general adjustment to life than those not diverted.

> This diversion can be accomplished within existing resources available for handling this kind of case.

The intent of the project is to keep the child out of the juvenile hall, keep the family problem out of the court, and still offer counseling and help to the family.

This approach relies on the following features:

> Immediate, intensive handling of cases rather than piecemeal adjudication; avoidance of compartmentalized service by the creation of a prevention and diversion unit handling cases from beginning to end; spending the majority of

[10] See note 7 *supra*.

staff time in the initial stages of the case—when it is in crisis—rather than weeks or months later; the provision of special training to probation staff involved; the provision of ongoing consultative services on a periodic basis to enable staff to continue to improve their crisis handling skills; avoidance entirely of court; avoidance of juvenile hall through counseling and the use of alternative placements that are both temporary and voluntary; maintenance of a 24-hour, 7 day-a-week telephone crisis service[11]; closer ties with outside referral services.

This approach to the problem of delinquency prevention is based on an extensive analysis of the experience of Sacramento County. During 1969, Sacramento County Probation Department and the Center on Administration of Criminal Justice, University of California, Davis, conducted a demonstration project to examine detention decision making at both the intake and court levels. Part of the project entailed extensive interviewing of juveniles detained on 601 offenses and their parents. Interviews were conducted after intake proceedings, but prior to the court detention hearing. Reasons for detention were examined along with family problems.

In situations where parents did not want their child released to their custody or where the juvenile did not want to return home, alternative placement possibilities were examined with the juvenile and his parents prior to the detention hearing. In many of these situations, alternatives were discovered that were satisfactory to both the minor and his parents. Based on information to this effect presented by the project personnel to the court at the detention hearing minors were released to these alternative placements pending their jurisdictional and dispositional hearings. Follow-up data indicated that these placements proved successful and that several resulted in permanent placements.

Based on the results of this demonstration which indicated the extensive workload involved in handling 601 cases and the possibilities of delinquency prevention through diversion of these cases from the system, the present diversion plan was developed.

Also entering into the development of this plan was the growing body of evidence that crisis counseling and short-term casework are one of the most effective ways of dealing with problems arising out of family situations. One recent study, for example, concluded that:

> Planned, short-term treatment yields results at least as good as, and possibly better than, open-ended treatment of longer duration.

> Improvement associated with short-term treatment lasts just as long as that produced by long-term services.

> Short-term treatment can be used successfully under most conditions if its objectives are appropriately limited.[12]

---

[11] See "Project Operation" *infra*.

[12] U.S. Department of Health, Education and Welfare, Social and Rehabilitation Service, "Short-term vs. Extended Casework," III Research Demonstration Service No. 1 (August 15, 1969). See also W. Reid and A. Shyne, *Brief and Extended Casework* (1968).

The report indicated that "extended casework was three times as costly as short-term, with no better results to show for it." In explaining these results the report stated that the brevity of the service period may have "mobilized the caseworker's energies and caused a more active, efficient and focused approach" while at the same time calling forth "an extra effort from the client, producing a better outcome."

A highly successful program in Denver, Colorado, demonstrated the potential of family crisis therapy as an effective alternative to psychiatric hospitalization.[13]

Projects such as the highly successful family crisis counseling program developed for police officers by the Psychology Department of the City College of New York have demonstrated the utility of using these techniques at the first level of contact in the criminal justice system.[14]

PROJECT OPERATION

The 601 diversion project began handling cases on October 26, 1970. For purposes of the experiment the project handles cases on four days of the week with the regular intake unit handling the other three days. Days are rotated monthly.

On project days when a referral on a 601 matter is received—whether from the police, the schools, the parents, or whomever—the project staff arranges a family session to discuss the problem. Every effort is made to ensure that this session is held as soon as possible and most are held within the first hour or two after referral. Through the use of family counseling techniques the project counselor seeks to develop the idea that the problem is one that should be addressed by the family as a whole. Locking up the youth as a method of solving problems is discouraged and a return home with a commitment by all to try to work through the problem is encouraged. If the underlying emotions are too strong to permit the youth's return home immediately, an attempt is made to locate an alternative place for the youth to stay temporarily. This is a voluntary procedure which requires the consent of both the parents and the youth.

Families are encouraged to return for a second discussion with the counselor and depending upon the nature of the problem for a third, fourth, or fifth session. Normally, the maximum number of sessions is five. Sessions rarely last less than one hour and often go as long as two or two and one-half hours. First sessions take place when the problem arises. Since the project staff remains on duty until 2:00 A.M., a few begin after midnight. Crisis line service after project closing hours is handled through referral by the probation department switchboard to the home of the probation counselor. This service has not been used a great deal but its availability is important in conveying the counselor's concern to the family.

[13] D. Langsley and D. Kaplan, *The Treatment of Families in Crisis Intervention* (1968).

[14] M. Bard, *Training Police as Specialists in Family Crisis Intervention,* Final Report (no date) (mimeo).

STAFF

The unit staff consists of a supervisor and six deputy probation officers. The unit supervisor has approximately ten years' experience and his assistant seven years' experience. The deputies range from no experience in a probation setting to approximately four years of experience. There are three male and three female deputies. The three deputies without probation experience all have some previous experience in a social service agency.

TRAINING

The techniques of crisis intervention and family crisis counseling are crucial to the concept of the project. Normally these are techniques employed by therapists who have undergone long periods of training. Moreover, the application of these techniques at the intake point of probation present some novel and difficult questions. The training portion of the project is therefore one of its most crucial aspects. Project training involves two phases: initial training and ongoing training.

Initial training was conducted during a one-week period. This included demonstrations of actual family counseling by a number of different therapists, intensive discussion, and role playing of the kinds of problems which counselors were expected to face.

The ongoing portion of the training is built around weekly consultations with the project psychiatrists and the project psychologist.

In these sessions the project counselors have opportunities to observe, discuss, and work with the project consultants. Other training sessions have focused on the role that other agencies play in helping to deal with family situations.

CASES HANDLED

The project does not handle all 601 cases. Out-of-county and out-of-state cases, cases in which the juvenile already has a case pending in court or a warrant outstanding, cases involving youths who are in court placement, and cases involving youths who are already on probation for serious criminal offenses were excluded from project coverage because of administrative and other problems involved in their handling. Some citation and other noncustody referrals are also excluded from the project as not requiring handling as intensive as that of the project. For the first nine project months about 40 percent of all 601 referrals were excluded from the project for these reasons.

RESULTS

Results of the project to date are highly promising. During its first nine months the project handled 803 referrals involving opportunities for diversion but filed only eighteen petitions. Court processing was thus necessary in only 2.2 percent of these referrals as opposed to 30.4 percent in a three-month preproject period and 21.3 percent of the referrals handled in the normal manner in the control group.[15]

Referrals and Petitions—First Nine Project Months

	Number of Referrals	Number of Petitions	Percent
Preproject period (July 1 to September 30, 1970)	362	110	30.4
Control cases	558	119	21.3
Project cases	803	18	2.2

Available data concerning repeat offenses indicate that the project group is doing better than either the preproject sample or the control group. Youths handled during the first four months of the project were followed up for a period of seven months after initial handling to determine the number of repeat offenses. At the end of this period, 45.5 percent of the control group had been rebooked for either a 601 or 602 offense while the comparable figure for the project group was 35.0 percent. This represents an improvement of over 23 percent in the rate of repeat offenses.

Perhaps even more significant is that for repeat offenses involving criminal conduct (section 602), the improvement was even greater. For this category the repeat rate for the control group was 23.4 percent and 15.3 percent for the project group. This is a drop in the rate of repeated offenses of 34.6 percent.

Percent of Juveniles Rebooked within Seven Months
(cases initially handled October 26, 1970, to February 28, 1971)

	601 or 602	602 Only
Preproject period	48.6	27.0
Control cases	45.5	23.4
Project cases	35.0	15.3

Data concerning overnight detention indicate that project youths initially require overnight detention in less than 10 percent of the cases while the figure for control cases is over 60 percent. The control group spent an average of 5.3 nights in detention per youth while the project group had an average of 0.1 night in detention per youth as a result of initial handling.

[15] Because the same youth may be referred to the probation department more than once, the number of referrals exceeds the number of individuals. The number of petitions filed includes only those filed when there was an opportunity for diversion. It does not include those filed after a case has once been to court, as there is then no further opportunity for diversion and does not include those filed on a 602 referral, as these are not within the scope of the project. If these are included, seven-month follow-up data indicate that 34 percent of all control group youths and 14 percent of all project group youths ultimately went to court.

COST OF SERVICE

Original projections for the project indicated that crisis counseling could be performed within the cost allocations required for more traditional service, assuming that complete case costs including intake, court, and supervision were included within the totals for traditional service. Based on the project's record to date in diverting cases out of juvenile court and in reducing juvenile hall detention and recidivism, a comparison of project and control costs indicates that diversion is less expensive than the more traditional procedures. The average total cost, for example, for project handling of a case, not including repeat bookings, was $29 as compared with an average cost of $222 for control cases. If the cost of repeat bookings is included, the average project cost per project case is $170 and the average control group cost $405.

CONCLUSION

Diversion is "an opportunity, not a solution."[16] It is a concept that seems to carry with it "the possibility of reallocating existing resources for programs that promise greater success in bringing about correction and the social restoration of offenders."[17]

The Sacramento Project is just such a reallocation. Its record is not yet complete. The results to date, however, are a powerful demonstration of the value of the diversion concept in combination with the use of family crisis counseling at the point of probation intake. Because the approach makes use of existing personnel, it can be created without the addition of major new resources. Because it is both specialized and reasonably self-sufficient, it has the ability to make more effective use of other community resources while at the same time not becoming dependent upon them. For jurisdictions with reasonably strong probation services, it can do in fact what so many programs claim, that is, pay for itself.

The project is at the heart a combination of a potent counseling technique and an organizational form that maximizes its use at an immediate, early point when it will do the most good. No one of these components taken singly is likely to be especially effective. Taken together, however, the combination offers a promising, fresh approach to an old and troubling problem.

---

[16] Allen Breed, "Diversion: Program, Rationalization or Excuse," speech before 19th National Institute on Crime and Delinquency, June 19, 1972.

[17] *Ibid.*

CONCLUDING NOTES: OTHER AREAS OF CONCERN IN DIVERSION

It is clear that there is considerable and increasing philosophical support for the diversion of some offenders from the criminal justice system and that the recent publications of the National Advisory Commission on Criminal Justice Standards and Goals (NAC) have given impetus to the development of diversion programs nationwide. The NAC, appointed in 1971 by the Law Enforcement Assistance Administration and chaired by Governor Russell W. Peterson of Delaware, published six reports in 1973. These documents set forth criminal justice standards and goals for crime reduction and prevention at the State and local level. Three of the six reports have specific segments or chapters covering diversion, and the other reports implicitly support the diversion concept. Although the standards and goals cannot be mandated for implementation to the States or local levels of government, it is certain that major attention will be given to those recommendations and that diversion will play a significant role in the administration of justice in the United States in the next decade. In the words of the NAC, "[e]ach local jurisdiction, in cooperation with related State agencies, should develop and implement by 1975 formally organized programs of diversion that can be applied in the criminal justice process from the time an illegal act occurs to adjudication." Diversion, as viewed by the NAC, is a legitimate and appropriate part of the criminal justice system.

The transition, however, from a philosophical orientation to operational programs will be complex, but if diversion is to become a viable alternative to entry into and/or penetration of the justice system, potential difficulties must be identified and addressed and issues must be resolved. Systemwide planning is required or there is a distinct probability that diversion programs will become as fragmented and disjointed as those justice system practices which, in some measure, themselves led to the diversion movement.

Four areas require particular attention. There are needs to explicitly:

1. Determine the guidelines which define those offenders who are eligible or ineligible for diversion, those agencies which are appropriate to receive those who are diverted, and programmatic activities of the agencies which receive diverted cases.
2. Identify or develop, and mobilize resources in a community, determine techniques for increasing community "tolerance" levels, enhance the delivery system for these resources, and make more equitable the availability of resources to diverse types of communities.
3. Determine the impact of diversion practices on the justice system overall as well as its component parts, and examine the need for possible administrative, organizational, and legal changes.

4. Prepare a complete methodology for evaluating the effectiveness of diversion, keeping in mind that being "progressive" is not synonymous with being "successful."

DIVERSION GUIDELINES

The need for diversion guidelines is critical. Unless there are agreed-upon standards for practice and procedure and general consensus on philosophy, diversion will surely become the source of continuing and substantial inequities. Basic questions—such as who is (or is not) to be diverted, by whom, on what basis, and to what programmatic activities—should be answered by some shared understandings. Without such common understandings, the justice system—through increased use of nonsystematic diversion—may become more confused, autonomous, and fragmented.

Some minimum standards are needed, for example, to guide the *selection of individuals* for diversion. Diversion practices may be exclusionary and identify types of offenders who are deemed ineligible, such as those with a history of violence or felony offenders. Or practice may be permissive and allow that all offenders who may benefit from non-justice-system treatment be considered eligible, regardless of other considerations. Diversion may be restricted to adjudicated offenders or it may include nonadjudicated offenders. If the former, diversion is from the system after entry; if the latter, diversion is an alternative to entry into the system. Both raise substantial legal issues.

Determinations as to time frames are required, i.e., the optimum time for diversion, the length of time or duration of diversion, and so on. Guidelines are also needed as to actions to be taken if the offender diverted fails to comply with the actual or implied conditions of diversion or if it appears that the diversion plan is inappropriate.

Meaningful standards are necessary for the *selection of agencies* to receive those who are diverted. Diversion need not necessarily be made to private agencies; it may be appropriate for diversion to be to those public agencies which normally have been either minimally or not at all concerned with the offender population. And it may be appropriate for diversion to be to individuals rather than agencies. The selection of agencies requires community inventories; these, in turn, may indicate the need for new private and/or public agencies or combinations/consortiums/conglomerates of established agencies which address needs of offenders. Of equal significance is the complex and politically sensitive problem of sifting through a wide variety of potential diversion agencies, including those with "unusual" or nontraditional characteristics, such as those with an ex-offender or ex-addict staff. Underlying many of these guidelines are fiscal considerations —including possible requirements for subsidies to agencies which handle those who are diverted. A delicate issue arises from public support of private agencies in terms of performance objectives and standards, constraints, and expectations. The subsidy issue is made even more complex as the need arises to determine which public agency at what level of government pays the subsidies to these new partners in the justice system.

There is, of course, a requirement to examine the *programmatic activities* of the agencies which receive diverted offenders. While an inventory of these various programs and some estimate of their effectiveness are essential to rational diversion practice, a basic question emerges as to whether offenders should be diverted if appropriate (or at least similar) programs exist within the justice system. And if such programs already exist in the justice system, the advantages, if any, which accrue by transfer of these programs and clientele to community-based, non-justice-system organizations must be determined.

The movement of programs and offenders to non-justice-system organizations will require new roles for justice- and non-justice-system personnel. As an example, the probation or parole officer realistically might be required to become a catalyst and seek to activate a community and its caretakers to absorb the offender as a member of that community. This would require a complete knowledge of community resources and a diagnosis of clientele needs. There would be an emphasis on reducing the alienation of the offender from his community by impairing the continued maintenance of a criminal identity and encouraging community identity. The officer would no longer find employment for the offender, but instead direct him into the normal channels of job seeking in the community. Residential, marital, medical, financial, or other problems would be addressed by assisting the offender engage those community resources which deal with these problem areas. This new role, then, might be one of ensuring a process of community, not correctional absorption. Again illustrating interrelationships of these issues, note that the "new role" phenomenon itself raises questions about training for and acceptance of the role and methods or techniques of implementation.

THE COMMUNITY

Several issues arise as one examines the role and resources of the community. Not at all insignificant is the complex issue of imbalance among communities to accept cases which are diverted and to provide necessary services and resources. Some communities have distinct economic advantages over others—and it is clear that diversion has an economic, as well as a motivation, base. Middle- and upper-class communities and their citizens, socially and economically secure, often have available financial resources to mobilize a wide range of services, ranging from psychiatric care through private schools. The differences in resource levels need scrutiny, for it would be socially disastrous to deny diversion to those who are economically disadvantaged. Without plans to balance resource requirements with the delivery of services, the poor and the disadvantaged will continue to flow into and through the justice agencies.

A parallel community-based problem occurs where there is a low community tolerance for diversion. Numerous examples of low- or nontolerance may be cited, ranging from open through latent resistance and hostility directed against self-help groups and agency halfway houses. And besides the very difficult "how," there is the related question of "who" is responsible for dealing with community fears and anxieties. Is every justice agency seeking to divert offenders responsible for the development of its own resources or is an overall plan among cooperating agencies more rational? And, if a plan is appropriate, who designs and implements it, and how are activities financed and monitored?

IMPACT OF DIVERSION

Although changes in the justice system will be an inevitable consequence of an increased use of diversion, there is a possibility that the changes will be both unplanned and unsystematic. These changes may range from administrative and organizational restructuring and modification in procedure and policy, on one hand, through major changes in the populations which are serviced by the justice systems, on the other.

As justice agencies become partners with communities, there may be requirements for all agencies to implement organizational change to include new bureaus or divisions of "community service." This might require new personnel or reassignment of personnel, development and acceptance of and training for new roles such as those of diagnostician and/or catalyst, additional funding and different kinds of facilities, and new understandings within the agencies and communities themselves. Permanent linkages with community organizations may be required and force traditional pyramid-shaped hierarchical organizational models to be flattened. New information systems may be needed, and continuing involvement with or monitoring of diverted cases may be desirable.

The large-scale diversion of offenders—either from or after entry into the justice system—may have other consequences for the justice agencies. If substantial numbers of offenders are diverted by local law enforcement to community-based agencies, there will be reduced inputs to prosecution, adjudication, and correctional agencies. Lessened inputs will alleviate some of the backlog in the judicial system and reduce caseload pressure in probation and parole and the size of institutional populations. While these occurrences are desirable, at some point in time the bureaucratic instinct for survival may be threatened and reactions protective of the establishment may set in. Of greater significance, however, is that increased diversion may leave the justice system with a unique clientele of hardened, recalcitrant, difficult offenders who seem unlikely to "make it" in the community. These offenders may have complex problems requiring long-range treatment, and they may represent a major threat to and be rejected by their communities. In addition to creating major management problems, these offenders will require new and different programs, facilities, and staff for treatment. In short, extensive diversion may not only "threaten" the justice establishment with new roles and reorganization; it may change the justice system population and alter the system itself.

PLANNING AND EVALUATION

There are yet other important aspects of diversion which require attention—planning and evaluation. A lack of midrange and strategic planning and systematic evaluation have long been major defects in justice operations from law enforcement through corrections. The movement toward diversion of offenders mandates that planning and evaluation not be "tacked on" to operational processes, but rather be built-in, continually updated, and constantly reviewed. The questions about planning and evaluation are familiar—criteria must be established; funds must be made available; personnel, software, and hardware must be obtained; methodologies developed; responsibilities delineated. Without such planning and evaluation, it appears certain that diversion practices will produce more chaos than clarity and consistency.

SUMMARY

A fragmented justice system which has been neither just nor efficient, the increasing demands of the citizenry to be participants in the affairs of government including the justice system, and recognition that the community is an appropriate base for many justice operations have spearheaded the movement toward diversion. But even as there is increasing momentum toward diversion, in part product of the National Advisory Commission on Criminal Justice Standards and Goals, it is clear that there is a pressing need for more comprehensive operational guidelines, shared understandings between justice and nonjustice agencies, examination of the role and resources of the community, planning and evaluation, and study of the long-range impact of diversion on both the justice system and society.

Diversion is both a challenge and an opportunity. As a potentially major mechanism of the justice system, diversion will require considerable attention. Although changes in the justice system are indicated, movement to untested and ill-defined alternatives is inappropriate.

APPENDICES

DIVERSION*

National Advisory Commission
on Criminal Justice Standards and Goals

In 1973, the National Advisory Commission on Criminal Justice Standards and Goals explicitly noted and legitimated the new concern with diversion. Reprinted here are the standards for police, court, and correctional diversion in that order. For amplification, the reader is referred to the original Commission reports.

* From *Police*, Standard 4.3, National Advisory Commission on Criminal Justice Standards and Goals (Washington, D.C.: U.S. Government Printing Office, 1973), pp. 80–82.

STANDARD 4.3   DIVERSION

Every police agency, where permitted by law, immediately should divert from the criminal and juvenile justice systems any individual who comes to the attention of the police, and for whom the purpose of the criminal or juvenile process would be inappropriate, or in whose case other resources would be more effective. All diversion dispositions should be made pursuant to written agency policy that ensures fairness and uniformity of treatment.

1.   Police chief executives may develop written policies and procedures which allow, in appropriate cases, for juveniles who come to the attention of the agency to be diverted from the juvenile justice process. Such policies and procedures should be prepared in cooperation with other elements of the juvenile justice system.

2.   These policies and procedures should allow for processing mentally ill persons who come to the attention of the agency, should be prepared in cooperation with mental health authorities and courts, and should provide for mental health agency referral of those persons who are in need of professional assistance but are not taken into custody.

3.   These policies should allow for effective alternatives when arrest for some misdemeanor offenses would be inappropriate.

Commentary

Police efforts to divert suspected offenders from the criminal justice system are centered primarily upon the selection of alternatives to formal wardship and delinquency proceedings for juveniles. The police traditionally have counseled and released youths to their parents in lieu of instituting formal proceedings. It has been estimated, in fact, that roughly half of all juvenile offenders are released without formal petitions being filed. Recently, however, increasing use of police referrals to other agencies within the community has benefited youngsters by obtaining professional help for them without delinquency or wardship proceedings.

Police diversion practices have varied greatly from agency to agency. In 1969 Malcolm Klein of the University of Southern California conducted a study of forty-eight police agencies in Los Angeles County;[1] this study revealed diversion rates ranging from a high of 82 percent to a low of 2 percent. While the final decision to divert a youth from the system may depend on the circumstances of the individual case, the study illustrates that agency policy probably has a great effect upon the decision.

Police agencies should establish policies to encourage the diversion of young potential offenders from the criminal justice system; policies should include criteria for determining on a case-by-case basis whether to file a petition or seek an informal disposition.

Diversion presupposes the development of effective alternatives. Police agencies should identify youth service bureaus and other formal and informal community agencies that would provide assistance and counseling to referred juveniles.

To insure accountability, and to monitor and evaluate the outcome of referrals, police agencies must follow through on diversion cases. The problem was stated in the *Juvenile Delinquency Task Force Report* of the President's 1967 Crime Commission:

> The juvenile may not arrive at the selected place of service, or he may be refused service without the referring official's finding out in time to take other steps. Even where there is a well-articulated referral system with smoothly operating procedures, sheer number of cases may substantially lessen its effectiveness. If the time lapse between apprehension and referral is a matter of days, the subsequent follow-up by a selected community resource may occur at a point when the juvenile and his family have surmounted their initial fear, anger, or regret and concern, and the contact is regarded as an unwelcome reminder of past unpleasantness instead of an avenue of help in time of crises.[2]

Most diversion decisions should be made by trained juvenile officers, who should have responsibility for follow-up on referrals. However, there should be no return to the discredited practice of having juvenile officers act as hearing officers in the juvenile justice process.

The Mentally Ill

Police frequently encounter situations in which they must deal with mentally ill persons who pose a danger to themselves or others. The authority of the police to initiate commitment proceedings is based upon common law and upon statutes in most States.

[1] Malcolm W. Klein, "Police Processing of Juvenile Offenders: Toward the Development of Juvenile System Rates," report to Los Angeles County Criminal Justice Planning Board, 1970.

[2] President's Commission on Law Enforcement and Administration of Justice, *The Challenge of Crime in a Free Society* (Washington, D.C.: U.S. Government Printing Office, 1967), p. 18.

While there is some movement to establish specialized agencies to serve as intake points for mental health agencies, the police probably will continue to be confronted regularly with mental health problems. For these reasons, it is essential that police agencies establish and maintain liaison with courts and mental health agencies to develop policies and procedures that insure uniformity and effectiveness in processing mentally ill persons who come to the attention of police agencies.

In Los Angeles, Calif., where the police serve as the primary intake point for mental health agencies, a special unit in the police department has been established to review all mental cases prior to initiating seventy-two-hour involuntary detention, evaluation, and treatment. During 1971, the unit reviewed 2,714 cases and referred 2,100 cases to the psychiatric clinic for professional evaluation. In addition, the unit made over 2,300 voluntary referrals by telephone to mental health clinics.

Police agencies should be able to make effective referrals of persons who need professional assistance but who are not taken into protective custody. Under an ambitious referral program in Dayton, Ohio, the police department, in connection with its team policing project, contracted with a local community health center to provide on-call intervention services for a full range of mental health problems. Persons in need of mental health care are referred to the center, or center personnel are called to the patient's home.[3]

Diversion under Special Circumstances

Although most police diversion cases involve the informal disposition of juvenile matters, some other occasions arise in which certain individuals should not be subjected to the criminal process. For example, an aged or mentally retarded person who has committed a relatively minor offense should not be arrested or prosecuted when a person or agency is willing to assume responsibility for the offender's future conduct. Such decisions to divert, while frequently made by field policemen, should be made according to written agency policy where permitted by statute.

Police experience has shown that certain types of conduct, such as those manifested by the mentally ill, alcoholics, and juveniles, may be dealt with best by diversion from the criminal or juvenile justice system at any stage of the process. Agencies should exercise leadership in such cases. However, police experience also reveals that other conduct, particularly so-called victimless crime, is best dealt with through the criminal justice system. Nevertheless, in exceptional victimless crime cases, in which the purpose of the criminal justice system would be inappropriate or other resources would be more effective, judicial diversion should be authorized by law to avoid criminal sanctions.

Other Reports of the Commission

The reader is referred to the other reports of the Commission and particularly the Community Crime Prevention, Courts and Corrections reports, which contain extensive discussions of diversion under varying definitions.

[3] "Law Enforcement and MH Agencies Team-up in Ohio," *Psychiatric News* (August 18, 1971).

The reader is particularly referred to the discussion of Youth Services Bureaus in the Community Crime Prevention report. These bureaus should be considered by the police as a major tool in the diversion of juveniles from the justice system.

GENERAL CRITERIA FOR DIVERSION*

National Advisory Commission on Criminal Justice Standards and Goals

* From *Courts*, Standards 2.1 and 2.2, National Advisory Commission on Criminal Justice Standards and Goals (Washington, D.C.: U.S. Government Printing Office, 1973), pp. 32–41.

STANDARD 2.1   GENERAL CRITERIA FOR DIVERSION

In appropriate cases offenders should be diverted into noncriminal programs before formal trial or conviction.

Such diversion is appropriate where there is a substantial likelihood that conviction could be obtained and the benefits to society from channeling an offender into an available noncriminal diversion program outweigh any harm done to society by abandoning criminal prosecution. Among the factors that should be considered favorable to diversion are: (1) the relative youth of the offender; (2) the willingness of the victim to have no conviction sought; (3) any likelihood that the offender suffers from a mental illness or psychological abnormality which was related to his crime and for which treatment is available; and (4) any likelihood that the crime was significantly related to any other condition or situation such as unemployment or family problems that would be subject to change by participation in a diversion program.

Among the factors that should be considered unfavorable to diversion are: (1) any history of the use of physical violence toward others; (2) involvement with syndicated crime; (3) a history of antisocial conduct indicating that such conduct has become an ingrained part of the defendant's life-style and would be particularly resistant to change; and (4) any special need to pursue criminal prosecution as a means of discouraging others from committing similar offenses.

Another factor to be considered in evaluating the cost to society is that the limited contact a diverted offender has with the criminal justice system may have the desired deterrent effect.

Commentary

This standard advocates diversion as a legitimate and appropriate part of the criminal justice system. It also suggests a general approach toward determining which offenders are appropriate for diversion. The criteria for invoking diversion must vary according to the nature of the program and the type of criminal activity.

Given the limited state of knowledge regarding the effectiveness of diversion and its impact on the ability of the criminal justice system to deter crime, the most appropriate approach is to examine carefully existing programs that have been found acceptable in practice and to develop further programs incorporating the most promising aspects of those which seem successful. This standard embodies the major general considerations for diversion programs that are currently in use.

Most of the current diversion programs are informal and are neither required nor specifically authorized by statute. They represent an exercise of the broad discretion of officials in administering criminal justice. The discretionary decisions are influenced by many factors, particularly the scarcity of existing system resources in the face of an overabundance of cases. Diversion often occurs not because of a desire to help the offender or to protect society, but because of the pragmatic realization that there are not enough resources to pursue formal prosecution. As these standards envision an ideal situation in which caseload and resources are balanced, the simple desirability of alleviating caseload pressure is not a sufficient basis for exercising a diversion decision.

Variety of Rationales

Existing programs also reveal a variety of rationales for diversion not related to caseload pressure. For example, prosecution for minor charges against youthful first offenders often is regarded as needlessly creating a potentially harmful criminal record. Such offenders often are diverted to minimize the negative effects of conviction and to make available counseling or other assistance. Diversion also may occur when it is believed that noncriminal disposition will more appropriately meet the needs or inclinations of the victim. Thus prosecution of petty property offenses may be deferred if the defendant agrees to make restitution.

Diversion occurs most often following the commission of crimes considered to pose little danger to society. However, in some situations cases are diverted even though the behavior is violent (such as intrafamily assault) or the person is potentially dangerous (such as violent, mentally ill persons). Diversion of family assault cases can be regarded as a reaction to caseload pressure and to the notion that full prosecution of the case will aggravate the underlying marital situation. With respect to mentally ill persons who are potentially dangerous, diversion in the form of commitment to public mental health facilities provides more appropriate treatment for the offender as well as a potentially longer term of confinement than is available under criminal statutes.

Diversion of an offender assumes that some act justifying criminal intervention has occurred. Often the facts are clear or the defendant admits his guilt. In situations where it is not clear that guilt could be established, however, care must be taken that diversion is not invoked for individuals who have committed no crime.

Two Prerequisites

It is impossible to specify all of the factors that might be regarded as indicating the desirability of diversion. There are, however, two common prerequisites for diversion: (1) undesirability of criminal prosecution because of undue harm to the defendant or his underlying problem, because of the apparent futility of prosecution in preventing future offenses, or because formal prosecution fails to meet the needs of the victim; and (2) availability of assistance, such as treatment, counseling, or mediation procedures. Given these general prerequisites, there is substantial room for variation among specific factors. Should diversion apply only to the first offense? Should addicts be diverted following all crimes or only following crimes such as use or possession of narcotics? These and many other specific questions cannot be answered in general terms; they must be considered in the context of the substantive areas under consideration and answered in light of the policies which individual jurisdictions wish to follow.

Diversion ordinarily should not be an ad hoc matter. Occasionally a defendant may on his own initiative arrange for a diversion program, as by obtaining private psychiatric treatment. Defense counsel should be encouraged to develop possible alternatives to formal prosecution and to present these alternatives to the prosecutor with a request that formal charges be suspended. By virtue of his professional and personal contacts in the community, a prosecutor sometimes may become aware of assistance that could be offered on a diversion basis.

But in many areas the need is for specific ongoing programs with well-defined procedures and criteria for selecting defendants to be diverted and for supplying them with services following diversion. Many problems underlying the commission of crimes are prevalent enough to justify specialized programs that provide assistance to many persons. An ad hoc approach to programs is much less efficient. In addition, defendants are entitled to equal access to diversion programs. This right can be respected only by the development of regular methods for determining the appropriateness of diversion in each case. In many cases diversion should be attempted only when an ongoing program of established value is available to handle the diverted offenders. The uses of specialized diversion programs are discussed in the remainder of this commentary.

Police Decision

In one category of situations, the diversion decision ordinarily will be made before the case is presented to the prosecutor. Usually it will be made by the police. Such diversion programs are beyond the direct purview of the Courts Report. But the relationship between the court process and such programs is so close that no discussion of the first can ignore the second. At present, many of the problems of the lower courts are attributable in part to the caseloads they are forced to assume. To the extent that precharge diversion programs alleviate caseload pressures, they are of direct concern to the courts.

The threat of criminal prosecution should not be used improperly by prosecutors who wish to encourage diversion. Since diversion may in some cases reduce the deterrent effect produced by formal processing of offenders, the prosecutor has a responsibility to insure that formal prosecution is used when such action might prevent future offenses. For these reasons, the Courts Report must be concerned to an extent with precharge diversion programs, such as those utilized in the following situations:

1. Public intoxication. Despite the unwillingness of the U.S. Supreme Court in *Powell* v. *Texas,* 392 U.S. 514 (1968) to hold that prosecution of a chronic alcoholic for public intoxication necessarily violates the eighth amendment prohibition against cruel and unusual punishment, it is clear that the criminal justice system has proven ineffective to many individuals with alcohol-related problems. In this area the goal of diversion programs should be to determine, at the earliest point possible, which of those individuals apprehended for public intoxication should be processed as criminal defendants and which should not. It ordinarily should be possible for this determination to be made by the police officer. If an officer sees a person who is intoxicated and unable to function adequately, he should be authorized to decide whether there is a substantial likelihood that the intoxication is symptomatic of an underlying alcohol-related problem. If he so determines, he should be authorized to take the individual to a detoxification center in lieu of booking him for public intoxication or some similar criminal offense. Once the individual is accepted by the detoxification center, there should be no possibility of criminal prosecution.

Care must be taken to establish a method of admission to detoxification centers that permits police officers to shift responsibility for a person presented as rapidly and easily as possible. In the absence of such procedures, police officers are unlikely to exercise their diversion responsibilities often enough.[1]

Once the individual has been accepted by the detoxification center, the direct relationship between him and the criminal justice system terminates. But the responsibility of the criminal justice system does not end there. Because of the potential danger of unjustified detention of those diverted to such centers or to other programs, the detoxification center should detain the individual against his will only until he recovers from the direct effects of the intoxication, or for three days, whichever is shorter. The treatment center also should interview each person so detained and refer him to other agencies providing counseling and treatment for alcoholism, or to programs for persons with vocational, psychiatric, medical, or social problems.

Coercion should not be used to require participation in diversion programs, however. The experience of the Vera Institute Project is that 60 to 70 percent of persons referred accept the referral on a voluntary basis, and that a much higher percentage accepts medical services only when offered.[2] Given the lack of evidence that nonvoluntary treatment is effective in combating the problems of individuals in this category, diversion would not be

[1] See Arthur Matthews, *Mental Disability and the Criminal Law* (Chicago: American Bar Foundation, 1970), p. 171.
[2] Raymond Nimmer, *Two Million Unnecessary Arrests* (Chicago: American Bar Foundation, 1971), p. 140.

appropriate if its results were to channel offenders into longer-term treatment programs.[3]

2. Assaults involving husband and wife. Experience has shown that, in many cases of assaults involving husband and wife where no serious injury has been inflicted, attempts to invoke the criminal process are of little use. On the other hand, such assaults may indicate underlying individual or family problems and thus should not be ignored.

In most cases, diversion should begin prior to a formal response to the complaint. When, as in some communities, diversion is not considered until the filing of formal charges, the high frequency of noncriminal dispositions suggests that diversion at an earlier stage would have been more appropriate.[4]

In jurisdictions experiencing a high rate of family assault complaints, police units specially trained to handle family disputes with a minimum of violence should be established. Such units should answer complaints relating to incidents of assault and battery between husband and wife. Police officers should attempt to calm such disputes without the use of violence or arrest, and should arrest only if severe injury has occurred or if arrest of one of the disputants is the only way to calm the dispute. After the dispute is calmed, officers should determine whether referral to family or other counseling sessions is advisable. If so, they should recommend specific programs. Records should be kept of such calls, and if repeated disturbances occur, the disputants should be referred to a family court with criminal jurisdiction over intrafamily assaults.

The New York Police Department's Family Crisis Intervention Unit, sponsored by the Vera Institute, has become a model for similar programs developed by a number of metropolitan police departments. These programs train officers to evaluate disruptive situations and settle them as amicably as possible without resorting to arrest. A pilot project in New York demonstrated that such programs can accomplish their diversion objectives effectively with no increased risk to police officers. In addition, it suggested that such programs also have the side effect of improving police-community relations.[5]

3. Mentally ill minor offenders. If an individual who is clearly mentally ill commits a minor criminal act, there is no legitimate reason to delay his entry into the mental health system pending an acquittal on grounds of insanity or even pending a prosecutor's decision that the defendant should be diverted. Diversion of such individuals should be a police task. Police

[3] See Keith S. Ditman, George C. Crawford, Edward W. Forgy, Herbert Moskowitz, and Craig McAndrew, "A Controlled Experiment on the Use of Court Probation for Drunk Arrests," *American Journal of Psychiatry* 125 (August 1967): 170, suggesting that compulsory referrals to Alcoholics Anonymous or an alcoholism clinic were no more effective in reducing recidivism than was taking no action whatsoever.

[4] See Raymond Parnas, "Judicial Response to Intra-Family Violence," *Minnesota Law Review* 54 (January 1970): 585.

[5] Morton Bard, "Family Intervention Police Teams as a Community Mental Health Resource," *Journal of Criminal Law, Criminology and Police Science* 60 (June 1969): 247.

officers should participate in special training programs designed to train them to recognize symptoms of mental illness.[6]

If a police officer encounters a person he would otherwise arrest for a misdemeanor, and the person appears to be mentally ill, the officer should be authorized to refer the individual to a mental health facility for evaluation. The mental health facility should have authority to seek involuntary hospitalization of the individual when appropriate, but such commitment should not be a prerequisite for diversion.

Such programs require local facilities with a professional staff available twenty-four hours a day and equipped to make evaluations whenever necessary. Equally important to a successful diversion program of this nature, however, is the development of a procedure whereby police officers can obtain a rapid and reliable evaluation of a person, followed by a willingness on the part of mental health facility personnel to take further responsibility for securing treatment, on an involuntary basis if necessary.[7] Police officers need to be relieved of their responsibility for an offender at the earliest possible time. In the absence of a procedure to this effect, police officers will tend to book the individual and leave to jail personnel the responsibility for securing mental health assistance. Such delay is unnecessary, as well as harmful, to diversion efforts.

In the situations described above, diversion would be effectuated by the police. In other situations, diversion should occur at a later stage of the criminal justice process, and the decision as to whether to divert a particular offender should be made by the prosecutor's staff.

Delayed Diversion

Several factors characterize situations in which diversion should be delayed until that point. First, they tend to involve serious offenses. Since the offender has actually demonstrated that he presents a significant danger to the community, the decision to divert him from the criminal justice system poses an even greater threat to community security. Thus the diversion decision should be delayed until more information is available and until the prosecutor himself can evaluate the desirability of prosecution. Second, the programs into which offenders are diverted tend to involve more significant deprivations of liberty than those discussed above. In view of the negative result of an unjustified diversion and the corresponding need to protect defendants, more formality is appropriate. This greater formality can only be provided if diversion is postponed until the case reaches the more formal stages of processing.

In regard to the more serious situations, diversion decisions need to be made on a case-by-case basis. As in the situations described above, however,

[6] An example of the type of police training material that is available, but that needs further development, is the booklet published by the National Association of Mental Health, entitled *How to Recognize and Handle Abnormal People* (1964). Films based upon this manual also are available from the United States Public Health Service Audio Visual Facility in Atlanta, Georgia. These titles include: "Booked for Safekeeping," "The Cry for Help," "The Mask," and "Under Pressure."

[7] See Matthews, *loc. cit.*

there are categories of situations in which specific programs need to be developed in order to make diversion a realistic alternative in particular cases. These are discussed below.

1. Fraud.   Fraud and similar white collar offenses account for a high percentage of many prosecutors' caseloads. Each year in Chicago, for example, a special unit of the State's Attorney's Office of Cook County, the Fraud and Complaint Division, handles about 10,000 cases; the entire office handles only 5,000 felony prosecutions yearly.[8]

In Detroit, the police use a diversion system under which some white collar offenders are diverted into a program that requires restitution as an alternative to criminal prosecution. This program differs from most diversion programs in that it is operated by a criminal justice agency; the prosecutor's office itself assumes responsibility for assuring that the offender participates by making restitution. If a prosecutor's office is large enough and if the number of consumer fraud complaints so justifies, a special unit should be established to deal with fraud complaints.

If a complaint for a fraud offense involves a defendant with few prior complaints against him, the defendant indicates a willingness to make restitution, and the victim indicates a willingness to accept this resolution of the complaint, then the prosecutor's office should enter into an agreement for the suspension of criminal prosecution upon the condition that restitution is made. By this method, the overwhelming majority of cases can be handled informally and with the approval of all concerned.

In Chicago, for example, the 10,000 cases handled yearly by the Fraud and Complaint Division result in the recovery of approximately $1,500,000. Only 800 to 900 complaints ultimately lead to formal prosecution. Judging from the Chicago experience, bad-check complaints can be expected to make up at least half of the cases handled in such a program. But swindles concerning automobile transactions and even building construction also will be involved.

Many prosecutors apparently are reluctant to give publicity to such programs because they feel they will be labeled collection bureaus rather than prosecutorial agencies. There also is some fear that publicity might weaken the deterrent impact of convictions when prosecution is completed. But it also is likely that lack of publicity leaves many victims unaware of this method of obtaining restitution. Individuals who are unwilling to seek formal conviction may be willing to seek restitution in this manner. Moreover, publicizing these programs may increase public awareness of fraudulent schemes and bring more violations to official attention. In addition to publicizing its program, the Chicago Faud and Complaint Department has established mobile units to provide decentralized services to neighborhoods and communities within Cook County.[9]

2. Mentally ill serious offenders.   In theory, a defendant who was mentally ill at the time of his offense is entitled to be channeled into the

---

[8] See D. McIntyre, ed., *Law Enforcement in the Metropolis* (1967); F. Miller, *Prosecution, The Decision to Charge or Not to Charge* (1969).
[9] *Ibid.*

mental health system by asserting at trial the defense of insanity. If he is still mentally ill and dangerous at the time of acquittal on insanity grounds, he is subject to postacquittal commitment. In addition, mentally ill defendants often are diverted by informal means, many times on the grounds that they are incompetent to stand trial. Following treatment, prosecutions often are dropped or the charges drastically reduced. Similar practices in Michigan are documented in an article by Lewin.[10]

It would be preferable if the matter of diversion were faced directly, and more structured diversion programs for such offenders established. Specifically, each court should have available a mental health unit staffed with personnel able to evaluate offenders. This mental health unit should be authorized to examine an offender at the request of the prosecution or defense, at the suggestion of the court itself, or on its own initiative. The results of any such examination should be made available to all parties. If, following such an examination and report, the prosecution and the defense agree that the offense was the result of mental illness, they should agree to suspend prosecution on the condition that the defendant participate in a treatment program.

3. Drug abuse. Given the wide disagreement regarding the appropriate response to drug-related offenses, general statements about diversion programs for such offenders are difficult to make. It is clear, however, that at least some of these offenders are dealt with best through noncriminal programs. At this point, the Commission recommends experimentation with programs limited to situations in which all of the following characteristics apply: (1) the offense does not involve violence to another person; (2) the offender is addicted to the use of drugs and the offense is related to this addiction, either by having been committed during drug intoxication or by being part of the offender's pattern of use of drugs (e.g., possession of drugs) or of obtaining drugs (e.g., concealment of drugs, theft of property to obtain money to purchase drugs, sale of drugs as a means of raising money to purchase drugs for own use); (3) the offender does not have a history of serious long-term criminal activity; (4) appropriate treatment programs are available; and (5) the treatment program has agreed to take the offender on a diversion basis. In many situations, the benefits of diversion will outweigh any decrease in the deterrent impact of seeking formal conviction.

4. Youthful offenders. The offender who is too old for juvenile court jurisdiction but too young to deserve the full impact of a criminal conviction has been an especially troublesome problem for the criminal justice system. It is in this area that diversion can provide an especially attractive middle ground. The effectiveness of efforts in this direction can be predicted to some extent on the basis of the results of Project Crossroads, the pilot project in Washington, D.C.[11] Participation in this program was limited to individuals between the ages of sixteen and twenty-six charged with misdemeanors

[10] Lewin, "Incompetency To Stand Trial: Legal and Ethical Aspects of an Abused Doctrine," *Law and the Social Order* (1969): 233.

[11] John Holahan, *A Benefit–Cost Analysis of Project Crossroads* (Washington, D.C.: National Committee for Children and Youth, 1970).

and less serious felonies, who had no previous adult record, and who were either unemployed or whose jobs were in jeopardy as a result of the criminal charges against them. Each participant was given counseling and personal assistance, job training and placement, and remedial educational assistance. Although only 30 percent had been employed during 80 percent of the twelve months preceding participation in the project, more than 50 percent were employed for 80 percent of the year following participation. Moreover, their wages were substantially higher after participation than before.

Most important, the diversion programs apparently had a significant impact upon their criminality. Such experience strongly suggests at least experimental use of diversion programs for relatively young offenders whose criminality is not part of an established life-style. Consideration must be given to the possibility that diversion programs have a strong deterrent effect while criminal conviction, by closing employment doors and causing other hardships, may increase the likelihood of future crimes.

5. Unemployed offenders. Many people do not consider the mere unemployment of the offender a mitigating factor. Yet, from a purely pragmatic point of view, the experience of the Vera Institute's Manhattan Court Employment Project suggests that unemployment be considered a major factor favoring diversion, and that specific programs be established for selected unemployed offenders.

Useful Model

The Manhattan Court Employment Project[12] provides a useful model for such programs. Papers relating to each arrested defendant brought to criminal court for arraignment are reviewed by project personnel. If a defendant appears eligible, he is interviewed. Both the defendant and his lawyer are asked whether they would agree to the defendant's participation in the program. Under the project's criteria, those selected must: (1) not be alcoholics or heavy narcotics users; (2) not be engaged in activities— legitimate or otherwise—that produce more income than the types of jobs to which the project will refer them; (3) be unemployed or earning less than $125 per week; (4) be residents of areas not too remote from the project; (5) not be charged with homicide, rape or other sex offense, kidnaping, or arson; and (6) not have a record of more than one continuous year in a penal institution. Only about 20 of the 1,000 cases coming to court daily are selected for the program.

Once eligibility is established, the approval of the prosecutor is sought. If this is forthcoming, the prosecution is adjourned for ninety days and the defendant is released on his own recognizance to participate. At the end of the ninety-day period, one of three dispositions will be made: the charges will be dismissed; the adjournment will be continued so that the defendant can participate further; or, if no progress has been made or seems likely, the participant will be removed from the program and the prosecution resumed.

[12] Vera Institute of Justice, *Programs in Criminal Justice Reform* (New York: Vera Institute of Justice, 1972), pp. 79–91.

After entering the project, the defendant is interviewed by a counselor who generally comes from the defendant's neighborhood and who often has served a long prison term himself. This counselor will be responsible for the defendant while he participates in the project and after he leaves it. Each counselor carries a caseload of fifteen to twenty-five participants. The defendant may participate in weekly group counseling sessions in addition to periodic meetings with his counselor. The group sessions are designed to help participants identify, understand, and express their feelings, convince them that they can succeed in society, and show them how to do so. Each participant also confers with a career developer, who assists him in formulating vocational objectives and in locating employment. The career developer refers the participant to active lists of cooperating employers. About 44 percent of these referrals lead to jobs. If one referral is unsuccessful, the career developer works with the participant to make the next referral more successful.

Increased Employability

During the first year, dismissal of charges was recommended and accepted for only 39 percent of the participants; by the third year, the rate had increased to 61 percent. The participants' employability increased greatly. Of the 100 participants selected for a follow-up study, only thirty had been employed when they entered the project. Of the eighty-seven who could be located, seventy were found to be still employed. Moreover, the criminality of the participants was significantly reduced; the rearrest figures were significantly lower than those for a comparison group selected from the general court population.

The project not only was more successful than traditional methods in reducing criminality of offenders, but it also was cheaper. The project cost $860 per participant. Pretrial detention costs $1,000 per ninety days; prison costs totaled $5,000 per year, and parole costs totaled more than $1,800 annually.

Based on this experience, it is clear that further development of such projects is in order. Diversion programs should be created that offer employment assistance and personal counseling for offenders with the following characteristics: (1) relative youth; (2) no pending charge of a serious nature, such as homicide, forcible rape, or kidnaping; (3) unemployed, or employed in a job providing compensation clearly inadequate for reasonable comfort; (4) not engaged in any high-income activity, whether legal or not; (5) no record of long-term stays in penal institutions; and (6) not an alcoholic or heavy narcotic user.

The categories discussed here are merely illustrative. Diversion of other offenders also may be appropriate. Determination that an offender comes within one of the illustrative categories discussed here should not resolve the diversion question. Prosecution still might be appropriate for a number of reasons, such as community demand for harsh disposition of such offenders, or a need to deter such activity. As the standard makes clear, diversion is appropriate only when, considering all factors, the total benefits to be derived from diversion outweigh those to be derived from prosecution.

STANDARD 2.2   PROCEDURE FOR DIVERSION PROGRAMS

The appropriate authority should make the decision to divert as soon as adequate information can be obtained.

Guidelines for making diversion decisions should be established and made public. Where it is contemplated that the diversion decision will be made by police officers or similar individuals, the guidelines should be promulgated by the police or other agency concerned after consultation with the prosecutor and after giving all suggestions due consideration. Where the diversion decision is to be made by the prosecutor's office, the guidelines should be promulgated by that office.

When a defendant is diverted in a manner not involving a diversion agreement between the defendant and the prosecution, a written statement of the fact of, and reason for, the diversion should be made and retained. When a defendant who comes under a category of offenders for whom diversion regularly is considered is not diverted, a written statement of the reasons should be retained.

Where the diversion program involves significant deprivation of an offender's liberty, diversion should be permitted only under a court-approved diversion agreement providing for suspension of criminal proceedings on the condition that the defendant participate in the diversion program. Procedures should be developed for the formulation of such agreements and their approval by the court. These procedures should contain the following features:

1.   Emphasis should be placed on the offender's right to be represented by counsel during negotiations for diversion and entry and approval of the agreement.

2.   Suspension of criminal prosecution for longer than one year should not be permitted.

3.   An agreement that provides for a substantial period of institutionalization should not be approved unless the court specifically finds that the defendant is subject to nonvoluntary detention in the institution under noncriminal statutory authorizations for such institutionalization.

4.   The agreement submitted to the court should contain a full statement of those things expected of the defendant and the reason for diverting the defendant.

5.   The court should approve an offered agreement only if it would be approved under the applicable criteria if it were a negotiated plea of guilty.

6.   Upon expiration of the agreement, the court should dismiss the prosecution, and no future prosecution based on the conduct underlying the initial charge should be permitted.

7.   For the duration of the agreement, the prosecutor should have the discretionary authority to determine whether the offender is performing his duties adequately under the agreement and, if he determines that the offender is not, to reinstate the prosecution.

Whenever a diversion decision is made by the prosecutor's office, the staff member making it should specify in writing the basis for the decision, whether or not the defendant is diverted. These statements, as well as those made in cases not requiring a formal agreement for diversion, should be collected and subjected to periodic review by the prosecutor's office to insure that diversion programs are operating as intended.

The decision by the prosecutor not to divert a particular defendant should not be subject to judicial review.

Commentary

In view of the variety of diversion programs that can be developed, few general rules for making diversion decisions can be formulated. Pursuant to the Commission's general objective of improving administrative decision making by regularizing internal procedure and raising the visibility of this decision making, however, this standard directs that where the possibility of diversion is contemplated, guidelines be drafted for making the diversion decision in specific cases. Here, as in screening and negotiating pleas of guilty, the discretion of the decision-making officials should be structured by written regulations to obviate whimsical and erratic decisions.

Where it is contemplated that the diversion decision will be made by the prosecutor or a member of his staff, the guidelines should be promulgated by the prosecutor's office. If diversion is to be to a program or agency outside the prosecutor's office, consultation with that program or agency is essential. Special attention should be given to determining which individuals the program or agency will accept under the circumstances of a pending criminal prosecution. Where it is contemplated that the diversion decision will be made by someone outside the prosecutor's office, guidelines should be developed by that agency after consultation with the prosecutor's office. For example, when intoxicated persons are diverted, police officers are likely to make the diversion decision, under guidelines developed by the police. In these cases, consultation with the program or agencies to which the offenders will be diverted is essential.

The standard also attempts to structure the making of the diversion decision in another way. Where a defendant is diverted and a court-approved agreement is entered into, a written record exists. But the standard requires that even though no court-approved agreement is involved—as when diversion decisions are made by police officers—written statements of the reasons be made. Even when a court agreement is involved, the standard calls for the prosecutor to maintain his own record of the reason for his decision. In both situations, such a record need be made only if diversion actually were considered (e.g., a defendant suggested a program to the prosecutor and asked that charges be suspended) or when the defendant was within a category of offenders for which diversion should be routinely considered (e.g., the charge is public intoxication or possession of narcotics for personal use). By structuring the decision-making process and raising its visibility, the commission hopes to stimulate internal regularity in diversion decisions that would make outside supervision unnecessary.[1]

---

[1] See Kenneth Culp Davis, *Discretionary Justice, A Preliminary Inquiry* (Baton Rouge: Louisiana State University Press, 1969).

Deprivation of Liberty

The standard requires that a court-approved agreement is necessary for the conditional suspension of a prosecution only when the diversion program involves actual deprivation of liberty. This is a less stringent requirement than that proposed by the American Law Institute's Council, which recommended that such agreements be required in all cases.[2] In view of the potential limiting impact upon prosecutorial discretion, the danger of extensive litigation over decisions to reinstate prosecutions, and the burden of the formalities involved, the Commission thought that the formal procedure of court-approved agreement was justifiably required only in limited situations.

The standard also provides general guidelines for the procedure that should be followed for entry into an agreement for a conditional suspension of prosecution. A defendant in this position is usually entitled, as a matter of constitutional right, to representation by counsel. But the sense of the standard is that, given the special value that counsel can serve in the negotiation process, special efforts should be taken to assure that a defendant fully understands the value of counsel before waiving his right to it.

The one-year limitation on suspension agreements is consistent with that recommended by the Council of the American Law Institute.[3] If a longer period of enforced treatment is sought, the appropriate procedure is a negotiated plea of guilty arrived at under the more stringent procedural safeguards applicable there.

Many of the same objectives sought through diversion can be accomplished if the sentencing judge had authority to sentence a convicted offender to a diversion program and the jurisdiction had an expungement statute to permit removal of formal records of conviction following successful participation in such a program. The formality of the guilty plea process would provide the safeguards that the Commission feels are needed to minimize the chance that a person whose guilt cannot be established by the prosecution would be compelled to submit to a long-term program.

The limitation upon full-time institutionalization is intended to limit the extent to which diversion can be used to broaden the criteria generally applicable to such programs. If, for example, the criterion applicable to civil commitment to a psychiatric facility is dangerousness to others because of mental illness, it seems appropriate to limit the period of time an offender can be hospitalized if such dangerousness cannot be shown. However, this will seldom be the case.

Court approval should be given only if the agreement would be approved if it involved a guilty plea. This is appropriate in view of the similarities between the two situations—both involve submission to programs under the threat of more formal action by the State.

---

[2] See American Law Institute, *A Model Code of Pre-Arraignment Procedure,* Tent. Draft No. 5 (1972), §320.5.

[3] *Ibid.,* §320.5(1)(b).

Final dismissal "with prejudice," as provided in subparagraph 6, is undoubtedly an understood provision of all suspension agreements. It should, however, be formalized and fulfillment of the agreement should be formally acknowledged to avoid later disputes concerning the matter.

Different Approach

Subparagraph 7, which provides for the discretionary right of the prosecutor to declare the agreement violated by the defendant and to reinstate prosecution, differs from the approach recommended by the American Law Institute's Council. The American Law Institute's proposal requires that a prosecutor who believes that a suspended prosecution agreement has been violated offer the defendant a hearing before the prosecutor to determine whether a violation has occurred and, if so, whether the prosecution should be reactivated. The rules of evidence do not apply, but the defendant is entitled to representation by counsel and the right to confront and cross-examine witnesses. The prosecutor's decision to reinstate a prosecution following such a hearing is subject to judicial review only to the extent that a defendant is entitled to the opportunity to establish that the decision is not supported by the record taken of the hearing; new or additional evidence may be taken before the court.[4]

While the Commission felt that it would be desirable for the prosecutor to give a defendant whose prosecution was to be reinstated an opportunity to argue against such action, it did not think that such a detailed procedure should be required in all cases. The standard, then, is not intended to discourage or disparage such procedures, but merely to recommend that they not be required in each case as a formal matter. If guidelines are established, the Commission believes that defendants' rights to fair treatment can be protected adequately by reliance upon the prosecutor's discretion. In addition, the danger that reinstatement would give rise to protracted litigation over the prosecutor's fundamental right to prosecute might well discourage the prosecutor from entering into such agreements in the first place. Thus the position in the standard is consistent with the Commission's basic position of encouraging use of diversion in appropriate cases.

---

[4] *Ibid.*, §320.9.

USE OF DIVERSION*

National Advisory Commission
on Criminal Justice Standards and Goals

* From *Corrections*, Standard 3.1, National Advisory Commission on Criminal Justice Standards and Goals (Washington, D.C.: U.S. Government Printing Office, 1973), pp. 95–97.

STANDARD 3.1   USE OF DIVERSION

Each local jurisdiction, in cooperation with related State agencies, should develop and implement by 1975 formally organized programs of diversion that can be applied in the criminal justice process from the time an illegal act occurs to adjudication.

1.   The planning process and the identification of diversion services to be provided should follow generally and be associated with "total system planning" as outlined in Standard 9.1.

   a.   With planning data available, the responsible authorities at each step in the criminal justice process where diversion may occur should develop priorities, lines of responsibility, courses of procedure, and other policies to serve as guidelines to its use.

   b.   Mechanisms for review and evaluation of policies and practices should be established.

   c.   Criminal justice agencies should seek the cooperation and resources of other community agencies to which persons can be diverted for services relating to their problems and needs.

2.   Each diversion program should operate under a set of written guidelines that insure periodic review of policies and decisions. The guidelines should specify:

   a.   The objectives of the program and the types of cases to which it is to apply.

   b.   The means to be used to evaluate the outcome of diversion decisions.

   c.   A requirement that the official making the diversion decision state in writing the basis for his determination, denying or approving diversion in the case of each offender.

   d.   A requirement that the agency operating diversion programs maintain a current and complete listing of various resource dispositions available to diversion decision makers.

3.   The factors to be used in determining whether an offender, following arrest but prior to adjudication, should be selected for diversion to a noncriminal program, should include the following:

   a.   Prosecution toward conviction may cause undue harm to the defendant or exacerbate the social problems that led to his criminal acts.

   b.   Services to meet the offender's needs and problems are unavailable within the criminal justice system or may be provided more effectively outside the system.

   c.   The arrest has already served as a desired deterrent.

   d.   The needs and interests of the victim and society are served better by diversion than by official processing.

e. The offender does not present a substantial danger to others.

f. The offender voluntarily accepts the offered alternative to further justice system processing.

g. The facts of the case sufficiently establish that the defendant committed the alleged act.

Commentary

Alternatives to criminalization should be developed for use from the time an illegal act occurs to adjudication. These procedures should be preferred over traditional punitive measures for those offenders who do not present a serious threat to others.

Diversion programs should be a part of the same planning process that is performed for the rest of the criminal justice process, and particularly corrections. The methodology is outlined in Standard 9.1, Total System Planning. Planning for diversion should include the procedures to be used and the points at which diversion may occur. As with other correctional programs, systematic review and evaluation of policies and procedures should be provided for. The community should be represented in the planning process, and the community resources that may be used in the program identified and enlisted.

A number of factors justify noncriminal treatment, counseling, or restitution programs. The existing system has failed to achieve reformation in any large number of cases; it is discriminatory in nature; and it is costly in relation to outcomes. Personal values, costs, and humanitarian interests also contribute to the arguments for diversion.

Most of the diversion processes operating today are informal and are not mandated by statute. On the contrary, they are the result of ambiguities in existing legislation as well as the broad administrative discretion of officials administering criminal justice. The discretionary decisions are influenced by a variety of factors, but of most importance is the scarcity of system resources. Diversion often occurs because of the pragmatic and pressing realization that there are not enough resources to handle the potential, if not actual, caseload.

It is impossible to specify all of the factors which might be desirable in determining whether or not diversion is a correct alternative. In general, however, there seem to be guiding principles which help determine the desirability of diversion to formal justice system processing. They relate to existing programs, visibility, stated goals, methods for measuring success, and, finally, the willingness of specific communities to participate in the development of rational, community-based alternatives to justice system processing.

If diversion programs are to perform as they are intended, then the decisions of those referring to these programs must be subject to review and evaluation. In a similar vein, decision makers cannot make referrals outside their system unless they have necessary information about alternative programs and the authority to make decisions referring cases out of the system. Guidelines outline the information necessary to meet the requirements of both of these conditions.

The first step in establishing accountability is to disclose the basis of decisions. Too often the rationale for discretionary decisions is undisclosed and unstated. Simply requiring written statements for each decision forces the process to become more open while it also permits administrative or judicial review. Review can be through the courts, the legislature, or whatever source seems most appropriate in seeing that goals have been achieved and standards complied with.

INDEX

Adams, Thomas F., 80
Akers, Ronald L., 69
Allen, Francis A., 9
Ashford, Ann E., 98, 310

Bard, Morton, 335, 352
Baron, Roger, 329
Barrett, David R., 210
Barstis, A., 179, 182, 190
Bates, Ronald, 307
Bauzer, Riva, 77, 89, 115, 311, 315, 325, 327
Bazelon, David L., 223
Beam, Kenneth, 141
Becker, Howard S., 68, 110, 159, 168, 197
Berger, P. K., 321
Bess, Bruce, 240
Bittner, Egon, 320
Black, Donald J., 90, 111, 114, 116–17, 144
Blauch, Lloyd E., 175
Blumer, Herbert, 68–69
Blumstein, Alfred, 76, 124
Bodine, George E., 115
Bodine, Terry, 87
Bonacich, Edna, 86, 320
Borden, D., 183
Bordua, David J., 6, 77, 110–12, 114–15, 146, 311, 321
Briar, Scott, 90, 113–14, 144, 177, 187, 197, 279
Brotman, Richard, 40
Brown, William J. T., 210
Buckner, H. Taylor, 110
Bufe, Noel, 100, 314
Burges, Robert L., 69

Calof, Judith, 43
Cameron, Mary O., 170, 171
Carr, Lowell, 125
Carter, Robert M., 75, 79, 92, 149, 224, 307, 314
Chambliss, William J., 77, 81
Chricos, Theodore G., 76
Cicourel, Aaron V., 84, 96, 114, 125, 145, 315
Clemmer, Donald, 169
Cloward, Richard A., 197
Cohen, Albert, 69
Colden, C. D., 77
Constantino, Carl J., 190
Cottrell, Leonard S., Jr., 75, 89, 96, 100, 159, 223
Courtless, Thomas F., 74, 179, 180, 181
Cramer, John M., 210
Cramer, M. Richard, 86, 320
Crawfod, George C., 352
Cressey, Donald R., 2, 67, 69, 75, 94, 302, 329
Cumming, Elaine, 121, 321
Cumming, Ian, 121

Dana, Lewis, 130
Davis, Kenneth Culp, 359
Dawson, Robert O., 89
DeFleur, Melvin, 69
Deutscher, Irwin, 118
Dickson, William J., 168–69, 172
Dinitz, Simon, 159
Ditman, Keith S., 46, 352
Dix, George E., 89
Dole, Vincent P., 43
Donnelly, Richard C., 197
Drury, Fred, 240

Durkheim, Emile, 110
Duxbury, Elaine, 71, 103

Eastman, George, 209
Eaton, Joseph, 173
Edell, Laura, 121
Eisner, Victor, 53–54, 314
Eldefonso, Edward, 78
Empey, LaMar T., 74, 78, 278
Ennis, Philip H., 74
Erikson, Kai, 159, 168

Feeney, Floyd, 329
Ferdinand, Theodore N., 113–14
Ferster, Elyce Zenoff, 74, 177, 179–81
Fleton, Joseph B., 183
Forgy, Edward W., 352
Foster, Jack Donald, 159
Freed, D., 179, 181, 188
Freedman, Alfred H., 40, 43
Frost, Thomas M., 209

Gandy, John M., 120–21
Gemignani, Robert J., 55, 278
Gibbons, Don C., 87, 89, 91, 157, 311
Gibbs, Jack P., 68, 110
Glaser, Daniel, 69, 314, 323
Glueck, Eleanor, 184
Glueck, Sheldon, 184
Gold, Martin, 92, 98, 315
Goldman, Nathan, 51, 77, 80–81, 89,
    115, 315
Goldstein, Joseph, 198
Graham, Donald, 234, 299–300
Grimes, A. J., 321
Gusfield, Joseph, 184

Hackler, James C., 109–10
Hagan, John L., 109–10
Hall, Jerome, 132
Hamann, Albert, 208
Harlan, Justice, 124, 125
Harlow, Eleanor, 299
Hetrick, Emery S., 48
Hunsicker, Patricia Ann, 239

Jackson, Phillip D., 76
Jacobson, Lenore F., 173

Jameson, Samuel H., 223

Kadish, S. H., 198
Kahn, Alfred J., 133, 137
Kaplan, D., 335
Kaplan, Leonard V., 35
Kenney, John P., 78
Kitsuse, John I., 68, 96, 159, 168
Klein, Malcolm W., 73, 76–77, 82–84, 90,
    92, 94, 115, 299, 307, 314–15,
    323, 325, 346
Klemke, Lloyd W., 167, 171, 173
Kobetz, Richard W., 78, 177–78, 207,
    216
Kobrin, Solomon, 76, 156, 307, 323
Kolnick, J. S., 49
Kuh, Richard H., 36, 40

Labin, Susan, 307
LaFave, Wayne R., 94, 198
Langsley, D., 335
Lapiere, Richard T., 118
Larson, Richard, 76
Lasswell, Harold D., 197
Lazarsfeld, Paul, 321
Lemert, Edwin M., 68, 75, 82, 87, 89–90,
    93, 96–97, 101–3, 106, 110, 123,
    128, 130, 134, 138, 156–57, 159,
    167–70, 225, 279, 314, 330
Lerman, Paul, 79, 88
Levine, Sol, 95
Lincoln, Suzanne Bugas, 321
Lindesmith, Alfred R., 40
Lohman, Joseph D., 85, 307
Lombroso, Cesare, 97
Lopez-Rey, Manuel, 129
Lubeck, Steven G., 278
Lucas, Campbell M., 105
Luchterhand, Elmer G., 113–14

MacIver, Robert M., 84, 95
Martin, John M., 102, 279, 281, 283
Martin, Richard I., 325
Matthews, Arthur, 351, 353
Mattick, Hans W., 263, 265
Matza, David, 69, 88, 321
Mays, J. B., 142–43
McAndrew, Craig, 352
McCune, Shirley, 125
McDermott, Robert A., 2, 67, 302, 329

McEachern, Alex W., 76–77, 89, 98, 115,
    155, 307, 310–11, 315, 323, 325,
    327
McIntyre, D., 354
McKay, Malcom V., 52
McLean, R. I., 240, 247
McSally, B. F., 197
Mead, George Herbert, 68–69, 110
Merwin, Donald, 299
Miller, Frank W., 89, 354
Mills, Robert B., 48
Mitchell, Richard, 307
Monahan, Thomas P., 51
Moore, Eugene Arthur, 52
Morris, Norval, 263
Moskowitz, Herbert, 352

Nettler, Gwynn, 110
Newman, J. Robert, 98, 310
Nimmer, Raymond, 351
Norman, Sherwood, 102, 179, 182, 190
Nye, F. Ivan, 131

O'Connor, George W., 142, 147
O'Connor, Gerald G., 98, 310
Ohlin, Lloyd E., 69, 197, 248, 321
Ohmart, Howard, 93
Ottman, D., 184

Parker, William H., 142
Parnas, Raymond L., 89, 352
Pearl, Arthur, 157
Peterson, Russell W., 339
Pilavin, Irving, 90, 113–14, 144, 177,
    187, 197, 279
Pitchess, Peter J., 221, 239
Platt, Anthony, 128
Playfair, Giles, 172
Polk, Kenneth, 102–3, 156
Porterfield, Austin, 131
Pound, Roscoe, 87, 127–28
Powers, Edwin, 131
Price, Hugh B., 49
Pursuit, Dan G., 78

Quinney, Richard, 69

Rabiner, Edward L., 43
Range, Charles E., 152

Reckless, Walter C., 159, 169
Rector, Milton G., 52
Reid, W., 334
Reiss, Albert J., Jr., 90, 111–12, 114,
    116–17, 144, 321
Robinson, Sophia, 132
Roethlisberger, Fritz J., 168–69, 172
Romasco, Anne, 75, 89, 96, 100, 223
Rosenheim, Margaret K., 25, 263, 279
Rosenthal, Robert, 173
Rubin, Sol, 36–38, 40, 137, 197
Rubin, Ted, 87, 93, 103, 278

Sager, Clifford J., 43
Sanders, Wiley B., 73
Scheff, Thomas J., 168, 173
Schiering, David, 102
Schur, Edwin M., 110, 159, 322
Schwartz, Richard D., 97, 172, 197
Selling, Thorsten, 89
Seymour, John A., 100, 103–4, 220, 263,
    276
Sheridan, William, 25, 27–28, 134, 180,
    190
Shirley, Mary, 131
Short, James F., 69, 131
Shyne, A., 334
Sigurdson, Herbert, 76, 307, 323
Sington, Derrick, 172
Skoler, Daniel S., 125
Skolnick, Jerome H., 97, 172, 197
Snethen, Edith Nash, 74, 179
Somers, R. H., 317
Spergel, Irving A., 85, 92–93
Steinan, Leslie, 35
Sternberg, David, 42
Sundeen, Richard A., Jr., 90, 307, 312,
    314
Susini, Jean, 154
Sutermeister, Robert, 280
Sutherland, Edwin H., 69, 169

Taft, Donald, 169
Tannenbaum, Frank, 68, 110, 159,
    169–71, 197
Tao, L. S., 48
Taylor, Edward M., 98, 310
Teele, James E., 95
Terry, Ralph M., 115
Terry, Robert M., 88
Thomas, Charles C., 142

Thomas, W. I., 69, 165
Thornton, Warren, 329
Thorsell, Bernard A., 167
Twain, David, 299

Underwood, William A., 53

Vera Institute, 251–52, 256, 352, 356
Vinter, Robert D., 126, 278–79
Vorenberg, Elizabeth W., 219, 248, 321
Vorenberg, James, 219, 248, 321

Wald, Patricia M., 179, 181, 184, 188
Waldo, Gordon P., 76
Walker, Nigel, 91
Walsh, J. L., 316
Wambaugh, Joseph, 88
Ward, David A., 75, 94

Warren, R. L., 316
Watson, Nelson A., 142, 147
Wattenberg, William W., 100, 314
Weil, Robert J., 173
Werthman, Carl, 135
Westley, William, 112–13
Wheeler, Stanton, 75, 83, 86, 89, 95–96, 100, 118, 147, 159, 223, 311, 315, 320
White, Richardson, Jr., 25
Wicker, Allan W., 118
Wilson, James Q., 6, 51, 83, 85–86, 90, 118–21, 147, 311, 315, 320
Wilson, O. W., 142
Winters, John E., 210
Witmer, Helen, 131
Wolfgang, Marvin E., 89
Wood, Roland W., 40
Wooten, Barbara, 38
Wurzburger, Rebecca, 234, 299–300

Zola, Irving K., 86, 320